# RUSSIA, MY NATIVE LAND

*Also by Gregory P. Tschebotarioff*

author of:

> *Soil Mechanics, Foundations and Earth Structures*
> (also translated into Spanish and Japanese)

> "Retaining Structures," Chapter 5 in *Foundation Engineering*
> (edited by Gerald A. Leonards)

co-author of:

> "Soil and Foundation Engineering in the U.S.S.R.,"
>> *Highway Research Board Special Report No. 60,*
>> National Academy of Sciences, Washington, D.C., 1960,
>> pp. 1–45; 182–188.

editor of the following English translations from the Russian:

> "Bases and Foundations in Frozen Soil" by N. A. Tsytovich,
>> *Highway Research Board Special Report No. 58,*
>> National Academy of Sciences, Washington, D.C., 93 p.
> *Dynamics of Bases and Foundations* by D. D. Barkan

(Dr. Tschebotarioff is also the author of 80 articles and discussions in professional engineering journals. His publications in the historico-political field are listed in this book as References 63 to 69 inclusive)

*A U.S. Engineer Reminisces
and Looks at the Present*

# RUSSIA,
# MY
# NATIVE
# LAND

Gregory P. Tschebotarioff

*McGraw-Hill Book Company*

NEW YORK
LONDON
TORONTO

Library of Congress Catalog Card Number: 64-21632

First Edition

65376

*To my dear American wife*

# CONTENTS

Foreword                                    ix

Introduction                                xiii

On Spelling and Terminology                 xxi

Acknowledgments                             xxv

Part        IMPERIAL RUSSIA
I           AND THE FEBRUARY
            1917 REVOLUTION

Chapter 1   Setting of Our Family Life
            Before World War I              3

*1. Our Family Background, 3; 2. Family Interest
in History, 11; 3. My Early Education, 19; 4. Some
Russian Army Customs, 27; 5. Imperial Russia's
Upper Social Strata, 32; 6. Relations with For-
eigners, 36; 7. Rumblings of Approaching World
War, 38.*

Chapter 2   The First Thirty Months of the War   42

*1. Outline of the Military Operations, 42; 2. The
Palace Hospital at Tsárskoye Seló, 52; 3. The Imperial Law School in Wartime, 64; 4. The Miháilovsky Artillery School, 69; 5. The Guard Horse
Artillery Reserve Battery, 73.*

Chapter 3   Facing Austro-Germans after the
            February 1917 Revolution        79

*1. Don Cossack Guard Battery on Eve of Revolu-
tion, 79; 2. Military Situation after the February
1917 Revolution, 84; 3. Don Cossack Guard Battery
after the February 1917 Revolution, 89; 4. Cossack
"Self-Determination," 98.*

Part     RUSSIAN
 II      CIVIL WAR, 1917–1920

*Chapter 4*   "The Ten Days That Shook the
             World"—As I Saw Them          107

             *1. Bolshevik Seizure of Power at Petrográd, 107;
             2. Cossack Attack on the Púlkovo Heights, 109;
             3. Who Captured Whom in Gátchino's Bolshói
             Palace?, 121; 4. General Krassnóv Held at Smólny
             by the Reds, 129.*

*Chapter 5*   Fighting the Reds in the Don
             Under Atamán Kaledín           139

             *1. Return of the Guard Battery to the Don, 139;
             2. Pro-Red Mutiny in the Don, 144; 3. With a
             White Partizán Detachment, 159; 4. Capture and
             Escape, 171.*

*Chapter 6*   Bolshevik-Held Petrograd in
             Spring and Summer 1918         183

             *1. Travel North, 183; 2. Life at Tsárskoye Seló, 184;
             3. Letters from Tobólsk, 190; 4. My Engineering
             Studies, 198; 5. Travel South to the Don via the
             Ukraine, 200.*

*Chapter 7*   The Don Under the
             Atamán General Krassnóv        208

             *1. Anti-Red Uprising in the Don, Spring, 1918, 208;
             2. Our Life at Novocherkássk, 212; 3. General
             Krassnóv's Personality and Attitudes, 213; 4. The
             Don Between the German and the Volunteer
             Armies, 218; 5. Interpreting English for the Ata-
             mán after November 1918, 225; 6. The Resignation
             of Atamán Krassnóv, 237.*

*Chapter 8*　In the Ranks of the Grand
　　　　　Army of the Don, 1919–1920　　239

*1. Northward Advance with the 2nd Don Cossack
Battery, 239; 2. Aide-de-Camp to Inspector of
Artillery, 253; 3. Orders to Proceed Abroad, 267;
4. End of White Resistance in the Crimea—and Its
Aftermath, 269.*

Part　EMIGRATION AND
III　"FORTY YEARS AFTER"

*Chapter 9*　Life in Emigration Abroad　　273

*1. Interpreter to the Don Cadet Corps in Egypt, 275;
2. Engineering Studies and Work on Three Conti-
nents, 284; 3. Some Socio-Political Observations
during my Wanderings, 291; 4. Cossack Émigré
Politics before and during World War II, 298;
5. My First Contacts with Soviet Engineering Colleagues, 308.*

*Chapter 10*　1959 Visit to Soviet Union
　　　　　with U.S. Exchange Delegation　　316

*1. Reception in the United States of Soviet Founda-
tion Engineering Delegation, 316; 2. Reception in
the U.S.S.R. of the U.S. Exchange Delegation, 326;
3. At the Stalingrád Dam across the Volga, 334;
4. New Construction, 338; 5. Moscow University, 339; 6. Revisiting old Haunts, 341; 7. Impressions of Kíev and the Ukraine, 350.*

Epilogue　　357

Appendix　　365

References　　368

Name Index　　373

Subject Index　　380

*Illustrations, 32 pages, Figures 1 through 73*

# Foreword

Among the factors tending to impede the formation of a balanced understanding of Russian problems in American public opinion, not the least has been the fact that among the millions of people who came to this country from Eastern Europe on the great tide of immigration from that area that marked the end of the last century and the beginning of this one, so few were genuine Russians and so many were members of non-Russian nationalities who had suffered in one way or another under Tsarist imperialism or Tsarist oppression. For decades on end, Jews alone made up the overwhelming majority of those who received immigration visas on the "Russian" quota. Finns, Poles and members of other non "Great Russian" elements also came in large numbers. The "Great Russian," on the other hand, was a rarity among the immigrants. Thus, the tone of much that was said and written about Russia in this country tended to be set by people who had bitter memories and negative feelings with relation to the Russians as a nation.

This situation combined with, and contributed to, a similar distortion with relation to the non-national ideological issues which divided people in the area of the traditional Russian state. There was, of course, from the outset a natural tendency for Americans to sympathize with any opposition, revolutionary or otherwise, directed against a wholly autocratic and monarchical system of government. Beyond that, serious American students of Russia (not least the namesake of the writer of these lines: George Kennan, 1845–1923) found their sympathy and interest attracted, time and time again, by the Russian oppositionists and revolutionists, and tended to constitute themselves the spokesmen and defenders of the latter, particularly since there was often no other way that their views and feelings could find expression at all before world public opinion. And the one-sided nature of the immigration to this country contributed to the resulting imbalance; for the Russian revolutionary movement of the decades immediately preceding the Revolution was made up in its greater part by people of the non-Russian nationalities, in whose feelings toward the Tsar's regime both national and ideological resentments had a part.

It is not to deny the tremendous stupidities committed by the Tsar's Government with relation to the non-Russian national elements within the Empire, nor is it to deny the evils of the early industrialism and

the disaffection of the intelligentsia by which Russia was so griev-
ously affected around the turn of the century, if one points out that
an American opinion fed so largely on the views of the anti-Russian,
anti-Tsarist and anticapitalist elements within the territory of the old
Empire could scarcely have been a well-balanced one. All these shortcomings of the Tsarist system and of Russia's national development
did indeed exist, and did indeed deserve the sympathy and concern
of others. But they were not all that there was. In the view of Russia thus created, a number of important features of the Russian scene
were inevitably given the short end of the stick—such things as Russian national pride, those curious elements of tolerance which seemed
always to be woven into the warp of Tsarist autocracy, the tremendous economic and educational advance that marked the final years
of the dynasty before the First World War, and the brilliant fireworks
of cultural productivity of all sorts which illuminated the Russian
scene as the old Empire went to its doom.

Out of this distorted image of prerevolutionary realities have come
certain of the real and serious failures of understanding with relation
to the Revolution itself and the ensuing Soviet period. Of these, the
most serious has no doubt been the assumption that the prerevolutionary Russia was both an underdeveloped and an undeveloping
country to which neither popular education nor economic development could conceivably have been brought on a scale commensurate
with the needs of the modern age other than by the huge cruelties and
sacrifices of a Stalin era. But scarcely less serious has been the widespread underestimation by Americans of the strength and legitimacy
of Russian national feeling, an underestimation which has made it
difficult for people to understand the ambiguity in the attitude of the
average Russian towards the Soviet regime—the curious way in which
national pride is mingled with shame or uneasiness over the enduring
deficiencies of the Soviet system, and the resulting sensitivity to foreign criticism (of which there has been no lack in the United States
in recent years) that appears to disparage people as well as ideology,
the nation as well as the system.

It is a good thing, in these circumstances, that the available memoir literature should now be supplemented by the reminiscences of
one who has managed to combine a devoted and constructive attitude
towards his American citizenship of later years with memories of a
Russian boyhood and youth in which the more positive aspects of
prerevolutionary Russia come fully to the fore. One is faced with a

sense of incomprehension, as one reads this account, over the political schizophrenia of a civilization which had so much to give to one portion of its youth and was yet so violently rejected by another. But this is the way it was. All those who have lived long in Russia have had occasion to observe that when the question is placed as to which of two contrary and seemingly irreconcilable phenomena in Russian life is the true one, the answer is invariably: both. And so it is in this instance. The physiognomy of Tsarist civilization which emerges from the pages of these memoirs is scarcely to be reconciled with that physiognomy which the revolutionists found so unacceptable. But it existed too, and it is important that Americans of this generation should be reminded of it.

These reminiscences relate to a number of periods or episodes: the author's boyhood life in the family of a Don Cossack Guard officer (and later staff officer) at Tsárskoye Seló; his mother's association with the Empress and her daughters in common hospital work during the war; Kerensky's unsuccessful effort to whip up armed resistance to the Bolsheviki in the days immediately following the second revolution of 1917; the failure of the effort of General Kaledin, shortly thereafter, to organize Cossack resistance to the Bolsheviki in the Don territory; the ensuing civil war in the south of Russia; and finally, experiences in the emigration and renewed contacts with Russia in the 1950s. In each of these fields Professor Tschebotarioff has something to add to the historical record—something which is either new or has fallen into forgetfulness or is not easily accessible to the average English-language reader. Particular importance attaches to the description of experiences in the civil war, in which the basic deficiencies of the anti-Communist forces—their disunity, their lack of popular support, the confusion in their relations with the Western Allies, and in general, the unfortunate effect of the recent war effort on Russia's political life—come clearly to the fore. But special mention should also be made of the manner in which this account disposes of certain misconceptions which have been perpetrated in this country with regard to the significance of the Cossack resistance to the Bolsheviki in 1917: notably the impression that this effort reflected a disposition on the part of a majority of the people of an entire great section of the former Russian empire to become permanently detached from the body of the traditional Russian state and to set up a wholly independent existence. This historical myth, which gained sufficient currency in this country to become embodied in a congressional resolution of 1959, should not survive the clarifying light cast upon it in these pages.

A special word of credit is due to the author of the memoirs for the effort he has made to make them accurate and explicit in detail. One senses here the hand of the trained scientist and engineer; and a welcome one it is in this sort of document. No one who has had to wade through any portion of the sweeping generalities and extravagant ex parte claims which characterize so much of Russian memoir literature will fail to be grateful to Professor Tschebotarioff for his scrupulous and meticulous attention to detail.

*George F. Kennan*

*I have labored carefully not to
mock, lament, or execrate, but
to understand human actions; . . . .*

SPINOZA *

# Introduction

At the end of January, 1937, I was comfortably installed in one of the Graduate College apartments at Princeton, sometimes used to house bachelor faculty members. I had just arrived from
Cairo, where I had resigned my engineering position with the Egyptian Government in answer to a call from Princeton University.

On one of the first evenings there was a knock on my door and a
young student appeared to interview me for the *Daily Princetonian.*

This was his first assignment in journalistic work, he told me, and he
had forgotten his notebook. Could I give him some paper to jot down
his notes? Also, there were two "kittens," as he put it, waiting for
him outside the Graduate College, so would I, please, tell him as
quickly as possible all about my adventures during the Civil War in
Russia? His eyes gleamed with expectation.

I had a dreadful vision of a fantastically garbled account appearing
in print if I only just opened my mouth on that topic. So, I hedged
as best I could.

A day or two later the *Daily Princetonian* carried a headline on its
front page: FORMER COSSACK FIGHTER JOINS FACULTY. TSCHEBOTA-
REFF AVOIDS WAR EXPERIENCES.†

Since then American friends who at times heard me reminisce repeatedly urged me to write down some of the events I had witnessed.
Many of them are of historical interest and important details related
to them either have not been described at all or have been garbled
both in Red and in White publications, although in different and frequently conflicting ways.

Until recently I thought of this writing as something for me to do
after my retirement. I intended not to limit myself then to a disconnected description of isolated events I took part in, but to try giving
a picture of many facets of Russian life, character and ambitions con-

---

* Spinoza, *Tractatus Theologico-Politicus,* Chapter 1 (see Ref. 12, p. 137).
† *Daily Princetonian,* January 29, 1937.

cerning which I found appalling misconceptions to be prevalent among the American public. During the past quarter of a century I have given much thought to this matter.

These present misconceptions have a most detrimental effect on American attitudes towards Russians as Russians, and mark a profound change in these attitudes during the past eighty years. The friendly relations which existed before that and which reached their high point during the American Civil War were strongly affected by a number of subsequent events.

Probably one of the most important factors was the composition of the European immigration to the United States since the last quarter of the nineteenth century. The influence of this immigration gradually changed the outlook of the entire country. It came from many European states and nationalities, the majority of which, however, had one trait in common—ancient enmities and prejudices towards Russia, even though in each case the reasons for hostile biases were different.

Prior to 1917 very few Great Russians * came to settle in the United States. After World War I, Russians themselves,—both Red and White—contributed to an unfavorable image of their country and people in the Western world: the Reds by exaggerating the shortcomings of Imperial Russia to excuse their own failures and to justify their own far greater excesses; the *émigré* Whites by dwelling almost entirely on the Red brutality and by refusing to admit that anything positive had been achieved in the U.S.S.R.

The immigration after World War II further accentuated this unbalanced picture as a result of a completely indefensible clause of the Yalta agreement. That clause obligated the Western Allies to forcibly repatriate to the Soviet Union all persons who had left its borders after 1939 and who were found in the occupied zones of Nazi Germany and of its satellites. For that reason very few former Soviet Russians or Ukrainians managed to escape extradition to the Reds unless they had collaborated with pro-Nazi groups which helped them hide their true past after the downfall of Hitler.

The naive trust placed by some American World War II leaders in "dear old Joe" Stalin, the ruthless Georgian dictator of the Soviet Union, led to bitter disappointment and a swing to an opposite extreme in Washington.

* See p. xxi for explanation of term.

An organized campaign set in to arouse American public opinion. The understandable fear of continued Communist aggression was amalgamated with the anti-Russian biases of many recent arrivals to this country and resulted in a widespread confusion of the terms "Russian," "Communist," and "Imperialist." In some cases this confusion appears to have been instigated deliberately and led to grotesque aberrations climaxed by the so-called Captive Nations law, U.S. Public Law 86–90, unanimously voted by the U.S. Congress in July, 1959.

Very few Americans realize that this law is not limited to bona-fide nations, such as Poland, Hungary and others mentioned in part of the Yalta agreement violated by Stalin. Actually, P.L. 86–90 called in effect for the complete dismemberment of Russian territories according to an overall geographical pattern which closely resembles the one advanced in the past by Nazi and Kaiser Wilhelm invaders of the Soviet Union and of Russia who wanted their political subjugation and economic control.

In the purely military sphere, the United States appears to have avoided the classic error of preparing itself to fight the last war all over again, but it has not done so in its political approach to things Russian. The basic premises of P.L. 86–90 repeat not only the fundamental errors of Hitler, but of some of his predecessors in past invasions of Russia as well.

Public Law 86–90 even commits the United States to help some mythical nations, such as "Cossackia" and "Idel-Ural," in "the recovery of their freedom and independence." The very name "Cossackia" was "discovered" in Central Europe between the two world wars. It therefore seemed both easy and incumbent on me, as a former Don Cossack officer and an American citizen for over twenty years, to expose the fraudulent hoax of which the United States Congress has become a victim—a very willing one, it is true.

However, all my requests to be allowed to testify under oath before relevant Congressional committees were rebuffed. None of my published letters to editors nor my published articles and addresses * produced visible results. The main reason for this appeared to lie in the almost complete lack of real knowledge among native Americans concerning things Russian, and especially concerning the spirit behind the conflicts which shaped historical events in Eastern Europe.

* Refs. 63, 64, 65, 66, 67, 68, 69.

I was deeply and, in the final analysis, favorably impressed by a 1959 visit to the Soviet Union which I made as a member of the U.S. Foundation Engineering Exchange delegation appointed by the President of the National Academy of Sciences in Washington, D.C. This first visit to my native land after forty years' absence convinced me, among other things, that the proverbial Western lack of understanding of the spirit behind past Russian historical events extends to contemporary developments there as well.

I find it puzzling how such an intelligent, well-informed and basically decent man as Winston Churchill could speak of Russia, apparently in all seriousness, as "a mystery wrapped in an enigma." There is nothing mysterious about past or present Russian reactions to Western moves. Russia's terrible human losses in World War I produced a violent popular revulsion against the ruling classes whose lack of foresight had permitted this suffering to occur. The virus of Marxism, imported from the West, thus found a temporarily fertile soil. This situation led to one of the greatest upheavals in history, and for a number of years after the victory of communism there Russia was a very sick country. Many short-sighted actions of Western nations in the years to come, culminating in the Nazi invasion, only served to prolong the sick state of Russia and to retard its return to sane and normal relations with the outside world. Few people in America understand this. It seems to me that the trouble here is not just lack of understanding in the West of the meaning of distant events, but also lack of imagination needed to visualize human reactions springing from a set of circumstances different from one's own experiences.

And yet the fate of the world in this nuclear age may depend on a better mutual understanding between Russians and the West. Differentiation between the national aspirations of Russians as people and the aims of communism, as an international ideology brought to Russia from the West, is of crucial importance in this respect. Indeed, if it is true that all aggressive Communist actions of the past forty years are only a natural expression of permanent national characteristics of the Russians as people (this is the thesis of the man who wrote our Public Law 86–90 *), then the idea of preparing the dismemberment of Russia, even at the risk of a world-wide nuclear holocaust, may not appear completely insane. However, if the menace to world peace is rooted in past Communist ideology, then things are not hope-

---

* See *Congressional Record,* January 21, 1960, p. 919.

less since the influence of ideologies and their substance as well change with time. I maintain that the latter is the true situation.

Having grown up in a Russian military family close to the seat of Imperial power, and having served in the Russian armies, I *know* that all presently popular talk of past *Russian* aspirations for world domination is utter nonsense.* I also see much evidence of changes in Communist attitudes within the Soviet Union and of promise of continued changes for the better. This process will inevitably develop further if left to itself, and can only be materially slowed down by menacing threats from abroad.

The problem is a very complex one and cannot be even outlined in a few pages. Hence my decision to proceed with this book about which I have been thinking for many years.

As I am writing these lines, I am approaching the age when I can retire from academic teaching. However, university retirement pay being what it is, it will not be possible for me to give up my consulting engineering activities so long as I am of sound mind and body. I have therefore decided to abandon my original plans of writing my reminiscences in retirement, and to do this now, expanding the scope of the book to include my recent impressions of the Soviet Union.

I will try to concentrate on the human aspects and meaning of events I have witnessed during the "half century plus" of my conscious life, using my personal experiences mainly as a framework. The first and last decades will receive particular attention.

The book will be divided into three parts: Part I will consist of the first three of the ten chapters of the book and will cover the period up to the beginning of the Civil War in November, 1917. Part II (five chapters: 4, 5, 6, 7, and 8) will describe the Civil War itself. Part III will have two chapters. The first, Chapter 9, will merely provide a short connecting link with recent experiences in Chapter 10 which will describe my 1959 impressions of the Soviet Union.

I was fortunate in having preserved some documents which helped me refresh my memory, for instance: the *Poslouzhnóy Spísok* (official Service Record) of my father; a diary, or to be more precise, a journal belonging to my mother, covering the period from June 14, 1915, to January 1, 1918; several personal letters to me from the former Don Atamán, General Piótr Krassnóv, written abroad between 1922 and 1941; and other materials. I have also checked my recollections

---

* See pp. 13, 16, 18, and Refs. 7, 21 and 22.

against various published documents; for instance, the official records assembled by the Don Historical Commission in Belgrade; the memoirs of Marshal Joffre of France, General Ludendorff of Germany, American and British military attachés, and of others. Looking over, in the New York Public Library, microfilms of 1913–1914 St. Petersburg newspapers which we used to receive at home also helped to confirm and to document many points I remembered. I shall therefore refer to supporting materials as I develop my narrative.

I am very grateful to the McGraw-Hill Book Company for its agreement not to press me for a revised second edition of my earlier engineering book * until I have completed the present historico-political one.

I doubt that my present effort will win much acclaim. Hostile reactions of the recently proliferated breed of professional "Russia-haters" are of course to be expected, but many other groups will probably dislike parts of it—different ones in each case. For instance, some of my German friends may dislike being reminded of the fact that aggressive actions for the dismemberment of Russia and for its Teutonic colonization began long before Hitler, that they were only revived in Kaiser Wilhelm's days when organized planning began, and that World War I started at a moment when Germany was obviously best prepared for it militarily and industrially as compared to Russia. Some Roman Catholics may also dislike reminders of past invasions of Russia which their militant extremists had promoted. However, these are all facts which should be generally known and kept in mind in the West, since the present welcome reconciliation between Teuton and Gaul in the fold of Rome is insufficient to insure the peace and the survival of the world. It is essential that it be followed by a similar reconciliation between Teuton and Slav, Christian and Jew, and between the Roman Catholic and the Eastern Orthodox Churches.

Some Russian Reds also may find unpalatable parts of my account, namely those of Civil War episodes, which will contradict parts of their own published official versions. On the other hand, some Russian Whites still blindly adhere to the doctrine of "irreconcilability"—although not without some external encouragement and pressure from foreign propagandists with more zeal than foresight, it is true. They and their friends are likely to resent my writing about some favorable

---

* *Soil Mechanics, Foundations and Earth Structures,* which was number 15 on the best-seller list of all McGraw-Hill engineering books for 1952. Translated into Spanish and Japanese.

impressions I brought back from my 1959 visit to the Soviet Union, just as some of them disliked the very idea of my having gone there at all, even as a member of an official U.S. delegation.

I cannot blame those of either side whose judgment is inevitably beclouded by deep emotional recollections of relatives who tragically perished in the terrible turmoils which swept across the greatly suffering land of our birth. I consider myself exceptionally lucky that both my parents died a natural death, only indirectly caused by the Revolution—that is, from typhus. None of my relatives perished except in open combat and I myself always felt that I had hit my opponents no less hard than they had hit me and mine. Moreover, I passed unscathed through several difficult situations, in some cases due to the fact that past kindness is seldom forgotten and is often repaid.* Finally, I am certain that people I knew who did perish as martyrs during this second "Time of Troubles" loved Russia above all and that they would never have wanted their memories misused to promote hatred for Russia abroad and to prepare new miseries not only for its peoples, but for the entire world as well.

Nor can I agree with those of us who claim that we, emigrés from Russia, being guests of America, should not criticize any actions of its government or Congress related to Russia. As my Chapter 9 will show, I am greatly indebted to many Westerners, and especially to numerous individual Americans for friendly help in my time of need. Probably the greatest gift America has bestowed on me is my dear wife, born Florence Dorothy Bill. Coming of an Anglo-Saxon and Scotch-Irish family which has lived on this continent for some three hundred years, she helped me understand many facets of American life which seem so strange to someone who was not born and raised here. Without this help and her loving sympathy I doubt that I could have successfully weathered the many mental and other pressures to which a person of Russian origin is all too often subjected when attempting to participate in the mainstream of intellectual life abroad. That is why this book is dedicated to her.

I feel that it is the direct duty of American citizens of Russian origin not to remain silent when they witness systematic and deliberate misinformation of American public opinion on subjects concerning Russia which affect world peace, since they are among the few who know the true facts.

* See pp. 172–176, 181–182, 187–188.

Some Ukrainian separatist critics have angrily written to me: "You are an American citizen, yet your heart is still in Moscow!" This is only partially true—part of my heart certainly does remain in Russia, but the other part is right here in America. My resulting desire to help bring about better understanding and improved relations between the two countries cannot be considered inimical to the interests of either nation since continued conflict can only end in "co-annihilation," to use an apt remark by United States Senator Fulbright.

In this book I will deal mainly with what is wrong about Western attitudes towards Russia, not because I think Russia was always right, but because hundreds of recent Western publications have been exaggerating Russia's shortcomings, both past and present, real as well as imaginary. I therefore feel that the limited space now available to me should best be used to present to the American public how foolish all this propaganda of hatred and fear looks to a man of Russian background.

I will start by trying to show how erroneous are many concepts about old Imperial Russia which are popular now in this country. I shall do this not because I favor monarchism (this is a politically dead issue, in my opinion) but because one cannot understand the present without knowing the past.

I am confident that many Americans will appreciate this approach. I will feel that my efforts have not been in vain if they prompt some people here and in other Western countries to take another and closer look at their attitudes towards the Russian people and towards "Rossíya"!

*Begun: June, 1962*
*Completed: December, 1963*
*Princeton, New Jersey*

*Gregory P. Tschebotarioff*

# On Spelling and Terminology

In the course of my narrative I intend occasionally to use original Russian words (in addition to their English translation) when the full flavor and/or exact significance of their meaning cannot be otherwise conveyed to those readers who do know at least some Russian. These Russian words will be printed in the Latin alphabet, generally using the transliteration system of the New York Public Library. There are several other such systems, however. A few lines of explanation may be useful in this connection.

The Russian alphabet was originally derived from the ancient Greek. This was also the case of the alphabets of other Slavic nations, Serbs and Bulgars, to whom Christianity came from Byzantium. The modern Ukrainian * alphabet is similar, too. On the other hand, Slavic nations to which Christianity came from Rome—Poles, Czecho-Slovaks, Croats and Slovenes—use the Latin alphabet.

Approximately two-thirds of the letters of the Russian alphabet are derived directly from the Greek, some of them being similar to the Latin ones. The remaining third or so of the letters is specifically Russian. The sounds which they represent can be conveyed in the Latin alphabet only by a combination of letters, the combination varying with the language used.

I will illustrate the point by giving and partially analyzing my full name, as it is printed in Russian:

Григорий Порфирьевич Чеботарев

According to the New York Public Library system, with signs of accentuation added, this would be transcribed as:

Grigóriy Porphýrievich Chebotarióv

The first is my Christian name (Gregory), as given me at baptism. The second is my patrimonial name, my father's Christian name

---

* Until the twentieth century, the Ukrainians were usually referred to as *Maloróssy*—meaning "Little Russians"—to distinguish them from the much more numerous *Velikoróssy* or "Great Russians" of North and Central Russia. The Ukrainian language is no more different from the Great Russian language than, say, Plattdeutsch is from Hochdeutsch. The third branch of the Russian people are the *Byelorussians,* meaning "White Russians." This ancient name has nothing to do with the political views of the inhabitants of the region on Poland's eastern borders.

having been Porphýry—Porphýrievich is its genitive form, meaning "of Porphýry."

Most people are familiar with the elements of algebra and its mathematical symbols. They will recognize the first letter of my patrimonial name printed above in Russian as the Greek letter $\pi$— that is, "pi." The second letter $o$ has the same significance as in the Latin alphabet. The third letter, which looks like the Latin "p," is derived from the Greek $\rho$—that is, "ro"—and is so pronounced. The fourth letter is also derived from the Greek $\phi$—that is, "phi"—and also is so pronounced.

However, the last letter of my patrimonial name and the first letter of the family name Ч—which looks like a figure four—is a purely Russian letter, the sound of which has to be reproduced in the Latin alphabet in different ways, depending on the language used. Thus, in Italian the letter "C" will suffice; in English "Ch" will have to be used; in French, "Tch"; in German, "Tsch"; in Polish, "Cz," and so forth.

My first important document in the Latin alphabet was my 1925 degree of *Diplom-Ingenieur* from Berlin. Therefore, my name was spelled on it phonetically in German, beginning with the letters "Tsch." I moved to America twelve years later and could have easily changed my name or its spelling when I became a United States citizen in February, 1941, but by that time I had already published a number of technical engineering papers with my name spelled, as on my diploma, beginning with "Tsch." I realized that keeping this spelling would cause some difficulties in everyday life—actually many Americans who first saw my name in print could not get much further than a choked-off hiss: "Tss-s-ch-ch . . . ," until they realized that "Ts" should not be pronounced.

However, I preferred to cope with this kind of unpleasantness rather than create confusion as to the authorship of my previous papers which would have been inevitable had I formally dropped the "Ts." My early papers would have been then catalogued in various lists and indexes under the letter "T" and my later ones under the letter "C."

The spelling of the last syllable of my name also posed some problems, although much lesser ones. The ending ЕВ of many Russian names is pronounced "ióv" or "ióff." Not realizing that the letter "e" will not be similarly pronounced in a Latin-alphabet ending, many Russian *émigrés* spelled their endings "ev" or "eff" when first confronted by the necessity of spelling their names abroad. I did the latter. However, when I took my final citizenship papers in 1941, I changed the ending of my last name to "ióff" to make it more phonetical. My already long last name became still longer by one letter. The judge was therefore at first much surprised by my wish, until I explained that I did not care to have my name pronounced too differently from what it was in the two wars I had fought in.

In the text of this book, when referring to myself before leaving Russia, and to my late parents, I will use the phonetic spelling "Chebotarióv," rather than my present legal spelling, which is more difficult to read in English.

There is no middle name in Russian. Only one Christian name is given at baptism by the Eastern Orthodox Church. Feeling that my last name was enough of a mouthful for most Americans, I decided to abbreviate my patrimonial name to the middle initial "P." which is now part of my legal American name. However, both Red and White Russians would usually address me as Grigóriy Porphýrievich because no legal formalities or foreign customs can change the name of one's father and because the polite way to address someone in Russian was and still is by his Christian and patrimonial names. Since this form of address will be frequently quoted in my book, I will explain it somewhat further. I think that the best way to do so is by giving examples.

Since my paternal grandfather's name was like mine, that is, Gregory, my father would be addressed as "Porphýry Grigórievich." My maternal grandfather's name was "Iván Stepánovich Doubiágsky." Since in Russian the ending of the genitive and of other cases is different for the masculine and the feminine genders, my maternal uncle would be spoken of as "Nikolái Ivánovich Doubiágsky," and my mother as "Valentína Ivánovna Doubiágskaya" before marriage, and "Chebotarióva" after her marriage.

In Russian one never addresses a person by his first name as is customary in America. A diminutive form of the first name is however often used, but only by relatives, pals among classmates and other *very* close friends. Thus my paternal uncle, Iván Grigórievich, could be referred to as uncle "Ványa"; my maternal uncle Nikolái as uncle "Kótya" (although the usual abbreviation is "Kólya"); I as "Grísha"; my mother as "Válya"; and my sister, also christened "Valentína," as "Álya"—so that mother and daughter would know who was being called at home.

When people were on sufficiently intimate terms to address each other by such diminutive names, they would also say *ty* (thou) to each other, rather than the formal *vy* (you). This represented an intermediate form of familiarity. For instance, all officers of the same unit would say "thou" to each other, but the older men would address the younger by their little names whereas the younger men would still address their seniors by their first and patrimonial names, even while saying "thou." Both in military and in civilian circles they could do this *only* after a senior or older man was the *first* to propose a drink *na ty*—very much in the same way Germans drink *Bruderschaft* before saying *Du* to each other instead of *Sie*.

Many of the names of Russians I will mention later on are of West European origin. Some of them I have seen spelled only in Russian and will therefore have to transliterate their names as best I can, without assurance that the spelling will be the one they would have used.

There is one very important point of terminology which I would like to mention since it has led to much confusion of concepts in the West, where there is only one word, "Russian," to designate both a person of that race and a citizen of the country. The Russian language however makes the necessary distinction between the two: the term *Rússky* was and is used to designate a person of the Russian race whereas the term *Rossíysky* was applied to a citizen of the multinational *Rossíyskaya Impériya*, or briefly *Rossíya*, in very much the same way one would now speak of a citizen of the U.S.S.R. as being as *Soviétsky* citizen.

The borderline between the two concepts was not always clearly drawn, it is true. For instance, one could speak either of *Rússkye Voyská* or of *Rossíyskye Voyská* when referring to Russian troops, but one would not say *Rússkaya Impériya* when referring to the entire country.

In any case, the Russian language permits differentiation, when needed, between the two concepts, which is not possible in English or in other Western languages. I will therefore occasionally use the term *Rossíya* when I have to emphasize that I mean the multinational community of peoples forming the Russian state, rather than just the Russian people, as I have done on p. xx.

# Acknowledgments

I have already written on p. xix about the great debt I owe to my wife for having morally supported me at times which were most trying. The help she gave me in improving the style of the manuscript of this book was considerable.

My father-in-law, Alfred Hoyt Bill, the author of a number of books on American history,* has drawn my attention to valuable data on past Russo-American relations which give a very different picture of them and of Russia itself than appears in some of the modern utterances inspired by "cold-war" attitudes. Of particular interest for me were the books (Refs. 21 and 22) by F. V. Greene, who served as the American Military Attaché to the United States legation at St. Petersburg in 1876–1877 and who showed sympathetic understanding for Russian actions, aims and ambitions.†

I cannot thank individually all the Russian *émigrés* who wrote me literally hundreds of letters from all over the world, praising my exposure of calumnies against the people and the country of our birth. I take this opportunity to thank them all now, realizing at the same time that many of them will not fully share all of the political views which are expressed in this book.

Dr. George Vernádsky, professor emeritus of Russian History at Yale University, gave me valuable advice and help.

I am particularly indebted to Mr. Mark E. Weinbaum, editor of the liberal New York anti-communist Russian-language daily *Nóvoye Rússkoye Slóvo*, ‡ who not only published my articles (Refs. 65a to 65f), but supported me editorially as well (Ref. 75). He continued this in spite of the resulting flood of personal vituperation against him in the "separatist" press. Being of Jewish origin, he had no interest in doing this except to maintain high standards of integrity

---

* Among them: *The Beleaguered City, Richmond, 1861–1865*, Alfred A. Knopf, New York, 1946, 313 pp.; *Rehearsal for Conflict. The Story of Our War with Mexico, 1846–1848*, Alfred A. Knopf, New York, 1947, 342 pp.; *The Campaign of Princeton, 1776–1777*, Princeton University Press, New Jersey, 1948, 145 pp.

† Thus on pages 261–265, 278–279 and 308 of his *Army Life in Russia* (Ref. 22) Greene gives a thoughtfully penetrating analysis of the events, some of which he witnessed with the Russian troops in the field, which led to the liberation by Russia of the Balkan Christians from Turkish misrule.

‡ It is one of the oldest foreign-language newspapers in the country and celebrated its fiftieth anniversary on April 24, 1960.

in the best traditions of responsible journalism when reporting or discussing historical and political facts.

Professor George F. Kennan, on his return to Princeton from his ambassadorship to Belgrade, very kindly took time from the pursuit of his numerous new duties and interests to read my entire manuscript. I am very grateful to him for this and for the very pertinent constructive criticisms and suggestions which he made and which I was glad to follow.

# Part I    IMPERIAL RUSSIA AND THE FEBRUARY 1917 REVOLUTION

# 1     Setting of Our Family Life before World War I

## 1. *Our Family Background*

I was born February 15/28,* 1899, at Pávlovsk, a little garrison town a couple of miles south of the Imperial residence, Tsárskoye Seló (which means "Tsar's village") and 17 miles south of St. Petersburg (now called Leningrad), which was then the capital of Imperial Russia.

My grandparents came from different areas of the country. I am therefore one half Don Cossack, one quarter Great Russian and one quarter Ukrainian. My family name is derived from the Ukrainian word *chebotár*, meaning "bootmaker." The word is generally used in that sense in the entire south of Russia, not only in the Ukraine, but to the east of it as well, where lie the Great Russian-speaking areas of the Don Cossacks. So there are Chebotarióvs who are Cossacks and there are many others who are not. The name occurs frequently all over Russia.

Both of my paternal grandparents were Don Cossacks, and my father, Porphýry Grigórievich Chebotarióv, was an officer of the Don Cossack Guard Battery stationed at Pávlovsk. He was a Captain at the time of my birth.

In view of many questions frequently asked of me abroad, I think I should say at the very start that Don Cossacks are *not* a form of mounted police, that they are *not* all members of male choirs, and that any phonetical resemblance to the word "Don" in Don Quixote and Don Juan is purely coincidental.

The Cossacks are a complex, peculiarly Russian, phenomenon without parallel or counterpart in the Western world. Essentially, the Cossacks were the descendants of former frontiersmen who still retained their ancient privileges of free men, including the ownership of large land reserves and the duty of keeping their own horses,

---

* The first date refers to the Julian calendar which was in general use in Russia until the Revolution. It is referred to now as the "old style," but is still used by the Eastern Orthodox Church. The second is the Gregorian calendar used in the West. According to the latter, once in three out of four centuries the month of February has only 28 and not 29 days every fourth year. Thus now, in the twentieth century, the difference between the two calendars is thirteen days.

3

saddles and arms in their dwellings in constant readiness for immediate action against foreign invaders.

Cossacks were generally called by the names of the rivers along which they settled, the oldest and largest group being those of the Don, the next largest, of the Kubán, then of the Térek and of the Urál, all of whom settled along rivers of these names at the time they were embattled frontiers. This is why their regions were called "Armies." All Cossacks used only the Great Russian language, except for some 60 percent of the Kubán Cossacks, who spoke Ukrainian and who were the descendants of a different type of Cossacks, the "Zaporózhtzi."

By the end of the nineteenth century, Russia's borders had moved to the east and to the south, far beyond the main Cossack settlements west of the Urál Mountains. Nevertheless, while forming an administrative part of the Russian empire for over one hundred years, the Cossacks retained much of their original way of life. Their regions were still called *Voiská* (Armies) although Cossacks no longer were in the majority there, constituting only some 47 percent of the total local population. This was a consequence of the development of mining, industry and commerce, which led to an influx of the *inogoródnyi* (out-of-towners) from the north and west. By comparison to these newcomers, most of the Cossacks were well-to-do—and, hence, conservative farmers. Although by the time of the Revolution they were only a minority in their Army Areas, there still were about three and a half million Cossacks in the Don Army Area (*Oblast Vóyska Donskógo*) alone.

In exchange for the repeated reaffirmation of their ancient privileges and rights on the land reserves of the area, the Don Cossacks supplied the Imperial Russian government with fifty-one Army and two Guard regiments of first-rate cavalry, with supporting horse artillery. Many of the horses for the remounts of the regular Russian cavalry also came from the Don steppes.

I do not know the history of our family very far back. What I do know of it may however be of general interest since it will be the first of many examples I shall cite showing that the upper social strata of Imperial Russia were very far from being the completely closed society they are frequently pictured.

My paternal great-grandfather, Yákov Chebotarióv, was a Cossack farmer of the Kazánskaya Stanítza (district) in the northern part of the Don Army Area. He distinguished himself during the

1831 war with the Poles when serving with a Don Cossack cavalry regiment. His unit was ordered to dismount and to attack on foot a fortified Polish position. The Cossack officers wore then, as all Russian Army officers did prior to World War I, grey overcoats which stood out clearly against the brown overcoats of the men. The Polish sharpshooters therefore had little trouble picking off the officers one by one. Deprived of its leaders, the Cossack advance faltered. Great-grandfather Yákov was then only a Corporal, but he assumed command of his entire unit, rallied his men, and stormed and captured the Polish position in hand-to-hand fighting. I seem to recall being told that it was a fortified key redoubt of Práha (the eastern suburb of Warsaw on the right bank of the Vistula) but I am not sure that I remember this point correctly.

For this action Great-grandfather was promoted officer and received the St. George Cross, the highest combat decoration of Imperial Russia. It was awarded only for battlefield valor, like the Victoria Cross in England or the Congressional Medal in the United States.

After the war Great-grandfather returned to his farm and raised a large family. As a member of the Order of St. George he enjoyed a number of privileges which helped him send his elder son south to Novocherkássk, the capital of the Don Cossacks. He made good there, became a Government official, and wrote his father that he wanted to show his gratitude by helping a younger brother get an education. A family council selected the next senior brother; however, he suffered an accident, having stumbled against a pitchfork during the harvest, and lost an eye as a result. The family decided that this would be too much of a handicap for him in his studies and that his younger brother, Grigóriy, my grandfather and namesake, should go instead. There was no time to prepare a new suit of city clothing for him, so he took off on foot for Novocherkássk, some 170 miles away, wearing the clothes tailored for his elder brother who happened to be smaller than he was. Later I met in the Don an old great-uncle who described to me with considerable humor all this as well as the sight presented by grandfather Grigóriy when he arrived in Novocherkássk with his sleeves over an inch too short.

This did not prevent him from completing his secondary education so well that he won a scholarship to the Technological Institute at St. Petersburg, completed his studies there with distinction, returned to the Don as an engineer, and then took part in the construction of the Southeastern railroad which ran from the Azóv Sea port city of

Rostóv-on-the-Don through Novocherkássk, to Vorónezh, beyond the northern borders of the Don area (see Map E, p. 142). This must have been in the late 1860s.

When the Southeastern railroad was opened, Grandfather was awarded the title of Army Captain and was given a grant of some land near Khartzísk on the Ukrainian border. Later this became part of the Donétz coal mining basin, but at first Grandfather rented it out for cattle grazing. As the story was told to me by my great-uncle, the cowherd arrived on foot one day at Novocherkássk and asked Grandfather what he would give him if he brought him coal from his land, some one hundred miles away. Grandfather promised him 100 roubles (about fifty gold dollars). The cowherd departed and some time later returned with a horse-drawn cartload of excellent anthracite coal. He had noticed a *soúslik* (prairie dog) come out of his hole on a hillside with blackened fur, dug down a few feet after him, and found the anthracite seam.

Grandfather gave him the hundred roubles as promised. In addition, to show his appreciation for the find, he appointed the cowherd manager of some small-scale digging to be started immediately.

Shortly afterwards Grandfather Grigóriy died of pneumonia. His widow, my grandmother Praskóvia Ivánovna, a Cossack (Kheráskova) by birth, remarried soon after. Her second husband was a retired Cossack cavalry general, Piótr Ríkovsky, who developed her coal mines into a large and profitable concern. They became known as the Ríkovskye Kópi, and kept that name even after they were bought for several million roubles by a French concern in the early 1900s.

My great-uncle told me of an episode which occurred there in the late 1870s or in the 1880s, well before the mines were sold. A Scotch mechanic by the name of Hughes had started a machine shop not far from the Ríkovsky mines, but on the Ukrainian side of the border. He too prospered and his shop developed into large iron works which right up to the time of the Revolution bore a russified version of his name—Yúzovka; but during the Georgian dictator's rule were renamed Stálino.

The Ríkovskys and the Hugheses at first were on good neighborly terms. Then one unfortunate day Hughes drove over to show off to his friends a pack of thoroughbred hounds he had just imported from England, forgetting about the tame bear who was chained to a post at the entrance to Grandmother's estate. The hounds went for the bear, who was already full grown at that time, and were all killed or maimed by him. Recriminations as to responsibility for this canine slaughter ended the friendship.

I have read somewhere that the Soviet Premier Nikíta Khrushchev had worked as a coal miner in that area in a place owned by French interests. It may have even been Grandmother's original mines. At any rate, I always understood that conditions of work in that general locality were pretty bad. The anthracite coal was of high quality, but it occurred in comparatively thin seams of some three feet thickness. It was therefore uneconomical to advance the headings in a way permitting the men to stand up; they had to crawl when working. Hence it is not altogether surprising that a very large proportion of the miners became ardent Bolsheviks during and after the Revolution.

After Grandmother's remarriage, my father, who was her second and youngest boy, was sent to board at the newly formed Don Cadet Corps at Novocherkássk and was left very much to his own devices from then on. His was the first class to graduate from the Corps and Father headed the list. As was customary each year in Russian schools of all levels, his name, as No. 1 of his class in order of grades received, was engraved in gold letters on a slab of white marble fixed to a wall of the big Hall of the Corps.

From the Novocherkássk Cadet Corps, Father went on to become a *yúnker* at the Miháilovsky Artillery School at St. Petersburg. I should explain here that the Russian Cadet Corps, of which there were quite a number, were militarized boarding establishments for general education—at the high school level in the American sense. They prepared boys for the professional military *Ouchílische*— schools on a similar level to the United States West Point Academy. Pupils at the latter were called *yúnker*, while *kadét*, in contrast to its use in the United States, designated only a preparatory level. Also, instead of just one school for the entire Army, there were separate three-year schools for the artillery and the engineers and several two-year schools for the cavalry and the infantry. Their graduates were promoted to Second Lieutenant, a rank which had different names in different branches of the services: *Kornét* in the regular cavalry, *Khoroúnzhi* in the Cossack troops and *Pod-poróuchik* in the infantry and regular artillery.

Unlike the United States, in Russia the name academy is reserved for the highest level of scientific and educational work. Three schools on such a level were: a General Staff Academy, the Mihailov-sky Artillery Academy and a Military Engineering Academy to which were sent outstanding men—but only after several years' service as officers with the troops. I believe that this restricted meaning of the word Academy still holds in the U.S.S.R.

Father graduated from the Mihailovsky Artillery School in 1893 second on the list; another Don Cossack and a friend of Father's, Alexándr Vassílievich Cheriachoúkin,* was first, so the latter's name was engraved on the marble slab of honor of the school for that year's class. Father then joined the Don Cossack Guard Battery as Second Lieutenant and remained with it until 1910, commanding it with the rank of Colonel from 1906 on. In 1895 he had been detached to the Mihailovsky Artillery Academy and completed its course two years later first on the list—so he got inscribed on their marble slab of honor. Graduates of the Academy were really full-fledged engineer technologists and had the choice of either being assigned in that capacity to military arsenals or of returning to their units. Father chose the latter.

Fig. 1 shows him in full parade uniform of a Colonel of the Cossack Guard Battery. The gold emblem on his right breast (where emblems of academic achievement were usually worn) indicates a graduate of the Mihailovsky Artillery Academy. The emblem of the Mihailovsky Artillery School (*ouchílische*) however did not rate as academic and was worn on the left side of the tunic, as was done with emblems of other similar schools or of military units served in pre-viously. It is barely visible in the picture.

My mother's picture (Fig. 2) was taken at about the same time as the adjoining one of my father. She was the daughter of Iván Stepánovich Doubiágsky who had served as an Army doctor in the Balkans during the war of 1877–1878, and who, at the time of her marriage and until his death (about 1905), was the senior medical doctor of the hospital at Pávlovsk. He was of Great Russian origin.

Fig. 3 shows him on the veranda of his Pávlovsk hospital residence with his family and friends. On the left is my maternal grandmother, Ólga Sergéyevna. I do not remember her maiden family name, but she came from Chougoúyev, a small town on the upper reaches of the Donétz River, 27 miles to the south of Khárkov, the main city of the Eastern Ukraine. I have often heard her refer to herself as a

---

* See Chapter 8 and Chapter 9.

"Khokhlúshka." * She had daughters by her first marriage who remained spinsters and hence kept their late father's name—Tikhomírov. One of them, Aunt Mánya, is the second from the left, and the other, Aunt Yúlia, is the fifth from the left in Fig. 3. I cannot identify the others. It is likely that one of the two women on the right is Ásya Erdély, with whom my maiden aunts were quite friendly and who used to come with them frequently to Pávlovsk. She was a harpist, and apparently quite a good one; she stayed in Russia after the Revolution and became a soloist of the Bolshói Theatre in Moscow.

My two Tikhomírov aunts were schoolteachers at St. Petersburg. They seemed to have connections in the artistic world and to be friendly with the Prokófiev family. I recall the indignant tone of their frequent narratives concerning the various trials and tribulations which the then upcoming Prokófiev was encountering in his struggle for recognition.

Until about the time that Figs. 1 and 2 were taken, my parents were quite well off. Judging by the shares of the Poltáva Land Bank which I found among my father's papers, my grandmother Ríkovsky had made him an outright gift of 200,000 roubles (100,000 gold dollars) some time before his marriage or as a wedding present. In addition, she was giving him a handsome annual allowance. This was absolutely needed for service in the Guards where an officer's pay barely covered his mess bills, a lot of entertaining being done there.

The Battery was pretty much of a show piece and participated in various military displays, examples of which are given by Figs. 4 and 5. The latter picture was taken in the inner courtyard of the Ekateríninsky Palace at Tsárskoye Seló, in front of its main building, just as Tsar Nicholas II, in his capacity of Honorary Colonel of the Battery, received a direct report from its Sergeant.

The horsemanship of the Battery can be judged from the fact that so far as I know it was the only unit permitted at some parades to dash at full career single file through the comparatively small closed-in courtyard and out through the narrow gate (seen in the background to the right of the Sergeant's head, in Fig. 5), with only inches to

---

* The feminine of *Khokhól,* a nickname for Ukrainians, used in the rest of Russia very much the same way that one uses in America the word "hoosier" to designate a native of the state of Indiana. There was nothing offensive or contemptuous about it, in spite of contrary assertions of anti-Russian propagandists in this country.

spare between the axle hubs of its guns and the delicate wrought-iron lattice work of the historic gate.

Father owned two riding horses, Mother one, and I had a pony. In addition, we had two harness horses with carriage and sleigh and an automobile of French make as early as 1907. This was quite a novelty at the time.

We frequently spent summer vacations abroad, mainly in France. I do not remember much of Nice or of Biarritz, where we had spent two summers earlier, but I do remember a few things about St. Malo and adjoining Paramé where we stayed in 1906.

Relations between Father and his mother, however, gradually deteriorated. It all seems to have started when Grandmother Ríkovsky realized some time after the birth of a daughter that she would not have a male heir from her second marriage. As her second husband was getting old, she suddenly decided that Father should resign from the Guards and prepare himself to take over the management of the coal mines. Even if this had required additional studies, it would not have been too unusual; for instance, I know of an officer of the Leib-Guard Cossack Regiment, Borodín, who decided that he did not like peacetime service, resigned, entered the Górny (Mining) Institute at St. Petersburg and became an engineer after graduation. At the start of World War I he, however, rejoined his old regiment. Things should have been easier for Father, since many of his courses at the Artillery Academy could have probably been fully or partially credited to him.

Father however declined to follow his mother's wishes. She had taken little personal interest in him while he was growing up—he had achieved much through his own efforts and took a genuine interest in his profession of artilleryman. Grandmother did not take kindly to this. She was pretty much of an authoritarian matriarch, whose great wealth had accustomed her to having her wishes complied with by her relatives. Father's elder brother however sided with him. Relations gradually soured and finally came to a complete break between the Ríkovskys and Grandmother's two sons from her first marriage, whom she disinherited.

Father indicated to his superiors his interest in a position where he would not be required to absorb large prestige expenses. He was first given the command of a Don Cossack *Divizión*—that is, of two batteries located at Chougoúev in the Ukraine, which also happened to be the birthplace of my maternal grandmother, as mentioned earlier.

We spent a summer there with him, but returned north in the fall and rented an apartment at Tsárskoye Seló, where I started going to school. We knew that father would soon be called there to fill a vacancy of Senior Instructor at the Officers' Artillery School. Officers, usually captains, before receiving the command of a battery had to take one year of refresher courses at its Tsárskoye Seló buildings in the winter and at its shooting range at Loúga, some 90 miles to the south, in the summer.

In 1912 Father was transferred to the personal staff of the Grand Duke Sergéy Miháilovich, the Inspector General of the Artillery of the Russian armies. He had the post of Officer for Special Assignments. The first major duty he had was to examine all artillery officers in the Western Military Districts of Russia on their knowledge of the maintenance and repairs of their field guns. He spent several months traveling from one garrison town to another. Later, I frequently met artillery officers who, on hearing my name, immediately asked if I was related to the Colonel Chebotarióv whose arrival they had waited for with such trepidation. His reports were supposed to have considerable weight when promotions were considered and apparently Father had a reputation of being pretty tough where service and technical matters were concerned.

Father's second assignment on the Grand Duke's staff was much more interesting. He spent several months in the Balkans studying the use of heavy artillery by the Serbian and Greek armies during the 1912–1913 wars which these countries waged first against Turkey and then against Bulgaria.*

## 2. *Family Interest in History*

Father set me an example and stimulated my interest in history. In 1905, when the seventy-fifth anniversary of the Don Cossack Guard Battery was celebrated, he wrote and published at his own expense a well-illustrated 192-page volume of its history, of which I was fortunate to obtain a copy abroad. I list it as Ref. 4, which gives the full official name of the Battery. The numeral "6" in its name refers to its number on the Guard Horse Artillery Brigade which provided artillery support to the thirteen regiments of Guard

---

* The latter war was largely the result of German intrigues aided by King Ferdinand of Bulgaria who by birth was the German Prince of Coburg. Later, the same dynasty even succeeded in bringing Bulgaria to Germany's side after the Russian reverses of 1915 in World War I.

Cavalry, of which three were Cossack regiments. Although listed as "6th," our battery was the only Cossack unit in the Guard Horse Artillery.

All units of the Guards had the prefix of German origin—*Leib-Guard* (Body-Guard)—to their full official titles, but this was an honorary designation which had been only partially valid for some of its oldest units even in the distant past.

By the time of the reign of Nicholas II, the functions of his personal bodyguard were performed by a unit known as His Majesty's Own *Konvóy* and by His Majesty's Own *Svódny Polk*—that is, "Composite Regiment". The latter was formed in the decade before World War I of particularly reliable corporals picked from various units of the Guards and of the Army. The Konvóy consisted of two *sótnya* (meaning literally "hundred"—that is, squadrons), one of Kubán and the other of Térek Cossacks.

Both the Kubán and the Térek Cossacks of the Konvóy wore their traditional dress—the *cherkésska*—a long wide-sleeved coat reaching below the knees with several visible cartridge pockets across the chest. Since they appeared near the Tsar in most official photographs, the erroneous idea seems to have gained wide acceptance abroad that this was a typical Cossack dress worn by all of them. This is not so. It is a dress originally worn by most Caucasian mountaineers, who were contained in the northern foothills by the Kubán and the Térek Cossacks settled there for that purpose. These and only these Cossacks adopted the Caucasian mountain dress,* giving it the name of the warlike Moslem tribe of the Cherkéss (Circassians) who were their principal opponents.

The Don, the Urál and the several Siberian Cossack armies however wore the same type of uniform as did the rest of the Russian Army, except for wide trousers slightly hanging over their top boots, with a colored two-and-a-half inch wide stripe down the sides—red for the Don, violet for the Urál, yellow for the Transbaikál, and so on. In the Guard units the trouser stripes were omitted. However, one could always tell a Cossack by the cocky angle at which he would usually wear his cap and by the lock of hair which protruded from under its edge—it was one of the traditional Cossack privileges not to have their hair close cropped as was done for the rest of the Russian Army.

* See Fig. 38 and Fig. 39.

Let us now go back to my father's history of the Don Cossack Guard Battery (Ref. 4). One item of general historical interest it contained was realized by me only many years later when I read in this country about "Lincoln's Cossack General"—Brig. Gen. John Basil Turchin (see Refs. 49 and 70). He was supposed to have been a Don Cossack Artillery officer and to have served in the Imperial Guards before emigrating to America in 1856, where he shortened his name. Father's book has a list of all past officers of the Battery which gives their names, from where and when they joined the battery and when and for what post they left the Battery. Under No. 12 I found Turchin, listed by his original name of Iván Vassílievich Turchanínoff.

The main items of general historical interest contained in Father's book refer to the Turkish campaign of 1877–1878 and to the Abyssinian expedition of 1898.

Few Americans realize the intense feelings of genuine sympathy which existed among all classes of Russians for their Slavic and Greek Christian brethren in the Balkans who for centuries had been subjugated by the Moslem Turks. As a thirteen-year-old boy I yelled myself hoarse in the streets of St. Petersburg during demonstrations in support of the 1912 anti-Turkish Balkan coalition. I can assert that the mass participation by persons of all ages in these demonstrations was quite genuine and spontaneous.

The Turkish War of 1877–1878 is known in Russia and in the Balkan Slavic countries as the *Osvoboditelnaya Voyná* (War of Liberation). An intelligent, understanding and far-sighted appraisal of Russia's role in the Balkans is given by the contemporary American Military Attaché, F. V. Greene * (see Refs. 21 and 22). He spent the entire campaign of 1877–1878 with the Russian armies.

Father was intensely interested in that campaign. He had a copy made of the painting (shown by Fig. 6) and hung it in the drawing room of our apartment. The original was in the palace of the Grand Duke Mikhaíl Alexándrovich. It shows an episode of the war during a march of General Rauch's column along a mountain path which the Turks had not fortified, believing that it could not be negotiated. The Don Cossack Guard Battery did lose a caisson, as shown in the picture, but the rest got through outflanking the Turks and forcing them to abandon their fortified positions. F. V. Greene, on page 170

---

* Direct descendant of Washington's able lieutenant, Nathaniel Greene, Commander of the Army of the South in the American Revolution.

of Ref. 21, lists the same units of Rauch's column as does my father on page 100 of his book (Ref. 4).

In our drawing room also hung a larger painting for which Father had personally commissioned and paid. It depicted another episode of the same Turkish campaign. The Sergeant of the Don Cossack Guard Battery, Avédikoff, had to stay in a Bulgarian village behind the rapidly advancing detachment of the 2nd Guard Cavalry Division (of which the Battery formed part) to repair the broken axle of a two-wheel cart which contained the Battery's cash box. He had only eight of his Cossacks with him. By the time repairs were completed, there were retreating Turkish troops on all sides of the village, but the Turks were as yet unaware of his presence.

Sergeant Avédikoff decided to break out of encirclement by suddenly attacking what appeared to be the weakest Turkish unit, an infantry company of over sixty men. He mobilized the male inhabitants of the village, although they were unarmed, and told them to move up along a ravine in the rear of the Turks and to cheer when he charged, to create the impression of large Russian reinforcements nearby. The Bulgar peasants, who hated their Turkish oppressors, willingly obliged. Four of Avédikoff's eight Cossacks were to attack from a different direction. With the remaining four Cossacks, he rode up along another gully to intercept the Turks. When they were close by he suddenly rode out, shooting the Turkish officer and two of his men just as the invisible Bulgars raised a frightful din in the rear of the remaining Turks, who all promptly surrendered. So Avédikoff brought back Turkish prisoners with the Battery's cash box!

Sergeant Avédikoff received the soldier's St. George Cross and was promoted officer. Fig. 7 shows him as a second lieutenant of a Don Cossack Army regiment—it was not customary for a man to remain as an officer in the same unit he had served while in the ranks. The Guards Battery gave him a rousing send-off from its San Stephano position at the gates of Constantinople.

Father commissioned a painter, Mr. Bákmanson, to make a special trip to Bulgaria, where in a village called Derbént there still were many Bulgarian peasants who remembered Avédikoff's attack twenty-five years earlier. So the painting in our drawing room was a very accurate representation of the attack and, of course, showed the same season.

Cossacks were frequently selected for particularly difficult assignments. An example of this is provided by the expedition which the

Imperial Russian Geographical Society sent in 1898 to Abyssinia. There seem to have been strong political overtones to the action. This was a time of intense African rivalry between England and France, and of growing cooperation between France and Russia. The Abyssinian Church was a branch of the Coptic Christians which belonged to the Eastern Orthodox Creed. Abyssinia therefore had considerable religious affinity for Russia.

The bodyguard of the expedition consisted of picked officers and men from the two Guard Don Cossack regiments and the Guard Cossack Battery. It was commanded by Colonel Artamónov of the Atamánsky Regiment. He and two of his men, one of whom was Corporal Schedróff of our battery (Fig. 8), accompanied a 1,500-man Abyssinian elite detachment of the Dadiazmatcha (General) Tassáma, which formed one of the several columns sent by the Negus (King) Menelik (according to the Paris *l'Illustration,* Ref. 24) in order to *reculer* (roll back) the frontiers of his possessions. Its destination was the region of the White Nile. Somewhere on the way they met a French officer who, however, fell sick by the time they reached the confluence of the river Sobat and Nile. He was therefore unable to attempt swimming the Nile to raise the French flag on its left bank, according to Father's account (page 165 of Ref. 4), to: "assert the rights of France on a large region." Colonel Artamónov, a Corporal of his regiment, Arkhípov, and the Corporal of the Guard Battery, Schedróff, did it for him. Schedróff's narrative of their dangerous crossing is given verbatim in Father's book (Ref. 4).

This seems to have been a supporting operation for the major one at Fashoda, a point on the Nile some one hundred miles to the north. Fashoda was occupied by a French officer, Commandant Marchand, from the French Sudan on July 10, 1898, an action which almost involved France in a war with England. Kitchener played an on-the-spot role in the development of events. France finally backed down and Marchand evacuated Fashoda December 11, 1898. I think it more than a coincidence that the Russian Geographical Expedition left Abyssinia soon after that (in the spring of 1899) and returned to St. Petersburg.

Colonel Artamónov and his two Cossacks were personally received and decorated by the Tsar in a special audience. The Imperial Geographical Society, in its session of May 15, 1899, also awarded them a medal. Judging by the photo, Fig. 8, Corporal Schedróff picked up a third medal somewhere along the line. The two silver chains on his right breast, however, connect to silver watches won by him in his battery. In the Russian Army it was customary to award such watches as prizes for pistol marksmanship, for *djigitóvka* (fancy stunt-riding), for horseback sabre exercises and other similar competitions of men from various units.

It is interesting to note that the French account of the Nile crossing appeared in the Paris *l'Illustration* only over a year later—on January 13, 1900 (Ref. 24). Apart from some apparently inevitable Western journalistic *klúkva*,* (Corporal Schedróff was made into the "Brigadier Sochtchedroff" and Colonel Artamónov, a Don Cossack, into a "scion of a very ancient family of boyars"), the French account gave full credit to the personal courage of the three men. Thus they wrote:

> ". . . there were no boats; neither the Abyssinian soldiers, nor the local Negroes would agree at any price to swim across the wide, deep and rapid river inhabited by hippopotamuses and crocodiles."

In view of the international politics involved, I do not think it surprising that the *l'Illustration* never even mentioned the raising of the French flag nor the presence of a sick French officer with Tassáma's detachment. Somewhat lamely, the article attributed the feat of Artamónov and his men to the need of "pushing a reconnaissance to the left bank" of the Nile. Anyone reading this account might get the impression that the whole thing was a purely Abyssinian affair, resulting from a personal whim of the Negus Menelik, supported by some courageous Russians who just happened to be around. I think that the entire case provides a good illustration of the staunch way Imperial Russia helped its Allies without clamoring for special recognition of its actions.

At the start of the 1904–1905 Russo-Japanese war a new type of field gun was introduced in the Russian Army to replace an older

---

* A small northern plant with edible red berries. It is somewhat similar to but smaller than the American cranberry. It became a synonym for silly nonsense written abroad about Russia after a Frenchman wrote a book about a short trip of his to Russia which contained a number of surprising observations including the description of a refreshing nap he took in the shade of a majestic klúkva. Particularly outrageous nonsense was since then designated as a "most shady klúkva" or a "most spreading klúkva." I was interested to note that the expression is still sometimes used in the Soviet Union, and in the same sense (for instance, see page 1379 of Ref. 48).

model seen in Fig. 4. The harness for the horses however remained unchanged. The Guard Battery was the first Cossack unit to receive the new gun. A team of twelve volunteer-instructors, specially trained by my father, was then sent to the front to help the Cossack batteries there familiarize themselves with the new field pieces. This team, wearing the wide black fur caps of the Far Eastern Army, is shown in Fig. 9.

The last four years before World War I happened to provide anniversaries of three separate previous invasions of Russia from the West during the preceding three centuries. They were all commemorated by numerous ceremonies which deeply impressed on my mind the relevant historical facts.

In 1909 was celebrated the bicentennial of the battle of Poltáva, where in 1709 Peter the Great decisively defeated Charles XII of Sweden who had invaded the Ukraine in the mistaken belief that his secret ally, the treacherous Hetman Mazépa, would swing the local population to his side.

In 1912 occurred the centenary of Napoleon's 1812 invasion of Russia, of the indecisive battle of Borodinó, of the burning of Moscow and of Napoleon's disastrous winter retreat.

The year 1913 was particularly rich in historical anniversaries. First came the tercentenary of the Polish invasion * in support of a pretender to the Russian throne who had secretly embraced Roman Catholicism; their capture of Moscow; the uprising of the local population which killed the pretender and, finally, the termination of Russia's "Time of Troubles" by the election to the throne of Mikhaíl Fyódorovich who in 1613 became the first Tsar of the Románov dynasty.

Then came the centenary of the 1813 battle of Leipzig where the Leib-Guard Cossack Regiment covered itself with glory. General Latour-Maubourg's brigade of French Cuirassiers had crashed through Prussian infantry, had overrun a Prussian battery and were thundering up a slope of a mound with nothing between them and the three Allied sovereigns—the Russian and the Austrian Emperors and the King of Prussia—who were watching the battle from its top. However, the Don Cossacks of the Guard were behind the mound. Tsar Alexander I ordered them to counterattack.

* It had strong overtones of a religious crusade, having been sponsored by the Jesuits in an attempt forcibly to convert Russia to Roman Catholicism (see page 116 of Ref. 72).

This they did successfully, using their lances and threw the Cuirassiers back in what is probably one of the most spectacular cavalry charges in military history. I do not know of any other which had such a "full house" of high level brass watching it. *

As a reward for this feat the regiment had the special honor of triumphantly entering Paris in March, 1814, at the head of the three Allied armies preceding even the three monarchs.

Fig. 10 reproduces an English print of the period which shows the last ranks of the Don Cossacks of the Guard passing under the Porte Saint Martin ahead of Tsar Alexander I, his Allied monarchs and their armies.

The Parisians did not seem to have kept hostile memories of that regiment, which stayed as part of the occupation forces of the city for several months. Fig. 11 reproduces a French cartoon of the period —a bashful young Don Cossack Guard officer is being restrained by his faithful orderly from meeting some Parisian hussies.

By Imperial order the name LEIPZIG was engraved on the regimental standards, and the day of their charge—October 4 (old style) —was made the regimental holiday.

The Guard Battery was always very closely associated with the Leib-Guard Cossack Regiment. The St. Petersburg *Rússky Invalíd* published on the 1913 centennial anniversary of their charge a poem by my father dedicated "To the Heroes of Leipzig," (Ref. 5). It was reprinted later in Paris by the Museum of the Regiment (Ref. 40), and again in 1963 at the sesquicentennial anniversary.

Fig. 12 shows how a later-day Frenchman, the famous painter Edouard Detaille, saw that regiment (Ref. 10). This is the way these fine men really looked, and as I knew them.

The Napoleonic wars provide one of many examples which refute the arguments that world domination is a *Russian* tradition rather than an aim of Communist extremists. If this were so, then the Russian armies, after chasing Napoleon from Moscow in 1812 to Paris in 1814, would not have gone home shortly after that. They were no longer on the scene the following year, and it will doubtless be remembered that Wellington was alone at Waterloo in 1815 to cope with Napoleon's return from his exile at Elba.

---

* A Colonel Chebotarióv was killed in that attack. He was not a relative of ours.

### 3. My Early Education

Pávlovsk of my childrood days was quite a small town. Three batteries were the only units stationed there at the time. It livened up quite a bit in the summer when many people came from St. Petersburg to their *dáchas* (summer cottages). There were then excellent daily symphony and other concerts either in the open air or in a large hall (see Ref. 36) which adjoined the railroad station and the vast park which was open to the public. It attracted many excursionists from the nation's Capital.

Pávlovsk formed part of the personal estate of the Grand Duke Konstantín Konstantínovich. We were very friendly with the family of his Town Manager, a retired General of the Guard Horse Artillery, Edouárd Edouárdovich Heéring. They had the courtesy of the Grand Duke's private palace grounds (see later photo, Fig. 61) * and I frequently played tennis with them there.

The Grand Duke was a highly educated and literary-minded person who published several quite good poems and plays under the nom de plume "K. R." He held the post of Inspector General and was in charge of all the military Cadet Corps.

On the occasion of a birthday of his elder daughter, he staged at his Pávlovsk palace a play he had written for her—*Wedding of the Sun and the Spring*—and invited children of officers garrisoned at Pávlovsk and in its vicinity to participate with his own children in the roles of various flowers, plants and animals of the play. I was then seven or eight years old and was given the role of the third of four *golovástiks* (tadpoles). We wore grey tights, a grey body made of stiff papier-mâché with a long fin-like tail on its back, great bulging bright-colored eyes over a slot for our face, and slots at breast level for our hands. It took several grownups to help one get in or out of these contraptions which were made to order and were tightly fitted. We then had to hop a simple step together while singing in our squeaky voices (I still remember the first four lines).

The occasion was one to remember since the Tsar and his family were in the front row and a large part of the audience were Románov relatives of the Grand Duke.

There were no schools at Pávlovsk, so until the age of ten all my studies were conducted at home, mainly under Mother's personal

---

* The palace had been designed at the end of the eighteenth century by a Scotch architect, Cameron (see Ref. 36).

guidance. She did a lot of studying herself so as to teach me effectively, but seemed to take it in her stride. Like Father, she had graduated first in her class and had received a gold medal at the Pávlovsky * Institút at St. Petersburg.

Special attention was paid to teaching me foreign languages. Father did not want me to become a professional soldier and favored the idea of a career for me in the consular branch of the Imperial Foreign Service, which did not require personal prestige expenses.

At the age of five I got a French governess for two years. When I was seven she was replaced by an English governess who also lived in our apartment. My French was kept up by a visiting teacher. At the age of nine I received a German tutor and kept up my French and my English by special lessons. My regular Russian studies and formal yearly check examinations continued without interruption so that I was one of the youngest boys in my class when I actually did go to school. Since that time I have been able to switch or to translate from any one of the four languages to the other.

All this meant very strenuous work. I cannot say that I relished it at the time, but my general training and especially my knowledge of languages, proved most useful to me after the Revolution, and many was the time when I thought gratefully of my parents who made me acquire this knowledge. At the age and by the method I was taught, a foreign language is assimilated without too much effort, in very much the same way a child learns his own language.

Some twenty years later I thought of emigrating to South America and started studying Spanish at the Berlitz School in Bremen, Germany. These were evening group classes—I was then an engineer, and during the day worked in an office at reinforced-concrete designs. I made very little progress in Spanish and gave it up. I am therefore convinced that the reason so many Russians speak a number of languages fluently does not lie in any special aptitude of ours, but is to be found in the method and timing of instruction which was followed in many educated and moderately well-off Russian families.

Exposure to several different foreign teachers has the added advantage of letting undue influences on an impressionable child cancel each other out. I do not remember much about my French governess, except that she was an ultra-ardent patriot who easily inspired me to

* Both the town and the Institút were named after their founder, the Emperor Paul (1796–1801).

share her feelings and views. When she was replaced by an English girl, I at first flatly refused to have anything to do with a representative of the nation who had burned Jeanne d'Arc. Father then forbade anyone to speak to me in any language. This, plus the fact that Miss Edith Hadland was a very sweet person, finally won me over.

Dealing with people of different nationalities, with the different meanings they attributed to the same expressions and seeing the varying approaches of our elders to them, was quite an educational experience in itself. I will give some examples:

One of my friends, Níka Coúriss, on learning the meaning of the English expression "to pull someone's leg," decided to put it to good use on his younger sister's French governess, an elderly spinster of majestic proportions and bearing. *"Mademoiselle, permettez moi de vous tirer la jambe?* (Permit me to pull your leg)"*, queried my friend. *"Mais vous n'oserez pas!* (But you won't dare!)" was the indignant reply. "I've done it! I've done it!" my pal said with glee as he danced away.

On an earlier occasion, some of my friends and I were witnessing a parade at Tsárskoye Seló with two English governesses (on the same grounds which are seen in Fig. 5). There were stands for guests behind the group of high officers on the right of that photo. It was a sunny day and the bright and varied colors of the parade uniforms of different units made a cheerful and pretty picture. However, the two English girls were perhaps feeling homesick, and were loudly exchanging remarks about these silly Russians who wore such uniforms in the era of machine guns. Finally, to our great joy, a well-groomed elderly civilian who sat behind us bent over and remarked with perfect courtesy in English: "The red coats and the bear skins at London parades are *much* more practical, aren't they?"

The closest we came to an open clash with any of our foreign tutors was in 1913 when I joined two of my friends and their tutors for an extended bicycle trip. I was then fourteen. Níka Coúriss, sixteen, had with him his good-natured lanky English tutor, Mr. Fry, and Mítya Heéring, thirteen, was accompanied by his German tutor, a most unpleasant fellow. I remember only his nickname, *Pouchegláz,* (Popeye), because of his bulging eyes. He was a student at what is now the Esthonian University town of Tartu. Its Russian name is Yúriev, but at the time it was operated by the Baltic Germans and was called Dorpat. Most of the courses at Dorpat University were given in German. Popeye, although a citizen of Rossíya, continuously wore a typical German student cap with the colors of some student corporation from within the German Empire. Our first stop was at Krásnoye Seló (Red Village), the site of the summer camp of the Imperial Guards where we were put up by the officers of one of the regular batteries of the Guard Horse Artillery. We all had lunch at the mess and learned there that the huge new four-engine plane, *"Rússky Vítyaz,"* of the Russian designer Igor Sikórsky * had just landed at the vast maneuver grounds. A year later it lifted sixteen passengers, surpassing by far anything done up to that time. This was the era of arguments between proponents of the lighter-than-air ships and of heavier-than-air planes. Popeye would not admit a future for anything but the Zeppelins, whereas we naturally were all enthusiastic about Sikórsky's pioneering successes. Popeye not only would not go with us to look at Sikórsky's plane, but forbade us to go without him. Our problem was solved with the help of two young lieutenants who had been incensed by Popeye's arrogant behavior at lunch. They lured him away to look at their horses in the stables, while we let the air out of the tires of both our tutors, removed their hand-pumps to prevent pursuit, and sped off on our bicycles. There was a military guard around the *"Rússky Vítyaz,"* but the commanding officer, on hearing our story, decided we deserved a special reward. He personally escorted us on board and into the spacious cabin of the ship. Popeye was fit to be tied when we returned, but Mr. Fry took our side and told him that he got what he had been asking for.

Some strange foreign characters tried their hand at tutoring in Russia. The most peculiar one I had was an Englishman by the name of Mr. Mays. I was about twelve then. Mr. Mays had been a merchant marine captain in the past and described himself as a confirmed "rolling stone" who never stayed anywhere for more than three months. He did not get a chance to stay that long with us, however. When I told Father about some of the adventures Mr. Mays had while running guns for the Japanese and for the Boers before that, he decided that he would have to give Mr. Mays two weeks' notice. Father wanted me to understand that this was not because Mr. Mays had worked for the Japanese at the time they were at war with

---

* Most Americans know Ígor Sikórsky only as a successful helicopter designer in this country. Very few people now remember that his greatest achievement was the first multiengine plane in the world, while he was still a Russian citizen. "Rússky Vítyaz "means "Russian Knight."

us, but solely because Mr. Mays had worked for the Boers when they were at war with his own country, England. And yet Father personally, like most Russians, sympathized with the Boers and not with the English. When Mr. Mays tried to explain his past behavior to Father by saying that "money does not smell," Father paid him his two weeks' salary on the spot and told him to pack his bags and leave immediately.

At the time, most Russian schools for general education followed the German pattern and were similarly named: the "Gymnázia" emphasized classical studies and the "Reál School" concentrated on the natural sciences. There was a school of each type at Tsárskoye Seló. I joined the Gymnázia there at midyear 1909–1910 and stayed for two years. The school's building looked then very much as it did when I saw it again half a century later (see Fig. 60). While we lived at Pávlovsk, which was less than 2 miles away, our coachman drove me over in the morning and came back to pick me up in the afternoon.

The social origins of the members in my class were varied. For instance, it included a Prince Poutiátin and a boy by the name of Vikéntiev, the son of a local *izvóschik* (cabby). The two were frequently fighting, and it was usually Vikéntiev who started it, by following Poutiátin around chanting repetitiously: *"Ty nye kniáz, a griáz"* (Thou art not a prince, but mud). This son of a cabby became an infantry officer at the start of the War; he was quite a bit older than I, and was therefore able to volunteer earlier than I could. When I ran into him in 1916 I noticed that his chest was covered with ribbons of combat decorations and that he had several stripes on his sleeve indicating the number of times he had been wounded.

Among the other boys in the class was one by the name of Solomón, apparently of Jewish origin, who belonged however to the Russian Orthodox faith and was a *dvorianín,* that is, a member of the nobility. We also had one of the several sons of the local Jewish photographer, Ótsoup, whose business competed with the official court photographer, Hahn. All four boys I mentioned above emigrated after the Revolution.

A boy of whom I heard again later was Knípper, the nephew of the famous actress, Knípper-Chékhova, widow of the writer Chékhov. He remained in the Soviet Union and became prominent as a musician. Some time after the start of World War II, I was listening to records of Soviet war songs played at a friend's house in Princeton. One, *"Poliúshko-Póle"* ("Meadowland"), I found quite stirring. First one heard the faint distant beat of approaching horses' hooves, coming closer and closer as the angrily fierce song of their riders going to meet the invading Germans also increased in power and volume—then it all slowly faded away in the distance. I looked at the record—the composer's name was that of my former classmate, Lev Knípper.

One name in the school which later became notorious in a very sinister way was that of the nephew of our German teacher, Rosenberg. He was not in my class and I remember him only vaguely as a fellow who kept very much to himself, but who for some reason was a frequent target for snowballs. It was he who in World War II organized and headed Hitler's infamous *Ost-Ministerium*.

At midyear 1911–1912 I was admitted to the senior of three preparatory classes of the Imperial Ouchílische Pravovédeniya (School of Jurisprudence) at St. Petersburg. For purposes of brevity I will refer to it from here on as the Law School. It was one of two "schools for the privileged" there, which meant that it accepted only the children of hereditary nobility. Its military counterpart was the Corps des Pages.

The senior class was called the First; together with the Second and Third classes it formed the three-year university level "Senior Course"; the gold braid on the collars of the students' uniforms distinguished them from the students of the four-year high school level "Junior Course"—the Fourth, Fifth, Sixth and Seventh classes—who had silver braid on their collars, as I have in Fig. 15. This photo shows me as a sixteen-year-old of the Fifth class. The color of my cuffs and collar was green. This distinguished the Law School from the Imperial Lyceum which had the same organizational setup and uniforms as we had, but whose color was red.

Outside of their walls, in winter students of both schools had to wear spotlessly white pigskin gloves and three-cornered hats—somewhat like those worn by senior naval officers of most countries with their full dress uniforms. An English governess just arrived at St. Petersburg is supposed to have expressed surprise at the youth and number of what she thought were Russian admirals in the streets.

This garb must have been well-suited to the days when all students of the school could afford to move about town in a *likhách*—this is, an expensive cab or sleigh with a particularly swift horse. But it was most impractical in crowded electric streetcars—the mode of conveyance which for financial reasons had to be used by myself and by many of my classmates.

The school was under military discipline. Traditionally, the Director was a retired major general and the Inspector of Students, a retired colonel. When I was at school the Director was General Mitskévich, a Pole, and the Inspector of Students was Colonel Goltgáuer, a Baltic German. Both wore their uniforms. We had to give the military salute not only to them, but to any boy of a senior class we might happen to meet on the street.

Originally the school was supposed to train officials for the Ministry of Justice. Actually very few graduates chose it for their profession, but many went into the Foreign Service. The school was founded by a German Prince of Oldenburg, who married the sister of Tsar Alexander I, stayed on in Russia, and was given the rights of a member of the Russian Imperial family and the title of Prinz Oldenbúrgsky. His son, bearer of the same title, was the *Popechítel*—which was in effect something like a dictatorial one-man Board of Trustees of the school.

Our Oldenbúrgsky had the reputation, putting it mildly, of being quite an eccentric. For instance, during the 1904–1905 revolutionary ferment in Russia, he felt that the Director of the School was not doing enough to combat leftwing trends within its walls. So he promptly authorized the boys themselves to expel or to impose lesser punishments on any of their classmates if this were done by class vote. Class presidents were elected to serve as liaison with the Director and with the senior First class. The latter could hold inquiries and review any harsh penalties imposed. If it approved them, there was to be no recourse, the Director was merely notified as to what they were.

Within a few months every breath of leftwing thought was eradicated from the school. Since there was no longer anyone for the witch-hunters to pursue, they began turning their pent-up energies towards what in America is called "hazing" and in Russia was called *tsouk*.

I find it most interesting that democratic America tolerates customs in many of its universities and schools which the overwhelming majority of intellectuals in Imperial Russia protested and considered degrading to human dignity.

The *tsouk* reached its maximum development six years or so after it started, which was at about the time I and my classmates were in the lowest class (the Seventh)—so we took the brunt of it. From then on a reaction set in against it.

There was nothing very terrible about it, it was just an awful nuisance. One would have to stand at attention when asked silly questions and answer by equally silly prescribed sentences. For instance, to the question: "When is the soul of a *riábchik* * degraded?," —the proper answer was: "When it finds itself in the stomach of the Director of the School, Major General Mitskévich." One of my classmates was required to sit on top of a cupboard in a wastepaper basket and supposedly imitate Buddha by holding up his hands with their palms pressed together, Hindu style, at the level of his chin and at the same time rhythmically, like a metronome, incline his head sidewise first towards one and then towards the other shoulder. This went on for several minutes.

During evening prep, senior boys entertained themselves by ordering a selected victim among their juniors to write an essay of a specified length and within a specified time. It did not have to make any sense, because the topics assigned were not supposed to have any. Thus I was once required to write a six-page essay in twenty minutes on "The Influence of Children from the Negro Tribe of Nyam-Nyams on the Movement of Electric Street Cars along the Névsky."

The dormitories of the four "Junior Course" classes were all located in one very long room above the main entrance to the school on the Fontánka River, opposite the parklike Summer Gardens in the center of St. Petersburg. When we were in the Seventh class, we could get to our belongings, kept in small cupboards next to our beds, only by passing the beds of the Sixth class. This we were required to do by solemnly marching past, arms stiffly stretched out downwards, palms turned inwards along the side seams of the trouser legs, head turned to attention towards the beds, repeating before each bed, whether occupied or not: *Pozvólte Proytí!* (Permit me to pass). Frequently there would be some loafer around who, just as one had reached the end of the row of beds, would lazily drawl the order: *Obr-ra-átno!* (Back!)" and would chase one back and forth in this manner until he got tired of it.

Most of this hazing went on after classes, when the day boys had gone home. There was a sharp difference between them and the boarders. Numerically, they were about evenly divided. The parents of most boarders lived in far away parts of the Empire and had little influence on the development of their children. In the cases I witnessed, the

---

* A game bird, like a tiny woodcock, which does not seem to exist in America. Its German name is *Rebhuhn*. It is considered a great delicacy.

tone was unfortunately set for them by a clique of not too attractive characters. The day boys were quite different and much more intellectual. I formed a number of friendships among them and decided to stop being a boarder, to live at home and to commute daily from Tsárskoye Seló. This I did for three and a half years until graduation from the Junior Course in 1916.

Mother was at first opposed to this, fearing that it would be too strenuous for me. Certainly it was not easy, over an hour being wasted on the trip each way. But, somewhat unexpectedly, Father immediately supported my request.

It turned out that he himself had refused to put up with the *tsouk* in the past at the only other place I have heard of as having practised it in Russia—at the Nikoláyevsky Cavalry School in St. Petersburg. This school was his first choice after graduating from the Don Cadet Corps at Novocherkássk. The freshman class of the Cavalry School was referred to there as *Zvyéri* (Wild Beasts), a term used in the same way as "plebes" for the freshmen of the United States West Point Academy.

On his very first day at that school Father was stopped by an upperclassman asking him: "Wild beast, what is the horizon of a garbage dump?" Father's answer was: "Certainly wider than yours." There was quite a row about this, as an upshot of which Father asked to be transferred to what had been his second choice—the Miháilovsky Artillery School. There had never been any *tsouk* there, and its authorities were glad to have Father—the top man of his class. The Cavalry School administration was also glad to let him go, considering him a rebel against their school's tradition.

### 4. *Some Russian Army Customs*

Once something became recognized as a "tradition" of a military unit, it was usually upheld by all higher authorities as building *esprit de corps* and pride, and hence assuring a high morale. Traditions could, however, be somewhat peculiar.

For instance, the Leib-Guard Pávlovsky Regiment of infantry had been formed in the days of Emperor Paul, who had an upturned nose. So only officers and men with turned-up noses were selected for it then. This became a regimental tradition. I have a slightly turned-up nose myself and the standard joke for people meeting me was to ask why I wasn't serving in the Pávlovsky Regiment.

The *tsouk* (hazing) had somehow become a tradition of the Nikoláyevsky Cavalry School. A serious clash developed over it soon after Father's transfer to the Artillery School. For the first time it was not just isolated Cossacks who were individually exposed to it, but a well-knit group of the first class to graduate from the Don Cadet Corps. They had all grown up together. Part of the Cavalry School's tradition was the wearing of particularly well-cut snappy uniforms ordered from special expensive tailors and paid for by the young men themselves. Some of the newly arrived group of Cossacks did not have the money to do this. Two of the upperclassmen, already exasperated at the rebuffs suffered during their attempts to "haze" the Cossacks, one night cut into shreds the top boots of one of them, considering that they did not meet the traditional high standards for style of the school.

Yet it was all the poor fellow could afford. The point of the upperclassmen was that if this was so, he should not have come to the school at all. The other Cossacks found out who the two upperclassmen were, cornered them somewhere, and gave them such a whipping with their *nagáikas* * that the pair had to be hospitalized. When the question, "Who did this?" was asked of the lined-up squadron, every Cossack in it, over twenty of them, stepped forward. Each one of them had taken at least one whack at their captives, so there should be no question of any individual responsibility. Any stern action against all of them would have caused deep resentment in the Don.

The dilemma which confronted the authorities was finally resolved by the formation of an entirely separate Cossack squadron within the school. It bore the customary Cossack name of *Sótnya,* meaning "hundred"; its members wore the red-colored side stripes of the Don on their wide trousers and had a newly established tradition of no hazing. All this took place alongside the opposite *tsouk* tradition of the somewhat foppish old *eskadrón* of officer candidates for the regular cavalry in the same school.

In a way this was typical of the diversity in the composition of the various individual units of the Russian Army. This diversity was maintained by the custom which required the formal acceptance of a candidate by the society of officers of a given unit before a junior

* A Cossack riding whip which consists of a short (15 inches or so) wooden handle, frequently silver-inlaid, with a single 2-foot leather thong hinged at its end. Statements published in this country that Cossacks used cat-o'-nine-tails on revolutionary demonstrators (*Life,* Feb. 3, 1958, p. 10) are utter nonsense. I never saw or heard of such an implement in Russia in my day or in that of my father.

officer was actually assigned to it. The idea was to ensure a friendly and congenial atmosphere. In the Guards and in some of the older and more distinguished Army units this custom even extended to the wives of officers. If a man decided to marry a girl of a background considered uncongenial to the rest, he could be requested by his fellow officers to transfer somewhere else. Usually no objections were raised to marriage connections with professional families (doctors, engineers or industrialists), even if they did not belong to the nobility. Actresses were not objected to if they left the professional stage after marriage—amateur acting was generally popular. But in the Guards the line was drawn on connections with merchants. I have frequently heard of officers having to transfer from the Guards because of marrying some rich Moscow *koupchikha*.* The idea concerning merchant families seems to have been in part that commerce cannot be engaged in successfully without besmirching one's honor by cheating or by other shady practices, and in part, on disapproval of marriages for money.

The *chéstnoye slóvo* (word of honor) meant what it said. If an officer was shown to have broken his word, he would be expelled from his unit and few people would ever shake hands with him again.

Political police connections were strongly frowned upon. The gendarmes—the politico-military police force of the Empire—wore uniforms similar to those of the Regular Army, but junior officers of the latter and of the Guards frequently did not salute gendarme officers of higher rank. Many Americans have expressed incredulous surprise on hearing this from me, since it conflicted with some of their ingrained misconceptions about old Russia. I shall therefore quote from Ref. 28, vol. 2, pages 169–170, a book written in 1891 by George Kennan † who strongly criticized many of the Siberian exile practices of Imperial Russia in the days of Alexander III.

Speaking of a Captain Nikólin, the gendarme commandant of the political prisons at the convict mines at Kara, Kennan noted that he "made [an] unfavorable impression" and went on to say:

". . . but I was not prepared, nevertheless, for the contemptuous, almost insulting coldness of the reception given to him by Major Pótulof, . . ."

---

* Feminine of *koupétz* (merchant).
† The uncle of George F. Kennan, the distinguished present-day American diplomat who is one of the few really competent American experts on Russia.

Pótulof was a Regular Army officer and Governor of the prisons at Kara. Kennan adds:

". . . Nikólin was generally hated and despised, by the regular Army officers at the post, as a secret spy and informer. . . ."

These feelings on the part of the officers annoyed the police, and the telephones of even Guard officers were frequently tapped. Often my father, on hearing tell-tale scratching noises in his receiver would angrily exclaim into the mouthpiece: "Again some *svóloch* (a swear word) is listening in!"

The approval by the officers of a unit was also required for the admission of a *Volno-opredelyáuschiysya*, an untranslatable, but (for a Russian when spelled in Russian) not unpronounceable term used to designate a man in the old Russian Army to whom were accorded the special privileges of an educated draftee, irrespective of his origin. They wore the same uniforms as the other privates, except for a special distinguishing border along the edges of their shoulder straps. However, they either had separate messes or they messed together with the officers. Also, they formed separate sections in the *Ouchébnaya Kománda* (training section) of their unit where promising men were prepared for wartime reserve officer status.

All this shows a commendable respect for and encouragement of education, even in old Russia. But I do not think these measures were good since they made our intellectuals miss unique opportunities for intimate contacts with representatives of the mass of simple people from whom they too could learn much. An amusing incident happened in 1912—or 1913—in the 22nd Artillery Brigade, if I remember correctly. An old sergeant was putting his Training Section, squad by squad, through some field exercise. The first squad was composed of simple country boys whose naturally developed practical common sense and previous open-air life helped them to grasp easily what they had to do, and to actually do it. The next squad, composed exclusively of city-bred and educated boys, botched everything. The exasperated sergeant, a peasant himself, lined them up and bellowed: "This is not a university here for you. (*Mozgámi voróchat pridyótsya.*) You will have to make your brains move!" One of his offended charges had connections with the leftwing press, so the incident got written up as proof of the "retrograde" and anti-intellectual attitudes of the Army. This produced much hilarity among all officers, including my father, who happened to hear of the case. After years of con-

tacts with university students in various countries, I too feel that
this much-maligned Sergeant actually was a very wise and observant
man.

Generally speaking, there was no more adherence in the Russian
Army to the dead letter of a Regulation than there was in the British
Army, for example,—as I was very much surprised to discover in
1920–1921 in Egypt. A sentence from an order by Tsar Peter the
Great was occasionally quoted by Russian officers in this connection:
"Do not hold on to a Regulation (*Oustáv*) as a blind man holds on
to a wall."

Also, in contrast to some Western armies, a disregard of combat
orders usually was not penalized if it led to success. I have often
heard a relevant slogan: *Pobedíteley nye soúdyat!* (Victors are not
court-martialed!), which appears to have originated during the eighteenth century wars with Turkey. The Russian Commander-in-Chief,
Field Marshal Roumiántsev, is supposed to have decided to teach
what he thought would be a lesson to the up-coming young General
Souvórov * whom he disliked for his cockiness. He sent Souvórov to
lay siege in 1773 to the Turkish fortress Tourtukái with strict orders
not to risk an attack, since it was garrisoned by superior forces.
Souvórov found that the Turks had plenty of supplies and were well-
housed, whereas his small force would have to live off the devastated
surrounding countryside. So he stormed and took the fortress by a
sudden surprise attack in direct disobedience of his orders. To make
things worse, Souvórov did not formally report his action to Roumiántsev, but did so by a two-line verse:

> *Sláva Bógou, Sláva Vam,*
> *Tourtoukai vziat, y ya tam.*

that is:

> Glory to God, Glory to you,
> Tourtoukai is taken, and I am there too.

The enraged Field Marshal ordered him court-martialed, but, since
Souvórov was a General, such an order had to be approved by the
reigning Monarch. Catherine II dismissed it by writing on it the
sentence about victors which I have quoted and which became proverbial. In some ways this was a healthy tradition, but many a young

---

* Souvórov subsequently became one of the greatest military leaders in Russian
history (see Ref. 15).

officer paid by his life while trying some daring exploit contrary to orders—I witnessed one such case (see p. 117).

The pay of Russian Army officers was probably the lowest of any European country. Outside of the Guards and of a few other units, the majority had no private means and had a very hard time making ends meet. Their service was one of "Duty" with a capital "D" in the defense of their country which had suffered so much in the past from foreign invasions and which was yet to suffer still more.

### 5. Imperial Russia's Upper Social Strata

St. Petersburg society was very far from being exclusively of Great Russian or even of just Russian or Róssiyan origin. The variety of foreign names encountered was almost as great as it is today in the United States. A great number of people came to both countries from different foreign lands, liked the place, stayed there and became assimilated. The main difference lay in the fact that in Russia this immigration was of an upperclass type, whereas the majority of immigrants to America were mainly laborers.

Tsar Nicholas II himself had only a few drops of Russian blood in him. His mother, the dowager Empress Mariya Fyódorovna, widow of Tsar Alexander III, was born a Danish Princess, Dagmar, and all three of his direct ancestors before that (Alexander II, Nicholas I, Paul I) took German princesses for spouses. Emperor Paul's mother, Catherine II, was a German. Therefore Nicholas II was $\frac{1}{2}$ Danish, at least $15\frac{1}{32}$ German, and at best $\frac{1}{32}$ Russian. I say "at best" on the assumption that the real father of Tsar Paul may possibly have been one of Catherine IIs Russian favorites. If one accepts the official version that his father actually was the unfortunate Tsar Peter III, who also was part German, then there may have been less than 1 percent Russian blood in the last Tsar, Nicholas II.

The Germans I have met in Russia were of two distinct types. The first lived in large groups which kept their national identity and their ties to their German *Vaterland*. The Baltic Germans belonged to this group. They formed the upper crust of the Baltic Provinces of the Russian Empire, where they had lorded it for centuries over the local Esthonians and Latvians.* Most of these Baltic Germans con-

---

* The national independence of Esthonia and Latvia was established for the first time after World War I as part of the *"Cordon Sanitaire"* against the Soviet Union.

sidered that they owed their allegiance to the Throne and not to Russia or to Rossíya as such. To this same first category belonged the Volga Germans, farmer-colonists who in the reign of Catherine II were allowed to migrate from Germany and settle as one large group along the middle reaches of the Volga River.

On the other hand there were many Germans who had emigrated to Russia as individuals at various times and who had become completely russified. A few of both groups were in an intermediate position—I have known some of them who, while in Russia, seemed to feel more like Germans, but later, when they found themselves in Germany after the Revolution, felt more like Russians.

Persons of other than German descent were more isolated from their original homelands and appeared to lose their national identities much more completely. There were many such people in Russia.

First, there were quite a number of Frenchmen, mainly descendants of French nobles who fled to Russia from the guillotine. My maternal uncle, Nikolái Doubiágsky, married a girl by the name of Clapier de Colongue. She knew less French than I did. My sister used to play with a little girl who lived on the same street at Tsárskoye Seló. Her father, Chaperon de la Raye, was a Leib-Guard Cuirassier officer. When in December, 1916, I joined the Reserve Battery of the Guard Horse Artillery, two of my young fellow officers had French names—Chatelain and Andreau. In the group of four families which joined together with us at Tsárskoye Seló to provide dancing lessons for their children, one also had a French name—Corbet.

My last Brigade Commander of the Guard Horse Artillery was Baron Vladímir Ivánovich Vélho, of Portuguese descent, who could not speak a word of Portuguese.

The father of my Pávlovsk childhood friends—the Heérings—was of German descent, but his wife was born Baroness Ramsey. Her ancestors were of Scottish origin, who came to Russia via Sweden.

I knew an engineering student of the Institute I went to at Petrográd (Fig. 58) whose name was Loewenhaupt. He was a descendant of the Swedish General Loewenhaupt, the second-in-command of Charles XII, who surrendered at Poltáva in 1709 and then stayed on in Russia.* Another engineering student I knew of the same Institute was Andreoletti; his father was an Italian tunneling expert who

---

* After that battle Tsar Peter the Great was host to the Swedish officers he had captured and chivalrously toasted them as his teachers—referring to his earlier defeat at Nárva.

came to work on railroad construction in the Caucasus and who had then settled in Russia.

I have already mentioned a family friend of my aunts, the harpist, Ásya Erdély. She was of Hungarian origin. So was one of my officers at the Miháilovsky Artillery School, Captain Shokóly.

My friend, Mítya Heéring, married a girl of the Creighton family. I do not know how long they had been in Russia, but after the Civil War I gave English lessons to one of her relatives, Colonel Creighton of the 4th Leib-Guard Rifles Regiment when we both were for a while at the same camp at Tel el Kebir in Egypt. From there he established contact with the branch of his family which had remained in England and they invited him to join them. So he wanted to be in a position to converse with them when he got there.

The variety of nationalities and of the ensuing inter-marriages in the upper strata of old Russia was not limited to foreigners; many persons of the minority branches of the multinational Empire found their way to the very top.

My Director of the Artillery School was General Karachán, a Tartar; my Battery Commander was Colonel Neviadómsky, a Pole. Among my classmates and others I knew at the Imperial Law School, I remember Prince Gedróitz, of Royal Lithuanian ancestry; three brothers Kadjár, nephews of the last Persian Shah of that dynasty; Prince Makínsky, a Tartar; Prince Mkheídze, a Georgian; an Armenian, whose full name I do not remember—except that it began with the nobility prefix of "Ter"; Sevastópoulo, of Greek descent; also numerous Ukrainians who did not consider themselves anything but Russian, two brothers Pollán who were of French origin; and several boys of German origin—Baron Tizenhausen, von Pfaffius and others. One of my best friends and Tsárskoye Seló neighbors, Níka Coúriss, was the son of a retired Leib-Guard Hussar Colonel of Lithuanian origin.

The Leib-Guard Cavalry Brigade stationed at Warsaw was entirely Polish, was officered by Polish aristocracy, and at the start of World War I was commanded by General Baron Mannerheim, of Swedish origin, who later became Finland's famous Field Marshal. Guard units of the St. Petersburg area were at one time commanded by a Moslem Tartar, Khan Nakhichevánsky. Col. Robert McCormick mentions, on page 47 of Ref. 38, the surprise he felt on being introduced on his arrival to Russia in 1915 to the Leib-Guard officer who was to accompany him to the front. McCormick thought at first he must be Japanese; he was Prince Toundoútov, a Buddhist Kalmuck. Among prominent St. Petersburg families were the Abazá, who were Circassians, and the Kochubéys, Ukrainians whose ancestor had been treacherously murdered by Charles XIIs secret ally, Mazépa. Doubtless many other examples could be cited.

It is true that most of the above were members of minority nobilities. But the way to the top was partially open to anyone through Government service. An outstanding example is General Anton Deníkin, who commanded an army under the Tsar in World War I and then was the Supreme Commander of the Volunteer (White) Army in the ensuing Civil War. He was the grandson of a serf. Any person who became an officer in the Army or in the Civil Service became a *dvorianín* (a member of the nobility) for life and was addressed as "Your Well-Born," corresponding to the German *Euer Wohlgeboren.* A Colonel would be addressed as "Your Highly Well-Born," again a copy of the German *Euer Hochwohlgeboren,* still in official use at the time in Kaiser Wilhelm's Germany. This custom was not of Russian origin and there were many jokes about the miraculous way the quality of one's birth improved with one's rank. Finally, a General or a civilian official of equivalent rank was addressed as "Your Excellency."

An Army or Civil Service General's rank, or that of a Colonel in the Guards, gave one the right to become a member of the hereditary nobility.

Cossacks occupied a very special position within Imperial Russia as free men who had never known serfdom. Thus my father began his service in the Cossack Guards, although he was not a member of the Rossíyan nobility. But he was in a position to send me to the Imperial Law School only by the end of 1911 when all formalities for his becoming a hereditary *dvorianín* were completed—they were started soon after he was promoted Colonel and assumed command of the Cossack Guard Battery in 1906.

Most Cossacks were well-to-do and hence conservative farmers who were relatively immune to revolutionary propaganda. The Imperial Government took undue advantage of this fact and preferred to use Cossack rather than other less politically reliable troops when quelling disorders. The Cossacks resented this and I have heard of petitions sent through their commanders requesting that Cossack units be used against demonstrators no more frequently than regular cavalry. Except in the Guards, this does not seem to have had much effect, however.

The attitude of St. Petersburg society towards the Cossacks was a mixture of respect for their fighting qualities and of patronizing condescension towards the *kazachki* who could always be counted upon to do the dirty work for them. Cossack reaction was to look down on what they considered to be foppish sissies. It is well expressed by a story about General Baklánov. He was a Cossack commander in the mid-nineteenth-century conquest of the Caucasian Moslem mountaineers who were leaning towards their co-religionist Turkey. Baklánov's valor and exploits made him a legendary figure and Tsar Alexander II expressed the wish to see him in St. Petersburg. The Tsar recognized the tall Cossack behind a crowd of courtiers at the first reception he attended and asked why he was not in front. Baklánov is supposed to have answered: "Your Majesty, we Cossacks are used to being in the front ranks only in battle!"

### 6. *Relations with Foreigners*

One often reads now about supposedly innate and unreasonable Russian distrust of all foreigners. This is not correct. In the days of my youth Russians did distrust some foreigners, but only nationals of hostile powers—and with good reason. Representatives of friendly countries were, on the contrary, received with open arms. As a boy I had the opportunity to observe both types of reception, especially during the summer of 1912, part of which I spent with Father at the Loúga camp of the Officers' Artillery School, 85 miles south of St. Petersburg.

Father, who was a Senior Instructor there, was very busy with his officer-refresher courses, so I and a cadet, the son of another instructor, spent a lot of time with our neighbor, Captain Novogrebélsky. He was in charge of the vast firing range and frequently took us around it on his inspection trips in a small open gasoline-driven trolley along narrow-gage railroad tracks which crisscrossed the range. One day Novogrebélsky, who was a Roman Catholic Pole, was simply fuming about the impending arrival of the Norwegian Military Attaché. He was incensed at having to show "this cousin of the Germans," as he put it, the moving targets and other new installations on his range. On the next day he was in a better mood, explaining that arrangements had been made for the Horse Artillery group—

with a reputation for very hard drinking—to first entertain the visitor at lunch. So my cadet friend and I decided to watch the fun and installed ourselves in the cover of a clump of bushes near the officers' mess. The Norwegian officer, in uniform, arrived on time, inspected the horses held by orderlies in readiness for him to mount, and then entered the mess building. Through the open windows we could hear loud toasts, cheers, and then singing as the lunch dragged on. Finally, a horse-drawn carriage was ordered, and the Norwegian was carried out by several orderlies. A couple of Russian officers escorted him to the railroad station and laid him out, as comfortably as possible, but still dead drunk, in a reserved first-class compartment of a train bound for St. Petersburg.

Several weeks later the procedure was repeated with one of the German Assistant Military Attachés. His superiors must have been forewarned by the reception of the Norwegian and therefore sent down quite a prize drinker, who succeeded finally in emerging from the mess and in mounting his horse with only a few of his hosts in a position to accompany him. They then rode out to observe the gunnery exercise but, as Captain Novogrebélsky happily told us the next day, the German officer failed in his efforts to raise his field glasses to his eyes.

Quite different was the attitude towards officers of friendly nations —Bulgars, French and Serbians. The same Captain Novogrebélsky arranged a special treat for me and my cadet friend. With two Bulgarian officers we were allowed to occupy a reinforced concrete and armored steel pillbox built right among the artillery targets. We rode out to it well ahead of the time for the start of the firing and sent our horses and orderlies away. The pillbox had a long horizontal slot on the side opposite to that of the firing batteries, and through it one could see the targets, some of which were only a few feet away. No high explosive shells and only antipersonnel shrapnel of the type which is filled with spherical lead bullets were to be used that day; the soil was sandy, so there was no danger of shell fragments flying backwards or of bullets ricocheting back into the open slot, which could however be closed by armor plate with periscope-like viewers if necessary.

It was a terrific thrill for thirteen-year-olds to have shrapnel burst overhead, hails of bullets whizz past, and to see and hear bullets hit all around us. Equally interesting was the time spent waiting with the two Bulgars, whose uniforms looked very much like those of the

Russian Army. We found that we could more or less understand each other when they spoke Bulgarian and we Russian, so similar are the two Slavic languages.

A numerous French military mission was attached to the Russian Army on an exchange basis. One of its officers, Captain Lavergne, wearing his French Army uniform, went through the regular course of the Officers' Artillery School. He was assigned to the group which worked under my father and was a frequent guest at our home. I also remember his superior, Colonel Nollet, being entertained at lunch by my parents. I still have a little gold trinket presented as a souvenir to my father by his group of officers when they graduated. It is covered with Russian alphabet initials; however, one is in the Latin alphabet: "G.L."—for Lavergne.

Father returned from his 1913 mission to the Balkans an enthusiastic admirer of the Serbian Army and people. He had established many personal contacts and friendships in Serbia and reciprocated the hospitality he had received by entertaining at our Tsárskoye Seló home many Serbs who came to St. Petersburg. They included a number of Serbian artillery officers, but I also recall the striking white-haired figure of Spaláykovich, the eminent Serbian diplomat.

I have kept a Royal Serbian decoration which was awarded to Father at that time—the Order of St. Savva, third class. I liked the inscription on it, in old Church Slavonic, which is equally understandable both to Serbs and to Russians: *Trudóm Svoím Vse Priobreté*—that is, "By your Labor shall you Earn Everything."

## 7. *Rumblings of Approaching World War*

From about the age of ten I was usually allowed to lunch and to dine with the grownups, even when we had guests, on the condition that I should be seen but not heard. This was not too difficult for me, since it permitted listening to most interesting conversations. Mother had established and firmly enforced the rule that not more than ten minutes professional artillery shop talk would be tolerated at any party; but there was no limit on discussions of international affairs or of military and general history, subjects in which she herself was keenly interested.

The Balkan Wars of 1912–1913 in a way were a preliminary round for World War I. The Germans, in a virulent revival of their traditional policy of *Drang nach Osten*—that is, "Thrust to the East"—were heavily counting on the help of Turkey. The Turkish Army was reorganized by a German military mission headed by General Liman von Sanders, who eventually became a Turkish Field Marshal with the title of Pasha. His presence alone, in the eyes of some Germans, judging by my teachers of that language, was sufficient to guarantee the defeat of the Slavo-Greek coalition, whose armies had received Russian and French help.

The crushing defeat of the Turks and the final liberation of the last areas in Europe inhabited by Slav and by Greek Eastern Orthodox Christians under the Turkish yoke was a great setback for the *Drang nach Osten* trends in Berlin and in Vienna.

In addition, Austria-Hungary became seriously worried about the effect of Serbia's growth on her own subject Yugoslav peoples and on her other Slavic nations, especially the Czechs, who were restless under the domination of Austro-Germans and of Hungarians—the two ruling races of the Hapsburg Empire. The military press of Austria-Hungary was advocating vigorous counteroffensives, the crushing and conquest of Serbia, and the dismemberment of Russia, considering these countries to be the living inspiration for Slavic unrest in their Empire. All this was reported in the St. Petersburg newspapers which we received at home. Plans were openly debated in Austria as to whether Russia should be cut up into eight, twelve or even fifty bits and pieces (Ref. 44b).

In furtherance of these aims, a campaign was intensified in Vienna which appears to have been first initiated there in the 1890s. It consisted in trying to foment anti-Russian feelings among the Ukrainians living in the Austrian province of Galicia—less than 10 percent of all Ukranians lived there, as compared to more than 90 percent in Russia (see Map F, p. 353). By creating an Ukrainian university at Lvov (Lemberg) and by other similar measures, the Austro-Hungarians attempted to transform the Ukrainian branch of the Russian nation into a separate and distinct "oppressed" nation and then to spread the seeds of separatist ideas within the borders of Russia itself. This campaign was successful only among the part of the Galician Ukrainians which had either embraced Roman Catholicism directly or which had recognized the supremacy of the Pope while keeping the outward rites of the Eastern Church—the latter group being called "Uniates."

However, a large proportion of the population in Eastern Galicia and in the adjoining mountain areas of Hungary refused to give up their Eastern Orthodox faith and insisted on continuing to use the written Russian language as their own for literary purposes. They called themselves "Carpatho-Russians." Many of them emigrated to America, and they and their descendants living here still designate themselves by the name (Refs. 16 and 62). There still are older men among them who bear personal witness to the persecutions they endured.

The campaign of persecutions and intimidations was intensified in the five years preceding World War I both in Austria (of which Galicia formed an administrative part) and in Hungary. These developments were reported in the Russian press and caused great indignation all over the country, especially in view of the privileged position enjoyed by Germans in Russia.

In Germany "proper" these Austrian measures hostile to Russia received full support. Chancellor Bethmann-Hollweg made a speech emphasizing the *Rassengegensaetze* (racial contradictions) between the Slavs and the Germans, and Bismarck was quoted as having said that "Slavdom should not be permitted to raise its dirty head" (Ref. 44c). German legislatures supported measures to accelerate German colonization of Polish-owned lands in the eastern provinces of Prussia (Ref. 44i). The question whether Russia could be made into a German colony was debated and affirmed in parts of the German press (Ref. 44g).

In this connection, the impending expiration of the 1905 Russo-German trade treaty caused lively debates on both sides of the border. Russia had been compelled to accept this treaty at the time when it was greatly weakened by the Russo-Japanese war and by internal revolutionary disorders; the treaty enabled Germany to import Russian foodstuffs at extremely low prices, handicapping Russia's industrial development, which was stimulated by the granting of the 1905 constitution and by the creation of the *Doúma* (Parliament).

Demands for a complete revision of the trade treaty were growing in Russia in preparation for the start of negotiations in 1914 prior to its expiration in 1916. The German press was insisting on its renewal without any changes (Refs. 44f, 44g, 44h, 44j).

In 1912 the German Reichstag voted enormous credits for a drastic and rapid strengthening of the striking power of its armies, especially for a great increase in heavy artillery, which was to be completed before 1915. These measures were only partially due to Turkey's defeat and resulting weakening, and at the time were also attributed to Germany's desire to bring pressure on Russia during the 1915 negotiations for the trade treaty renewal.

My father's on-the-spot study of the use of heavy artillery in the Balkan Wars of 1912–1913 had convinced him of the decisive role it could play in the next war. I often heard him express great anxiety about the advantage which accrued to Germany through Russia's slowness in responding to Germany's gigantic armament program of 1912. It was only in 1914 that Russia's answering armament program was enacted. When completed in 1917 it would have brought Russia's heavy artillery almost but not quite to the level reached by Germany in 1914–1915 (Ref. 18).

I fully endorse the conclusions of the Russian *émigré* military historian, General N. N. Golovíne, who wrote on page 186 of Ref. 18, at the end of his analysis of the Russian 1914 program:

"One can assume with a considerable degree of probability, that fear of the completion of this reorganization was one of the substantive motives which forced the German General Staff to select the year 1914 for its 'Preventive War.'"

Before the outbreak of World War I in the Fall of 1914, I heard my father and his friends express fear that this would actually happen at that time, since it was the most favorable moment for Germany.

The shooting of the Archduke Franz Ferdinand at Sarajevo must have been very welcome for the Berlin militarists. Had it not happened, another pretext surely would have been found to invade Serbia.

# The First Thirty Months of the War

## 1. *Outline of the Military Operations*

I have often met Americans whose only knowledge of Russia's role in World War I was that it had been disastrously defeated at Tannenberg. I have yet to meet an American who did not look surprised on hearing that this Russian defeat was relatively minor in the general scale of things, that it was calculatedly risked, and that this Russian sacrifice assured the victory of the Marne for its Western Allies and hence the loss of World War I by Germany.

Russia did lose almost three Army Corps at Tannenberg, but their deliberately rapid and risky advance into the fortified forested lake area of East Prussia made the German High Command lose its nerve and withdraw two Army Corps from the Western Front. Their absence from that front at the crucial phase of the Battle of the Marne permitted the "Miracle of the Marne" when the French stopped the onrushing Germans in their tracks. Marshal Joffre, the French Commander-in-Chief, gratefully recognizes all this in his memoirs. I will quote him, as well as other contemporary military authorities, since my own recollections of these events as they were known on the Russian side have often been met with incredulity in this country.

The German Schlieffen plan for the war, named after General Count von Schlieffen who worked it out and who headed the German General Staff until 1906, was well-known both in France and in Russia. The plan was based on the fact that the Russian mobilization, because of vaster spaces, greater distances and fewer railroads in the country, would take a couple of weeks longer than the German one. Von Schlieffen therefore proposed to concentrate the bulk of the German forces in the West and to crush France by what is now known as a "Blitz"—that is, lightning—attack before the Russian armies could advance too far into Prussia,—then to turn the entire force of Germany against them with the help of the Austro-Hungarians.

The French were understandably worried by this and urged the Russian command, if war came, to respond immediately to a German attack on France by invading Germany at any cost well before the slow Russian mobilization was completed. According to Marshal Joffre this' was agreed to in principle as early as 1911. On page 57 of his memoirs (Ref. 27) the Marshal describes the visit to France of the Russian Chief of Staff, General Jilínsky, and notes: "Our Allies agreed not to wait until their Armies were completely concentrated before acting." This was reaffirmed during Joffre's own visit to Russia in August, 1913. The Marshal has this to say about it on page 59 of Ref. 27:

> "The Grand Duke * assured me that my request would be satisfied. He fully understood the necessity of the Russian Army taking the offensive rapidly, whatever risks such an attitude might seem to involve; for it was essential to bring some relief to our front at any price, supposing that the Germans would attempt at the opening of hostilities to crush our forces. The event proved in what a generous and loyal manner this great gentleman kept his word; I feel it my duty to say this here, and I will have occasion to repeat it further on. France should never forget the service which our Allies rendered her."

Things developed as had been expected and feared in Franco-Russian military circles. By violating Belgium's neutrality, Germany was able to invade rapidly the north of France, with overwhelming forces. Imperial Russia kept her promise and two Russian armies invaded East Prussia well before the beginning of the crucial Battle of the Marne in the West, which was a very dangerous operation (see Maps A, p. 44 and C p. 89). The First Russian Army, under General Rennenkampf, had to advance westward quite separately from the Second Army, under General Samsónov. A fortified German line of lakes separated the two Russian armies. Samsónov's northward attack had to proceed by separate columns with insufficient heavy artillery into fortified forested territory where every inch of ground was well-known to the enemy and where an extensive railroad network permitted the Germans to concentrate and to shift their inferior forces rapidly along short interior lines from one critical point of the front to another. Von Ludendorff notes on page 68 of Ref. 37: ". . . we had succeeded in assembling on the battle-field a force nearly as strong as that of the foe." This battle is known in Russia

---

* Nikolái Nikoláyevich, who was the Commander-in-Chief of all Russian armies at the start of World War I.

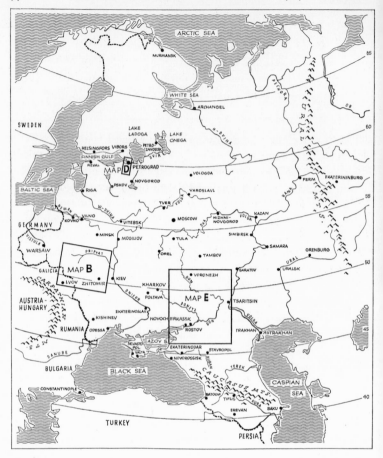

Map A. European borders of Imperial Russia. (Compare with Map G, p. 354. *See p. 80 for Map B, p. 111 for Map D, and p. 142 for Map E.*

as "The Battle of the Masurian Lakes," a more appropriate name than Tannenberg.*

* Tannenberg is situated some distance behind the site of the actual fighting. The Germans gave its name to their 1914 victory, apparently to wipe out all memories of the crushing defeat suffered five centuries earlier by the Teutonic Knights at the hands of the Poles and Lithuanians during the First Battle of Tannenberg in 1410, which stopped the *Drang nach Osten* of that day. Ludendorff however claims he suggested the name because the Germans won that earlier battle! (Ref. 37, page 68.)

There can be be no question that the two German commanders, von Hindenburg and von Ludendorff, made brilliant use of the special advantages of their position, and that the two Russian commanders made a number of tactical blunders. However, the importance of the latter is completely overshadowed by the monumental strategic blunder of the German High Command in not only removing two German Army Corps from France, but in doing so from the key right flank of their armies, whereupon von Kluck's army lacked the reserves needed to overwhelm the French counterattack on that flank. Had it not been for this, the odds are that Germany would have crushed France right then, in accordance with the Schlieffen plan, and would have won the war.

In this connection, Marshal Joffre writes the following in his memoirs, Ref. 27. On page 222 he mentions his consternation on the interception (on August 17/30) of a German radio message, according to which:

"Three Russian army corps have been completely destroyed and two corps commanders have been taken along with 70,000 prisoners; . . . ."

The French marshal goes on to say on the same page:

"And yet, in spite of this catastrophe, the Russians had rendered us exactly the service I had expected of them; for, as I learned the next morning, at the very moment that this bad news arrived from Tannenberg, two German army corps were leaving our front on the way to East Prussia."

On page 223, under the date of August 18/31, 1914, he continues:

". . . by far the most important news was that which arrived from Belgium, reporting the movement of German troop trains from the west to the east and stating that their passage through Berlin had been confirmed. Thirty-two trains had been counted, moving evidently in the direction of Russia. Thus, there could be no doubt that the reaction of the Russian offensive was beginning to make itself felt on the French front, and that the pressure of the enemy on our forces must inevitably diminish."

The German Chief of Staff on their Eastern Front, General von Ludendorff, acknowledges this on pages 69–70 of his memoirs (Ref. 37) as follows:

> "The decision to weaken the forces on the Western front was premature, but, of course, we in the East could not know that, for the reports from the West were favorable. But it was particularly fateful that the reinforcements destined for the Eastern front were drawn from the right wing, which was fighting for a decision, . . ."

Simultaneously with the offensive of the two armies in East Prussia, four other Russian armies, the Fourth, the Fifth, the Third and the Eighth (page 48 of Ref. 31) were concentrated on the Southwestern Front and started a successful offensive against the bulk of the Austro-Hungarian armies (which was assembled in Galicia) in the directions shown by the arrows on Map C, p. 89.

My father was with them. At the start of the war he had been given the command of the 58th Artillery Brigade. It was attached to the 58th Infantry Division which was a so-called "second-line" outfit; that is, it did not exist in peacetime, but was formed during mobilization mainly from reservists with the cadres being provided by the "parent" division. This was the 5th, which was stationed in the Ukrainian city of Zhitómir, partway between Kíev and the Austro-Hungarian border (see Map B, p. 80).

The formation of the 58th Division was rapidly completed, and it took part in the first headon clashes in Galicia between the advancing Russians and the counterattacking Austro-Hungarians. The latter probably knew that the 58th was a second-line unit and hurled at it their best troops, the Tyrolean Alpine Rifles, in an unsuccessful attempt to breach the Russian front at that point. On August 13/26, 1914, these crack German-Austrian mountaineers forced back the reservists of the 58th three times. Each time, however, the infantry reformed their ranks under the cover of the forty-eight field guns of Father's Brigade which he had massed close behind the crest of a key ridge and which beat back the Tyroleans by a hurricane of fire over their open sights. For this action Father was awarded the Cross of St. Vladímir, 4th class, with swords, the next highest Russian combat decoration after the St. George.

The Galician operation was a complete overall success. The defeated Austro-Hungarians suffered heavy losses, abandoned most of that province, and retreated to the Carpathian mountain passes. Behind them they left the garrisoned fortress of Peremýshl (Fig. 13), which is sometimes known by its Polish name of "Przemysl." The 58th was assigned to the besieging Army. Because of the lack of siege or even of heavy artillery, no attempt was made to reduce the fortress by bombardment or by storm. Six months later the garrison attempted to break out through a sector of the ring which had closed around them. They were beaten back solely by artillery fire, never reaching the Russian trenches. On the next day (March 9/22, 1915) Peremýshl surrendered with its 117,000 defenders. Father was in command of all the artillery of the sector attacked, and for that action was promoted to the rank of Major General.

The 58th was then sent into the Carpathian Mountains, the key passes of which led from Galicia into Hungary and had been captured by Russian troops. Fig. 14 shows Father on the Hungarian slopes of the Ouzhók Pass near the ancient Russian town of Oúzhgorod, called Uzcok by the Hungarians. Father and other Russian officers have told me of the strong emotion they felt on finding deep in enemy territory Carpatho-Russian villages which for centuries had held out in their mountains and kept their national identity and Eastern Orthodox religion in spite of recurrent waves of persecutions.

Meanwhile, to the north, a seesaw struggle with the Germans continued. They had been unable to exploit their success of the Masurian Lakes (Tannenberg) and could not breach the adjoining fortified Russian line of the Narew River in Poland which stretched along the southern border of East Prussia. Parts of East Prussia even remained in Russian hands until March, 1915 (Ludendorff, Ref. 37, pages 134–163 of Ref. 37). The Austro-German offensive, which was launched against Warsaw from Silesia in the late autumn of 1914, was thrown back. This situation continued until May, 1915, that is, for about nine months after the start of the war.

Things changed radically after that. The Western Front in France had become fairly stabilized, and the trench warfare which had set in there permitted the Germans to move to the east considerable forces not only to relieve Russian pressure on Austria-Hungary which had placed the Dual Monarchy in a most precarious position, but also ". . . to try and obtain a decision against Russia," according to General Ludendorff (page 165 of Ref. 37).

The element which governed the outcome of the subsequent operations in 1915 was the fact that Russian reserves of ammunition had not been planned for a long war and were about to give out. This was also the case with all other belligerents. However, the well-developed industries of Germany and of the Western Allies permitted them rapidly to replenish their supplies. This the predominantly agricultural economy of Russia could not do, and it was not until 1916 that the industries of England and of France were in a position to start sending some military supplies to Russia.

Under these circumstances the natural strategy of slow retreat and of trading space for time was adopted by the Russian High Command. Austrian Galicia and Russian Poland formed a salient which had to be abandoned first. To slow down the German advance, the fortress of Novogeórgievsk, straddling the Vistula northwest of Warsaw, not only was not evacuated, but was even reinforced. The 58th Division was among the units ordered into the fortress.

Father immediately realized the hopelessness of this enterprise and sent home all valuables and mementos he had with him. His special messenger arrived at Tsárskoye Seló on July 14/27, 1915. According to Ref. 37, page 184, the investment of the fortress was completed thirteen days later, that is, on August 9 (new style; July 27, old style).

We were all terribly upset, especially since the sacrifice of these troops seemed such a useless one in view of the earlier experiences of the Belgian fortresses which were able to hold out for only a few days. The new German heavy-siege artillery, which included 42-cm. (16.8-inch) guns, apparently howitzers, rapidly reduced them. I was interested to read recently General Ludendorff's comments on Novogeórgievsk (page 184 of Ref. 37):

> "It is astonishing that the Grand Duke * should have let it come to this, whereas, later on, Brest-Litóvsk and Gródno were evacuated. He ought to have told himself that it was impossible to hold the fortress, and that the condition of the fortifications was not good enough to withstand heavy high-angle fire."

The 58th was assigned to man some of the forts south of the Vistula where Father was placed in command of all the artillery. The German general, von Beseler, who earlier had captured the Belgian fortress of Antwerp, directed his attack on the forts north of the

* See note on p. 42.

river on which the fire of his heavy-siege artillery was concentrated. After these forts were captured, the rear of the southern forts was open and they too surrendered eleven days after the investment, on August 7/20, 1915.

Father later told me that the German frontline officers behaved quite decently. The Commander of the opposing German division sent his Aide-de-Camp to invite the higher officers of the 58th to his Headquarters. Their departure was, however, delayed until he could send over his own transportation—he had not expected to find that in the 58th anything that could be of use to the enemy had been destroyed before the surrender, including the horses, which were all shot. Nevertheless the German General and his staff officers did not sit down to their meal until the Russian officers arrived, several hours late.

But in the German rear, Father told me, things were quite different. After a brief internment at Neisse in Silesia, on the river of the same name now much in the news because it forms the present border between Poland and East Germany, Father was transferred to a prisonlike old castle at Moewe on the lower Vistula in East Prussia. It was one of the semipenal type of places of internment where the Germans claimed to have introduced a particularly harsh regime in retaliation for the alleged mistreatment of German prisoners in Russia. Father told me that this seems to have been only a pretext, and that the real purpose was to bring pressure on officers of Ukrainian, Cossack, Tartar and of other Russian minority origins who had refused to accept various blandishments offered by the Germans in other special camps and who rejected separatist propaganda for the planned dismemberment of Russia intensively carried on in such camps by Kaiser Wilhelm's government.

By the time winter set in late in 1915, the German advance was finally stopped approximately on the very same lines which not only were held right up to the March 1917 Revolution, but which in places were even pushed back in 1916. But this comparatively short retreat (see Map C, p. 89) was accomplished in 1915 at tremendous human cost, where the lack of arms and of ammunition had to be compensated for by the sacrifice of human lives in continuous delaying and holding actions. It is this terrible human holocaust that was mainly responsible for the popular feelings which produced the Revolution and the ensuing success of Bolshevik ideas.

In my mother's journal (page 75 of Ref. 6a) I find the following entry under the date of February 28/March 12, 1916:

"In the evening I was impressed by a chat with an old *izvóschik* [cabby], . . .

'The French hit them not the way we do—may the Lord bring them health. They [French] mow them down in rows, while we are sending our men barehanded to their death. The government we have, may the devil take it—the people all around *ozvyeryél* [are getting bestial from rage], and what is that new country that has declared war on us, even though small—Bulgaria even though small has caused us one-half million losses. It is men we have lost, not money—money will not buy men. . . .' "

Mother adds:

"Here was the voice of the people, the mood of the political clubs —of the *cháynaya* [the teahouse]."

At that time munitions were already beginning to arrive from France and from England, but this could not eradicate the deep anger throughout the country at the sufferings already caused mainly by Russia's lack of industrial preparation for the war.

Nevertheless, no serious disorders, desertions or other breaches of discipline occurred until the February 1917 Revolution removed all elements of restraint. In the summer of 1916 the Imperial Russian Command was even able to mount a very successful largescale offensive, which is known as the Broussílov offensive, by the name of the General who then commanded the Southwestern Front of the Russian armies. Its importance can be judged from the following comment in Marshal Joffre's memoirs (Ref. 27, page 467):

". . . the offensive which the Austrians had opened in the Trentino had assumed disquieting proportions, and the Russians, upon the request of Italy, had decided to advance the date of their attack, which was now fixed for June 4th."

Here again, the Imperial Russian Army came to the rescue of an ally in need, without sparing itself. According to the British Military Attaché, General Knox, in less than two months of the offensive, Russia lost 450,000 men even though inflicting at least 50 percent higher losses on their opponents (see Ref. 31, pages 460–461). The scale of this operation alone completely dwarfs Tannenberg.

This 1916 Russian offensive helped the Allied cause not only in north Italy, but in France as well. General Ludendorff, by then the Quartermaster General of the entire German Army, on page 258 of his memoirs (see Ref. 37) speaks of: "Russia's amazing victories over the Austro-Hungarian troops," and on page 260 goes on to say:

"Austria gradually broke off the Italian offensive, and sent troops to the Eastern front. The Italian Army now started a counteroffensive in the Tyrol. The face of the war had changed completely."

The British Military Attaché, Major General Knox, writes on page 446 of his book (Ref. 31):

"The Austrians had been driven back from lengths aggregating 195 miles of a line of 255 miles that they had fortified for upwards of nine months, and they had been driven back by an army with technical equipment far inferior to their own.

"The sudden success of an enemy, whom they thought they had decisively beaten in 1915, came as a rude and unexpected shock to the strategists of Berlin. The moment, too, was uncomfortable, for the attack on Verdun was still in full progress and was making ever-increasing inroads on German man-power. The Germans, however, came promptly to the help of their ally."

On page 551 of his Ref. 31, General Knox continues:

" 'Brusílov's offensive' was the outstanding military event of the year. In the extent of territory regained, in the number of the enemy killed and taken prisoner and in the number of enemy units absorbed, it surpassed other allied offensives. Russia, owing to this advance, and the bait of Rumania, absorbed enormous enemy forces. The following figures speak for themselves. England and France were opposed on July 1st, the date of the commencement of the Somme offensive, by 1,300 battalions. On January 1, 1917, the number was 1,327 battalions. Russia was opposed in the Eastern theatre on June 4th, the date of the commencement of Brusílov's offensive, by 509 German and 534 Austrian battalions; on January 1, 1917, she was occupying 854 German battalions, 708 Austrian battalions and twenty-four Turkish battalions—an enemy increase in the Eastern theatre of 345 German, 174 Austrian and twenty-four Turkish battalions, as compared with an increase of only twenty-seven German battalions in the Western theatre. This contribution to the Allied cause was attained with equipment that would have been laughed at in the Western theatre, and Russia paid the price in blood. Brusílov's armies lost 375,000 men in twenty-seven days in June, and their losses till the end of October exceeded a million."

Thus official British data shows that on the eve of the February 1917 Revolution the Imperial Russian Army pinned down on its front twenty percent more enemy troops than did the combined forces of England and of France.

General Knox is perfectly right in saying on page 551 (Ref. 31) that:

"On the eve of the Revolution the prospects for the 1917 campaign were brighter than they had been in March, 1916, for the campaign of that year."

It was the general disorganization in the wake of the March 1917 Revolution that brought to nought Russia's sacrifices. Next to the psychological trauma induced by the terrible *human* losses of the war, no other single factor contributed more to the general revolt of the masses against their rulers than did the rumors which built up around the tragic figure of the Empress Alexándra Fyódorovna. A quirk of fate gave me the opportunity to gain some insight into the real nature of the relevant events.

## 2. *The Palace Hospital at Tsárskoye Seló*

At the very start of the war Mother became a *sestrá milosérdiya* (a sister of mercy), or nurse. The photo Fig. 15 shows our wartime family about a year later. Mother is in the uniform she wore almost continuously for four years. I am in my Imperial Law School uniform, and my little sister, Alya, is almost overshadowed by her doll and by my French bulldog, Gribouille, usually known simply as "Boúlka." Not in the picture are my sister's French governess and the maid who also served as cook at home.

I will use the word "sister," throughout my narrative, since it expresses much better than the somewhat impersonal "nurse," the warm gratitude which all classes of the population showed towards the women who were caring for their numerous wounded. They were addressed directly as *sestrá*, and the wounded soldiers themselves frequently used the affectionate diminutive *sestrítza* when speaking to or of them.

At the start of the war practically all society ladies donned the sisters of mercy uniform and many, but not all, took their work seriously. My mother, because of her father having been a medical doctor, had a professional approach towards her duties. Also, she was one of the very few ladies at Tsárskoye Seló who already had some experience, having volunteered for hospital work during the Russo-Japanese war of 1904–1905 and having taken formal training courses at that time.

This latter circumstance is probably the reason why, although not belonging to Court circles, she was nevertheless asked to join a group of Tsárskoye Seló ladies to work together with the Empress and her two elder daughters, the Grand Duchesses Olga Nikoláyevna and Tatiána Nikoláyevna—who were aged nineteen and seventeen, respectively, at the start of the war. The two other daughters, Maríya and Anastasíya, were considered too young for hospital work.

A special small hospital was set up for the Empress. It was located in an isolated one-story building (originally a ward for contagious diseases, I believe), in the parklike garden of the main Palace Hospital, a three-story structure which in peacetime served the needs of the local civilian population. It was supported by Palace funds, hence its name.

The large main Palace Hospital building was assigned at the start of the war to the care of wounded soldiers. Its small annex, where the Empress was to work, cared mainly for wounded officers, but some soldiers were treated there too. It had its own operating room and staff, but shared the chief surgeon and doctor with the main hospital. Special rooms were provided for the personal use of the Empress and the two Grand Duchesses.

Very soon Mother was appointed senior sister of that annex and of its operating room. The photo, Fig. 16, shows her sitting next to the Empress; the woman on the other side of the wife of the Tsar is the chief surgeon, Princess Véra Ignátievna Gedróitz, a distant relative of my classmate at the Imperial Law School and, like him, of Royal Lithuanian descent. She was a most remarkable woman and a very fine person, who tried to oppose Ánna Alexándrovna Víroubova's (the lady-in-waiting) most unfortunate influence on the Empress. I do not recall now who S. I. Dobrovólskaya and U. F. Lvóva were outside the hospital. V. A. [Varvára Afanásyevna] Vilchkóvskaya worked there continuously until the Revolution. She was the wife of a retired Colonel Vilchkóvsky who headed some branch of the civil administration of Tsárskoye Seló.

Mother began keeping her diary the day she received at the hospital Father's message with his estimate of what awaited him in the fortress of Novogeórgievsk, to which he had been ordered with the 58th Division. Her diary * (see Ref. 6a) begins thus:

"On July 14 [27, 1915] Grísha telephoned. A messenger has arrived from Father, letters, a package. Grishoúk brought it on his bicycle about 10 A.M. I will never forget the bitter feeling of pain. Why does fate send this trial too? The prospect of a siege, complete isolation and captivity;—just what I had been insanely afraid of . . . The Grand Duchesses are touchingly attentive. . . ."

I think I should give some explanatory background data at this point. The Empress Alexándra Fyódorovna was born and grew up a German Princess of Hesse. After her marriage she embraced the Russian Orthodox faith and seems to have made a real effort to understand and to adapt herself to her new homeland. Unfortunately, like so many other Westerners, she made the mistake of believing that the mystic features in the Russian Orthodox church service solely reflected the real nature of the Russian people. Personal misfortunes drove her to grotesque extremes in her spiritual mysticism. An important factor in this connection was the illness of her only son and heir to the throne, the Tsesarévich Alexéi.

He had hemophilia, and the slightest cut produced continuous bleeding which endangered his life. Medical doctors were unable to cure it, but a sinister semiliterate Siberian peasant, Grigóriy Efímovich Raspútin, either actually did help him, or at least succeeded in persuading the Empress that this was the case. At the palace he successfully acted the role of a holy man, and the Empress refused to believe true reports of his dissolute life at St. Petersburg, which was generally known. It was inevitable that his debauchery outside the Palace led people to believe that he must behave similarly within the

---

* Strictly speaking, it is a journal, rather than a diary, since Mother did not make daily entries, but wrote only when she had a moment to spare, which was not often.

Palace walls. He seems to have even at times deliberately encouraged this impression.

The net result was immeasurable harm done to the prestige of the Imperial Throne throughout the country at a critical period of its history. In this respect the Raspútin affair seems to have been a repetition, but on a much grander scale, of the *Collier de la Reine,* ("The Queen's Necklace")—the scandal which innocently involved Marie Antoinette, the last Queen of France. Her background and her tragic fate have many other similarities with those of Alexándra Fyódorovna, the last Empress of Russia.

I once met, or to be more precise, bumped into, Raspútin. On the way home after class from St. Petersburg I had already entered the railway car on the train for Tsárskoye Seló when I realized that I had forgotten to buy the evening paper. I dashed out of the car just as Raspútin was about to get in. I was in my Imperial Law School uniform—three-cornered hat, white kid gloves, and all that—so Raspútin stepped aside, as two fellows who looked like his bodyguards moved up closer to him—apparently "just in case." As I passed Raspútin our eyes met and I will never forget the uncomfortable feeling I experienced—since then I have been convinced that he had hypnotic powers.

Mother realized that she was witnessing happenings, details of which were likely to be of importance later on. On pages 6 and 7 of her diary (see Ref. 6a) she wrote under the date of July 26 (August 8), 1915:

"To distract my thoughts I shall jot down 'historically' interesting moments during the past year: The Empress and the Grand Duchesses began to work in August [*1914*]—at first they were so distant. We kissed their hand when greeting them, and that was all. Véra Ignát [*ievna Gedróitz*] gave a one-half hour lecture in their room; A. A. [*Víroubova*] was always there; then they went to the bandaging room, the Princesses to that of the soldiers; the Empress and A. A. [*Víroubova*] to that of the officers. . . .

"November and December [*1914*] were a period of particularly touching cult of the Empress—she came so close to the life of the officers so simply, nicely and kindly . . . sat at their bedsides, was interested in everything—even in details of their life.

"Early in December [*1914*] they went traveling. On the way they sent wonderful telegrams from the sisters—Al[exándra], Ólga, Tatiána * and Anne [Víroubova]—the latter unnecessarily; she has no 'choútkost' [sensitivity]—'We are missing our dear wounded to whom we have become so accustomed.' They sent jam, inscribed 'from the three sisters' [sestrítz]. They returned on the 13th [26th] and the Empress took to bed. Enlargement of the heart, weariness and some severe insult at Moscow. We did not see her until Christmas."

Tsar Nicholas II had the reputation of being swayed by the last person who happened to talk to him. He seems to have been a very kind and well-intentioned man, an excellent father and husband—very fine attributes which are, however, insufficient as qualifications for the role of a successful autocrat, a role urged upon him by his misguided wife. I have often heard it said that he would have made a firstrate regimental commander—the implication being that this was about the maximum responsibility that he was fitted to assume.

Apparently at first he had agreed on the need to clamp down on Raspútin and actually did so. But he did not follow up by action against Raspútin's main supporter at Court and confidante of the Empress, A. A. Víroubova. Increasing outside pressure on him to do something about her, too, only made him come to the defense of his wife, apparently as a point of personal and family loyalty, to take action against most of her known critics and even to reverse himself about Raspútin. Both the criticisms and the Tsar's unreasonable reaction to them increased in intensity from then on, finally making a Revolution inevitable. It was in the air long before the actual event.

The turning point was the Tsar's fatal decision to assume personal command of all Russian armies in the field—an action urged upon him by the Empress.

Mother felt great personal sympathy for the Empress. She certainly had many problems. On page 2 of her diary (see Ref. 6a), Mother wrote under the date of July 17[30, 1915]:

---

* They always wrote many letters from their frequent trips. I have kept a total of ninety-six personal messages addressed to my mother: twenty-two from the Empress, thirty-two from Ólga Nikoláyevna, and forty-two from Tatiána Nikoláyevna. Of these, eighteen letters were mailed after the Revolution, including eleven from their Siberian exile at Tobólsk (see Figs. 20, 27 and 28).

"And how at times her girls, with their characteristic vivacity, can hurt her. Véra Ign[*átievna Gedróitz*] was reporting about the wedding of Auder[?]—'at Pávl[*ovsk*], his old grandmother lives there,—a German,'—and then added, smiling:—'the latter [*fact*] is carefully concealed.'—'Of course he has to conceal it, I quite understand him, she may perhaps be a real bloodthirsty German,' burst out O[*lga*] N[*ikoláyevna*]."

The Empress seemed to have more than the usual share of mother-in-law troubles with the Danish-born Dowager Empress Maríya Fyódorovna, who completely distrusted her. On page 42 of Mother's diary for October 24/November 6, 1915, I find:

"An interesting and frank remark escaped the Gosudárynya during the last visit of the Gosudár: [*written in the diary in French*]:

" 'He has gone to Petrográd to see his mother—he must talk, they have so much to say to each other. If I come, she remains silent.' "

On page 41, under the same date, Mother gives the following description of a visit of the Empress to the hospital and her own comments about it:

"She stayed for a long time in the diningroom with her handwork —one of the princesses played pingpong, the other checkers [*with convalescing officers*], some were reading, some were chatting— everything was simple and cosy. The Gosud [*árynya*] said to Var[*vára*] Af[*anásyevna Vilchkóvskaya*] [*written in the diary in French*]:

" 'Look how the little ones are having fun—how restful this simple life is—and the big gatherings of high society—*brrr*. I come away from them all worn out—I have to force myself to chat and to see people who, I know quite well, are against me, who work against me. These intrigues and hatreds—how painful and tiring it all is. Recently I was finally rid of a few of them, but only when there were proofs (Orlóv, one would think, and Djounkóvsky?) * And when I withdraw from that society, I arrange my life as I wish. People say, *"C'est une exaltée*. They judge badly

* Mother's comment, in Russian.

people I love and yet in order to judge one must know everything and in detail. Often I feel what kind of persons approach
me just by their look and whether I can trust them or not.' "

"Poor, unfortunate [Mother continued], this is how I always pictured her—herself pure and good, wholesome and simple. She is
depressed by the conventions and make-believe of high society
and she cannot believe in the dirt of Gr. [*Raspútin*]—as a result
[*there*] are enemies in the upper strata and distrust in the lower
ones. If only they could see her and know her to be what we
know she is!"

Most of Mother's friends belonged to "society," but not to Court
circles. I remember her at home at first often defending the Empress
as a human being and getting the reply, that she, Mother, was under
the personal *obayániye* (charm) of the Imperial Family, and therefore did not believe that the Empress was harming the country.
Mother did finally change her mind about the Empress, but was
not on close enough terms with her to try to do anything about it.
Throughout the diary one can see the gradual change of Mother's
initial admiration for the Empress. However her affection for the
two Grand Duchesses never wavered.

On page 61 for January 22 [*February 9, 1916*] Mother referred
to rumors about the impending divorce of the Tsar. It turned out to
be just wishful thinking, with Mother commenting:

". . . And yet what a fine gesture this would have been—to enter
a convent; all accusations of pro-Germanism would have immediately dropped away, all ugly rumors about Gr. [*Raspútin*]
would have been silenced and maybe the children and the throne
itself saved from a great danger."

This was written over a year before the Revolution. Knowing the
causes of popular distrust, Mother became more and more worried
as one mistaken step of the Empress followed another.

Although the Empress visited the hospital only occasionally, the
two elder Grand Duchesses did so continuously, and my mother
became quite friendly with, and fond of, them. They seemed to like
to do real work and to be away from their gilded cage in the Palace.
On pages 3 and 4, July 17/30, 1915, Mother wrote:

"They touchingly love their father. They came in for the boiling
of silk on foot. '*Papoúlya* brought us but did not want to drive

in; we walked from the gate'—T[*atyána*] N[*ikoláyevna*]. During the unwinding we all sat side-by-side, chatting; they questioned about Porphírenka,* the children; how we lived at Krásnoye [*summer camp of the Guards*], where we traveled. They left after 11, offered to give me a lift by car; I thanked, a container for silk had yet to be boiled, I fussed with it till half past midnight.

"On the 20th they came again to finish the preparation of compresses.

"On the 21st Zaliv. [?] operation went quite well, T[*atyána*] N[*ikoláyevna*] handed the silk and O[*lga*] N[*ikoláyevna*] the instruments—I the materials. In the evening they came again to clean the instruments; we all sat in a corner of the preparation room, very crowded; they themselves opened the windows; themselves brought the silk. O[*lga*] N[*ikoláyevna*] again said:

" 'Mamá sends you, V[*alentína*] I[*vánovna*], special greetings . . . It is good here . . . is it not strange, we would not have known you, had there been no war.'

"They diligently scrubbed with soap and alcohol, themselves carried to the containers the ready instruments. Officers were surprised—'there are orderlies, why do you spoil your hands!' "

They certainly tried to do their full share of the operation room work. On page 64, January 28/February 12, 1916, Mother noted:

"Today 'Papá' again leaves for the Army. I thought of making use of this time to boil silk since T[*atiána*] N[*ikoláyevna*] would certainly be occupied—I fear the poor thing is getting too tired. But she guessed: 'Well, just tell me, please, what is the hurry. How cunning you are—at first I could not understand—there are no emergency operations—why can you breathe carbolic acid —and I can't?'—She insisted. We left it until next week. Gosud [*árynya*] permitted."

They were not used to meeting people—on page 60 for January 16/29, 1916, I find this entry:

"Today T[*atiána*] N[*ikoláyevna*], after finishing bandage changing in our section went together with me to the upper one for Popóv's change of bandages—the dear child is so terribly shy

* Diminutive of "Porphýry," my father's name.

when she has to walk past a mass of sisters—she grasped my hand
—'I am so terribly embarrassed and frightened—I do not know
whom I greeted and whom not.' "

This shyness when first meeting strangers was paralleled by intense
interest in the way of life of ordinary people, about which they knew
next to nothing. One day, the lady-in-waiting who usually picked up
the two Grand Duchesses at the hospital was prevented by something
from doing so and just sent the carriage along. The two girls seized
the opportunity to do some exploring of the world around them on
their own, and ordered the carriage to stop near the Gostínny Dvor,
an arcade of shops, with the aim of buying something. They were
not recognized in their nurse's uniforms (Fig. 17). However, they
very soon realized that not only had they no money with them, but
that they did not know how to go about buying something. The next
day they questioned Mother as to how this was done. The story is
not in my mother's diary, but it has stuck in my memory—I was so
amazed that there could be people who had never bought anything
in all their life.

One evening at home I answered the telephone. A man's voice
asked if this was number 222,* told me to wait a minute, then an
unfamiliar young female voice asked for "Valentína Ivánovna" (my
mother), adding: "And who is this? Is this Grísha?" I was then
sixteen and bristled at having a strange girl call me by my diminutive, so my reply was: "And who are *you*?" "Tatiána Nikoláyevna,"
was the answer. I could not quite believe that I was really speaking
to the daughter of the Tsar and rather foolishly asked again: "Who?"
"Sister Románova the Second," the voice said. I was then only able
to mumble something unintelligible, and called Mother to the phone.

Apparently the two Grand Duchesses knew all about the families
of the Staff and of the wounded at the hospital. They spent as much
of their free time there as they could, chatting with the officers (Fig.
18). Inevitably, some mild flirtations developed, which caused occasional worried comments in Mother's journal. She seems to have taken
her duties of informal chaperone very seriously and to have been
determined to prevent any gossip whatsoever about the two girls she
had grown so fond of.

* Our phone number at Tsárskoye Seló. This one was easy to recall, but I still
remember my uncle Ványa's (Father's brother) phone number at St. Petersburg:
105.41. I mention this because I have heard people abroad express surprise that
there could be "that many" telephones in the old Russian Capital.

In Mother's diary I find a number of references to Raspútin's murder which occurred in mid-December—on the 17th [*30, 1916*]. Most of the facts are generally known, including the comparatively mild, but politically disastrous reprisals which followed. I will however quote two relevant passages:

From page 107, entry of December 30, 1916/January 12, 1917:

". . . a new outburst of wild rabid hatred—all classes speak about her with foam at the mouth. She has won meanwhile—Trépov, Ignátiev have been dismissed—she meant what she said: 'I have suffered enough, I can't any more. One must twist them into a ram's horn.' Well, it seems that blood spilled even for a great purpose does not bring happiness—on the contrary—new bitterness, a flare-up of reaction. . . ."

From page 120, February 5/18, 1917:

"The following sentence escaped from Olga some days ago: 'Maybe it was necessary to kill him, but not so terribly—we are a *seméyka* [*family*], one is ashamed to admit they are relatives.' *
"The autopsy showed that his lungs were full of water. His arms were raised and rigid—he was drowned while still alive."

On the day of Raspútin's murder, but apparently before the Empress knew of it, she received in audience at the Palace a good friend of our family, the wife of General Mrozóvsky, then in command of the Moscow Military District. On page 105 for December 30, 1916/January 12, 1917 Mother mentions in connection with the events of December 17/30, 1916:

"Mánechka Mroz[*óvsky*] was received—she was impressed by her [*the Empress's*] nervousness and bitterness—
'my foot will never be in Moscow—I will go where I am appreciated—the simple folk love me—and Moscow, Petrográd—"awful towns," ' (this was said in English) . . ."

This is where lies the real drama of the situation and the greatest sin of Víroubova—the Empress appears to have been misled by her to sincerely believe that the mass of the simple people were on her side.

* The Grand Duke Dimítry Pávlovich was one of the three murderers; the other two were Pourishkévich, a rightwing member of the Doúma, and Prince Yussúpov, a famous tennis champion.

About that time the Grand Duchess Tatiána Nikoláyevna thought of the idea of getting my father transferred from the German prison to a neutral country. This was very nice of her, but I doubt that Father would have accepted it. Mother certainly was upset at the possible implications of what the Empress told her about it, obviously with the kindest of intentions. On page 117 (three weeks before the Revolution) Mother wrote, on February 5/18, 1917:

"Two days ago the Gosoudárynya unexpectedly came to see us, for the first time after the 'event' [*i.e., the murder of Raspútin*]. In good spirits, kind, at times thinks about something and has a somewhat absent expression. She came up to me, kindly: 'The sisters [*of the Russian Red Cross exchange-inspection Mission to Germany*] visited me. They said they had seen your husband. I think it will be possible to arrange his transfer to a neutral country. If the doctors won't do it, maybe I will succeed.' "This last detail worried me,—an indirect confirmation of rumors about interference [*in relations with Germany*]. I do not believe and will never believe that the motivating force is a wish to help them [*the Germans*]. The only explanation which seems to be true: a complete destruction of Germ[*any*] would bring with it the overthrow of the Hohenzol[*lerns*]—that support of monarchies in Europe on which they rely should the son's throne become shaky."

I think that Mother's tentative explanation probably is the correct one. However, I do not believe that accounts published in this country about the influence the Empress allegedly had on military campaign decisions could possibly be correct. The caliber of the top men at Imperial Headquarters, like the Generals Alexéiev, Brussílov and others, was not such as to permit anything of the kind to develop.

During the second half of the 1915 summer, I spent six weeks or so working at the Palace Hospital. Mother had spoken to me about the need for help in its main building where there was a great influx of recently wounded soldiers—it was the time of the great and costly delaying retreat of the Russian armies. She then introduced me to Princess Gedróitz as: "our new volunteer." The surgeon scrutinized me for a moment, then told me to report at the main operation room a couple of hours later.

It turned out that the amputation of a gangrenous leg of a recently arrived soldier was scheduled then. Princess Gedróitz ordered me to hold down with both hands the rather revolting looking and smelling purple and green thing (I had been given rubber gloves) while she, assisted by a group of nurses, cut the flesh away just above the knee and turned it up so that it could later be turned back and formed into a cushion over the bone which she sawed off higher up. She told me to carry the leg away to a bucket in a corner of the room, then called me back immediately and looked me straight in the eyes. Apparently she was satisfied with what she saw and told me that I was appointed temporary operation room orderly. I do not believe that there was any real need for me to hold the gangrenous leg down since it was strapped to the table and the patient was under ether; she simply wanted to test my nerves before assigning me to the job.

I spent there the remaining six weeks of my summer vacation from school, witnessing quite a number of operations which ranged in complexity from various kinds of amputations to a trepanation of the skull. My main job was to transfer the wounded from their beds to a rolling table, roll them to the operation room, transfer them to the table there and, after the end of the operation, repeat all this in reverse order. Most able-bodied men were in the Army, and a group of boys were working as orderlies in the hospital. I was one of the more husky ones and was accordingly called upon to do much of the heavy lifting.

The most trying of all such tasks was the moving for changes of bandages of wounded with shell-splintered thigh bones. These were all casualties of German high-explosive fragmentation anti-personnel shells. The men were wounded during the frequent Russian bayonet counterattacks, which were carried out as delaying actions without benefit of artillery support since the reserves of shells had run out. The wounded had their injured legs under traction in stiff-wire baskets. Two boys were supposed to do the moving of one wounded, but we found it impossible to synchronize our movements so as not to cause agonizing pain to soldiers with splintered thigh bones. Finally we found that the following was the best way to go about it. The wounded man would sit up and put his arms around my neck; I would then pass one arm lengthwise under the part of his body "where the back loses its noble name," with the palm of the hand supporting the upper end of the wire basket which encased his leg, the other end and the uninjured leg being supported by my other arm. It was then possible to lift the wounded man, who usually was emaciated and had lost a lot of weight, and to swing him around onto the rolling table without causing groans of pain.

Occasionally I had time to chat with the wounded, who came from all over the country, to read to them letters from home with news of friends and relatives who had been either killed or maimed too, and to write replies. It is only then that I fully realized the terrible sacrifices which the peoples of Russia had been called upon to make, and the widespread bitterness because of the fact that many of these sacrifices could have been avoided by better preparation. It is also then that I developed a deep respect and enduring love for the people of my native land.

### 3. The Imperial Law School in Wartime

My operation room orderly work at the Tsárskoye Seló Palace Hospital became possible only during the second half of the 1915 summer, because the first half was taken up by another form of war work. Prince Oldenbúrgsky * had temporarily transformed the entire Law School into a factory for the production of bandage-type antigas masks.

Oldenbúrgsky held some very high position in the Russian Red Cross and had been entrusted with the production of these devices on what nowadays would be called a "crash basis." They were to give emergency protection against poison gases which the Germans had introduced as a new form of warfare and had actually used against Russian positions near Warsaw. He was encountering organizational difficulties in getting things going, largely because of shortages of trained manpower. So, with a suddenness typical of him, he decided to mobilize several schools, including our Law School, of which he was the sole trustee.

He told us this in the middle of a Latin examination, which he promptly cancelled on the spot, to our immeasurable joy. This exam was particularly feared by all of us since we expected retribution for the various pranks we had played during the year on our teacher, a man by the name of Voldemár. He was very short—I would say not much over five feet tall—and seemed to be acutely conscious of this fact. He tried to correct it by wearing specially made highheeled

* See p. 25.

shoes and a type of crew haircut which was known in Russia as *yózhik* (hedgehog). The hair was trimmed to stand up vertically, usually not more than an inch high,—but Voldemár's was at least two inches. In addition he had the queer notion that Latin should be taught as if it were a living language, by methods in some ways similar to those used in a modern Berlitz school. I still feel like shivering when I recall him gibbering away at me in Latin. All these peculiarities made him a natural target for every kind of joke and prank that boys are capable of thinking up.

I mention all this because by the 1930s he had become the Prime Minister Voldemáras of independent Lithuania and, I am told, exhibited dictatorial rightwing tendencies. I have always wondered how he could rule a country when he had seldom been able to maintain order in our class of some fifty boys.

The examination in the spring of 1915 was an exception, and, like most examinations in Russian schools, was carried on not only with decorum, but with some pomp. Voldemár and another teacher sat behind a large table covered with green cloth. On it were spread out the *billyéty* (cards), the number of which exceeded somewhat that of the boys in the class.

It was customary to divide a course up into the number of *billyéty* to be used, and to write on each card the part of the course it covered and specific questions referring to it. Each boy was called up in alphabetical order, would draw a card from the stack fanned out face down on the green cloth and would proceed to one of the three or four blackboards set up along the wall behind the examiners. He was then given a few minutes to quietly think over the questions he had drawn. He gave his answers orally but could write out on the board any part he might wish to.

The examination was already under way when suddenly Oldenbúrgsky came in. The boy on duty for the day gave the customary order: *"Vstat! Smírno!* (Stand Up! To Attention!)."* The Prince was a big ruddy-faced elderly man who, although retired, always wore his general's uniform. He briefly announced that the school would become an anti-gas device factory, that no exams would be held, and then left to make the rounds of the other classes.

Voldemár did not take this literally and proceeded with the exam. But within a few minutes after Oldenbúrgsky's departure, trucks began rolling up and unloading work tables, other equipment and supplies. We could see them being carried in past the big glass paneled doors of our classroom, but still the exam dragged on. My name is close to the end of a list in the Russian alphabet, and I was beginning to get worried. By checking off the parts of the course already covered in the exam I could see that the remaining cards were bound to contain the topics with which I was least familiar. But Oldenbúrgsky arrived in the unusual role of saving angel. He appeared again, as unexpectedly as before, and emitted an angry bellow on seeing that his orders had not been complied with. Shaking at Voldemár a heavy cane he always carried, Oldenbúrgsky roared that this was no time for Latin when men were dying at the front; the yearly average grades were to be used; any exam grades already given were to be ignored. With that he swung his cane, swept all exam cards and lists off the table onto the floor, and ordered us out of the room. We went out—with quite a cheer!

The entire school went to work with great enthusiasm—there were no weekend or Sunday rest periods. Each boy had to choose one of some twelve specialties: to cut up gauze into 3-inch wide strips of approximately 2 feet length (the ends of which could be tied together on the back of a man's head); to sew onto the middle of the strip a pad of folded gauze (which would come opposite a soldier's mouth); to place in the strip two gauze plugs for the nostrils; to tightly fold the whole thing into a small cylinder; to soak it in a solution of some chemical; to tightly wrap it in wax paper (this is what I did); to place the package in a 5-inch square sheet of impregnated cloth, three edges of which had been covered with some kind of glue; then to fold the cloth over and press together by a small roller its glue-covered edges. The result was a small air-tight package which, when ripped open, could afford for a few hours some protection against poison gas.

In six weeks our school alone produced some 160,000 such packages. This, together with work elsewhere, met the immediate needs. Rush work on this primitive emergency device was then discontinued as more sophisticated models became available.

The following school year (1915–1916) was uneventful except for an incident in which I got involved and which I will narrate since it illustrates the peculiar relationship which existed between the Russian press of that day and some influential rightwing persons.

I have already described the *tsouk*,* or hazing, to which we had

* See pp. 25–28.

been subjected four years earlier. The majority of our class disliked it intensely and took effective steps to eradicate this nonsense when we became the seniors of the "Junior Course," that is, of the classes for general education. Yet we got accused by the press of having done exactly the opposite, and were prevented by our superiors from publicly correcting the record. This is how it happened:

One of the boys in our class was very unpopular with the rest of us for very good reasons which I will not go into except to say that they had nothing to do with politics of any kind. I will call him Z. As we were all walking down a corridor one day after the end of classes, Z. tried to rush by to get home in a hurry. In so doing, he bumped into Buturlín, a boy of my class, who responded by giving Z. a shove which sent him reeling against me. I pushed him away against another classmate, Kárpov, who also got into the spirit of the thing. Seconds later we were propelling Z. down the hall, bouncing him (as he snarled and cursed) back and forth among the three of us. When we let him go he shouted some threats about getting even with us, but we paid no attention to what seemed just one of his customary displays of bad temper.

On the next day all three of us were suddenly placed under arrest in separate isolated cells. Colonel Goltgáuer entered mine shortly afterwards and offered me the choice between an apology to Z. and expulsion from the school. Mr. Z., Sr., had called on the Director and threatened to write a letter to the newspapers unless we apologized to his son. Apparently Z., Jr., had told his father (who was quite prominent in the world of art, and generally respected) that we had been persecuting him because of his refusal to join in the hazing of boys in the younger classes. This, of course, was completely false. I said so and flatly refused to apologize. Later, I heard that both Buturlín and Kárpov also refused. More than that, when the rest of the class learned of what had happened, they formally voted not only to forbid us to apologize, but to expel Z. from the school. This vote was investigated and approved by the seniors of the university classes of the school and was officially communicated to the Director. According to the procedure set up earlier by Prince Oldenbúrgsky (see page 25), expulsion of Z., Jr., thereby became mandatory. He never reappeared again in the school.

Meanwhile, Mr. Z., Sr., carried out his threat and wrote a letter which was published by one of the leading Russian newspapers giving a horrendous picture of the persecutions to which his noble son had allegedly been subjected. Very wisely, he did not mention our names in the letter, so we were unable to take legal action through our parents. But neither would Prince Oldenbúrgsky allow any action by the school, perhaps because the various incidents of hazing mentioned by Z. actually had occurred in past years—even though before Z., Jr., had joined the school and therefore had no connection whatsoever with him or with us.

Mr. Z., Sr.'s, letter proved a real boon to various columnists and writers of editorials. They had been having a lean and frustrating time because of censorship concerning Raspútin and related juicy affairs, so this provided a welcome outlet for their pentup indignation. Article after article appeared even in the conservative press condemning the allegedly savage mores of the Imperial Law School, although even the occurrences mentioned were no more savage than the hazing in many American universities.

Worried alumni residing at Petrográd called an informal meeting and questioned various other members of our class—my two pals and I were still under arrest. The alumni recommended our immediate release and official publication of the true facts. The Director then had to release us without any demerits. Oldenbúrgsky approved of this but ordered that the press be ignored—*Sobáka láyet, vyéter nósit* was the way he put it; that is, "The dog barks, but the wind carries it [the bark] away." This Russian peasant proverb was frequently used and expresses well the politically inept attitude towards the press, so characteristic of many rightwing leaders of old Russia. Granted that the behavior of parts of the press all too frequently deserved such contempt, there still must have been decent journalists who would have disseminated the true facts if only given access to them.

In spite of the additional burden imposed on me by the daily commuting from Tsárskoye Seló, I took part in discussion groups with some of my classmates, who, like me, were not living at the school. My recollection of the quotation from Spinoza at the start of my Introduction dates from then. As I remember it in Russian, it read: *Human actions should not be ridiculed, or condemned, or praised, but only understood.* At about the same time I became interested in the philosophy of the Yogi, a circumstance which later on was the indirect cause of unexpected help given me in a very tight spot.

Chess was very popular as recreation at the school. It received a great boost among us just before the War when a World Chess Tournament was held at St. Petersburg and the third place—just behind such giants of chess as Lasker and Capablanca—was won by Alékhin, then in the senior university class of our school. He later became a World Champion himself, but he then represented France where he had settled after the Revolution.

After our graduation in the Spring of 1916, practically our entire class of over fifty boys entered the Army, the majority volunteering without being called. Only three or four physically handicapped boys did not make it.

### 4. *The Mihdilovsky Artillery School*

My age at graduation from the classes for general education of the Imperial Law School was seventeen years and three months. Anyone under eighteen who volunteered for active service had to produce written permission from his parents before being accepted, but my mother flatly refused to give it to me, on the grounds that in Father's absence she could not shoulder this responsibility alone. Obviously, the German Military Censorship would never pass on to my father any such request from me. I seemed to be checkmated, but chance came to my help.

After his internment in Germany, Father, like other prisoners of war, was allowed to send and to receive one letter a month, in addition to a postcard—either every week or every two weeks, I forget which. He numbered all of them, so we knew if any got lost. In one of his very first letters, Father wrote that he was whiling away his time by writing poetry and dedicating it "to my dear Válya" (Mother's diminutive). She immediately realized what that meant. Shortly after they had become engaged, Father wrote a poem of the type called in Russia by its French name, *acrostiche*. The first letters of each line, when read vertically downwards, formed a sentence. In Father's poem it was the one I just mentioned. Nothing came out when we first tried this on Father's letter, but a short message was conveyed by reading the second letters of each line.

This gave me an idea. If Father could do this, why couldn't I do it too? A little practice showed me that I could. I suppose it would be much more difficult to do in a typed or printed epistle, but in long hand it was easy to inconspicuously change the length of the words in each line, to hyphenate them, and so on, until the desired result was obtained. In a few days my message was on its way saying that I had taken up poetry too, and asking by *acrostiche* Father's permission to volunteer.

Two or three months later came Father's reply: *Soglásen Ouslóviye Rodnóye Ouchílische Bataréya* (Agree; Condition My School Battery). In the Russian alphabet it took only thirty-five letters as compared to the forty-five letters of its above Latin alphabet transliteration.

There was nothing Mother could do but endorse Father's permission. I attached it, all covered with stamps of the German Military Censorship, to my formal application for admission to the Miháilovsky Artillery School at St. Petersburg, renamed Petrográd in a wave of anti-German feeling at the start of the war. My father was well-known in Russian artillery circles, and the way I got his permission made some impression on the authorities of the school. In May, 1916, I became a *yúnker*, that is, a cadet, of its 7th Accelerated Wartime Course.

This proved to be the happiest time of my life—hard, but well organized and directed work; sensible discipline and leadership; congenial fellow cadets; and bright hopes for my personal and for the country's future. The situation at the front had markedly improved—supplies were moving up, and the Brussílov offensive had been quite a success. We were too busy preparing ourselves to join the ranks at the front to pay much attention to the rumors about Raspútin and to other symptoms of the demoralization at the rear of the armies in the field.

The regular three-year course of the school had been reduced to seven months' duration by cutting out all general educational subjects, such as calculus and other forms of higher mathematics. The intensive training concentrated on teaching us how to maintain various types of field guns, how to man them and to direct their fire, how to do simple mapping, how to ride, and how to command our men.

It so happened that most of the *yúnker* in my course came out of civilian life—many of them mature men with professional experience as lawyers, engineers and so forth. I have heard our officers say that we formed a much more responsible and reliable group than did the almost parallel accelerated courses: for instance, the 6th and the 8th which followed it, where boys from the Cadet Corps (the militarized high schools) predominated.

I do not know just when this started, but by the time we joined the school the honor system had already become one of its traditions. We all adhered to it, considering that none of us had the right to help a fellow *yúnker* cheat during the numerous quizzes and examinations or even to tolerate anyone doing so, since the lives of other men would depend on how well we learned our job in the few months available. The administration of the school encouraged this tradition, but was prevented by existing Army regulations from recognizing it officially. So officers did not leave the classroom during written examinations, but their presence was a mere formality.*

I was one of the youngest in my course, but nevertheless, soon got the two stripes of a junior *portupéy-yúnker* (a cadet corporal) on my shoulder straps. My ability to ride had much to do with this since it contrasted me favorably with most of my classmates who had never ridden before, and who hence presented at first a rather sorry picture in the saddle. Later, during the summer camp at Krásnoye Seló, I was selected to ride the front pair of one of our six-horse field-gun teams. Usually a very big and heavy man had to be assigned to the rear pair, on which depended the braking effect when a moving gun team had to slow down; but a skillful rider had to be in the front pair. As compared to British and American guns, the Russian horse artillery had much longer traces between the rear and the middle pairs of horses (Fig. 4). The traces therefore had to be taut even on sharp turns, otherwise the hind legs of the middle pair of horses were apt to get entangled in them and bring the team to a fall, or at least, to an abrupt stop. It depended on the front rider to swiftly swing his pair of horses sideways on turns so that the traces never slackened. This type of harness called for superior horsemanship, but, although dangerous, permitted greater speed and maneuverability. This was quite an advantage in cavalry actions at the start of World War I and later during the Civil War.

Orderlies looked after the horses when the guns were unlimbered so that all of us could take turns at different posts of the gunners during target practice. In addition, each one of us got the opportunity to direct the fire of the Battery on a new target under the critical eye of our commander.

Other military schools were camped nearby and all were on friendly

---

* I was interested to find that the United States Army took a somewhat similar attitude towards the Princeton honor system in respect to Army engineering trainees sent there during World War II.

terms, including the Cossack *sótnya* of the Nikoláyevsky Cavalry School. But the regular *eskadrón* of the latter (see pp. 27 and 28) made itself rather unpopular with everybody. The infantry units were more or less reconciled to have them trot or gallop past on some country dirt road, choking them in clouds of dust and yelling the well-worn joke: *Pyekhóta nye pylí* (Infantry, don't kick up dust!). But the two artillery schools got quite annoyed at a prank the cavalrymen played on our neighbors, the Konstantínovsky Artillery School, which had been originally an infantry unit and got much ribbing as a result.

It was the birthday of the commander of the Nikoláyevsky School squadron. When that officer woke up in the morning, he was astounded to find in front of the doorstep of his cottage a 3-inch field gun pointed at it with a note of congratulations from his squadron attached to this birthday present. The night had been a very dark and stormy one, so some of his cavalrymen had crept up to the adjoining Konstantínovsky gun emplacement and quietly rolled the nearest field piece away. They got only a mild scolding for this, but things took a serious turn for the artillery *yúnker* who had been guarding the guns. He had taken refuge from the pelting rain in his sentry box and never noticed the theft. A court martial expelled him from the school for dereliction of sentry duty and sent him to the front as a Private.

I recall many other examples of youthful high jinks—so it was by no means all work and no play. Personally, I did not have much time for such play since soon after our arrival at the camp I got a special assignment which took up all of my limited free time.

Our school was frequently requested to try out and give an opinion concerning various new artillery devices. A British-made 4.5-inch light howitzer was sent to the school for that purpose accompanied by an English-language maintenance manual. One evening at roll call, any cadets who thought they might be able to make a technical translation from English were ordered to report immediately to a Captain Shokóly who was conducting the howitzer trials. Three of us turned up and I was put in charge of the translation job since I happened to be the only cadet corporal in the group. We slaved away at it till late into the night for a month or so and were about a third of the way through when suddenly arrived a Russian translation made in England by the manufacturers of the howitzer—Vickers Ltd., if I remember correctly. It was usable, so we were excused from translating the original further. However, a comparison by our officers of the work we had done with the official British translation showed ours to be by far the better one.

This finding gave us quite a boost with our commanders, and we became the favorites of Captain Shokóly who from then on used only us to try out various contraptions of which he was periodically placed in charge. This did not prove an unmitigated blessing, however. For instance, a new type of short-range flare to be fired at night from empty 3-inch shell casings went off prematurely as I was lighting the fuse and scorched my face so badly that I had to be sent to the hospital for a few days. I still have two black pellets embedded under the skin just above and below my left eye as a souvenir of the episode, but fortunately my eyesight was not impaired.

As our promotion was approaching in December, 1916, Captain Shokóly urged me to apply for a vacancy on the Russian Artillery Purchasing Mission to the United States, two of which had been made available to our school. Except for vacancies in the Guards and in a few other privileged units which were filled by direct application of a candidate to the commanding officer of the unit, all other available vacancies were posted by the school. The officer candidates then proceeded, in order of their class standing, to pick the ones they wanted from those remaining. I was not too far from the top and could have easily picked the assignment to America, especially since it required a knowledge of English, but I wanted to see front-line service. So I did not respond to Captain Shokóly's urging, entrenching myself behind the condition Father had placed when allowing me to volunteer that is, that I had to serve in the Don Cossack Guard Battery, which he had served in. A telegram from its commander, Colonel N. Oupórnikov, had already been received, giving the consent of the Battery's officers to my joining them.

## 5. *The Guard Horse Artillery Reserve Battery*

Our promotion to officer rank took place on December 22, 1916 (January 4, 1917), by formal Imperial Order, with all our names printed, as was usual, in the *Rússky Invalíd,* the official Army and veterans paper. The rank we got was that of *práporschik,* which can be translated as third lieutenant. It was just below the one usually given after the completion of a peacetime three-year course of the school, the graduates of which liked to wisecrack: "A chicken is not a bird, a práporschik is not an officer, and his wife is not a lady (bárynya)."

During the promotion ceremonies we all wore the officer uniforms of the units we were going to join. In the Cossack Guards it was, however, customary for a newly promoted officer to be formally assigned to some Army unit (in my case it was the 7th Don Battery), which he never even got to see, although wearing its uniform; the same Imperial Order listed him as "attached" to the Guards Battery. A year or so later, also by Imperial Order, he would be listed as formally assigned to the Guards Battery and given its uniform—the idea was a kind of probation period. So at the promotion ceremonies I wore the red stripes of all Don Cossack Army units on my trousers and the Russian letter D (for Don) with crossed guns above it on my epaulettes. All of us wore on the left breast of our uniforms the emblem (Fig. a) of the graduates of our school (see also Fig. b on p. 187).

*Figure a.* Gold plated emblem of graduates of the Miháilovsky Artillery School at Petrográd.

In the evening some twenty of us gave a dinner for our former section commander at the school, Captain Vysheslávtzev. It was arranged at the apartment of one of our classmates, Vladýkin, who had been a successful practicing lawyer in civilian life. On such occasions it was considered mandatory to drink one's former commander under the table—figuratively speaking, of course. Unfortunately, he proved to be quite tough. Our host was one of the first casualties and, by the time we got our Captain comfortably stretched out on a sofa, there were only two of us left to do so—a Latvian, whose name I do not remember, and myself. Both of us were still able to navigate, but somewhat uncertainly. I was rather pleased with this result, since it had been my first major encounter with alcohol, until to my horror I realized that it was already past five in the morning and that less than four hours were left for me to recuperate before reporting to the General commanding the Guard Horse Artillery, the Grand Duke Andréy Vladímirovich, who was then on leave from the front and staying at his Petrográd palace.

My Latvian classmate suggested pickled cucumbers as a good remedy—he had some at the apartment which he had kept since the time he too had been a lawyer. I clutched at this straw of hope. It was all right while we walked through the frosty snow-covered streets, but I again felt dizzy and sick the moment we entered his warm rooms. I was afraid to take a nap, since I might not be able to wake up. Prolonged periods of holding my head under a cold water faucet did not help much, nor did the cucumbers. It was therefore with quite some apprehension that I approached, on time for my appointment, the Grand Ducal Palace, which was one of a number along the embankment of the frozen Nevá River. I had to concentrate all my efforts on slowly walking in a straight line without swaying.

But the Grand Duke apparently knew well what promotion celebrations were like. A sympathetically smiling doorman told me that his orders for me were to sign the register and to report again for a personal interview with the Grand Duke a few days later—right after Christmas. This I did and was received very graciously. Andréy Vladímirovich had succeeded my father in the command of the Don Cossack Guard Battery in 1910 and kept an active interest in it now that he commanded the entire Brigade. He promised to see that I did not stay with its Reserve Battery at Pávlovsk for too long.

Meanwhile, I had already reported to its commander, Colonel Count Rehbinder. I was the only Cossack officer in his battery, which however included some thirty or so young Don Cossacks recently called to the colors. They were all at least two years older than I, but it was my job to train them with the help of a couple of seasoned Cossack corporals. I naturally relied heavily on the latter.

To economize, I continued to live at home at Tsárskoye Seló. Early in the morning a Cossack orderly would ride over from the Pávlovsk barracks with my horse on a lead; in the late afternoon I would return home and send him back with it. Occasionally I stayed overnight with some of my young fellow officers, especially after a party at the officer's mess. These were frequently held for officers on leave from the front, usually involved very heavy drinking and ended quite late—Fig. 19, shows me in the morning at Pávlovsk after one such party. As usual in the Guards, my salary barely sufficed to cover my share of the mess bill. Nevertheless, it did me good to see how well-liked my father had apparently been,—most senior officers who had known him wanted to drink "to thee" (see p. xxiv) with his son, and usually this happened early in the evening. These parties also taught one self-control—for an officer not to be able to hold his liquor was considered a cardinal sin.

Grandmother Rikovsky gave some welcome financial help. Apparently she had suffered some pangs of remorse at not having said good-bye to Father when he left for the front, especially so during the period when it was not known whether he had survived the siege and fall of Novogeórgievsk.

One event of special interest during my service at Pávlovsk happened shortly after my promotion to officer's rank, sometime between Christmas, 1916, and the New Year (old style)—eight to thirteen days after Rasputin's murder. Colonel Rehbinder called a meeting of all officers of his Reserve Battery and requested our views of the following problem: The Tsar had banished the Grand Duke Dimítry Pávlovich (one of the three murderers of Rasputin) to the Transcaucasian Front near Persia and had ordered a member of the Imperial Suite, Colonel Count Kutáysov, to "accompany" him there. Kutáysov had been an officer of our Guard Horse Artillery and therefore had the privilege of choosing whether he would wear on any given occasion the uniform of the Imperial Suite * or that of his former unit—in this case, of our Brigade. Its present commander, the Grand Duke Andréy Vladímirovich, wanted to know whether we felt that Colonel Kutáysov should be asked not to choose to wear our uniform while escorting Dimítry Pávlovich to Persia.

At officers' meetings of the Russian Army it was customary for the senior man present to state the problem and to ask for individual opinions in a reverse order to seniority, so as to avoid views of younger officers being influenced by those of their seniors. Since I was the junior of all present, the Colonel called on me to speak first.

I said that I had no idea as to what we should do, feeling rather silly as I said it . However, very soon it turned out that none of my

---

* Its members had a distinctive uniform; for example, in peacetime parades they wore white caracul caps (see Fig. 5).

seniors had any suggestions either. The meeting ended without any decision being taken one way or another.

The incident was typical of the mood of most officers at that time. Everyone felt that something had to be done to avoid impending political disaster, but nobody knew just what. There were persistent rumors that the former Commander-in-Chief, the Grand Duke Nikoláy Nikoláyevich, had been approached in his semiexile as Commander of the Caucasian Front against Turkey to obtain his consent to a Palace Revolution. This would have deposed and exiled Nicholas II and placed the Grand Duke at the head of the Government. But the fine old soldier is said to have refused even to consider doing any such thing in time of war. Had he agreed, I am certain that the overwhelming majority of the Guards and of the Army would have enthusiastically supported such action. There was no other potential conservative leader in sight, one evidence of which fact is provided by the Kutáysov incident I have just described. The gesture we were asked to take by the Grand Duke Andréy Vladímirovich amounted only to a completely futile expression of disapproval for our Supreme Commander without any possible positive effects but with many probable negative ones.

In mid-February 1917, Captain Iván Folimónov arrived from the Guards Battery to relieve me at Pávlovsk. On learning from Mother that I was leaving for the front, the Empress expressed the wish to receive me in a special audience. On February 18 (March 3), 1917, the eve of my departure, I reported at the Alexándrovsky Palace at Tsárskoye Seló, where the Imperial Family resided—the older and larger Ekateríninsky Palace (Fig. 5) was used only on ceremonial occasions.

I was asked to wait in a drawing room and happened to sit down on a sofa opposite a life-sized painting of Marie Antoinette with her children. I could not help wondering once more what the future held for the Empress and for her family.

About five minutes later I was ushered into another room nearby, where the Empress and Tatiána Nikoláyevna met me. Both wore their uniforms of sisters of mercy and stood during the short audience. The Empress asked most of the questions, but had a vacant tired look about her all the time which contrasted sharply with the keen and lively expression of her daughter's young face. I do not think the audience lasted more than five minutes. The Empress then handed me a little ikon, which I unfortunately lost later, and held out her hand, which I kissed. I then kissed the hand of Tatiána Niko-láyevna and wheeled around in the usual military fashion, clanking my spurs. A couple of seconds later, with my hand already on the door handle, I realized that I had committed a serious breach of palace etiquette which requires one never to turn one's back on Royalty during an audience. I should have retreated backwards until I reached the door. When I got home, I asked Mother to apologize for me later.

Ólga Nikoláyevna was not present at the audience, but sent Mother a note, a photocopy of which is shown here (see Fig. 20). In English translation it reads:

18 Feb. 1917

"Dear Valentína Ivánovna!

I am thinking of you today and kiss you very firmly. May the Lord preserve your Grísha.

*Sister O. Románova"*

# 3  Facing Austro-Germans after the February 1917 Revolution

## 1. *Don Cossack Guard Battery on Eve of Revolution*

In February, 1917, our battery was stationed on the Southwestern Front of the Russian armies. It formed part of the 3rd Guard Cavalry Division, which was then in reserve a hundred miles or so behind the front lines.

From Petrográd I traveled south to Kíev, changing trains there westward for Róvno, a town in the Ukrainian province of Volhýnia, close to the old Austro-Hungarian border. Then I had to go back by truck some 50 miles eastward along a paved road leading to Zhitómir (see Map B). Our unit was quartered in a large village close to that road.

The Battery was still in excellent shape insofar as the appearance of the men and horses was concerned and continued to be the show-piece it had always been. Robert R. McCormick (of *Chicago Tribune* fame), at the time a Major of the 1st Cavalry, Illinois National Guard, thus described his visit to our unit two years earlier, somewhere in the vicinity of Warsaw (pages 179–186 of Ref. 38):

"While I was visiting the Guards Corps the officers of a Kazák * battery of horse artillery gave a party.

"First [there] were mounted games. Fences had been erected, ditches dug, among other things a most severe in and out obstacle. There was something with which I was familiar. The performances of horses and men were splendid.

"Next followed a competition with the sabre, which consisted in cutting willow branches, slicing potatoes, and picking up on the point a bag of straw representing a man lying on the ground. If the drill had been one of a few picked men, it might not have been remarkable. The fact that all the men of a battery of artillery who had not recently practiced this particular exercise showed a universal excellence was an indication of the value of the soldiers.

* The word "Cossack" is pronounced "Kazák" in Russian. McCormick uses the latter transliteration throughout his book.

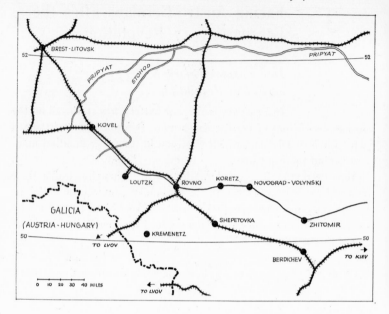

Map B.  Part of Western Ukraine. *See Map A, p. 44.*

"Then came rough-riding, beginning with such simple things as standing up on the saddle at full gallop and Roman riding, and two men picking up a third dismounted comrade, and a dismounted man leaping behind a galloping companion.

"This was followed by such gymnastics as I have never seen in any circus, the men swinging from the pommels of their saddles while the horses were in full gallop, and leaping from one side of their horses to the other side, and turning somersaults on the backs as on parallel bars, and—the greatest feat of all—a six-foot, 180-pound sergeant with a breast covered with decorations and Crosses of St. George performed all these things with a sabre clenched in his teeth. The last feat was picking up a handkerchief from the ground at full run. The Kazáks do not withdraw one foot from the stirrup and take the stirrup leather in the hand as we do in this trick, but fasten the stirrups together under the horse and lower themselves and pull themselves back in the saddle entirely with their legs. The trick of picking up the handkerchief was very badly done until the colonel of the Battery * took the hint and put five rubles in each handkerchief, after which there were no more failures.

". . . After my return from Russia I was astounded to hear from a European military officer that the Kazáks were an irregular body of guerillas, useful to harry a defeated army, but unable to contend with regular troops.

"The truth about this is that they are to regular troops what regular troops are to militia. Fortunately I have brought from Russia more than my opinion; whoever is unwilling to depart from his preconceived notions should see the moving pictures I have taken of a Kazák charge and of the English General Paget reviewing the Kazáks of the Guard.

"The Kazáks are frontiersmen. We know the superiority of frontiersmen over all other types of equal training. In addition to this the Kazáks are an hereditary military organization like the Samurai of Japan. Where other European troops are trained for three years these are trained from childhood. They bring to the army more personal military knowledge than the average soldier takes with him when he leaves after three years. They then undergo as much training as is given to the ignorant recruits.

"The result is that the Kazáks are a body of soldiers such as exist nowhere else in the world. I speak with confidence for I have been to see all the Allies' armies, I have been a horseman for twenty-five years and have played polo constantly in the last twelve.

"There is no *considerable* body of troops in the world that can, *mounted*, offer any serious resistance to the Kazáks."

This was the type of men—by then veterans of three years of war service—whom I was called upon to officer at the age of eighteen with only seven months' artillery school training and two months' reserve battery experience. However, most of the sergeants and corporals, and many of the men, had served under my father, who, luckily for me, appears to have been quite popular with them all. I think this is the main reason I got a lot of unsolicited and willing help.

* Anatóly Oupórnikov (note by the author).

Immediately after my arrival, the Battery Sergeant reported that a Cossack who had been my father's personal orderly asked permission to serve me in the same capacity. Naturally, I was only too glad to have him. He was a mature man who had rejoined his old unit on mobilization from the reserve; I am ashamed to say I have forgotten his name. He proved invaluable and took care of my belongings with a curious mixture of respectful deference to my rank and paternalistic benevolence because of his age. I am sure that, had we ever found ourselves in a similar situation, he would have acted like the Cossack orderly in the French cartoon of a century before shown in Fig. 11.

Relations with my fellow officers were also quite congenial. The Battery commander—Colonel Nikolái Nikoláyevich Oupórnikov *— had joined the Battery at the time my father was in command. Similarly it had so happened earlier that when my father joined the Battery in 1893 it was my present commander's father who was its Colonel. When my father made the formal call on him at his apartment, his small son (my Colonel) is supposed to have barked at him from under a table. This kind of reminiscence naturally helped ease the strain of my first days with this famous unit.

Most of the talk at the officer's mess however centered then on the promotion to officer's rank of one of our four *pod-khoroúnzhi* (sublieutenants),† a man by the name of Spiridónov. Our six-gun battery was divided into three two-gun sections and he was one of three *vzvódny ouriádnik* (sections corporals).

Spiridónov was selected for promotion over his rival, another sublieutenant and section corporal, Podtiólkov, to the latter's great disappointment. The promotion and farewell ceremonies had taken place a few days before my arrival—Spiridónov could not stay as an officer in the same unit where he had served in the ranks. Before he left for an Army battery, a dinner was given for him at our officer's mess, where he understandably made a few *faux pas* of etiquette. My fellow officers were still laughing about Spiridónov's table manners and were joking about signs of Podtiólkov's annoyance at not having been promoted. No one could have suspected at the time that within a year Podtiólkov would be leading a successful mutiny of the entire Don Area, that it would be Spiridónov who would capture him in

---

* A cousin of Anatóly Oupórnikov, who had commanded the Battery at the time of the visit described by Colonel McCormick in Ref. 38.

† A rank approximately corresponding to a non-commissioned officer. It ranked below a 3rd lieutenant (práporschik) but above a sergeant.

combat and who would then hang him, and that a Government of the Soviets—a term that no one had even heard of—would subsequently erect a monument to Podtiólkov's memory.

Five days or so after my arrival the entire 3rd Guard Cavalry Division, including our battery, was ordered to move up slowly closer to the front. As usual in such cases, *kvartiryéry,* or location teams, were sent ahead by each unit on each day's march to select and prepare suitable quarters for the night. Since an entire division was now moving, separate location teams were sent out by each of its two batteries and five regiments—two of the latter being Polish, and three, Cossack. One of the officers of the regimental teams was always placed in charge of the entire operation. The selection was done in rotation between the regiments—a Polish officer of the Leib-Guard Gródno Hussars happened to be placed in charge of location after the first day's march. I remember this well, since I was sent to represent our battery.

There was always a lot of skulduggery involved in such location operations, each officer trying to get the best possible quarters for his unit. If he let himself be particularly badly outwitted by his competitors, he would not be allowed to forget this by his fellow officers for a long time. I was well aware of this and of the disturbing fact that I would probably be outranked by all other officers on this job. So I was rather apprehensive as I rode out well before dawn towards my destination, at the head of a group of four Cossacks and a middleaged Corporal.

As I was brooding over my problem and wondering how to go about it, the Corporal rode up, saluted and asked permission to smoke.* When this was granted, he asked permission to ride alongside of me, and in a round-about way brought the ensuing conversation to the subject of our mission. He did this by reminiscing about similar location trips he and others had been on during the preceding three years of the war. It soon dawned on me that I was being given a case history lesson on the various tricks one had to watch for on our job and possible moves to counteract them. The Corporal had even gone to the trouble of ascertaining at the Battery office the name of the Polish officer who was to arbitrate things, and had collected

---

* In the old Russian Army it was customary even among officers for the second senior man of those present to ask permission of the senior officer to smoke. It was a form of courtesy strictly adhered to. If ladies were present at a party, the senior officer would always ask their individual permission to smoke.

among his friends a couple of stories about him which gave a clear picture of the man and of his idiosyncrasies. All this was done with the utmost tact and dignity worthy of a professional diplomat—there never was the slightest implication that he was suggesting anything to me. When his topic was exhausted, the Corporal gradually changed the subject, asked permission to sing and dropped back to lead the four Cossacks in a merry ribald song. My first mission ended in success.

I mention this incident because it is typical of numerous occasions which impressed me with the native intelligence and ability of Cossack and other simple Russian country folk.

A couple of days later the Battery passed through the town of Róvno, heading westward. On the third or fourth day of our move towards the front we crossed the line of positions where stationary fighting had been going on for almost a year until the successful Brussílov offensive of the preceding summer * drove the enemy back. Except for a few shattered trunks, not a tree was left standing for several miles in depth along the Austro-German and the Russian lines of trenches as a result of months of mutual shelling.

Suddenly, while on the march, the entire 3rd Guard Cavalry Division was ordered to turn around immediately, to proceed as quickly as possible back to Róvno, and to entrain there for an unknown destination. However, before we reached Róvno, the order was countermanded. It was only then that we learned of the revolutionary disturbances in Petrográd followed by the Tsar's abdication. The intention had been to send our entire division to Petrográd to quell the uprising, its Polish brigade apparently being considered just as reliable as the Cossack one. However, I doubt that the railroad personnel and workers would have let us reach our destination even if the Tsar had not abdicated.

## 2. Military Situation
### after the February 1917 Revolution

Food shortages appear to have been the immediate cause for the start of the Petrográd disturbances. There have been persistent rumors that these shortages were created deliberately by some moderate opponents of the late Tsar. Whether this was actually so has not been proved or disproved, and probably never will be

*See p. 51.

known. However, if these rumors are true, then certainly the promoters of these shortages, who hoped for reasonable changes once street mobs had the power to influence events, were most naive.

The general feeling of disgust with the Government of Tsar Nicholas II was so strong that there was practically no active opposition to the rioting, and the February–March 1917 Revolution succeeded with only a handful of casualties. It was even called at the time the great *bezkróvnaya* (bloodless) Revolution. The Cossacks did not oppose it either; on the contrary, one of the very few men killed was a police officer who was rough-handling a woman demonstrator when a Don Cossack of a mounted patrol * intervened on her behalf. The police officer then threatened the Cossack who drew his sword and cut him down.

The events at Petrográd are well-known and I shall not dwell on them but will concentrate on their after-effects on the Army at the front.

The Provisional Government which was formed after the February 1917 Revolution, and which the lawyer Kerensky came to head, consisted of men with little or no practical experience in government. They were mainly members of the former Doúma, or Parliament, which had however been elected under voting restrictions based on property owned. They therefore represented the middleclasses and had little authority over the street crowds. Hence they could not enforce their will on a rival governmental organization which was set up by radical leftwing groups—the "Soviets" (meaning, the Councils)—of Worker, Soldier and Peasant Deputies.

The Petrográd Soviet, shortly after the Tsar's abdication, issued the order which was to be disastrous to the Army at the front—the famous "Order No. 1." That order took away the disciplinary powers of all Russian Army officers because of fears of possible counterrevolutionary trends among them. Instead, such powers were vested in "Soviets" who had to be elected by the men of all units—from batteries and companies, through regiments, brigades, and corps, to armies and groups of armies (the latter called "fronts"). All this was done after three bloody years of a continuing war against the Austro-German coalition. Under the circumstances, the amazing thing is not that the Russian armies finally collapsed, but that it took them eight months (March to October 1917) to do so.

* From either the 4th or the 14th Don regiments which were then stationed at Petrográd.

The weak Provisional Government was unable to countermand this order and tried to live with it, in spite of its obvious absurdity and inevitably fatal consequences. The principle of "Freedom of Speech" was extended to the point where frontline officers did not have the right to arrest outside propagandists who came to address their men at meetings within the location of the military units and who called upon them, in anticipation of a revolution in Germany, to disobey operational orders, to stop fighting and to arrest officers unsympathetic to such ideas. The only thing officers could do was to try to talk back. Not many were temperamentally fitted even to attempt this— certainly most of the best combat commanders found the very idea degrading, and jeeringly referred to Kerensky as the "Persuader-in-Chief."

As a direct consequence of the "Order No. 1," the disintegration of the front after the 1917 Revolution proceeded slowly but inexorably. It was particularly rapid in the infantry, where by 1917 there were hardly any officers and men left who had been in the Regular Imperial Army prior to 1914, so great had been the losses during the 1915 retreat when the peacetime ammunition stockpiles were exhausted with no industry in the country to replenish them at the rate required. Space and human lives had had to be traded then for the time needed to get supplies from France and England. These were abundant in 1916, but by 1917 most officers in the infantry below the rank of colonel were in effect a motley assembly of civilians with not more than two or three months' training. Their men often had even less. The cavalry and the artillery had fared better—at least 50 to 60 percent of both officers and men still in their ranks had Regular pre-1914 Imperial Army training.

The few remaining old-line officers capable of maintaining order in the infantry were soon forced to leave their units and to abandon them to the leadership of semicivilian demagogues elected by the men to represent them and to rule them in their Soviets. The bitterness at the terrible and often unnecessary losses suffered by the infantry in the preceding years provided a fertile ground for vicious propaganda.

There can be no doubt that German agents took every advantage of this situation. The fact that Lenin and his entourage was enabled by the German High Command to avoid Allied lands by crossing Germany in a train with sealed cars and returning to Russia via Sweden from exile in Switzerland is generally known and has never been challenged. The German leaders did this apparently in the hope that Lenin's slogans, such as *Mir Khízhinam—Voyná Dvortzám* (Peace to the Huts—War to the Palaces), would poison and wreck the Russian Army without contaminating their own.

The Bolshevik propaganda could easily have been stopped under conditions of normal military discipline.* As it was, cases of murders of officers who in spite of anything tried to continue doing their duty were not infrequent. Some of them like the murder of many naval officers at the Kronstadt base, are suspected to have been promoted by German agents. This is entirely possible, even likely.

A great number of officers despaired of influencing their men and formed special *oudárny* (shock) battalions composed entirely of officers. These battalions spear-headed with suicidal valor the so-called Kerensky offensive in June-July 1917, and successfully accomplished their breakthrough assignments at key locations. Nevertheless, the offensive as a whole was a dismal failure. In spite of the abundance of shells which provided adequate artillery preparation, most of the infantry units were so demoralized by four months of incessant, open and unrestrained antiwar propaganda that they refused to budge.

The photos shown in Fig. 21 were taken a couple of weeks after the failure of the Kerensky offensive and provide a vivid picture of the sorry morale of the revolutionary troops. This is a photograph of a page from the Paris *l'Illustration*. At the bottom of that page it is stated that the pictures were taken at the end of July by the English photographer M. G. H. Mewes, correspondent for the *Daily Mirror* of London. At the top of the page it is indicated that these pictures were intended for publication as a "Supplement" to the September 8, 1917, *l'Illustration* of Paris. However, in many libraries they were bound with the December 22, 1917, issue, it being explained elsewhere in that number that French military censorship prevented the earlier September distribution. The entire "Supplement" is captioned THE CRISIS OF THE RUSSIAN ARMY and the sub-caption reads: *An Example of the Effects of Non-discipline in an Army*. The inscription below the top photograph reads: "Soldiers fleeing through a village, after having thrown down their arms, in a panic which a *provocateur*

---

* I have not heard of any cases of disobedience of World War I orders by any Russian Army units prior to the Revolution. I have however heard of cases of near-mutiny in the war-weary French Army prior to the November-1918 Armistice, which were ruthlessly suppressed by military courts.

created by shouting: 'The German cavalry has broken through.' " The caption below the bottom photograph is: "A soldier of the old school uses his rifle to stop two fugitives."

The photographs of Fig. 21 have been printed by American journals with erroneous captions stating that they represent fleeing "Tsarist" troops.* The significance of this period for the later development of events in Russia cannot be properly understood unless one realizes that it was the revolutionary imposition from the rear of freedom of propaganda among war-weary frontline troops and the removal of disciplinary powers from the officers that broke up the Russian Army.

Another factor which at the time had a negative influence on Russian events should be mentioned in this connection. It is quite paradoxical—the old Imperial Army had done *too well* its job of preventing the enemy from devastating Russian territories. Propaganda for a separate peace became easier as a result. It will be seen from Map C (p. 89) that at the time of the February 1917 Revolution, Poland, Lithuania and a large part of Latvia had been abandoned to the Austro-Germans, but that the latter had succeeded in occupying in addition only small strips of territory along the western fringes of Byelorussia and of the Ukraine. As a result, most of the population of Russia had no idea of what it was like to live under the heel of foreign conquerors. The inhabitants of the Ukraine learned this the hard way in 1918, after the Brest-Litovsk separate peace treaty between the Austro-Germans and the Soviets, a fact which accounts for the very large local support received there by the Bolsheviks during the subsequent stages of the Civil War.† During World War II the Soviet Army, in spite of its early defeats, was able to stage an overwhelmingly successful comeback for the very reason that the Nazi troops had succeeded in overrunning a much greater part of the country than had their 1918 predecessors (see Map C). News of their behavior and excesses therefore became much better known.

---

* *Life Magazine,* May 1, 1939. Although I provided *Life*'s editors with copies of the original French captions, they refused to print a correction of their caption: THE TSARIST ARMIES WERE RUNNING AWAY A LARGE PART OF THE TIME, AS HERE IN 1917 ON THE GERMAN FRONT. My letter on the matter was then printed in the Russian language New York Daily *Rossíya* on June 27, 1939.

More recently *Look* magazine made the same kind of mistake when reproducing this photograph on May 22, 1962, but printed my letter and correction on July 3, 1962.

† See p. 224.

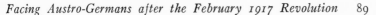

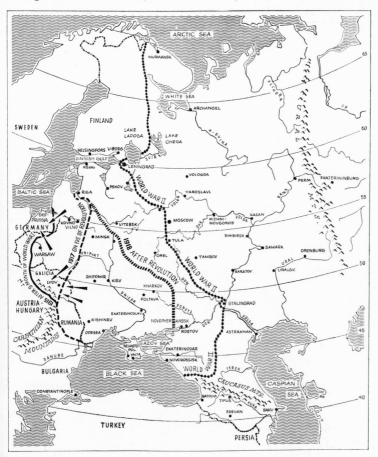

Map C. Lines of deepest German advance to the East during World
Wars I and II. Arrows indicate directions of Russian offensives at the start
of World War I.

### 3. *The Don Cossack Guard Battery*
### *after the February 1917 Revolution*

After the Tsar's abdication, the 3rd Guard Cavalry
Division turned back westwards from Róvno. The dismounted bulk
of the Division relieved some other units in the trenches along the
Stohód River to the east of Loutsk, but our battery was assigned to

antiaircraft duty on the outskirts of that town (Map B, p. 80).

We had to protect one of the three airfields around Loutzk. The mechanism for adapting our field guns to antiaircraft use was quite primitive. It consisted of a crib of timber railroad ties some 5 feet high with a vertical shaft at its center. A spare wheel was slipped onto that shaft so that it could be rotated in a horizontal plane; the two wheels of a field gun rested on this elevated horizontal wheel. The entire contraption permitted firing the guns at any point of the sky except for a 30 degree inverted cone right overhead. Since we had no range-finders, no appreciable accuracy of fire could be expected nor was achieved, and we only succeeded in forcing the German planes to fly above 5,000 feet or so, without actually hitting any.

At that time I unexpectedly acquired a completely different field of activity.

The Sergeant of our battery entered our officer's mess one day and reported unrest among the men, who requested their officers to explain to them the meaning of words they were hearing on all sides: "Socialism, Communism, Democracy, Constitutional Monarchy, Federation," and so on.

Problems of this kind were never a strong point of officers of the Imperial Guards. Colonel Oupórnikov looked with some dismay at his second in command; the latter turned to the next senior man, and the process was repeated until all eyes were fixed on the junior officer present, who happened to be myself. Obviously no one wanted the chore.

The Colonel voiced the general feeling by telling the Sergeant— I have forgotten his name—to assemble the men. Práporschik Chebotarióv would address them—he remembered this sort of thing better than anyone else, being the one most recently out of school.

Half an hour later I was perched on one of our field guns which was pointed skyward and was making a speech to over 100 Cossacks seated on the ground around me.

I was not entirely unprepared for the job although not by my school but by life at our home where I was used to hearing discussions of military history and of international politics. I was therefore able to give a more or less coherent account of the forms of government of England, France and of some other countries as compared to that of old Imperial Russia. It seems that both my senior officers and the men were satisfied with my performance because from then on I was repeatedly requested to speak. However, I was rather out of my depth where more profound matters of social dogma were concerned. Fortunately, I found help in the "Pod-Yessaoúl" (Captain) Kóssov. He had a rather remarkable background. A regular artillery officer, he decided after a year or so of service in the Imperial Guards, that he did not like peacetime service, resigned and went to study law at the Moscow University. When the war broke out in 1914, he immediately rejoined the Cossack Guard Battery. During the terrible days of the 1915 retreat, Kóssov, like many other cavalry and artillery officers of the Russian Army, volunteered to bolster the decimated ranks of the infantry and was severely wounded leading a counterattack. One of the German bullets pierced his throat, leaving him with a strong stutter. We became friends when he rejoined our Guards Battery early in April, 1917. Kóssov gave me a lot of coaching in making speeches to troop meetings and carrying on debates which his impediment prevented him from doing himself.

Some time after that, late in April or early in May 1917, our battery was ordered to move up to the Stohód River positions to bolster a thoroughly demoralized third-line infantry regiment which had a "six hundred plus" serial number. It adjoined on the north the positions of our dismounted 3rd Guard Cavalry Division at a rather critical location—where the river Stohód was crossed by the railroad and by the paved road from Loutzk to Kóvel (see Map B, p. 80). The infantry regiment was not doing any fighting at all and had begun fraternizing with the enemy; our assignment was to "liven things up."

In Russian, the word *Stohód* means "a hundred channels," and aptly describes the marshy nature of the terrain. The entire area is a southern extension of the famous Prípyat Marshes to the north—in most places ground water was no more than a couple of feet below the soil surface. For that reason all trenches and dugouts had to be built up above ground; an example is provided by the photo of our officer's dugout shown on Fig. 22. The roof and walls were covered with sod for purposes of camouflage from enemy air observation; beneath were several layers of heavy pine logs for protection against chance shell hits.

Shortly after our arrival I was making myself acquainted with the maze of our frontline trenches, and in the process of doing so wandered to one of our farthest outposts which was cut into the railroad embankment at a point where a small bridge had spanned one of the lesser channels of the Stohód River before it was blown up. A couple of hundred feet away on the other side of the channel was a similar German outpost. I found our infantrymen peacefully playing cards, not one of them performing sentry duty behind the slotted steel shields inserted into the sand bags at the top of the trench.

Looking through one of the slots I saw a German soldier's head and shoulders protruding above the breastworks of their trench. He was smoking a long pipe as he sunned himself and seemed to be enjoying the quiet surroundings. In accordance with our orders, I reached for one of the rifles which were leaning against the inside wall of our trench. The cardplayers stopped their game, but my two Cossack orderlies drew and cocked their service revolvers covering those of the infantrymen who had started to rise with angry mutterings. I took careful aim through the slot of the steel shield and pressed the trigger. This was the first time I had fired a heavy infantry rifle, so I was not prepared for the power of its recoil. By the time I got my eye back to the slot the German had of course vanished, but I could not tell whether I had hit him or whether he had just ducked a near miss.

But there was no doubt that the Austro-Germans resented this breach of a tacit armistice which had prevailed for some time on that sector with full encouragement on their part. Several of their machine guns opened up, making the dust fly from the tops of our sand bags. A couple of field batteries joined in a few minutes later. We stayed with the infantry outpost for an hour or so and left when the German fire subsided.

To say that our battery was unpopular with our own infantry would be something of an understatement. The Germans did not succeed in locating the well-camouflaged position of our field guns and soon gave up trying to silence us by direct fire. Instead, they countered any shooting we did by shelling the trenches of our infantry, who did not like this and sabotaged our work whenever they could.

For instance, one dark night I was on observation duty in one of the front trenches. Sounds of sledge hammer blows on wood stakes could be heard from the Austro-German side—they seemed to be repairing or extending their barbed-wire entanglements near their outpost at the railroad embankment which I have just mentioned. Our own outpost was quite close by; nevertheless, we had the place so well zeroed in that I confidently gave the target number to the Battery over the phone and ordered the two-gun squad on duty to first lob two rounds of antipersonnel shrapnel at it and follow up immediately with two rounds of high explosive shells. Just as the shells had softly rustled overhead and had burst in the darkness nearby, an angry voice was heard over our phone—my shells had been shorts which landed squarely on top of our own outpost causing casualties—dead and wounded. I left my observation post in a state of considerable mental anguish and rushed towards the outpost along a communication trench. On getting there I was immensely relieved when instead of corpses I found cheerful infantrymen who, for a change, seemed quite pleased by the fireworks provided for them. All eight shells had landed in the area of the German barbed wire where work had been going on—it had all been stopped. There were over a dozen telephones on the same hookup, so it was impossible to ascertain from where the false message had come. All I could do was to swear long and volubly into the phone for all on the line to hear.

I remember that night well for another reason. Our daylight artillery observation point was located at the top of a tree in a group of tall pines only a short distance behind our front trenches. It was well within sight and range of enemy rifle and machine gun fire and its safety depended solely on the effectiveness of the camouflage of its otherwise unprotected open platform. One had to climb to it up a rope ladder before dawn, pull the ladder up and quietly stay there until darkness fell again.

Just before dawn I got a phone call at the night observation post in the front trenches that something was delaying the officer who was scheduled to be on daylight observation duty. I was therefore ordered to take his place and to climb into the pinetree with a Cossack Corporal who would be waiting for me at its foot.

After a sleepless night on duty in the trenches I did not particularly enjoy the cramped quarters of the treetop platform. My soggy top boots started shrinking in the day's heat and were pressing on an inflamed rheumatic toe which had been bothering me for several days. With the help of the Corporal I managed to get them off and felt much better barefoot. I whiled the time away by scanning the enemy lines, but everything was quiet and nothing of interest could be seen through the powerful twin periscope-like artillery field glasses which were firmly attached to a thick branch of the pinetree, but which could be rotated a full circle on their base.

I had a chance to practice long-distance gunnery on a moving target—a lone two-horse supply wagon which was slowly plodding along an open road about 8,000 yards away. This was well beyond the range of our antipersonnel shrapnel and close to the limit range for the high-explosive shells of our field pieces. However, my third shell came close enough to make the driver put his horses into a brisk trot and the fourth apparently burst in uncomfortable proximity because the pace changed to a wild career towards a neighboring wood into which the supply wagon disappeared in a cloud of dust. The Austro-German batteries remained silent. Apparently their observers did not consider their Russian counterpart's action sufficiently offensive.

Their slumbering benevolence however got quite a jolt shortly afterwards. As I scanned the panorama before me, my eyes frequently returned to what appeared to have been the estate of a moderately wealthy landowner on a bit of comparatively high ground just behind the Austro-German frontline trenches. The house had been shelled into ruins, but a small adjoining parklike garden was intact. I could not help thinking how pleasant it must be to stretch out on the ground under those shady trees. . . . Suddenly I perked up—if I thought so, the enemy probably thought so too! From then on, I concentrated on watching that area. My elevation permitted me to see along some sections of the zigzag approach and communication trenches near the park. In the afternoon I noticed some one-way movement along them —all towards the park. It also looked as if some packages or baskets were being carried there,—I gradually became convinced that a picnic party was about to begin. I waited until the movement ceased and a little longer, so that,—if I was right and the Austro-Germans actually had the gall to hold a picnic in the open right under our very noses, everybody would have happily settled down to it. Then I alerted not just the two-gun squad on duty, but the entire six-gun battery. Colonel Oupórnikov was immediately on the phone. What on earth was going on? I am afraid I embellished somewhat what I had actually seen, so the economy-minded Colonel would not think that I was just acting on a hunch and stop me from proceeding.

The exact coordinates and the range of the park had already been obtained through actual shelling by the battery which had preceded us on that position, so I only had to give the target number and order two antipersonnel shrapnel, rapid fire. All six guns let go at once, immediately reloaded and fired again not more than two seconds after the first salvo. Then the order to check and adjust sights for high explosives—a matter of about five seconds for our veterans—and again: two shells, rapid fire. I could see that all twenty-four shells had burst in the small park. This happened in less than ten seconds, with no warning whatsoever, causing an enemy reaction which left no doubt as to their extreme annoyance. Within a few minutes every Austro-German battery and machine gun in the vicinity opened up on our infantry trenches and kept up a frightful din much longer than was usual in such cases. Also movements in the communication trenches near the park could be seen—it looked as if some stretchers were being carried out. It certainly appeared that casualties had been inflicted, but I did not learn their full extent until a chance conversation with a fellow engineering student five years later at Berlin.*

My actions may appear cold-blooded to a civilian reader, but a deadly war was on and it was our battery's special assignment not to let the enemy forget it. However our Colonel became reluctant to send me often to observation duty in the pinetree; he seemed to put me down as a trigger-happy youngster likely to waste precious ammunition. The latter was the only point that bothered him. Like many other officers who had to live through the dearth of shells during the terrible 1915 retreat, he just could not get accustomed to the idea that we now had more ammunition than we were ever likely to use up.

Some time during the summer of 1917, I forget exactly when, I had to do a tour of duty with our baggage train stationed over a hundred miles to the rear in the same Ukrainian village where I had first joined the Battery. I do not know how it got its name, *Samostryély,* literally meaning "Selfshooters"—this being the old Russian word for arquebuses. After a week of boredom there I was ready to believe that it had some connection with suicide—I was the only officer for many miles around. For recreation I exercised not only my own horse, but the second horses as well of some of my fellow officers who had two, but kept only one horse up at the front.

Having nothing else to do for the three weeks or so I stayed there, I took more interest than I would have otherwise in the deliberations of the "Soviet" of my men. This "Council" was elected in accordance with the disastrous Order No. 1 I have already outlined, but proved quite useful to me since in this case the Soviet concerned itself exclusively with what might be called internal household matters.

Earlier I have mentioned that all Cossacks owned their horses. There was a Government daily allowance for their upkeep, which could be spent in various ways at the discretion of the commanding officer. Knowing very little about the subject, I was content to leave

*See Chapter 9, p. 292.

it to the six or eight mature veterans the Cossacks of the baggage train had elected to their "Soviet." I promised to approve their decisions if they seemed reasonable, and attended their deliberations merely as an observer. The experience was most enlightening.

The discussions followed rather unorthodox patterns and most certainly did not conform to most recognized rules of western parliamentary procedure. However, after much heat had been generated, colorful language used, and many irrelevant side-issues and personal quarrels brought in and aired extensively, there usually emerged a consensus as to what should actually be done. The actions then taken made quite good sense as a rule.

Thus, in the matter of the allowance for the horses, our Cossacks first collected accurate information on the fodder prices which prevailed in the various villages of the area and debated the trends likely to develop in the near future. It then appeared that their best bet would be to rent some field where the owner would have difficulty in bringing in the hay himself because of manpower shortages; then to scythe part of it for hay, doing this themselves, and use the rest for grazing. With this scheme in mind, mounted patrols were sent out to scour the neighborhood. They reported back not only on the size of possibly suitable fields and on the quality of the grass, but also on the families and personalities of the owners, with an estimate as to how much of a tough bargainer each man was likely to prove. With three or four likely prospects selected in this manner, the entire Soviet of our baggage train proceeded to negotiate with each one of them in turn. After a few days of hard bargaining, they presented a written agreement for my approval.

I was quite impressed by that performance—no group of officers with General Staff training could have better planned and implemented this operation. I do not think that the characteristics which produced this result are limited to the naturally much more independent Cossacks; I have found that many Russian peasants have the same earthy common sense. In this connection I was interested to read many years later a book by Maxím Górky entitled *My Universities,*—by which he meant two Vólga River barges where his "professors" of human relations were his fellow bargees.

One of the members of the baggage train Soviet was a Cossack saddlemaker and repairman by the name of Kouznetzóv. He once

---

* The title of the English translation is: *My University Days,* Ref. 19.

noticed on my desk the Russian translation of a book *Ways of Achievement* by the Hindu Yogi Ramacharaka, and frequently discussed it with me. I was quite interested in its philosophy, especially by the view that what happens to a man in his life is partly predetermined by the after-effects of his own past actions as well as the actions of the people close to him and only in part by his own free will. As if to prove the correctness of this view, our friendly chats brought me later on unexpected help from Kouznetzóv at a critical moment.*

Many older officers found it difficult or even impossible to adjust themselves to the new conditions, although many tried to do so. For instance, Colonel Oupórnikov made an unsuccessful attempt to establish closer relations with the men, which in all Cossack troops had been much better anyway than in regular units. Cossack officers would not limit themselves to watching the singing and dancing of their men, which customarily took place most evenings after roll call and prayer, but actually took an active part in them.

But, as was already happening in the entire Russian Army, rank meant less and less with each passing day, in the Cossack units too, and leadership—whether for good or for bad—passed to those capable of exercising it by the sheer weight of their personalities.

Colonel Oupórnikov soon decided that the situation was quite hopeless and took leave of absence during which he obtained some nominal post in the rear. So he did not come back, nor did his very able second in command, Captain Konkóv, after being hospitalized with appendicitis.

Fig. 23 is probably the last photo of most of the officers † of the Battery in one group. It was taken after a party near the Stohód River dugout shown on Fig. 22 which we gave some time in May, 1917, to see Konkóv off.

The officers of Fig. 23, left to right, are: (front row) Captain Borís Oupórnikov, his brother Colonel Nikolái Oupórnikov, Captain Konkóv, and Captain Kóssov; (second row) myself, Lieutenant Zinóvy Krassnóv, Captain Nikolái Folimónov, and an orderly; (third row) three orderlies. The way the latter are demonstratively holding up their cigarettes is visual evidence of the slackening discipline. This

---

* See Chapter 5, p. 181.

† The two officers missing from the group are: Captain Iván Folimónov who was with Reserve Battery at Pávlovsk, and Lieutenant Khopiórsky who was on observation duty.

would have been unthinkable before the Revolution, even after a party.

### 4. Cossack "Self-Determination"

Continued maintenance of discipline and of the fighting spirit of Cossack troops required their removal from under the jurisdiction of the predominantly ultra leftwing Soviets at Army levels. The idea of achieving this by so-to-speak "out-Sovieting the Soviets" originated, of all places, among the regular officers of our Guard Cossack Brigade. One of its first proponents was Captain Kóssov of our battery whom I have already mentioned above.

It was Kóssov who thought up the use of the "self-determination" principle—proclaimed by the Russian Provisional Government in Petrográd—as an excuse for the creation of purely Cossack Soviets of frontline troops. The idea was to prevent the disintegration of Cossack units and help preserve order in the Russian state as a whole; there was no national separatism whatsoever about it.

The word "self-determination" had become almost a joke by the late summer of 1917. It was rumored that even small individual districts or towns were trying to "self-determine" themselves as an excuse for severing ties with places garrisoned by Bolshevik-led mobs of demoralized reservists, or with industrial centers run by leftwing workmen.

Most Cossack officers had enough moral authority over their men to maintain a reasonable degree of discipline in their units and still get the votes of their Soviets to back them. However, Cossack troops, like most of the cavalry, were then scattered all along the front from the Baltic to the Black Sea. A division was the largest all-Cossack formation at that time. Therefore, at the levels of an Army Soviet and higher, Cossacks could be and actually were regularly out-voted by the infantry delegates. The overwhelming majority of the latter had little or no inner discipline, which led to their rapid adherence to Bolshevik slogans for immediate separate peace. By 1917 there were hardly any officers and men left in the infantry who had been in the Regular Imperial Army prior to 1914, so great were the losses during the 1915 retreat when the peacetime ammunition stockpiles were exhausted with no industry in the country to replenish them at the rate required.

This movement for the creation of special Cossack Soviets caught on like wildfire all along the front. It was eminently successful in its objectives: the Cossack troops were among the last units of the Russian armies to leave the Austro-German front in December 1917 and were the only ones to come back as intact units to their home bases.

But it took quite an internal struggle to make it succeed. In our battery I gradually became the spokesman for the officers at political meetings and discussions with the men—Captain Kóssov acting as my chief mentor. My main opponent was sub-Lieutenant Podtiólkov.

His opposition did not present any serious problems at first, since he had no education. Nevertheless, he tried to butt in on any topic discussed. Thus, at one of my frequent meetings with the men, one of them asked me some question about socialism. Before I had a chance to try and answer it, Podtiólkov yelled: "Ordinary socialism, that's nothing (*yéto chto*) but u-u-utopism, that's the very best of all (*naipervéyshi*) socialisms." Even when talking nonsense, Podtiólkov's pentup feelings of real grievance made him sound impressive to a crowd. He was a man of enormous bulk, not fat but square-shouldered and well over six feet tall, with a powerful voice which always rang with genuine indignation. He had all the attributes of a successful rabble-rouser—a point which was apparently soon realized by Bolshevik propagandists in the area. Podtiólkov began to receive frequent visits from suspicious-looking characters and spent many hours in seclusion with them. The officers no longer had any right to do anything about such outsiders or even ascertain who they were.

It soon appeared that Podtiólkov was getting quite a bit of "grooming," for gradually both the substance and the wording of his outbursts became more coherent. Nevertheless, when it came to actual voting, I easily won out over him until the late fall.

Thus, after being nominated by Captain Kóssov, I was elected by the Battery to represent it at the All-Cossack Conference of the Osóbaya (Special) Army—the name of the Army which included the Guards, with headquarters at Loutzk. We met in that town sometime late in May or early in June. I do not remember much about the proceedings except that we held our meetings in a semiruined and abandoned church which had received several shell hits during the fighting of the preceding years. It must have been Catholic or Protestant for it had rows of built-in seats, in contrast to Russian Orthodox churches where everyone stands. I also recall the peculiar feeling I had when delivering a political speech from what had been a pulpit cantilevered from one of the massive interior pillars.

Much more interesting was the subsequent (July 1917) conference of some 200 delegates of Cossack units from the Southwestern Front (Group) of the Russian armies facing the Austro-Germans. I had been again elected by the Don Cossack Guard Battery to represent it. The conference was held at Berdíchev, a Ukrainian city with a large Jewish population to the southwest of Kíev, and some 25 miles to the south of Zhitómir. We opened the conference by a funeral service for several Cossacks who had just been killed in the streetfighting against the Bolsheviks in Petrográd.

The basic conservatism of the mass of the Cossacks led most of them in 1917 to support actively the democratic and moderately socialistic Provisional Government of Kerensky against the Bolsheviks, just as most Cossacks had helped ensure the stability of the Russian state under the tsars.

Thus it was mainly Don Cossack troops of the Petrográd garrison who put down the Bolshevik attempt to seize power from Kerensky in July 1917—the 4th and the 14th Don Cossack regiments and the reserve section of our Don Cossack Guard Battery.

On leaving the service, we were unpleasantly startled to find that the square in front of the Russian Orthodox cathedral was packed by crowds carrying red flags. Their spokesman, a Jewish workman, greeted us, however, as defenders of freedom against the "counter-revolutionaries from the left." As we marched away to the movie-house where our conference was to be held, the crowds followed singing the revolutionary funeral march: *"Vy Zhértvoyu páli v borbé rokovói"* ("You have Fallen Victims in the Fateful Struggle").

Before the Revolution the overwhelming majority of Jews were anti-Tsarist and hence hated the Cossacks for their actively staunch protection of the Russian monarchy. However, by mid-1917 most middleclass and moderately socialistic Russian Jews exhibited the friendliest of feelings towards Cossacks, who provided the only substantial bulwark in sight against the gathering onslaught of leftwing extremism.

We were given many other demonstrations of this changed attitude. For instance, a Jewish dentist who put several fillings in my teeth while I was at Berdíchev firmly refused to accept any payment from me for his work.

Delegates of various political parties and organizations came to address and to greet our Conference. The general theme was the need for a vigorous prosecution of the war until final victory over the Austro-Germans. The only discordant note was provided by an infantry soldier-delegate from the Main Soviet of the Southwestern Front, who obviously was a Bolshevik. The reaction to his speech by a Caucasian mountaineer who happened to be present, however, almost brought about his premature demise.

Special cavalry units of Moslem tribesmen from the Turkestan and the Caucasus were formed and incorporated into the Russian Army early in the war. The largest was the Touzémnaya (Native) Division, unofficially known throughout the Russian Army as the "Díkaya" (Wild) Division because of some of its dubious exploits when in the rear of the fighting lines.* To observe our Conference they had sent a young Lieutenant who had been only recently promoted from the ranks and who proudly wore his epaulettes on a new well-fitting grey *cherkésska* † with a decorative red *bashlík* (a kind of hood for cold weather) slung over his shoulders. Past blood feuds among his clansmen had only recently been sternly suppressed by the Russian authorities, but memories of such medieval customs were still strong in his hills; murder threats were not uttered nor taken lightly where he came from.

The Bolshevik delegate—like the other speakers—delivered his oration from the stage of the theatre where we held our meetings. His speech followed the usual pattern of his party in appealing to the rank-and-file present to refuse to fight any longer and to disavow their officers. Since the overwhelming majority of the delegates elected by the Cossacks to that Conference were officers or seasoned corporals and sergeants used to controlling themselves when hearing that sort of thing from the infantry, nobody seemed particularly upset and only occasional derisive remarks from the floor interrupted the speaker. The newly promoted officer of the Moslem tribesmen however reacted differently.

As the Bolshevik emissary reached the point in his speech where he called for the execution of officers who wanted to continue the war, a guttural voice was heard from the back of the floor, shouting in broken

---

* They had to be withdrawn from occupied East Prussia for that reason. It should be noted here that their dress conformed to the erroneous western ideas about Cossacks (see p. 12) so that most Germans thought these Moslem tribesmen *were* Cossacks. Service with the primitive "Wild" Division was considered romantic and hence was fashionable in Petrográd society. The Division was commanded by the Grand Duke Mikhaíl Alexándrovich, brother of the Tsar, and was officered in part by Guardsmen on leave. I heard amazing stories from one of them about his men.

† See p. 12.

Russian with a strong Caucasian accent: "You want kill *me?* I kill *you!*" As I turned around to see who it was, the hillsman was already racing down one of the aisles with his unsheathed sword in his hand. A fairly wide orchestra pit still separated him from the stage, so the Bolshevik stopped speaking, but at first stayed where he was, apparently feeling secure. However, the Caucasian displayed the agility of a mountain goat: without slowing down a bit he leapt so that one of his feet came on top of the orchestra pit railing from where he sailed through the air with a blood-curdling yell, his sword stretched out ahead and his red "bashlík" streaming behind him. This spurred the Bolshevik to even greater agility. He spun around and dived headlong through one of the paper-covered panels of the backdrop of the stage very much like in a circus hoop-diving stunt. There was a terrific crash as he fell to a lower floor level behind the stage. His moans were drowned out by Cossack applause and cheering which greeted the Caucasian's feat. The cheering soon changed to laughter at the baffled expression on the fiery mountaineer's face as he stopped with drawn sword before the gaping hole left in the paper backdrop by his quarry and then self-consciously turned with an embarrassed grin to face the ovation.

I do not know how badly hurt our "guest speaker" was—some backstage hands quickly carried him away. But the incident had a definite after-affect—no one else with strongly divergent views ventured to address us again.

The Cossack Conference decided to leave a permanent Executive Committee at the Headquarters of the Southwestern Front. I was elected to it, but declined to accept the appointment, returning to the Battery instead.

During one of my previous absences from the front lines I had missed some action. It must have been during the Kerensky mid-June offensive to the south, when a secondary offensive was attempted on our section of the Stohód River.

Our six-gun battery alone had fired over 3,000 rounds then, almost without interruption. Other batteries which had been brought up to that sector did the same. Most of the enemy frontline trenches and barbed wire were literally obliterated, and an all-officer shock-battalion had no difficulty in moving through them, but was then overwhelmed by Austro-German reinforcements. Our infantry did not give any support; instead, they held Bolshevik-inspired meetings and voted not to budge. The same thing happened at other points of planned reakthrough along the entire front of the Russian armies. The policy f permitting exposure of war-weary troops to unrestricted propaanda and allowing them to vote had produced the inevitable result.

After my return from the Berdíchev Cossack Conference, a period f intense boredom followed for me on the now completely slumberng Stohód positions. To make things worse I had to cancel a twoeek vacation trip to Kíev which I was to make in August. I had aved up some money for it and was looking forward to a nice time ith a girl in Kíev whom I had known for many years. Instead, I ad to stay in soggy trenches, having lost all my savings plus a ouple of months' salary at a card game of *chemin de fer*. I have ever again gambled for money.

Another consequence was that I could not afford to take my vacaion until the end of October, and then only by economizing and oing home to Tsárskoye Seló. I got there just before the momentous vents at Petrográd, 15 miles to the north.

# Part II    RUSSIAN CIVIL WAR
1917–1920

# 4

## "The Ten Days That Shook the World" —As I Saw Them

### 1. Bolshevik Seizure of Power at Petrográd

When I returned home on leave in October 1917 things had changed somewhat at Tsárskoye Seló since I left it eight months earlier on the eve of the Revolution. We still lived in a small rented house at No. 6 Zakharzhévskaya Street in a part of Tsárskoye Seló known as Sofía. Mother continued to work as senior sister of mercy at the same hospital, which had however been moved to another building and renamed "Hospital No. 3." The Empress and the Grand Duchesses had been prevented from working there since the March 1917 Revolution, and early in August had been exiled to Tobólsk in Siberia.*

My mother's friend, Mrs. Lýdia Fyódorovna Krassnóva, was staying with us. She was the wife of General Piótr Krassnóv, who was to play such a prominent role in the events which were about to unfold.

I found a mood of great anxiety at home. All around there was a feeling of expectation that something was about to happen and that things simply could not go on any longer the way they were going.

Kerensky's government no longer enjoyed the support of any groups that mattered, and its role in the Kornílov affair had finally lost it the allegiance of most of the remaining officers who still attempted to stem the tide of anarchy in their troops.

Long before that the reserve garrisons in Petrográd and in other cities had lost all semblance of discipline and spent their time attending political meetings, voting resolutions, and demonstrating through the streets in support of various political demands. Officers who attempted to restore some military order in their units were immediately branded as counterrevolutionaries and, at best, were forced to leave. Murders were frequent.

Continuation of the war with Germany was impossible under such conditions. Chaos in the rear contaminated the front. In this con-

---

* I will give some details of this in Chapter 6, p. 190.

nection, on pages 97–99 of Ref. 34, General Piótr Krassnóv wrote, with reference to the reserve garrisons of the rear:

". . . it is necessary to conclude peace as rapidly as possible and to dismiss and send back to their villages these masses who have become insane. . . ."

Very few people in the West realize even now how disastrously shortsighted were the Western Allies when they selfishly insisted that Russia stay on in the war at any cost in spite of the terrible wounds she had suffered in the common cause. George F. Kennan is the only American I know of who seems to have understood this (see Ref. 29). Continuation of the war by Russia made an internal victory of Bolshevism inevitable.

The so-called Kornílov uprising on August 27 (September 9), 1917, was a last desperate attempt to stop the disintegration of the Army. General Kornílov was not a monarchist or a counterrevolutionary (page 684 of Ref. 31). The son of a simple Siberian Cossack and of a Kirghíz (or Buriát) woman, he had inherited partly Mongolian features from his mother and prided himself on his humble origin. An able and courageous soldier, he realized that no army could function under the conditions tolerated by Kerensky's government. In his capacity of newly appointed Commander-in-Chief, General Kornílov therefore demanded the restoration of disciplinary powers of officers and sent the IIIrd Cavalry Corps to Petrográd to disband the local Soviet—where the disastrous Order No. 1 had originated (see p. 85)—and to disarm unruly reserve units of the local garrison. There are some indications that Kerensky at first went along with this, but then reversed himself and proclaimed General Kornílov a mutineer. Railroad workers refused to move the trains of the IIIrd Cavalry Corps and the whole action collapsed. The Corps Commander, General Krýmov, committed suicide and General Kornílov was arrested. From then on there was nothing to restrain Bolshevik propaganda for a separate peace.

By the time I arrived in Tsárskoye Seló towards the end of October 1917, rumors were circulating everywhere about the impending armed seizure of power at Petrográd by the Bolsheviks. A former Imperial Law School classmate of mine was on leave there from his Cossack regiment at the front, and we decided to join forces in trying to find a place where we could volunteer to fight the Reds should they attempt an uprising. We were quite appalled at what we found as we toured the city. There was talk everywhere about the impending Bolshevik insurrection, but nowhere was anything serious being done to prepare to meet it—demoralization was general and complete. The only place where we got some encouragement was at the offices of the Union of Cossack Armies.

One late afternoon my friend telephoned me from Petrográd; it looked as if things were about to start. I took the first train from Tsárskoye Seló, picked my friend up at his apartment, and proceeded with him to the Union of Cossack Armies, only to find its offices closed. Somebody told us that a center of resistance was being organized at the Winter Palace. So we walked towards it along the Névsky Prospékt—Petrográd's main artery. Halfway down, we were stopped by a line of Red Guards—armed workmen's militia—which was drawn across the street. We were told we could not go any farther until the Kerensky supporters at the Winter Palace were overcome. It was already evening and quite dark. In order not to attract undue attention we bought tickets to an operetta which was still playing as usual in a side street. Every few minutes one of us would step to the door to reconnoiter. Every once in a while some desultory firing was heard. Then there was silence. Soon after, the line of Red Guards barring the Névsky was withdrawn and traffic was resumed. The only units which had defended Kerensky's regime at the Winter Palace were a women's battalion and some cadets from Oranienbaum who all soon surrendered. Such was the ignominious end of the rule of Kerensky's government at Petrográd on October 25 (November 7), 1917.

## 2. *Cossack Attack on the Púlkovo Heights*

We did not know it at the time, but Kerensky had succeeded in escaping from Petrográd and fleeing to the area of Óstrov and Pskov (the latter a town some 170 miles to the southwest) where the headquarters of the IIIrd Cavalry Corps were located. It was the only unit nearby which had kept some military cohesion and which Kerensky rightly felt might remain loyal, but by an irony of fate, this was the same IIIrd Cavalry Corps which Kerensky had branded as counterrevolutionary during the Kornílov affair only two months earlier. General Piótr Krassnóv was appointed to command it after General Krýmov had committed suicide when his advance on Petrográd had been stalled. It was General Krassnóv whom Kerensky now summoned to march the same IIIrd Corps again on Petrográd

In view of this background, the fact that Kerensky's order was obeyed at all is one more proof of the stabilizing role that the Cossacks tended to play in the affairs of the Russian state. General Krassnóv expressed as follows what he felt when he decided to obey Kerensky's order:*

". . . it is not to Kerensky that I am going, but to the land of my birth (*ródina*), to the Great Russia which I cannot forsake. And if Russia is with Kerensky, I will go with him. Him I shall hate and curse, but I shall go to serve and die for Russia. She elected him, she followed him, she had been unable to find a more capable leader—I shall go help him if he is for Russia."

Unfortunately for Kerensky, he was now powerless to reverse the measures he had permitted earlier with the purpose of assuring the impotence of the IIIrd Cavalry Corps. After the failure of Kornílov's march on Petrográd two months before, the various units of the distrusted Corps were purposely scattered over a wide area to hinder any sudden move it might wish to take on its own. As a result, General Krassnóv had only some 700 horsemen with a few field guns at hand when Kerensky came to him for help (page 155 of Ref. 34).

I will now proceed with my narrative of the events as I remember them and will quote some references to indicate to what extent they agree or disagree with my own recollections. These references are: my mother's diary, Ref. 6; General Krassnóv's published account, Ref. 34; John Reed's "Ten Days That Shook the World," Ref. 52, from which I adapted the title of this chapter; and official Soviet documents, Refs. 13 and 45.

I should mention that in 1917–1918 I had written down some of the descriptions which follow, but had to destroy them later in the Don. Thus, what I am writing now is not merely forty-five-year-old recollections, but is an attempt to reconstitute what I had already written once and what I had then repeatedly discussed with other participants of these events.

The first inkling we had at our Tsárskoye Seló home that the Bolshevik success at Petrográd would be contested came over our tele-

---

* See page 149 of Ref. 34. This statement of General Krassnóv's was written in 1920 and is one of several which should be noted, since anti-Russian propaganda in the West now falsely attempts to represent him as having been a "Cossackian" separatist when he was Don Atamán in 1918 (see pp. 208–238).

phone in the evening of October 27 (November 9). A man's voice asked for Mrs. Krassnóva, who immediately recognized her husband. Speaking in a casual manner without identifying himself further he remarked that he was at Gátchino—a small town some 14 miles to the south (see Map D).

Mother noted this as follows, October 27/November 9, page 47 of Ref. 6.

"Sad and resigned we [*Mrs. Krassnóva and she*] were sitting and sewing in the drawingroom when suddenly the telephone rang from Gát[*chino*] . . . P[*iótr*] N[*ikoláyevich Krassnóv*]—'stay

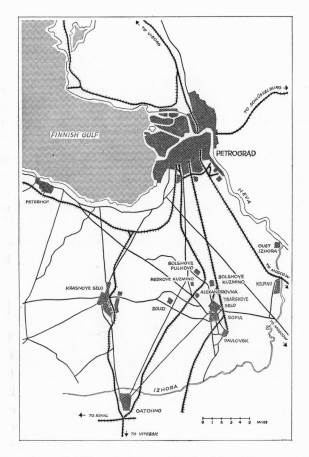

Map D. Vicinity of Petrográd. *See Map A, p. 44.*

at home tomorrow, don't even think of going to Petrográd—
things won't be good there tomorrow, and in Tsárskoye too much
may happen.' "

Mother added—"*So, va-banque.*" *

All this evidently meant that Krassnóv might attack and occupy
Tsárskoye Seló on the next day and anyone who went to Petrograd
would be cut off from home.

Soon after we heard quite an uproar in one of the neighboring
streets—a band was playing a lively march and a babble of shouts
and cheering accompanied it. We learned that it was one of the Guard
Rifle Reserve regiments marching off to meet Cossack "counterrevolutionaries" who were approaching from the south. Mrs. Krassnóva
naturally was in quite a state of nerves.

That same evening Mother continued on page 48 of her journal:

"The regiment left with its band playing for fratricidal combat.
A heavy cross has fallen to the lot of P[*iótr*] N[*ikoláyevich
Krassnóv*]. May the Lord help him! After all, this is the last
card, the last attempt to save Russia from anarchy, from the
shame of a humiliating craven peace! . . . It is now 2 o'clock
. . . I cannot sleep . . . a deadly complete silence is all around
. . . Many sad thoughts for Lidoúsha [*Mrs. Krassnóva*] cross
my mind . . . will the dear P[*iótr*] N[*ikoláyevich Krassnóv*]
be able to cope with his assignment . . . to take Petrográd . . .
it is no joke! May he only succeed in doing all this without too
much bloodshed . . . fraternal blood [*spilled*] will not be for-
given. . . ."

But early next morning fugitives began to appear. As I learned
afterwards the revolutionary reservists, who had never been in any
action whatsoever before, soon got tired of carrying their rifles and
piled them up on carts they requisitioned in one of the villages. When
they were passing at dawn through a wood, a Cossack patrol consisting of one officer and some sixteen horsemen rode out of it, separated the lazy "warriors" from the carts with their rifles and told
them to go home. On their return they could not very well admit all
this, of course, so the number of Cossacks whom they had encountered assumed huge proportions.

* French Monte Carlo roulette expression, used in Russia to designate a
situation when everything was staked on a single bet.

This was quite a help in scaring the demoralized rabble which comprised the reservist "garrison" of Tsárskoye Seló—estimated at 16,000 to 20,000 men. The official Soviet account (page 350 of Ref. 13) and the British Military Attaché (page 717 of Ref. 31) give the latter higher figure. After a few shrapnels burst over the nearest barracks at about 7 A.M. on October 28 (November 10), they all surrendered and Cossack patrols entered the town.

Krassnóv's headquarters were set up at the former palace of the Grand Duchess Marýa Pávlovna, only two or three blocks away from our house. I immediately reported there, and General Krassnóv appointed me his personal orderly officer. On page 51 of Mother's diary (Ref. 6b) I find the following entry:

> "Grishoúk left for the Headquarters (*Shtab*) around 9; he dropped in for a minute with the report that in the evening P[*iótr*] N[*ikoláyevich Krassnóv*] himself will come, that everything achieved so far was accomplished by 300 Cossacks with two field guns!!! . . . My heart shrank. . . ."

I did not feel any too happy either when I learned what the actual situation was. After his main forces had joined the advance guard which had captured Tsárskoye Seló, General Krassnóv had with him only the 9th and the 10th Don Cossack regiments, neither of which was at full strength, and a couple of squadrons of Siberian Cossacks. This gave him some 1,300 horsemen, and less than 900 riflemen in any dismounted action, since about a third of the men would have to stay with the horses, as actually had to be done in the subsequent action before Púlkovo. He also had ten 3-inch field guns of Cossack Horse Artillery, an armored train and a couple of armored cars.

The day of October 29 (November 11) was spent at Tsárskoye Seló consolidating the gains won there and waiting for reinforcements promised by Kerensky, which never came—various moves by railroad and other pro-Bolshevik groups prevented them. Only two field guns of the Reserve Battery of the Guard Horse Artillery with my old commander, Colonel Count Rehbinder, reported for service from nearby Pávlovsk, as well as an understrength reserve *sótnya* (squadron) of the Svódny Guard Cossack Regiment, also from Pávlovsk. It consisted of one officer and some forty young Urál and Siberian Cossacks.

General Krassnóv ordered an advance against Petrográd on October 30 (November 12). At first glance this may appear as sheer

lunacy, since its garrison consisted of some 200,000 reservists. However, their morale was so low that they were likely to prove worse
than useless in combat, as the 16,000 reservists of the Tsárskoye Seló
garrison had already shown. The numbers of the Red Guard volunteer detachments of workmen and sailors were not known, and their
stamina had never yet been tested in any field action. The only way
to find out was by actually testing it. In this respect General Krassnóv is perfectly right  in describing this first field battle of the Russian Civil War as a "forced reconnaissance" which he conducted (see
translation of Fig. 24 on p. 119 and pages 166-170 of Ref. 34).

He was encouraged to try it by some favorable factors. He could
rely on his men, especially on the 10th Don Cossack Regiment which
he had commanded and trained for about a year before the outbreak
of World War I in 1914. The men knew and trusted him—he had
won the officer's St. George Cross (Fig. 29) when he personally led
that dismounted regiment early in the war through barbed wire entanglements to capture entrenchments of Austro-Hungarian infantry.

Many units inside Petrográd were wavering, for instance—the 1st,
4th and 14th Don Cossack regiments stationed there. Energetic action
might bring them and many others back to the side of the Kerensky
government.

The one day of waiting for reinforcements at Tsárskoye Seló on
October 29 (November 11) however proved fatal in this respect.
General Krassnóv did not know that on that day the cadets (*yúnkers*)
of the Vladímirsky Infantry School and some other small units had
seized several key points inside Petrográd, but that Red Guard detachments overwhelmed them by the late afternoon (pages 36-362
of Ref. 13). Things might have perhaps turned out differently had
General Krassnóv advanced on the 29th instead of the 30th—as it
was, the Bolshevik command was able to meet him in the field with
their rear at Petrograd fully protected and their key Red Guard
volunteer units concentrated around the Púlkovo Heights some three
miles to the north of Tsárskoye Seló.

Púlkovo was the home of a world-famous astronomical observatory
of the same name located at the top of a hill. Various auxiliary buildings and parklike gardens surrounded the main structure (see Map
D, p. 111).

From there and from a line of adjoining villages intense rifle and
machine gun fire met the advancing Cossack patrols in the morning

of October 30 (November 12). General Krassnóv ordered several Cossack squadrons to dismount and to attempt a slow advance towards the Red positions. The General himself then walked with several officers of his staff from the village Alexándrovka to the northern edge of the village Rédkoye Kúzmino, where they stayed during the entire action. I was with them.

This was a vantage point from where one could clearly see large groups of Red Guards standing around on the southern slopes of the Púlkovo Heights to the north of us and moving to take up positions along the Púlkovo-Gátchino road to the northwest. Their dark coats stood out sharply against the brown autumn grass and indicated that most of them were not Regular Army reservists but were sailors and workmen. They obviously had a good combat morale—when shrapnel burst over them, they did not run the way most revolutionary reservists would but only dispersed from their original compact groups into skirmishing lines. They kept up a continuous fire, but their lack of training resulted in exceptionally poor marksmanship. No one in our group was hit although the *pe-ou* sound of bullets passing overhead was continuous, punctuated by an occasional *zi-ip* when they hit the ground or some obstacle.

General Krassnóv commented to the officers near him on the similarity between the Red fire and the panicky firing of the Austrians—and he named several battles in which the Austrians had been defeated by the Cossack units now engaged. The General always made it a point to say something that would raise the spirits of the men around him.

A two-gun section of one of the Cossack batteries unlimbered their pieces behind an adjoining house and then rolled them out by hand to take up a position in front of us. From there they occasionally aimed shells over their open sights at some particularly promising target.

In general, a strict economy of shells was observed—the same was true about the dismounted Cossacks. These veterans knew how to remain almost invisible, aided as they were by the greyish-brown color of their overcoats which blended perfectly with the surrounding terrain. It would have been difficult to guess that some three to five hundred riflemen were deployed in front of us before the hastily dug shallow Red trenches and the road ditches which they used for the same purpose. The great disparity in numbers did not permit trying to

close in on them—there must have been at least two or three thousand
Red Guards there. So our men stopped a few hundred yards away
from their opponents, at which distance their superior marksmanship
gave them a decided advantage. This accounts for the much greater
Red losses, as compared to ours.

Our side fired only sparingly, but the Reds did not. The general
effect was a dreadful din, which at a distance must have made things
sound much worse than they actually were. Mother wrote that same
evening (page 55 of Ref. 6b):

". . . I will never forget this day—this terrific battle, this wild
cannonade from eleven in the morning till seven in the evening,
and the knowledge that your beloved child is there. . . ."

Poor Mother continued to reproach herself that she had not somehow stopped me from going, even as she noted that I had refused to
listen. She even blamed herself in her diary for having wakened me
that morning—the alarm clock was in her room.

While things remained deadlocked, as described above, in our
center and on our left flank, they had gone much better on our right,
although we were at our weakest there. Our armored train was able
to operate along the railroad lines which existed in that sector—for
that reason only the half-strength reserve squadron of the Svódny
Guard Cossack regiment from Pávlovsk was assigned to support it.

It so happened that no Red Guards and only regular army reservists
from the Petrográd garrison were operating on our right. There were
at least a thousand of them, but they all fled after a few rounds of
shells fired at them by our armored train. Their commander, an infantry Captain whom they had forced to lead them, dropped into a
ditch from where he waved a white handkerchief until picked up by
a patrol of the Svódny Guard Cossack reservists. He was then brought
to General Krassnóv by their leader, a young Siberian Cossack
Lieutenant.

The latter seems to have been quite a hothead—he asked but was
refused General Krassnóv's permission to charge the Red Guards
(pages 167–168 of Ref. 34). Soon after, however, we heard a prolonged *hurra-a-ah* and the Siberian Lieutenant dashed past to the
right of us at the head of his forty young Cossacks with their sabres
drawn.

General Krassnóv was incensed. I still remember the anguish in his voice as he shouted repeatedly: "Who ordered the charge?" Nobody had. Apparently the young Lieutenant decided to disobey orders,* not realizing that the Red Guard volunteers were of quite different mettle than the demoralized infantry reservists he had just seen flee in panic. He paid by his life for his brashness.

A hurricane of fire met him. Every Red rifle and machine gun within range, including an armored car, seemed to be firing at once. One could not hear individual shots, just a continuous fluctuating roar. The amazing thing therefore was that there was only one man killed in the charge—the young Lieutenant himself. Eighteen of his men were wounded and all forty horses lost.

When their commander was killed while still several hundred feet away from the Reds, the native common sense of the young Cossacks asserted itself. They all dropped out of their saddles, whether wounded or not, and made their way back hugging the ground. This was the first time any of them had been under fire and it speaks well for the young fellows that they brought back not only all their wounded, but the body of their reckless commander as well.

Some of the unwounded riderless horses however kept going. The Reds stopped firing at them, but our own Cossack riflemen brought most of them down so that they would not become enemy prizes. This is why a number of horse carcasses lay around close to the ditches of the Púlkovo-Gátchino Road which formed the Red line, giving rise to the legend of ferocious hand-to-hand fighting along it.

The American Communist, John Reed, visited the battlefield the next day and wrote (page 220 of Ref. 52):

> "Those who participated in the fighting described to me how the sailors fought until they ran out of cartridges, and then stormed; how the untrained workmen rushed the charging Cossacks and tore them from their horses; how the anonymous hordes of the people, gathering in the darkness around the battle, rose like a tide and poured over the enemy. . . . Before midnight of Monday the Cossacks broke and were fleeing, leaving their artillery behind them, and the army of the proletariat, on a long ragged front, moved forward and rolled into Tsárskoye. . . ."

An official 1942 Soviet historical account even printed on page 387, Ref. 13 a drawing purporting to represent "The Battle of Púlkovo."

---

* This is the case I referred to on p. 32.

It shows rearing horses throwing their Cossack riders among Red Guard infantrymen and an armored car firing point-blank at them.

All this is pure fantasy. There had been no hand-to-hand fighting anywhere; the forty Cossacks who attempted the ill-fated charge never came closer than several hundred feet to the Red lines; at no time was there any sign that the Reds lacked ammunition. On the contrary, they seemed to be lavishly supplied with it and were using it wastefully; not a single field piece,* machine gun, wounded or dead Cossack was left behind; the retreat was accomplished under cover of darkness in complete order and the Reds followed hesitatingly, keeping up artillery and rifle fire on the Cossack positions long after they were abandoned. The electric lights were cut off at the Tsárskoye Seló power station, giving an advantage to the Cossack veterans who were accustomed to night movements and action.

The total Cossack losses of the day were only three killed and twenty-eight wounded (page 172 of Ref. 34)—the Red casualties appear to have exceeded four hundred. This is no reflection on their courage or stamina; on the contrary, the general feeling on our side was that they had performed extremely well for novices in the art of war.

The repulse of the foolish charge of the Siberian Cossack Lieutenant naturally greatly raised the spirit of the Reds, who began attempts to advance. Our riflemen slowly pulled back; by the evening they lined a railroad embankment passing through the village of Alexándrovka at the northern edge of the Tsárskoye Seló park.

It was in the shelter of this embankment that General Krassnóv began dictating to me his Orders to retreat, a photograph of the beginning and end of which is given by Fig. 24. This was the first time I had done such staff officer work, and my main concern was to make a more-or-less presentable-looking job of it. We soon moved to an abandoned house nearby where the rest of the Orders were written. I wrote them in a field dispatch book with four or five carbon copies. The original was kept by General Krassnóv and was presented by him a year later to my father in Novocherkássk,—I have it in my safe deposit box in the bank in Princeton. It has never been published. The English translation of the full text is as follows:

* I am not sure what happened to Colonel Count Rehbinder's two guns of the Guard Horse Artillery regular reserves. They did not come into action, nor were they ordered to retreat to Gátchino—they did return to their Pávlovsk barracks, with Rehbinder still in command, but I do not know when.

*Translation from the Russian*

Corps H.Q.

ORDERS TO

IIIrd CAVALRY CORPS

NO. 051

Village Alexándrovka                    October 30, 1917

"The forced reconnaissance undertaken by me from 12 hours until 18 hours today has ascertained that the opponent occupies a position from the village Kábozi, through the village Soúzi, to the village Bolshóye Púlkovo. The rebels consist of sailors, infantry units and red guards, their number is no less than two to three thousands. They have 3 armored cars, one of which is armed with guns, 2 field pieces. Their actions are very determined, the character of the battle leaves no doubt that they are directed by German officers. Since we not only do not receive reinforcements, but have no cartridges and shells, I consider that our position, threatened by a deep envelopment from the direction of Kólpino, especially taking into account [*end of upper part of text reproduced by Fig. 24*] the unreliability of the garrison of Tsárskoye Seló and the considerable battle fatigue of the Cossacks, does not permit us to take the offensive. We cannot remain in Tsárskoye Seló since our forces are insufficient to provide outposts and since we do not have ammunition to repel an attack. For that reason I have decided to retreat to the town of Gátchino as soon as darkness falls, and to await there the arrival of reinforcements."

For this:

"When darkness falls all combat units are to inconspicuously assemble at their horse holders and proceed to the town of Gátchino taking up quarters there in the area of the Baltic railroad, in the barracks of the Leib-Guard Cuirassier Regiment, in the riding-school building of the same regiment, and in the stables of the Palace Administration. Sentries and patrols are to be provided everywhere.

"1) *Protection*. For the defense of the town of Gátchino send out tomorrow at 6 in the morning by orders of the commander of the 1st Don Cossack Division a guard detachment of 2 *sótnyas* [squadrons] and 4 field guns which is to place 5 outposts on the bridges across the river Izhóra and have its reserve at the fork of the roads leading to Gátchino. In front of the bridges, at a distance of 800 paces, install roadblocks against armored cars, placing them under artillery cover, having established the range well in advance.

"2) *Liaison.* The guard detachment should be connected directly with me by telephone; in addition, install phones for liaison with me of the divisional headquarters and of the latter with regimental commanders. Be ready for an alert. The liaison installation should be completed by 6 in the morning.

"3) Replenish ammunition, filling the caissons and limbers, fill machine-gun belts and ammunition carts and issue 200 cartridges to every rifleman. All this should be done immediately. The location of the ammunition will be indicated by the commander of the Artillery of the Corps.

"4) Baggage trains should be with the units.

"5) The Proskúrovsky field ambulance detachment should [*be-beginning of lower part of text reproduced by Fig. 24*] take up quarters in the Bolshói Palace as per directions of the commandant.

"6) I am at Bolshói Palace, Room No. 20, third floor.

"7) *Successor:* Major General Khreschatítsky and Colonel Popóv.

> *"Commanding the IIIrd Cavalry Corps*
>
> *"Major General* [*Signed*] *Krassnóv*
>
> *"For Chief of Staff*
>
> *"(Lt.) Colonel* [*Signed*] *Popóv"*

General Krassnóv and the officers of his staff, including myself, then rode back to his Tsárskoye Seló headquarters. There Krassnóv gave me a car and requested me to pick up his wife at our home and drive her to an address in the town of Gátchino. This I proceeded to do.

All of Tsárkoye Seló was pitch dark, and Mrs. Krassnóva's things had to be hurriedly packed by candlelight. My grandmother Doubiágsky and my sister's French governess helped,—Mother was at her hospital which was standing by to receive wounded.

After depositing Mrs. Krassnóva at the Gátchino home of her relatives, I proceeded to the Bolshoí (Big) Palace where General Krassnóv's staff arrived shortly afterwards. I spent the night there, sleeping on a sofa.

### 3. Who Captured Whom in Gátchino's Bolshói Palace?

On the next morning (October 31/November 13) we learned that the Cossack rank-and-file had refused to replenish their ammunition supplies and to take up defensive positions along the Izhóra River, as had been ordered by General Krassnóv. The fact that not a single infantry unit had joined them, in spite of Kerensky's promises, had a most discouraging effect—they refused to continue alone the fratricidal struggle. The approaches to Gátchino were left unguarded, and first Bolshevik emissaries and then entire Red detachments began entering the town unhindered and unmolested.

Lodgings within Gátchino had been occupied by the Cossack units in accordance with the Orders of General Krassnóv. This meant that the main body of his troops was at some distance from his headquarters in the Bolshói Palace. Only a half-strength squadron of Yennisséy Cossacks, from the Siberian river of that name, were on guard duty there with him.

Two events of general interest stand out in my memory concerning our stay at the Gátchino Palace. To the best of my knowledge they have never been described in print, for reasons which I will try to analyze and outline briefly.

The first episode concerns General Krassnóv's actions after the arrival of the first Bolshevik emissary, the sailor Dybénko, just before Kerensky's disappearance. What I saw then convinced me that General Krassnóv had deliberately helped Kerensky escape from the Palace—in spite of his having later blamed Kerensky for alleged breach of faith in this connection, according to Soviet accounts (Document No. 1168: page 802 of Ref. 45).

The second episode is concerned with the brash attempt of the Red Commander-in-Chief, Colonel Mouravióv, accompanied by Trótzky, personally to seize General Krassnóv. Instead, both Mouravióv and Trótzky found themselves isolated for a while in our uncongenial company on the third floor of the Palace, with our armed Yennisséy Cossack sentries guarding the staircase landings. Red sailor sentries faced them below, where the first and second floors were held by the Bolsheviks. The manner in which the resulting deadlock was resolved is typical of the confused state of affairs at the start of the Russian Civil War.

I am not sure as to whether some of this happened on October

31/November 13, or on the next day—November 1/14. I have found some discrepancies in relevant references I have quoted in connection with this chapter. But this is not important, since there is no question as to the sequence in which things developed.

Kerensky had stayed at Gátchino throughout the Púlkovo battle. Before that he had made a brief appearance at Tsárskoye Seló during which he attempted to make a very foolish speech to one of the Army reserve units there. He called them "rebellious slaves" and other epithets, as a result of which the infantrymen, who had already laid down their arms, tried to pick them up again—for use against Kerensky, of course. The handful of Cossacks who were guarding the surrendered rifles had quite a lot of trouble quieting things down.

I saw Kerensky at that time—when he visited the Cossack Headquarters at Tsárskoye Seló. His unconvincingly theatrical poses and vague pronouncements in a somewhat hysterical voice left a most unfavorable impression with everyone there. It is true that this was just after the enraged infantry reservists had forced him to break off his speech and leave their barracks in a hurry.

The result of that visit was that General Krassnóv asked Kerensky to stay away from the immediate zone of military operations and leave the latter entirely to him. Kerensky was requested to concentrate on exercising from Gátchino his powers and prestige as legal head of the Provisional Government to redeem his pledges of providing reinforcements to Krassnóv's embattled Cossacks. From then on Kerensky stayed at the Gátchino Palace but found that he was powerless to keep his promise and get reinforcements to General Krassnóv.

The first Bolshevik emissary to arrive at Gátchino was the notorious sailor Dybénko.* He was a big, handsome, "jolly brigand" sort of fellow with an easy-going folksy manner which started him off well with the Cossack rank-and-file. Dybénko refused to negotiate with General Krassnóv or with any of the Cossack commanders, insisting that he would deal only with the Cossack Soviet.

This did not particularly disturb General Krassnóv since the Cossack Soviets (see p. 98) as a rule fully cooperated with their old commanders. In this case the highest Cossack Soviet present was that of the 1st Don Division, to which the 9th and the 10th regiments belonged. Its chairman was a Captain Azhógin (Ref. 34) and it had several reliable sergeants and corporals among its members.

* The name is Ukrainian.

One of these sergeants was assigned periodically to inform General Krassnóv on the progress of the discussions with Dybénko. I was in the room the General used for his office at the Palace when the Sergeant came in and reported that Dybénko was demanding the immediate arrest and delivery to him of Kerensky. The Cossacks in the Soviet were wavering. Most of them, especially the officers, disliked Kerensky intensely, considering that he had betrayed the IIIrd Corps in the days of the Kornílov affair (see p. 108). Krassnóv told the Sergeant that there could be no question of his agreeing to this.

Some time later the Sergeant came in again and reported that when the Cossack officers had aired their suspicions about the significance of Lenin's return from exile via Germany, Dybénko blandly proposed to arrest not only Lenin, but Trótzky as well if the Cossacks would arrest Kerensky. All three would then be placed before a People's Tribunal to answer the various charges against them. The proposal was patently fraudulent, but the idea caught the fancy of the Cossacks—it was no longer possible to keep their rank and file in line on this point.

The General pondered this and then told the Sergeant to be sure to prolong the discussions by any means he could think of by at least half-an-hour and under no circumstances agree to Kerensky's arrest before checking again with him.

After the Sergeant had left, General Krassnóv called his devoted Aide-de-Camp, Captain Koulgávov, to the table at which he was sitting. Koulgávov bent over and the two conversed in semi-whispers for a while. Then Koulgávov left. Some thirty minutes later he returned, came up to the General and again the two talked in low voices. Shortly after, the Sergeant came in again and Krassnóv told him that the Cossack Soviet could agree to arrest Kerensky.

The latter was nowhere to be found, but a search of the Palace led to the discovery in one of the rooms of a bound and gagged man in his underwear—he was one of Dybénko's own sailors. The only light he could throw on what happened to him was that someone, who must have silently emerged from a side room, suddenly threw a blanket over his head from behind as he was walking along one of the Palace corridors. Several men, whom he did not see, silently seized, gagged and blindfolded him, removed his clothing and left him lying securely trussed up on the floor.

According to page 1813 of Ref. 3 and other reports, Kerensky escaped from the Palace disguised as a sailor, but no mention was made as to how he got the clothing, nor, so far as I know, was the incident I have just mentioned ever described in print. There was no one in Kerensky's small entourage who looked as if he might have engineered this incident and gotten away with it—except the energetic and tough Captain Koulgávov. At some later date, with no one else present, I asked him point-blank whether he had done it. This he emphatically denied. Why should he have done anything to help the so-and-so Kerensky? But the way this excellent officer kept laughing as he said this, stroking his flowing moustache at the same time with a generally satisfied look of a "cat-that-had-eaten-a-canary," convinced me that he was denying under Krassnóv's orders a fact he had been pledged to keep secret. There are good reasons why Krassnóv should have wished it to remain that way.

Every ingrained instinct of an officer who, like General Krassnóv, was steeped in the best traditions and spirit of the old Russian Imperial Army would have rebelled at the idea of surrendering to a common enemy a man who had placed himself under his protection, no matter how much he disliked or despised that man. As I see it, it is conceivable that General Krassnóv might have himself arrested Kerensky, had he defeated the Bolsheviks and taken Petrográd, but he could not agree to betray him to the Reds.

Later events which I will describe showed that General Krassnóv had quite a gift for improvising unorthodox and expedient, but sometimes questionable, solutions of the difficult and unusual situations in which he frequently found himself. I believe that this is what he did at Gátchino in respect to Kerensky.

In his depositions to the Bolsheviks (Ref. 52, page 242; Ref. 3, pages 1810–1813; Document No. 1169: Ref. 45, page 803) Krassnóv stated that Kerensky had promised him to proceed to Petrográd for negotiations with the Reds, implying that his flight was completely unexpected. As Krassnóv himself correctly wrote later in Ref. 34 (see English translation in Ref. 3, page 1812), his own Cossacks were however terribly aroused against him—there were voices calling for his arrest on the charge that he had betrayed the Cossacks by giving Kerensky the opportunity to escape. Krassnóv obviously could not admit at the time that he had actually done so.

The only man held then was an orderly officer of Kerensky, a Práporschik (Third Lieutenant), Knírsha, who had not succeeded in getting away. By Krassnóv's order he was allowed to move about the Palace, but a Cossack guard with his rifle at the ready was to dog his footsteps and not for an instant leave him out of sight. Subsequently this Knírsha, a most obnoxious acting fellow, repeatedly provided moments of tragi-comic relief from the general tension.

I recall him bursting into Krassnóv's room, followed by his Cossack guard and by an Army Lieutenant, who had been appointed by Dybénko to serve as Red Commandant of the Palace, alongside of ours. According to General Krassnóv's memoirs (Ref. 34) his name was Tarássov-Rodiónov.

Addressing Krassnóv as "Your Excellency"—something he had not done before—Knírsha incoherently begged him in a hysterical voice not to surrender him to the Reds. The General asked Tarássov-Rodiónov to explain what it was all about. Calmly, the Red Lieutenant said that he had been ordered to take down in writing Knírsha's statements concerning the circumstances of Kerensky's flight and that he had summoned him for that purpose to his office. Knírsha's panic was caused by fear of retribution for what he had done to Tarássov-Rodiónov personally: The latter had been in command of a pro-Red company of reservists at the Gátchino Railroad Station which surrendered to the Cossacks (on October 27/November 9). To settle old personal scores Knírsha had kept him in solitary confinement without food for four days. "Don't be afraid, Práporschik," he said, "I am not a scoundrel like you are."

Rapidly changing from "Your Excellency" to "Comrade officers," Knírsha screamed: "Have you forgotten the pictures of the Viborg murders with a placard 'Officers Swimming School' over the place where officers, bound hand and foot, were thrown into the harbor? Don't turn me over to him!" At this point the bearded Yennisséy Cossack guard put his large paw-like hand on Knírsha's shoulder: *"Nye pouzháytess—Nye dam v obídou! Idyóm!* (Don't be scared, I won't let you be harmed! Let's go!)." As the trio left, the General turned to us: "What characters (*Típy*)! What a scene for my future novel!" *

The unsuccessful attempt by the Red command, with Trótzky's personal participation, to seize Krassnóv came about as follows: That indeed was a scene which could not be easily forgotten. The General

---

* A year later at Novocherkássk in the Don I asked Krassnóv whether he had written about any of this (I had) and was amazed to find that he had completely forgotten the details of the episode. However, the General then noted down some of the things I reminded him of and in Ref. 34, which was written in 1920, he does refer to his having told us "what a scene for my future novel." However, he does this in a somewhat different connection than the one I recall.

and some seven or eight of his Cossack officers, including myself, were having afternoon tea in one of the large third-floor rooms of the Gátchino Palace when an approaching hubbub of voices was heard in the corridor outside. The door to our room was flung open by a man in a Colonel's uniform and a motley crowd of some thirty Red Guards and sailors poured in after him. They carried rifles with fixed bayonets and many had machine gun belts draped over their shoulders. Two unarmed and fairly well dressed civilians were among them.

In a dramatic manner, the intruder loudly announced: "I, the Commander-in-Chief of our glorious proletarian troops, Colonel Mouravióv,* pronounce you, General, and all your staff arrested!"

Krassnóv's *sang-froid* was magnificent. Addressing his Chief-of-Staff, Colonel Popóv, in the silence which followed the Red's announcement, the General said firmly, but calmly: *"Pogovorítye s yétim merzávtzem!* (Talk to that scoundrel!)." He then turned to the officer who was sitting on his right and continued in a loud voice, which somehow managed not to sound affected, their conversation about some horseraces they had both seen in the past. The General was an excellent actor (the room could have been empty for all the concern he showed); he convincingly appeared to be oblivious of everything except his chat.

I glanced around. Everyone in our group had remained seated at the table, but all, except Krassnóv, had slightly turned their chairs to face the intruders. The right hands of all Cossack officers (again excepting Krassnóv) were in their pockets. Mine was too, clutching my automatic. The grimly determined expressions on the faces of my fellow-officers left no doubt as to what would happen if the Reds tried to move towards us. Their commander must have realized that too—also the obvious fact that he would be the first to be shot down if any firing started. He anxiously glanced back at his men who sensed his hesitation—the ones in front started backing, jamming the door behind them in the process. Out of the crowd stepped forward two or three of our Yennisséy Cossacks who had been on sentry duty downstairs when the Red mob rushed in, sweeping them along, but not disarming them in their hurry. The bearded Siberians now walked over to us and stood behind their seated officers, their rifles at the ready.

---

* I believe he was a gendarme officer (see p. 29) who a year later tried another about-face. The Reds, however, discovered his plan to switch to the side of Kolchák's White armies in Siberia and shot him for it.

The Red Colonel still stood halfway between the two opposing groups, but looked more and more uncomfortable. Our Chief-of-Staff, Colonel Popóv, slowly walked over towards him and inquired whether he was aware of the armistice that the Red emissary, the sailor Dybénko, had been negotiating. Mouravióv denied this and—when he heard that the terms included the arrest of Lenin and of Trótzky as well as of Kerensky—looked with dismay over his shoulder at the two unarmed civilians in his group, exclaiming: "How could comrade Dybénko have agreed to this!" Mouravióv then said that he regretted (*sozhaléyet*) not to have known any of this, or he would not have burst in the way he had done.

Colonel Popóv immediately seized on that and, turning to Krassnóv, formally reported: "Your Excellency, Colonel Mouravióv regrets his intrusion." "Oh, he regrets it? Well, I can talk to him then! But first get all this crowd out of the room!" And Krassnóv, as he turned to face Mouravióv, waved his arm towards the Red Guards and the sailors in the corner. He remained seated, leaning back with a relaxed air, one leg crossed over the other, his booted and spurred foot swinging slightly. The Red Colonel stood before him looking very much like a naughty boy facing his tutor. Krassnóv had clearly scored so far.

The Red Guards and sailors filed out of the room, but the two unarmed civilians stayed behind. It turned out that one of them was Trótzky * himself, and that the second was another member of the Council of People's Commissars, a Lithuanian by the name of Mitskévich. It was rapidly agreed that the third floor of the Palace was to remain in our sole occupation and that this was to be implemented immediately.

All Red Guards and sailors on our floor were gradually rounded up and were sent below by the efforts of joint Red and Cossack officer teams. Armed Yennisséy Cossack twin sentries were placed on the staircase landings with armed Red sailor twin guards a step or two below. Other sailors crowded behind.

Their mood was fairly jovial. As often happens with real fighting men after a battle, they did not seem to feel any rancor towards their opponents, and vice versa. I overheard the following exchange: "You are good fighters, Cossacks. Why don't you join us. Together we could beat anyone!" "You would have to do away with your black

---

* An alias; real name was Bronstein.

coats first,—you're much too easy to aim at now," retorted one of our Siberians. At that there was good-natured laughter from both sides of the sentry line on the stairway.

On returning to the room where our tea had been interrupted, I found our Captain Koulgávov arguing with Commissar Mitskévich. What were they aiming at, Koulgávov wanted to know, hadn't the French Revolution shown that universal freedom and equality was an unattainable dream? There was no question of that, replied the Lithuanian, what they were aiming at was the dictatorship of the proletariat—"You ruled before, now we will!"

Political debate was interrupted by the appearance of Kerensky's former orderly officer, Knírsha, still trailed by the same Yennisséy Cossack guard who had almost forcibly escorted him out of Krassnóv's room shortly before. Knírsha's mood had markedly improved since then. He was beaming all over as he announced: "Comrade Mitskévich, you have heard Comrade Trótzky order my release, but this man won't let me go!" Mitskévich haughtily told the Cossack to free Knírsha, but got the reply: *"A vy mnye chto, nachálstvo chto li boúdyete?* (And who are you, a boss of mine?)." He did not let Knírsha go until Krassnóv personally ordered him to do so. At the same time the General announced his promotion to corporal (*ouryádnik*) for devotion to duty. This was done in the presence of Trótzky and his group. I believe that this and other demonstrations of the sturdy Cossack spirit had much to do with the Reds deciding not to press things too far with us. We did not know it, but the fighting in Moscow had not yet ended.

At this point, the question could have well been raised as to who had actually captured and arrested whom. General Krassnóv and his Chief of Staff, Colonel Popóv, were closeted alone in a room with Trótzky, who had only his Red Colonel, Mouravióv, with him. Our armed sentries were all around them on the third floor, but we could never have gotten out of there by force, since the first and second floors were full of much more numerous armed Red Guards and sailors.

I do not know just what went on then between Krassnóv and Trótzky, but it is obvious that the General tried to use the advantage he had gained and attempted to negotiate. He had clearly shown that he was not going to let anyone push him around, especially in front of his subordinates, but he must have recognized the inevitability of compromise if any of us were to get out of there alive. It is then,

that is, at 1900 hours of November 1/14, that he must have made
and signed the deposition concerning Kerensky's escape which is
quoted as Document No. 1436 on pages 1810–1811 of Ref. 3 and as
Document No. 1169 on page 803 of Ref. 45. A careful reading of this
document will show that, although he does blame Kerensky for having escaped, only by implication does he deny having helped him
do so.

Some time later Trótzky and Mouravióv emerged from their conference with Krassnóv and left for Petrográd with their entourage
which now included Knírsha. It was announced that the General and
his Chief of Staff, Colonel Popóv, would follow them there on the
next morning for discussions with the rest of the Council of People's
Commissars. All of the other officers of his staff, including myself,
offered to accompany him there. On page 178 of his Ref. 34, Krassnóv wrote about this:

". . . but I asked to go with me only the son of my childhood
friend, Grísha Chebotarióv, who knew where my wife was and
who was to notify her, should anything happen. . . ."

### 4. *General Krassnóv Held at Smólny by the Reds*

The Red Lieutenant, Tarássov-Rodiónov, was to accompany the three of us to Petrográd. A car was provided for that
purpose and was waiting in a porte-cochère type of passage in the
walls of the Palace leading from a closed-in interior courtyard to a
big square in front of the building.

A crowd of sailors were standing in the courtyard, their rifles
stacked, and were listening to some speech by a prominent Bolshevik,
Roshál, who was haranguing them from the top of a truck. Infantry
reservists who had just arrived from Petrográd on foot were wandering about the square.

As we stepped out through a side door of the porte-cochère an in-
fantryman saw us and started yelling. Before we had time to get into
the car, a crowd of reservists had blocked the passage from the side
of the square. Angry shouts were heard: "We trudged all the way
from Petrográd . . . He gets a car . . . They will let him escape
too, like Kerensky. . . ." Some started loading their rifles.

In his memoirs, Ref. 34, Krassnóv made some not entirely complimentary remarks about Tarássov-Rodiónov's nervousness at that

moment. As I recollect what happened, this evaluation is not quite fair. Anyone would be nervous under the circumstances. However, the young Red lieutenant quickly made the General go back into the side door, standing between him and the menacing reservists until he was safely inside. He then called on the sailors for help—the latter willingly obliged upon an order from Roshál, who interrupted his harangue.

The sailor volunteers understandably felt contempt for the demoralized reserve infantry units who had fled at Púlkovo and who now, when all fighting was over, were back again at their noisy demonstrations. So the sailors dashed with fixed bayonets past our car and rapidly cleared the square in front of the Palace. We then got back into the car and quickly drove off. Only a couple of shots were fired after us, the bullets whizzing harmlessly by.

The road to Petrográd passed through Púlkovo and it was along it that the Reds had made their stand against us three days earlier. We looked with interest at the craters left by our shells and at the bloated corpses of Cossack horses shot down by our own fire.

The trip to Petrográd was uneventful. Colonel Popóv got into a political argument with our Red escort, Tarássov-Rodiónov, who, as a person, in my opinion, was quite likable. In the course of the conversation it turned out that not only he, but two of his brothers as well, had espoused radical ideas since early youth. That he nevertheless was accepted as a lieutenant in one of the infantry Guard regiments is another illustration of the complete dislocation of the customary order of things which resulted from the terrific battle casualties in the army during the preceding three years of war.

At Petrográd we drove to the Red Headquarters, which were located in the large buildings of the Smólny Institute, formerly a boarding school for girls of noble birth. We were all in uniform, with our sabres buckled on over our long cavalry-type topcoats. Tarássov-Rodiónov had asked us not to wear our service revolvers, but I had nevertheless taken with me my small automatic pistol, which fitted inconspicuously into my trouser pocket. None of us were searched and, in general, up to that point we were treated like delegates to a conference rather than prisoners.

At Smólny I was however separated from General Krassnóv and Colonel Popóv and was told that I would have to wait until they sent for me. I was then ushered into a large room which was full of officers and various other persons who had been arrested by the

Bolsheviks. Someone there recognized me and on seeing me enter wearing my sword mistakenly concluded that Krassnóv must have taken Petrográd and that I had come to free them. A flurry of pleased excitement resulted, but was replaced by deep gloom when I explained what the situation actually was.

I must have stayed in that room for at least an hour, keeping my topcoat on all the time, so as not to have to unbuckle my sword. A Red messenger finally arrived, saying that General Krassnóv wanted to see me. I followed him along several corridors which were swarming with armed and unarmed characters of proletarian appearance, into a small quite literally "smoke-filled" room, where the General and his Chief of Staff were sitting at a table. They had removed their topcoats and were conferring with several Reds, most of whom were civilians. I came to attention before the General, saluting him as smartly as I could.

Krassnóv told me, speaking slowly, and obviously weighing his words: "I have been asked to send you back to Gátchino to tell the troops there that I am staying here to continue negotiations. Of course you understand what you should say."

I did, the General had been arrested, but, naturally, I kept silent. I later learned that the Red argument was that nothing that Dybénko had said or agreed to was now valid, since by letting Kerensky escape, we had not fulfilled our part of the bargain.

Krassnóv continued: "I have composed a short written message for you to take along, but it has to be approved first by the Council of People's Commissars, where it now is and where you will receive it." After a slight pause, Krassnóv added: "And if you can, get Lýdia Fyódorovna * back to her apartment."

I then left with a Red officer and was asked to wait for Krassnóv's written message in front of the room where the Council of People's Commissars was meeting. There was a sign on its door: "Klássnaya Dáma," left over from the recent past when the building was a boarding school for girls. It was the same door which appears on the photograph bound opposite page 232 of John Reed's famous book, Ref. 52, and which is reproduced here as Fig. 25. However, the caption of that photograph incorrectly translates the sign which is visible on the door as meaning "Teacher's Room." Literally, it means "Class Lady." These were a species of female proctors whose job it was to

---

* Mrs. Krassnóva, his wife.

relieve the teachers from concern about discipline in a class of girls. Usually they were crotchety old spinsters or widows, who frequently sat at the very back of a classroom, facing the teacher and watching like hawks the behavior of their charges. In most cases they were enormously unpopular, and the name became a synonym in Russian society for pettily unpleasant attitudes. The fact that the new Red rulers started their formal meetings in a room thus inscribed of course provided a fertile field for sarcasm by their opponents during the Civil War which ensued.

I sat on a bench near the "Class Lady" door and chatted with the two Red Guard workmen who stood with fixed bayonets on each side of it, looking very much as they do in the photograph of John Reed's book. They did not know that I was a Cossack.

A couple of months earlier, the officers of the Cossack Guard Battery had voted to formally "accept" me as a regular officer, that is, to end the customary probation period (see p. 74). Since there could no longer be an Imperial Order confirming this, I was told to start immediately wearing the regular uniform of the Guard Horse Artillery. This meant that the broad red stripes of the Don Cossack army units on my trousers were removed and my shoulder straps were also changed (see Fig. b, p. 187).

Most of the Red officers at the time were still wearing their shoulder straps with the old insignia of rank. Thus only the shape of the hilt of my sword showed that I was a Cossack, a point lost on the militarily unsophisticated workmen-sentries, concerning which I naturally did not enlighten them.

They knew most of the men who went in and out of the room and told me who they were. I recall that one was the Commissar Lunachársky, but I was particularly interested to see Lenin * go into the room. He had a stubbly week-or-so-old growth on his chin and face, having shaved off his usual goatee-shaped beard when he went into hiding from Kerensky's agents after the failure of the July 1917 Bolshevik uprising. Apparently he started growing it again only when his present success was assured. Soviet paintings of the October-November 1917 events which I have seen portray him with his usual fullgrown beard, which definitely was not present when I saw him.

After a while, a Red officer came out of the room and told me that the transmission of General Krassnóv's written message to his troops

---

* An alias; real name was Ouliánov.

at Gátchino had not been approved by the Council of People's Commissars. However, I was authorized to proceed there and deliver the reassuring oral message he had given me.

The Red officer then led me to a car, a very fine open Rolls Royce, which, I was told, had belonged to the Grand Duke Mikhaíl Alexándrovich, the brother of the Tsar. Its chauffeur and his aide were ordered to take me to Gátchino, but were not told who I was. Nor did they know that the personal name-pass given me expired at 6 P.M., that is, a couple of hours later, permitting a trip in one direction only. In the general confusion of those days the Reds probably did not feel it necessary to take any special precautions with anyone who looked quite as young as I did then.

When we arrived at Gátchino, I ordered my two Red drivers to stop in the square in front of the Palace and to wait for me there. My general attitude was one of uncommunicative aloofness, to give them the impression that mine was some important mission which I was not at liberty to disclose. This did not prove too difficult, since they had seen me come out of the Bolshevik Smólny Headquarters.

In the Gátchino Palace, I told Colonel Márkov, a Cossack artillery officer who had been left in command there, all that I had seen and heard. In his office I changed the figure "6" on my Bolshevik pass to "o" and placed a "1" in front of it making it all look like "10," extending thereby the validity of the pass by a vital four hours. I then left the Palace and drove to the house where Mrs. Krassnóva was staying. It was already pitch dark.

There was an unpleasant moment when a patrol of Red sailors suddenly surrounded us with angry exclamations that Krassnóv himself was known to have visited that house. Bluff saw me through that one—not only my Smólny pass, but especially the unmistakably genuine proletarian cursing of my two Red drivers proved of great help.

The outcome was that Mrs. Krassnóva and her suitcases were safely installed in the car. In a letter to me sent almost twenty-three years later (August 21, 1940) she reminisced about this as follows:

". . . And do you remember that awful evening when you came to fetch me at my sister's in Gátchino and informed me that P[*iótr*] N[*ikoláyevich Krassnóv*] had been arrested by the Bolsheviks. I remember how I then wanted to stand up and felt that I could not—my feet did not obey me. Then I controlled myself and we drove to Petersburg through Púlkovo where carcasses of horses were lying along the sides of the road since the recent battle. What a difficult night it was, and how grateful I was to you that you were with me. . . ."

In Petrográd I took the precaution of not driving up to the doorway of the house in which Mrs. Krassnóva's apartment was located on the second or the third floor. Instead, the car was stopped before turning the last corner, the suitcases were left in it, and we walked to the house entrance and up the flight of stairs. There I rang the bell, knowing that a maid was staying at the apartment.

I was never more startled in my life than when the door opened immediately and two sailor sentries with fixed bayonets confronted me. General Krassnóv's voice could be heard from the drawingroom, which adjoined the hallway. There was nothing left to do but to wave the sailors aside, letting Mrs. Krassnóva walk in ahead of me.

After the first greetings of husband and wife were over, a Red officer whom I had seen at Smólny that morning inquired how I happened to get there, when it was well past six o'clock? My answer was that my pass had been extended, but he looked suspicious and went to the telephone to check with Red headquarters. Fortunately the telephone was in the General's study, two rooms away from the entrance hall.

I told the General that I had to be out of his apartment in less than a minute—Mrs. Krassnóva's suitcases would be left on the sidewalk round the corner. What was I to report to Colonel Márkov in Gátchino? The General replied that he had signed a pledge not to communicate with his troops, but he could not forbid me from reporting what I had seen. I saluted and left.

The most difficult moment came immediately after that, when I had to pass the Red sailor sentries in the hall, forcing myself to approach them with an unhurried step and an unconcerned air of authority. Apparently I succeeded in this, because they drew themselves up and one of them opened the door for me. I returned the salute and stepped out.

On the landing below I could not resist accelerating my pace, but slowed down again before rounding the corner. My Red drivers helped to quickly pile up Mrs. Krassnóva's luggage on the sidewalk, and we sped off again into the night on our way back to Gátchino. I felt anxious until we got out of Petrográd without being stopped. Further on, the telephone lines were still down.

In Gátchino I dismissed with thanks my car and its drivers and went to report to Colonel Márkov that he no longer could count on receiving instructions from General Krassnóv and would have to rely solely on his own judgment. I spent the night in his office, leaving at dawn. I could not be of any further use there, nor was it safe for me to stay, so first I headed for home at Tsárskoye Seló.

It did not seem too simple to get back there. No trains were running yet and I had to use the old frontline technique of walking to the Gátchino-Tsárskoye Seló highway and trying to hitchhike a ride. When a truck appeared in the distance I stepped out into the middle of the road with raised hand to stop it. As it pulled up, I was not entirely happy to find that it was packed full with standing armed Red guards, but again tried to appear unconcerned as I questioned them. It turned out that they were volunteer workmen on their way back to their factories near Oust-Izhóra—that meant that they would have to pass through Tsárskoye Seló. I asked them to give me a lift. I was asked: "And who are you? Shtabnói? [*from Headquarters?*]." I answered in the affirmative, of course without specifying which Headquarters, and climbed into the seat next to the truckdriver and the Red detachment commander. Discouraging further conversation did not prove too difficult.

Mother happened to be at home when I got back. There was a joyful reunion, and I spent some time telling her all about my adventures and listening to what had happened in my absence. She wrote it down shortly afterwards (Ref. 6).

I find a few discrepancies between her notes and my own recollections, as given above, but they are not important.

However, there are two discrepancies between my recollections and General Krassnóv's memoirs (Ref. 34).

A major discrepancy is the General's statement on page 183 of Ref. 34, if it is taken literally: "I sent Chebotarióv with a car to Gátchino so that my wife could move to Petrográd." This definitely was not the case, since otherwise I would not have had the trouble with changing the time on my Red pass. Perhaps General Krassnóv just forgot some details which seemed unimportant to him at the time among the many others he had to deal with, but which stuck better in my memory since they were the major ones I had to cope with.

But another explanation is possible. On page 190 of Ref. 34, the General states: "The present description has been made by me from

my diaries and from memory in July 1920." The Russian Civil War
was not entirely over then, but was definitely lost by the Whites—
only Baron Wrangell's troops were holding out in the Crimea. Krassnóv had already been abroad for some time and could not know
that his successor had sent me abroad too as interpreter (see Chapter 8). Krassnóv may have feared that I had fallen into the hands
of the Reds during the White retreat of 1919–1920, and did not wish
to write anything about my past activities that would have made
things more difficult for me had I survived and had I been left behind in the U.S.S.R. In his memoirs he does not even refer to me
by my rank, low as it was. On the other hand, when he knew that
I was safely abroad too, he wrote quite differently about this (see
Figs. 26 and 30). The reference to me in the latter photocopy as:
"the first Don partizán [*guerrilla*]" makes no sense unless it had in
mind my performance on November 2/15, 1917, after the first field
battle of the Russian Civil War three days earlier.

The translation from the Russian of Fig. 26 reads as follows:

"5 December 1927           "I was unable to learn anything
No. 698                    about Nik. Iv. Doubiágsky * and
Santeny                    I do not know where he is."
                                                      "P.K."

"Dear Grísha,

"Thank you for not forgetting us, old friends of your parents who
love you firmly and tenderly. I shall never forget the chivalrous
courage of your behaviour ten years ago in the terrible days of
November 1917, and how I am indebted to you for Lýdia Fyódorovna's † finding herself with me and my being able to get
her out of Petersburg, away from the Bolsheviks. . . ."

Things had been rather hectic at Tsárskoye Seló too. The electrical
engineer who had switched off the power, plunging the town into
darkness to the Cossack advantage during their retreat after the
Púlkovo battle, was brought dying to Mother's hospital. It was
claimed that he had shot himself, but Mother notes that the nature
of his head wound and the embarrassed behavior of the pro-Red soldiers who brought him in indicated that this was not so. There had
been a number of other murders in the town after the Bolsheviks

* The author's maternal uncle.
† Mrs. Krassnóva.

moved in. A priest who had initiated and led a religious procession through the streets during the battle was killed later.

Nobody had been touched at the hospital, because Mother, in her capacity of senior sister of mercy there, had personally called at the local Soviet demanding—and obtaining—a protective Red guard for the wounded to keep out various ruffians who were wandering about.

All of my friends were thoroughly scared however, as I soon discovered, even though none of them had taken part in any action on the Kerensky side—he was much too unpopular then among members of Petrográd society.

The leave from my battery was about to expire, and on the next day, November 4/17, I left for the Southwestern Front. My "vacation" was over.

Attached to my mother's diary (page 73 of Ref. 6b) is a letter written by me on November 12/25, 1917, shortly after my return to the Guards Battery. It describes how I traveled magnificently till Kíev (the capital of the Ukraine) having obtained at Mogilióv a place in a Staff railroad car with the help of an English officer with whom I became friendly on the way. The rest of the journey was much less agreeable and rapid in a car with broken window panes; nevertheless, I managed to get better accommodation than the other passengers, having occupied a place on the upper luggage shelf in good time, while the train was being assembled on the reserve tracks. Naturally, one had to climb in through the window. In spite of a number of incidents on the way—such as a tea kettle with boiling water turning over on my feet (my top boots saved me), an avalanche of suitcases almost burying a passenger as they fell from a broken luggage shelf, and numerous fistfights between exasperated travelers, I had reached the Battery quite safely.

Meanwhile, Mother had been permitted to visit the Krassnóvs at their Petrográd apartment. On page 71 of her diary, Ref. 6b, she writes:

"6th [*19th*] N[*ovember*]. Today I went to the city . . . [*Mother describes how she managed to get some money from her bank account*] . . . I visited Lidoúsha [*Mrs. Krassnóva*]. The poor things are living as if they were on coals—at the Smólny the promise to release them is being repeatedly delayed. At the moment it is scheduled for five in the morning tomorrow. Yesterday they were again taken to an interrogation—I am terribly

afraid that if they are released, they may be put out of the
way, as happened to the unfortunate Piótr Petróvich [*Karachán, an artillery general, who was murdered*]. Every time the
door bell rings, Lidoúsha shudders, expecting new misfortunes.
And how awful may be the moment of their departure—again a
raging crowd will gather, as it did in Gátchino. Hooliganlike-
looking Red Guards are wandering near the house. Once more I
appreciated my sister-of-mercy uniform—in any crowd the way
will be yielded, and help will be given to enter a streetcar. Today
an entire group of ferocious 'comrades' protected me in the
crush, demanded that the conductor return the change for my
ticket, and at the stop carefully helped me out, handing the
potatoes over the heads of others. And these same good-natured
men the day before had been martyrizing the *yúnkers* [*i.e., military cadets*], threw them into the water, howled and beat them—
judging by the stories they told in the streetcar."

The Krassnóvs were released by the Red command after all. As
I understand it, a strong point which influenced this decision in the
General's favor was the fact that he had been acting throughout
under the direct and personal orders of Kerensky, who at that time
could still claim to be his legal Commander in Chief. The events in
the Gátchino Palace where for a while we held Trótzky and Mouravióv on the third floor, but then let them go, also had some effect,
since they made the Reds feel that they had to reciprocate.

To page 73 of Mother's journal, Ref. 6b, together with my letter
of November 12/25, just mentioned, are attached letters dated November 13/26 from General Krassnóv and November 14/27 from his
wife. Both were mailed from the little town of Velíkye Loúki, near
Pskov, to the south of Petrográd, where they rejoined what was left
of the scattered and by then completely demoralized IIIrd Cavalry
Corps. The General wrote:

". . . how have you weathered this storm, this terrible whirl-
wind, which uproots old oaks, topples strong vigorous trees, and
after which rise again only weak reeds and proudly float to the
surface in the chaos of darkness and lawlessness *póshlyi* [*lowly*]
natures? How is the *mílyi* [*dear*] youth, Grigóriy Porfírievich?
How did he get back to his battery, and what awaited him
there . . ."

But the storm was only beginning.

# 5 Fighting the Reds in the Don Under Atamán Kaledín

## 1. Return of the Guard Battery to the Don

Our battery had been withdrawn from the Stohód River positions and was held in the general army reserves of the Southwestern Front. It was frequently moved about from one Ukrainian village to another.

The morale of the men in the Battery was very poor and was getting worse and worse as time went on. It improved temporarily when early in December 1917 (old style) arrived the news that the anti-Bolshevik Cossack government in the Don, headed by its Atamán, General Kaledín,* had decided to recall home all Cossack units. There was no longer any point in keeping them on the Austro-German front, which had completely disintegrated by that time. Most of the infantry had deserted and had gone home; the Bolshevik Government was firmly installed in Moscow and in Petrográd and was in the process of arranging a separate peace with the Central Powers. The Cossacks obviously could not continue the struggle alone.

The Brigade of Cossack Guards was thereupon concentrated in the area of Shepetóvka (Map B, p. 80), a large railroad junction, and entrained there. Our battery went in two or three trains with several squads of the Leib-Guard Atamánsky Regiment in each. They continuously kept an officer with a machine gun crew on the locomotives and a similar guard was installed on the rear platforms. Everyone was in constant readiness for an alert. The revolutionary turbulence of the Ukraine, which we crossed from west to east, made such precautions essential.

I think it took us almost two weeks to cover the eight hundred miles or so to the Don capital of Novocherkássk (see Maps A, p. 44, and E, p. 142). Time and again we had to use the threat of force to obtain changes of locomotives at various stations—the great majority of railroad workmen were violently pro-Bolshevik. Only here and

---

* The accent is here put on the last syllable as customary in the Don. In the north, his name is frequently pronounced Kalédin.

there did we encounter small groups of Ukrainian nationalists, who played an entirely insignificant role in the development of events.

We tried to avoid large Ukrainian cities, such as Kíev and Ekaterinosláv (present-day Dniepropetróvsk), which had large and strongly pro-Bolshevik workingclass populations. For that reason we crossed the Dniépr River over the Kichkáss Bridge, some distance to the south of Ekaterinosláv. It was here however that we barely averted disaster.

One morning I was awakened by a sudden decrease of speed and braking of our train, and by a long burst of machinegun fire from the direction of our locomotive. Then there was a sharp jolt as the motion was reversed, but our car appeared to have been derailed, since it slowly bumped over each railroad tie before finally stopping. We all got out to see what had happened. We were on a high curving embankment protruding from a sea of dense early-morning fog which enveloped its base and the surrounding fields. A large bridge loomed just ahead of us.

When the rising sun finally dispelled the fog, we found that the embankment we were on was unusually high; we were later told that this was the highest railroad fill in all South Russia at that time. It connected in a curve to the Kichkáss Bridge across the Dniépr River, which was fairly wide at that point. A railroad station was on the opposite (left) bank.

Local Ukrainian Bolsheviks had been forewarned of our approach and had tried to derail us. They held a locomotive under steam in readiness at the station, and when the rumbling of our approaching train was heard in the distance, sent it at us along our track—empty. The Red trainman jumped off it as it began gathering speed on their side of the bridge. The place for the collision could not have been better chosen from their point of view. The curvature of the embankment and of the track enhanced the probability of a derailment, which would have sent most of our train hurtling down along the high slopes, smashing the cars, the men and horses in them on the rocks below.

Fortunately for us, our Cossack Guards on the engine were wide awake. Our heavy machine gun there opened up immediately at the locomotive as it was sighted and continued firing at it as it rushed head on at them. Its boiler was riddled with bullets, lost much steam through the holes and, instead of continuing to gather speed, the locomotive slowed down because of lack of power. Other Cossacks of the

Guard prevented the terrified local engine driver from jumping off our locomotive, and forced him to apply the brakes. As a result the collision was comparatively mild. No one was hurt, but several cars, including the one I had been in, jumped the tracks. This immobilized our train.

We had no equipment with which to jack the cars back onto the rails. Foot patrols were sent across the bridge but found that the railroad yards there were completely deserted—even the station-master had fled, fearing reprisals.* We got some horses out of the cars with the help of an improvised ramp and sent mounted patrols out to the neighboring villages to seek out fugitive railroad employees, promising immunity and a bonus in cash to anyone who returned to his post. This worked, but we spent over a day on the right bank of the Dniépr River before we were able to resume our journey. The rest of it was uneventful.

On reaching the Don region, our train passed through the towns of Taganróg, Rostóv and Novocherkássk and continued north to the station Glubókaya (see Map E, p. 142) where we detrained, taking up quarters in the large *khútor* (village), Beriózov, a couple of miles away.

This was the first time I had been in the land of my Don Cossack forefathers and I was strongly and favorably impressed by the solid patriarchal way of life which still prevailed there in the countryside—especially because of the contrast it provided with the state of revolutionary anarchy we had left behind us in the Ukraine.

The home of my orderly happened to be only some 10 miles away, and I gave him leave to go there soon after we were quartered at Beriózov. He invited me and my friend, *Sótnik* (First Lieutenant) Zinóvy Krassnóv (not a relative of General Piótr Krassnóv) to visit him, so a few days later the two of us rode out alone across the frozen snow-covered steppe to his *khútor*. The country in that part of the Don region is undulating, with many ravines, very much like parts of northern Texas which I saw years later. We found the village to be comparatively small, only a dozen or so families living there in well-to-do style, that is, for Russian peasant farmers, of course. The

---

* The plight of the lower-level railroad administrative personnel in those days was tragic indeed. Most of them tried to stick to their jobs and keep traffic moving, obeying the orders of any political group which happened militarily to occupy their station at that moment. All too frequently this only led to their being shot when an opposing faction occupied their yards.

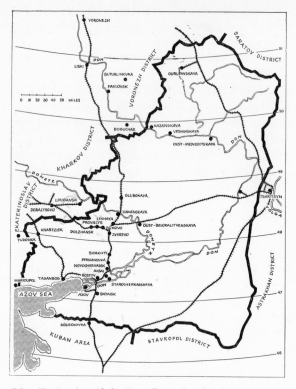

Map E.   Region of the Don Cossacks. *See Map A, p. 44.*

individual wooden houses were large and clean and surrounded by yards and barns.

My orderly's father was still living there and he acted host with perfect dignity and graciousness—very much the ruling patriarch of his family, used to exercising his authority. As in most Cossack homes, his service sword and a faded photograph of him in uniform hung in a place of honor on a wall.

His highest rank in the service was that of a corporal, nevertheless, at the end of the luncheon, Lieutenant Krassnóv, with customary Cossack deference to age, asked his permission to smoke. The old man was pleased to grant it to his guests, but did not smoke himself. When I stretched out my cigarette case to my orderly, to my amazement he declined with thanks. I could not imagine what had happened to him, having shared my cigarettes with him for the past ten months. However, when we walked out later into the yard, he asked me himself for a cigarette, explaining that it would have been discourteous for him (although he was in his thirties!) to smoke in his father's presence when the old man did not smoke himself.

The dinner was quite ceremonious. We were seated between two local elders, men in their sixties, both of whom were veterans of the Russo-Turkish war of 1877. For this occasion they wore their combat decorations and medals on their tunics of old-fashioned cut. A barrel of home-brewed *samogón* * (vodka) was rolled out and was served in tea-sized glasses. Toasts to our Guard Battery, to the village, to Don Cossacks in general, to our Atamán Kaledín and others were proposed and drunk in accordance with custom at one breath, the glass being then turned over one's head to show that nothing was left in it. I don't remember anything after the fourth or the fifth round. That was all right, since it was a point of honor for a village host to drink his guests to unconsciousness.

I came to the next morning in a comfortable bed with the most splitting headache I ever had before or since—there could be no doubt that the *samogón* had plenty of fusel oils left in it. Rubbing snow over my face and head helped somewhat, but both Zinóvy Krassnóv and I were glad when we finally mounted our horses and rode back to our quarters at Beriózov, enjoying the frosty air on the way.

Not all family reunions of returning frontline Cossacks were as harmonious as in the case of my orderly. The old Cossack in whose house I had a room told me a number of amusing stories of clashes which were occurring at Beriózov between representatives of the old patriarchal order and young Cossacks who had been influenced by Bolshevik ideas at the German front.

One young fellow came home on leave from his unit to his family house on our street. The first person he met there was his grandfather, whom he cheerfully addressed as "Comrade grandpa (*dyéd*)." The old man did not say a word in reply but took his *nagáyka* † off the

---

* Literally meaning "self-chased." Prior to 1914 the production of vodka was a State Monopoly in Imperial Russia, but it was stopped completely after the start of World War I. This led to home-built stills appearing in practically every village all over Russia. Usually the stuff did not have all of its fusel oils removed, which caused terrific hangovers.

† Cossack riding whip (see p. 28).

wall on which it was hanging and belabored his grandson with it until he apologized.

In another home the widowed mother used feminine guile instead of force. She sent her frontline son to her *lyédnik* * under the pretext of fetching something and then bolted and locked the door from the outside, letting him freeze there in the darkness until he promised to behave respectfully.

## 2. *Pro-Red Mutiny in the Don*

A glance is needed at developments in the Don region after the February 1917 Revolution in order to understand what was about to happen there—a brief sketch of Cossack origins has already been given by me on pp. 3 and 4.

Since the reign of Peter the Great, that is, for 200 years, the Atamáns of the Don Cossacks were appointed by the Tsars. Their role was essentially that of combined military and civilian governor of the entire area. After the fall of the Tsarist Government, a movement rapidly gained ground in the Don for the reintroduction of old Cossack customs and the election of an Atamán. (This paralleled similar developments among frontline Cossack troops, described on pp. 98–100). A *Voyskovóy Kroug,* meaning literally "Army Circle," but in effect a Cossack Parliament, met at Novocherkássk in June, 1917, and elected as their Atamán the General Alexéi Maxímovich Kaledín. He was a Don Cossack who had won fame as the Commander of the Imperial Russian Army which had successfully spearheaded the so-called Brussílov Breakthrough of 1916, and thereby substantially helped relieve the German pressure on Verdun and the Austro-Hungarian pressure on Italy (see pp. 50–52).

Kaledín followed a policy of support for the Russian Provisional Government in Petrográd headed by Kerensky. He had been elected by Don Cossacks only, who were an armed minority of the inhabitants of the region which bears their name.† Kaledín and the Don

---

* A sod-covered underground outdoor cellar filled with large blocks of ice sawed from rivers or ponds in the winter to permit preservation of food in the summer.

† Exact population figures are not available for that time. However, the processes which had reduced Cossacks to some 47 percent by the early 1890s (see p. 4 and Ref. 67) continued at an accelerated rate and it is reasonable to assume that by 1917 Cossacks did not exceed some 40 percent of the total number of inhabitants of their region.

Cossack regional government which he formed repeatedly tried to obtain cooperation of the non-Cossack majority of the area which largely consisted of factory and dock workers, coal miners and poorer peasants with less land than most Cossacks. However, these local non-Cossacks consistently elected Bolshevik sympathizers for their representatives. As a result, further elections in the Don were limited to the Cossack minority only. In an attempt to coordinate their anti-Bolshevik efforts, representatives of the Don, the Kubán, and the Térek Cossack armies met on October 20, 1917, and formed a "Yúgo-Vostóchnyi Soyúz" (Southeastern Alliance).* Its aim was to fight Bolshevik anarchy on the territory of the Alliance and to provide mutual support for the purpose of maintaining order and legality within the Alliance until the All-Russian Constituent Assembly met and determined Russia's future form of government and the status of the Cossack regions as well. Thus there was no separatism about the movement; on the contrary, it was aimed at maintaining the over-all unity of Russia.

The President of the "Voyskovóy Kroug" (Don Cossack Parliament), V. Kharlámov, was one of the two Don Cossack representatives on the governing body of the Southeastern Alliance. In Ref. 11, Vol. 2, pages 284–285, he makes the following relevant comments:

> "The creation of the Southeastern Alliance at the end of 1917 represents one of the attempts to organize the Cossacks on a country-wide scale for the purpose of counteraction to the raging popular masses. . . . The idea of state unity and the sovereignty of the future All-Russian Constituent Assembly were carefully protected by the Cossacks. . . ."

The non-Cossack majority of the area, which was largely of Russian and Ukrainian peasant stock, with some Armenians and Greeks in the cities, did not however take kindly to Cossack tutelage of

---

* A consultant to the United States Congress in the preparation of the no-torious so-called Captive Nations law, U.S. Public Law 86–90, states in a letter to *The New York Times*, February 9, 1960, that on this date (October 20, 1917): "Cossackia was established by the popular will of the people concerned." It should be noted that the term "Cossackia" was not heard of till some ten years later when it was "discovered" in Central Europe between the two world wars to promote the dismemberment of Russia in the coming conflict. There had been no such state in reality, nor was there ever any expression of the "popular will" in the area on the matter, see pp. 357–359, 361 for the tragic significance of this and other "errors" by our Congress.

regional affairs, nor to their historical claims to sole ownership of the area's natural resources.

Bolshevik ideas found a fertile ground in this situation. A Red Guard uprising took place in the industrial and port city of Rostóv at the mouth of the Don River, but was rapidly put down by White volunteer detachments a couple of weeks before our battery and other Cossack units returned from the German front.

The later informed consensus was that Atamán Kaledín should have done what the Reds did, namely, he should have disbanded the militarily useless war-weary frontline and reserve units who had lost all discipline, and he should then have formed new units around a hardcore of dedicated volunteers.

The formation of White volunteer detachments did go ahead in the Don, but almost exclusively under the auspices of a group of generals who were not Don Cossacks—Kornílov, Alexéyev and Deníkin—and to whom Atamán Kaledín had given asylum to permit the creation of their White troops. Dedicated officers from all over Russia made their way to their colors. Most of the younger men had to serve as privates and at the start many detachments of what became later the large Volunteer Army were composed solely of officers. Most of them were quartered at Rostóv.

A volunteer unit of some 500 men under Don Cossack Captain Chernetzóv was the first to be organized at Novocherkássk by Atamán Kaledín's government.

Atamán Kaledín had not been at the German front for several months and did not fully realize the extent to which the Cossack troops had been contaminated there by Bolshevik propaganda. He overestimated the importance of the fact that there had virtually been no desertions whatsoever from the German front among them, and that they had been the only organized units of the Russian Army to come home intact and only under orders. So he deployed the weary veterans who arrived first, including our battery, along the northern borders of the Don region. This proved to be a fatal mistake.

The Reds began concentrating opposite them their own volunteer Red Guards from the north and forming new units in the mining regions of the Ukraine to the west. They were, however, very careful not to cross the borders of the Don region.

Instead they sent swarms of propagandists who took the following line: The Bolsheviks had no quarrel with the Cossack rank-and-file.

. . . It was only Kornílov's volunteer White Guards that they wanted to oust from the Don before they became capable of offensive action. . . . If the Cossacks did not want to fight their Atamán Kaledín, why did they not just go home for a well-earned rest and let the Red Guards eliminate the Whites?

This propaganda line was remarkably successful. One could hear from reasonable and moderate Cossacks: "We can't fight all of Russia," or, "If you young officers are so eager to fight—well—go and fight. We will go home and watch you!" The end result was that most of the dependable men went home and mostly active or potential pro-Reds remained. The officers of the Battery sensed that they could no longer control coming events and the majority took or prolonged their leaves.

I had nowhere to go, not having had time to establish contact with relatives in the Don. So I stayed with the Battery at Beriózov, near Glubókaya in the north. Only one other young officer, Lieutenant Khopiórsky, stayed on with Colonel Souvórov who had been appointed to command the battery on its return to the Don.*

This was the situation in our battery when a surprise raid on the Red Headquarters of the Donétz mining basin by the Don Cossack Captain Chernetzóv triggered the up-to-then incipient pro-Red mutiny in our battery and other units of the northern front. It was the most daringly successful single exploit of the Russian Civil War that I know of, although its long-range results were more than questionable.

Captain Chernetzóv's 500-man *partizán* (guerrilla) detachment was living in four or five trains which were standing on reserve tracks of the Novocherkássk railroad station. The locomotive and some passenger cars which served as living quarters were in the center of each train; at their ends were uncovered freight cars, their walls reinforced with concrete which in combat could give additional protection to several 3-inch field guns and to heavy machineguns, some of which were housed in armored turrets. The subsequent exploits of Chernetzóv's guerrillas earned them the nickname of "railroad cavalry."

Through his intelligence agents, Captain Chernetzóv learned in January, 1918, that a conference of Red Guard commanders was taking place at the Ukrainian railroad junction Debáltzevo, in the

---

* Souvórov had begun his service under my father's command, but soon transferred to an army battery, apparently after finding that he could not afford the prestige expenses in the Guards.

pro-Red Donétz coal basin, some 30 miles away from the Don border and 100 miles from Novocherkássk (see Map E, p. 142). He immediately decided to wipe out there with one stroke the entire local High Command of the Reds. There does not seem to be any evidence to show whether he did this on his own, or with the knowledge and approval of Atamán Kaledín. Everything happened quite suddenly and unexpectedly.

At this time regular railroad traffic was still moving across the Don borders. In the evening of the day Chernetzóv heard about the Red conference, a regularly scheduled Rostóv-Debáltzevo passenger train steamed into the Novocherkássk station. As the railroad telegraph operator signaled its departure to the next station, he was suddenly seized by some of Chernetzóv's men who disconnected the telegraph and all telephones. Then, instead of the passenger train, Chernetzóv's semiarmored trains steamed out north, the one in the lead having its locomotive in front like an ordinary train.

The leading train stopped just short of the next railroad station building and several men in railroad uniforms got out and walked towards it. There, suddenly drawing their guns, they overpowered the telegraph operator. One of these Chernetzóv guerrillas was a railroad signal corps officer. He gave the departure signal of the supposed passenger train to the next station and immediately severed all telegraph and telephone lines. The process was repeated at each stop until Captain Chernetzóv's armed convoy arrived before Debáltzevo in the middle of the night with no one there suspecting that anything but a harmless passenger train had stopped at the edge of the station.

Chernetzóv's infantry disembarked from the rear trains unnoticed in the darkness and deployed in a wide circle around the lighted station settlement to intercept any fugitives. Then Chernetzóv himself suddenly steamed forward with the lead train, all his machine guns blazing away at the railroad station building. He had been correctly informed that the Red conference had been taking place in its main large waiting room, and that its numerous participants were sleeping on its floor.

I heard a vivid account of this from men I knew who were with Chernetzóv and who rushed in after him into the station's waiting room, guns at the ready, as he ordered: "Hands up!" All, except for the few dead and seriously wounded, complied; a man in front with a bullet through one arm struggled to hold it up with the other.

On Chernetzóv's order a couple of heavy machine guns were rolled in and were trained on the scared and silent crowd; then a list of some forty names of presumed leaders was read.

Chernetzóv announced that if by the time he finished counting ten these men did not step forward to surrender, the machineguns would open fire immediately and kill everyone in the place. He then started counting slowly amidst general silence. When he said "eight," several men stepped forward from the crowd and were taken aside to identify themselves; others were pushed forward by their "comrades." All of them were then taken out onto the railroad tracks and were all shot; I do not know what happened to the rest whose names were not on the list.

Chernetzóv quickly returned to Novocherkássk with his convoy.

There can be no doubt that Chernetzóv's raid thoroughly disrupted the military preparations of the Reds in the Donétz basin, since for at least two weeks after that they were unable to mount any offensive operations from that direction. But at the same time this raid triggered a pro-Red mutiny among the Don Cossack troops on the northern border and within less than two weeks Captain Chernetzóv was to be taken prisoner and cut down by the sabre of the leader of that mutiny, sub-Lieutenant Podtiólkov of our Guard Battery.

While Chernetzóv was attacking Debáltzevo, a conference of delegates of Don Cossack troops stationed on the northern border was taking place at Kámenskaya. This time it was Podtiólkov (see pp. 82; 99) who had been elected to represent our battery there.

I believe it must have been on January 11/24, 1918, within a day or two, that we heard the results of the Kámenskaya meeting. All officers and men were summoned by our battery Soviet to assemble at the Beriózov village schoolhouse to hear an important message which had just arrived from Podtiólkov. We went, knowing nothing about Chernetzóv's raid on Debáltzevo.

The large room of the schoolhouse was already packed with our men as Colonel Souvórov, Lieutenant Khopiórsky and I made our way through the crowd and sat down near a table occupied by three members of the battery Soviet. Its chairman, a semi-educated but very smart clerk, read the message from Podtiólkov which informed us of Chernetzóv's sudden attack on the Bolshevik headquarters at Debáltzevo, denounced him and Atamán Kaledín, and described what had subsequently happened at the Kámenskaya Conference. The delegates of the Cossack troops there had decided to take action themselves against Captain Chernetzóv's partizáns and the Atamán

Kaledín and to form a Don Military Revolutionary Committee for the purpose. They had elected as their chairman our sub-Lieutenant Podtiólkov.

In this capacity Podtiólkov now ordered the battery to get ready for action against the "counterrevolutionary" Whites to the south. Any officers who refused to lead the coming expedition were to be arrested and brought to his headquarters at Kámenskaya.

Our Cossacks shouted their approval. The chairman of the battery Soviet then turned to Colonel Souvórov and asked him whether he would comply with the order. Souvórov started on a rambling speech expressing his sympathy for their ideas and feelings but his disagreement with their "tactics."

The Chairman of the Soviet sensed his hesitation and interrupted him with a rapid string of questions which developed something like this: "You said, Mr. Colonel, that you sympathize with our ideas, didn't you?"—"Yes."—"Then you recognize our principles?"—"I do."—"In that case you will continue serving with us?"—"Yes."— "Of course you would not want to serve as a private, so, will you serve as our commander?"—"I will."—"Will you lead us into battle?" —"I . . . I . . . will."—"Will you fire on the White Guards?"— —"Ye--es."—"Hurrah to our Revolutionary Commander!"

When the ensuing hubbub had subsided, the Chairman of the battery Soviet turned to me with a smile of pleasure at my coming discomfiture. A number of other men who had tangled with me orally at past meetings also looked happy at what was coming. A particularly broad grin of anticipation was on the face of a Cossack who came from one of the poorest northern districts. His name was Ponomarióv. He was a ruddy faced somewhat plump man with little intelligence but a great store of pent-up hatred which frequently moved him to violent, but not very coherent, outbursts. At one time he used to end such outbursts by yelling a Bolshevik slogan of the period: "Enough! For three hundred years you have sucked our blood!"—a reference to the three centuries of rule by the Románov dynasty. However, Ponomarióv's far from anemic ruddy complexion used to give me the opportunity to start my comments by joking about the discrepancy between his appearance and his "bloodsucking" slogan. The Cossacks, who had a good sense of humor, used to roar with laughter on such occasions. The fellow loathed me as a result. Now he seemed to be figuratively "licking his chops."

The Chairman of the battery Soviet addressed me sarcastically: "And what do *you* have to say, Gospodín (Mr.) Práporschik?"

I got up and made a short speech: I said that the Battery meant more to me than it did to anyone else in the room; I had been born and I had spent my childhood there and had always been used to speak of it as *násha* (our) battery; I had begun my military service with them, but I could not fight with them against our lawful Atamán Kaledín. At the same time I certainly would not want to fight against them and I was therefore willing to promise to go home to Tsárskoye Seló in the north and abstain from participation in the fighting so long as they existed as a unit on the Red side—something that I was sure would not be for long. However, if they arrested me, I would escape and fight against them "with weapons in my hands."

This was pure nineteen-year-old bravado and a mistake, since I only had a very vague idea as to how I could escape. The thought had crossed my mind of hurling at any assailants a kerosene lamp which stood on the edge of the adjoining table and which had already been lit because of the gathering dusk, of firing a couple of shots close over their heads as I broke open the window behind me, then mounting one of the horses which were tethered in the yard, and trying to gallop in the approaching night through the steppe to my orderly's village nearby where I could count on further help to get away.

As I finished speaking, Ponomarióv roared, "He mocks us!" and started to rise from his seat in the front row of school desks shouting, "*Sorvát pogóny!* (Rip off his shoulder straps!)." This was considered a supreme insult to an officer and was frequently indulged in by revolutionary mobs in those days.

In an instinctive reaction, my right hand swiftly went to my trouser pocket and to the automatic in it. But, before I could draw my gun, a hysterical-sounding shout came from the back of the room: "*Tova-á-rischy! Ou nyegó bómba!* (Comrades! He has a bomb!)." I do not know who the man was who shouted, but there was something about his voice which made Ponomarióv and a couple of others who had started to rise plump back into their seats. I remained standing with my right hand in my pocket.

The Chairman of the Soviet pretended to busy himself with some papers on his desk, at the edge of which I was standing. Colonel Souvórov got up and went in the opposite direction through the adjoining door to the teachers' room, which had no other exit. Lieutenant Khopiórsky however stood up and, although no one had asked him and in spite of his being unarmed, announced his complete solidarity with me and remained standing at my side. He was a quiet fellow who had been shell-shocked a couple of years earlier on the German front and who had never participated in any of the debates at meetings with the men. For that reason, although he was my senior, he had been bypassed in the questioning. He now showed his mettle.

There was no reaction to his statement, but the Chairman of the Soviet politely asked me what was it I had in my pocket—a bomb or a revolver? I replied, also politely, that anyone who tried to attack me would soon find out. He then proposed to *"pereytí k ocheredným dyelám"* ("to pass on to the next item of business"). However, as he started talking about some trifling battery housekeeping problem, I could hear from the back of the room that revolvers from the detail guarding the field guns had been sent for; also several Cossacks had gone out into the schoolyard, and some of them started closing the wooden shutters of the windows behind me from the outside. It was obvious that I was trapped without any chance for escape.

Many an officer had found himself in somewhat similar situations in those days and had solved the problem by taking an unyielding stand and then shooting as many of his assailants as he could, reserving the last bullet for himself. Somehow this seemed silly to me at the moment. I had no hatred for any of our men and even liked the majority of them. Many thoughts flashed through my mind; however, of course I did not have the time to think the matter logically through then, but rather acted by impulse. My instinct told me that if I was to come out of all this without suffering personal indignity, I had to keep the initiative in my hands even when yielding.

An idea suddenly came to me. I whispered to Lieutenant Khopiórsky to go and ask Colonel Souvórov in the adjoining teachers' room to come out and order me to surrender. A moment later Souvórov emerged and in the silence which followed his appearance told me to surrender. I could not resist some braggadocio even then and loudly asked him: "How do you order me, as my former lawful commander?" When he said "yes" I handed my pistol over to him, saying that if he came to my lodgings with me, I would give him my sword.

As we walked away from the school building, followed in the darkness by a number of Cossacks, Souvórov was angrily telling me in a low voice: *"Soumashédshyi malchíshka!"* ("crazy kid"). "You al-

most got all of us murdered!" Why had I not acted as he did? He
went on to say how in the very first action he would place the Battery in a position where it would be easily shot to pieces. I remained
silent.

Khopiórsky roomed in the same house with me, so that the problem of guarding us after our arrest was simplified. Our orderlies
moved our cots into one room; a couple of sentries were placed outside the windows and the rest of the guard detail occupied the adjoining room.

I was very touched by the visit of the saddler Kouznetzóv, who
was admitted to see us in his capacity of a member of the battery
Soviet. However, all that he said was entirely personal: my belongings were bound to be plundered eventually, so would I give him as a
souvenir the book of the Yogi Ramacharaka which we had read and
discussed when I was with the baggage train a few months earlier in
the village Samostryély? (see p. 97). I, of course, presented it to
him.

On the next morning Khopiórsky and I left under guard for
Kámenskaya, taking only a small bundle of underwear and toilet
articles with us. So as not to remove our gold-braid shoulder straps
from our tunics and fur coats,* or to risk having them ripped off on
the way, we wore wide baggy canvas raincoats over them. We traveled by horse-drawn wagon to the station Gloubókaya (see Map E,
p. 142) and then, after a long wait, by train to Kámenskaya where
we arrived only after dark. Our Cossack guards looked very uncomfortable about this new relationship to their former officers and
the journey was accomplished in complete silence.

At Kámenskaya we were taken on foot to the Headquarters of the
Don Military Revolutionary Committee and into a large room where
through clouds of dense tobacco smoke we saw Podtiólkov sitting at a
table with a crowd of Cossacks around him.

Some of the men from other units started jeering at us—we, who
had not fought the Germans, now opposed them, frontline veterans!
The old ingrained *esprit de corps* of the Battery immediately asserted
itself. Not only Podtiólkov, but several others of our men in the room
loudly protested that we had indeed fought the Germans. "How come
they look so young?" asked someone in a much quieter tone. *"Nyé-
zhnago vospitániya!* (Delicate upbringing)," growled Podtiólkov.

---

* They were really sheepskin coats with the fur inside, the outside being cloth-
lined (see Fig. 19).

Then turning to me, Podtiólkov said, somewhat ominously, that he wanted to have a long talk with me, but was too busy at the moment. He then gave the order that we were to be taken to the local prison, placed in separate isolated cells and not permitted to communicate with each other or with anyone else. But Podtiólkov was never to see me again during the few remaining months of his life.

When we got to the prison building, our guards found that the order they had been given could not be carried out—every single cell there was already packed with people who had been arrested in the last two days. The sentries at the gate suggested that we be taken to the local hotel which had been requisitioned to serve as an auxiliary prison.

By the time we got to the hotel our guards were tired of tramping around the town and, without asking any further questions, they just ushered us in past the sentries at the door and then departed.

The hotel was a two-story building with a restaurant on the lower floor and some twenty or so rooms on the second. These were filled with Cossack officers who had been arrested by their men. We were assigned to a small room with a single bed. The two earlier "arrivals" of senior rank had first claim on it, so Khopiórsky and I slept on the floor on our fur coats.

The rooms were not locked and we could freely walk about the corridor, visit and chat with other prisoners and have meals at our own expense in the groundfloor restaurant. A guard detail occupied the vestibule; one sentry was posted at the door on the street; another stood watch at the door to the second floor lavatory to check that everyone who went in actually came out—the lavatory had a window opening on an inner courtyard and a low shed under it would have made escape comparatively easy. The sentries were provided by the Leib-Guard Atamánsky Regiment which had also joined the pro-Red rebels, but their attitude was similar to that of the guards from our battery—they were embarrassed at their novel role of jailors of their former commanders.

A couple of days passed uneventfully. We did not know it, but Atamán Kaledín's government at Novocherkássk was attempting negotiations with the rebels. These got nowhere and Captain Chernetzóv's White partizán detachment again took the offensive.

It must have been around noon of January 15/28 or 16/29, 1918, that the prisoners were electrified by news brought up to us from the restaurant by Captain Doubéntzov of the Leib-Guard Cossack Regiment. He had been sitting with another officer at a window table having lunch when a ruffianly looking fellow slouched up hurling curses and imprecations at them. He leaned against the plateglass windowpane, the palms of both hands pressing against it at chest level so that a sheet of paper stuck to the palm of his upper hand could not be seen from the outside. He finally obeyed orders to go away shouted at him by the sentry at the hotel door nearby, but only after a slight nod from Captain Doubéntzov showed him that the message written in large block letters on the paper stuck to his palm had been read. It said:

CHERNETZÓV TOOK ZVYÉREVO YESTERDAY. LI-KHÁYA TODAY. KÁMENSKAYA TOMORROW. THEY WILL TRANSFER YOU TO VORÓNEZH. ESCAPE WHO CAN.

Likháya was the first station 15 miles to the south of us, Zvyérevo the following one, further away. "They" obviously meant the local Bolsheviks, and Vorónezh was the seat of government of a non-Cossack province of the same name over one hundred and fifty miles to the north, where we could not expect the same "kid-glove" treatment we had been getting from our own Cossacks so far.

Sometime after dark that day a Bolshevik Commissar in civilian clothes came up to the second floor of our hotel and peremptorily ordered everyone there to put on their coats and line up in readiness for departure. Several officers immediately jumped on him, knocked him to the floor and piled up on top. Someone must have gotten his hands on the throat of the brash fellow because his frantic cries for help soon changed to a hoarse gurgle.

The first sentry to rush to his rescue was the Cossack who had been watching the door to the lavatory which was located around a bend in the corridor. I did not wait to learn the fate of the hapless commissar, but dashed for the now unguarded lavatory, followed by Khopiórsky and an Army medical doctor who must have realized what we were going to do. The windowpane which could be opened there was fairly small; so I gave my fur coat to Khopiórsky, passed one leg through the window and then, bending my head and shoulder with outstretched arm down to my knee, wriggled out through the opening onto the sill and jumped to the snow-covered wooden roof of the shed 3 or 4 feet below. Khopiórsky threw me our coats and then he and the doctor joined me on the ground. There we immediately put our coats on because of the bitter cold.

A quick survey of the inner courtyard was rather discouraging. The door to the street was of a porte-cochère type; it closed a one-story high cut in a part of the building which was two stories high. Thus there was no space to climb over it. It was locked and was of massive build.

Our best opportunity seemed to be at one end of the courtyard, where, for a short distance the adjoining enclosing structure was only one story high. The medical doctor had the lightest and shortest coat of all three of us, so we decided to have him go first. However, after we had helped him up to the roof, he did not help pull us up as had been agreed, but kept going, his boots making what sounded to us like an infernal noise as he ran along the tin-covered roof, jumped off into an adjoining garden and disappeared. I do not know who the so-and-so was, but I curse him whenever I think of that evening.

Khopiórsky was of much lighter build than I was, so I went ahead of him, mounting on his back as he bent over resting his hands on his knees and leaning sideways against the wall for support, so that I could pull myself up to the roof. From there I pulled him up after me.

Just as we were halfway across the tin-covered roof of the one-story section, a window of the adjoining one-story section opened, a revolver was pointed at us through it and a man's voice yelled: "*Vóry, stóy!* (Thieves, stop!)". I told him we were officers escaping from Bolshevik arrest, so would he, please, stop yelling, close the window and go back to bed. Unfortunately, he turned out to be pro-Bolshevik and started yelling all the louder. But, luckily, the outdoor sentries had been called into the prison-hotel to quell the riot there and could not hear him. So he left the window and went inside, still shouting.

At this point we did a most stupid thing. Instinctively we took the shortest distance to get out of this Bolshevik's possible line of fire. So, instead of going on and jumping off into the adjoining garden and escaping as the medic had done, we jumped back into the yard from where we had just climbed out, and only then realized that this time we were really trapped.

However, luck came to our rescue in the form of a girl who opened her second-floor window over the courtyard to see what all the noise was about. She seemed to take in the situation at a glance and told us to stay where we were, she would help us. A minute or so later she appeared wrapped in a shawl, unlocked the heavy porte-cochère door, let us out, and locked it behind us. We found ourselves on a deserted side street and walked rapidly away.

Later I learned that the girl was the mistress of the hotelowner. She knew that the key to the yard door was hanging on a nail over the bed of a German prisoner-of-war who served as handyman for the hotel. He was asleep when she tiptoed into his room, removed the key, and then, after letting us out, put it back without waking him. The German was known as a Bolshevik sympathizer, so he was believed when he swore as he was awakened by a search party sent to find us a few minutes after we had left that we could not have possibly gotten out of the yard.* So they concentrated on searching the yard, its sheds, and even climbed all over the second-floor roof to see if we were hiding behind some chimney.

Meanwhile, we had left through the fields on the outskirts of Kámenskaya and were heading south on the eastern side of the main north-south railway, using its embankment as our only guide since we had no compass and the sky was cloudy. Its silhouette was dimly visible in the darkness on our right. All streams were frozen over and were easy to cross. However, there was hardly any snow on the ground because of a recent thaw and this made walking very difficult. The railroad ran close to the top of a slope. We did not dare come too close to it since its tracks were likely to be patrolled; therefore we had to move further down along the slope and cross many steep gullies there. The stretches of land between the ravines had been ploughed, which made it hard to walk along the frozen rough surface. My top boots were rather loose-fitting, which was an advantage when riding in cold weather—the feet did not freeze. But now my heels were being constantly rubbed as my boots flopped up and down along them at each step. Before long I felt that they were wet from blisters which had formed and then ruptured; walking became more and more painful.

As time went on we moved more and more slowly since we figured that if Likháya had been taken by Chernetzóv that day, as predicted by his agent, there must now be a line of pro-Bolshevik outposts across the railroad somewhere south of Kámenskaya, that is, in the

---

* This was done after the riot in the hotel-prison had been subdued. Several other officers succeeded in escaping through the front door at that time, and later on as they were moved about in the next two days.

direction we were heading. We were soon proven right on that point.

A couple of hours before daybreak we were suddenly challenged. Fortunately, we had not stumbled right on to the outpost, but found ourselves three or four hundred feet down the slope away from it when they heard us. We gained another hundred feet or so while shouting back vague answers as to who we were, such as: *"S khoútora-a* (From the villa-a-ge)"—"Wha-a-t villa-a-ge?"—"Over the-e-re"—"Whe-e-re?" and so forth. When they ordered us to stop, threatening to shoot if we did not, we ran. Several bullets whizzed by, then they started running after us. In our long fur coats and my bleeding feet we were in no shape for this sort of competition, so we dropped into a clump of dry grass along a furrow and let them run by as we flattened ourselves out on the ground. There were three or four of them and they wandered about in the darkness, cursing, for some time. Then they gave up and went back towards the railroad. We then cautiously proceeded in what we thought was still a southerly direction.

Just before daybreak we found ourselves in front of a railway embankment and erroneously assumed that it was the line which ran from Likháya eastward to Tsarítzyn * (see Map E, p. 142). So we crossed it and continued at right angles to it. Actually, it was the same north-south main line which we had been following all day. After crossing it we found at daybreak that we were on a flat plateau at the top of the slope we had been following. Our original plan had been to hide during daylight in some gully covering ourselves by dry grass, and to stay there until sounds of gunfire gave us some idea where Chernetzóv's White guerrilla detachment was. This plan was no longer feasible now since all around was only slightly undulating steppe land with not a single ditch or other natural cover in sight.

There was however a small village ahead about a mile or so, on the side of the railroad from which we had come. It looked like a well-to-do Cossack settlement, so we headed for it and knocked at the door of a prosperous-looking house at its edge. Fortunately, our guess proved correct. Its owner, a Cossack of friendly disposition, took us in and briefed us as to the situation while we ate a hearty breakfast served by his wife.

Chernetzóv's White detachment had taken Likháya, three miles or so to the south of us, after a brief fight on the previous day. We

* Renamed first Stalingrád and then Volgográd later.

were virtually in no-man's land and mounted scout patrols of pro-Bolshevik Cossacks had ridden by only the previous evening. Just in case we met some while driving to Likháya, our host hid our uniforms under some hay at the bottom of his horse-drawn cart, gave us some of his own workclothing to wear and rehearsed with us the answers we were to give if stopped on the way.

These precautions proved unnecessary and an hour later we were approaching Likháya, which at that time consisted of only a few houses around the railway station and yards where we could see several trains of Chernetzóv's famous "railroad cavalry" under steam.

We were immediately taken to Captain Chernetzóv who questioned us at length about all we had observed at Kámenskaya. This was the only time I met the legendary guerrilla but my recollection of him is of a vivacious man of immense vitality who exuded great nervous energy.

Chernetzóv told me that I was to serve as his aide-de-camp during the attack on Kámenskaya which he was about to undertake. By way of an answer I removed first one top boot and then the other. Chernetzóv took one look at my blood-soaked socks and told me that I was granted a week's leave to recuperate; his medics would bandage my feet; a locomotive with one car would be leaving for Novocherkássk in a couple of hours and we could go with it.

As we waited, we walked about the platform and chatted with the guerrillas about their Debáltzevo raid and other recent actions. I met many old friends and acquaintances from the north who were now serving with Chernetzóv. His artillery was commanded by Captain Shokóly (see p. 72) of my old artillery school at Petrográd; a pointer of one of his field guns was my old Tsárskoye Seló "gymnázia" classmate, Solomón (see p. 23)—he had joined the Army somewhat later than I did and was only a yúnker of the Konstantínovsky Artillery School at the time. In general, most of Chernetzóv's guerrillas were non-Cossack volunteers who had made their way to the Don from the north.

### 3. *With a White Partizán Detachment*

Khopiórsky had relatives in Novocherkássk and stayed with them. I called on my former battery commander, Colonel Nikolái Oupórnikov, and was very cordially received by him and by his family. They lived in a large one-story stone house which they owned in the center of the town and put me up there. I enjoyed the opportunity to relax a little in comparative luxury and to relate my adventures.

The news that Chernetzóv had captured Kámenskaya and had put to flight its garrison of pro-Bolshevik Cossacks arrived on the next day and caused general rejoicing in the town. It was however soon followed by very bad news.

Chernetzóv had attempted rapidly to develop his success, but his opponents received Red Guard reinforcements and rallied under the command of a Cossack Colonel Gólubov in the area of the railroad station Glubókaya near which our battery had been quartered after its return from the German front.

In the course of the action which developed there, Captain Chernetzóv left his trains and personally led a flanking movement with some of his volunteer infantry. He himself was outflanked, however, his retreat was cut off and he was surrounded and captured. The former sub-Lieutenant of our Guard Battery, Podtiólkov, personally cut him down with his sabre after he had surrendered. The officers who accompanied Chernetzóv were also killed.*

I could not help feeling thankful to fate for my bloodied feet; had it not been for them I would have accompanied Chernetzóv too and certainly would not have been spared by Podtiólkov who, as I heard later, was quite incensed by the news that I had succeeded in escaping from under arrest at Kámenskaya.

A few days later Colonel Souvórov turned up in Novocherkássk, called on the Oupórnikovs, asked to see me, and with an awkward grin returned the automatic which I had surrendered to him about a week before during the mutiny in the village of Beriózov. At some stage of the battle near Glubókaya in which Chernetzóv had perished, Souvórov succeeded in abandoning his forced command of the turncoat pro-Red Guard battery and in galloping over to the White side.

Both Khopiórsky and I had meanwhile described in detail his perfidious behavior to all our friends and he was now given the "cold shoulder" by everyone. When the Don army was reconstituted several months later, there was not a single unit the officers of which would agree to have him serve with them.† He finally got an ap-

---

* There is an English language description of this episode on pages 612–617 of Ref. 56, *And Quiet Flows the Don*, by the Soviet writer Shólokhov. It tallies quite well with what I have heard of it.

† The Imperial Army customs described on p. 29 still largely remained in force in the Don.

pointment with a shady German-sponsored outfit known as the "Astrakhán Army." I do not know what happened to him subsequently.

After the Chernetzóv disaster, many Cossack officers at Novocherkássk felt that they were duty bound to step into the breach. One of them was Captain Iván Grigórievich Konkóv who decided to form a volunteer artillery *vzvod* (section), taking as his second in command Lieutenant Zinóvy Krassnóv. Both were former officers of our Guard Battery (see p. 97 and photo, Fig. 23).

I joined them and was assigned to serve as a pointer of one of the two 3-inch field guns of the section. These guns and their caissons were mounted on three open freight cars at the head of a train assigned to us—then followed an open freight car with two machine guns, two passenger cars for living quarters, the locomotive, and then three or four cars with horses.

I will never forget our departure to the "front" from Novocherkássk. After we had loaded the guns and horses from a special ramp at the rear of the station, our train was shunted alongside a passenger ramp on the other side of which were standing several open freight cars with bodies of Chernetzóv's guerrillas killed in the recent fighting. The corpses were frozen in the positions they had died in and were stacked like gnarled cordwood on the cars. This sight naturally had a depressing effect on our volunteers, most of whom were young students and schoolboys who were seeing dead bodies for the first time in their lives. I believe that the two trains were deliberately shunted alongside of each other across the same ramp by Bolshevik sympathizers, of whom there were many among the railway employees —a locomotive to move them apart could not be found until we were ready to leave for the north.

A small group of civilians were silently watching our preparations for departure. A simply dressed old woman suddenly came forward towards me, thrust a small folded piece of paper into my hand, saying, "This will protect you," and then turned around and left. I have no idea who she was or why it was me to whom she gave it.

It turned out to be a handwritten copy of what seemed to be an ancient prayer which Cossack women of the past must have given as a protective charm to their departing menfolk. I was deeply touched by the old woman's action, especially because of the circumstances under which she took it. I carried this prayer with me until the Civil War was over.

I still have it, keeping the frayed and almost crumbling 4½- by

2½-inch sheet of paper between two sheets of transparent plastic. Both sides are covered with not very legible writing, part of which can still be deciphered:

". . . Heavenly God . . . will save from the sword in battle . . . envelop by His mantle and take under His wing . . . protect from fear of terrors of the night, arrows that fly and the demon of midnight . . . may evil not come to thee nor wounds to thy body; His angels will be commanded to keep thee on all thy paths; they will lift thee on their arms when . . . thou treadest on a viper, a *basilisk* * or henchmen of the serpent . . . if thou callest out My name to Me, I shall hear thee . . . and shall glorify thee in the length of thy days. . . ."

Captain Konkóv had asked that his detachment be sent to any operational direction except that of Kámenskaya, since neither he, Lieutenant Krassnóv, nor I wanted to fire on any of our former men of the Guard Battery. Compliance with his wish was made easy by the fact that the greatest threat now came from the direction of Debáltzevo and the mining district around it to the west, from where an advance Red Guard detachment had occupied the station Goúkovo, thereby posing a threat to the junction Zvyérevo and thence to the rear of the remnants of Chernetzóv's guerrillas who were holding their own to the north in the Likháya-Kámenskaya area (see Map E, p. 142). Pressure on them had lessened. As we learned later, the action against Captain Chernetzóv and his brutal murder by Podtiólkov had shaken up many of the at first pro-Bolshevik Cossacks, most of whom now went home, leaving the fighting to the Red Guards. In particular, our Leib-Guard Cossack Battery had ceased to exist as a unit after Souvórov's defection.

That same night we arrived in Zvyérevo and prepared to give artillery support, when daylight came, to the attack on Goúkovo by the yúnker squadron of the Novocherkássk Cavalry School. We were to do this by firing our field pieces from the open freight cars on which they were mounted. This is what we had to do during the subsequent three weeks of fighting, never once having to disentrain our horses. This time, however, we did not have to fire at all. Goúkovo was cap-

---

* A Greek word which, according to the *Encyclopaedia Britannica* (1910), is: ". . . a name given by the ancients to a horrid monster of their own imagination, to which they attributed the most malignant powers and an equally fiendish appearance."

tured by a sudden surprise pre-dawn attack by the dismounted yún-kers. So we just steamed in and up to the station ramp which presented a grisly sight, strewn with enemy corpses.

To our surprise they were all clad in uniforms of the Austro-Hungarian army. This company of Reds was composed of some of the numerous prisoners of war who had joined the Bolsheviks and formed several so-called International Battalions. It was significant that they were spearheading the Red drive. It was generally believed at that time that this was done under secret orders of the Austro-German General Staffs, who wanted to prevent any pro-Allied groups from ousting the Bolsheviks and then continuing Russia in the war against the Central Powers. This particular company certainly looked to me like a Regular Army outfit,—their two slain officers wore their combat decorations and nearly all of the men had campaign badges pinned to their caps—for Izonzo and the like. Unfortunately, not a single survivor had been left to be questioned—the Russian Civil War was becoming quite savage.

The next day I saw another illustration of this. A Red Guard prisoner was brought in past our train by one of our infantrymen from a forward patrol—he was a shabby-looking young fellow. Suddenly, one of our own young volunteers jumped off the car, rushed up to the prisoner and held the muzzle of a revolver close to his head, repeating, his face distorted with hatred: "See this? . . . See this?" Before anyone could intervene, he pressed the trigger and killed the prisoner by a bullet through his brain. It turned out that shortly before that he had found the mutilated body of his uncle, a stationmaster who had been killed by the Reds for having co-operated with the Whites. The nephew was thirsting for vengeance. And so it went on—one act of brutality produced another, causing what nowadays would probably be called an "escalation" of reciprocal terror.

The incident happened as our trains, with Captain Konkóv's gun cars in the lead, slowly steamed from Goúkovo westward. Once we were briefly stopped by rifle and machine gun fire coming from a shallow cut along which the railroad curved through a low hill ahead of us. Konkóv gave the range and fuse setting and three or four shells from my field piece, which I aimed over open sights, burst in the cut and caused the survivors of the Red outpost to retreat before they could damage the tracks. As our train moved on, I saw for the first time closeby the corpses of men brought down by my own gun fire.

The next station, Proválye, was occupied by us soon after without opposition. We spent the night there.

On the following morning we moved on, but had to stop before reaching the next station, Dolzhánsk. Our mounted patrol reported that Red infantry had deployed before the station, so our trains, with our gun cars still in the lead, stopped some 400 yards behind a low ridge which overlooked Dolzhánsk. Some 150 infantrymen, our entire force, disentrained and advanced across the ridge. Rifle and machinegun fire met them.

Zinóvy Krassnóv went with our infantry, carrying a field telephone, as one of our men quickly laid out on the ground the connecting wire. We started shooting over the ridge with Zinóvy correcting our fire. The Reds, several hundred workmen volunteers from the neighboring coal mines, however held their ground before Dolzhánsk.

Soon after, line after line of deployed Red infantry appeared in the distance advancing towards us both on our left and our right. We were completely outflanked and our infantry was ordered to retreat back to the trains as fast as they could. The Reds before Dolzhánsk, which they had been attacking, immediately pressed after our men—we could tell this from the ever-shortening range telephoned to us by Lieutenant Krassnóv. We continued firing by guesswork for a while after he had to leave the ridge with our last infantrymen, but soon the first Reds appeared on the crest and we could fire at them by direct sighting.

Our regular Russian Army 3-inch guns had very fine optical sights with a periscopic arrangement protruding over the steel shield which effectively protected the gunners behind it from frontal fire. The sights had appreciable magnification and I could clearly see through them one of the first Reds appear on the crest, stop there kneeling on one knee, his rifle in his left hand, his right arm waving on his men behind him. A rapid turn of two adjustment wheels on my gun and he was in the center of the crosshairs of my sights. Seconds later the white puff of my shrapnel burst right in front of him; nothing moved there when the smoke cleared away.

Both our guns fired incessantly at the ridge to provide some cover for the retreat of our infantry, but we could not stop the stream of rifle fire which poured from it. We could be grateful for the high quality of the steel of which the shield of our gun was made—numerous rifle bullets whammed into it, leaving it pockmarked, but not pierced. Only one of my gunners—a sixteen-year-old boy—was lightly wounded in his forearm by a bullet fired at great distance by the Reds who were approaching on our left flank.

Our infantry, however, suffered heavily as they rapidly walked or ran towards the trains behind us—we lost more than half of them. I happened to look up from my sights just as a young officer was hit when he was running back past us some twenty yards to our right. He doubled up, his momentum making his limp body turn a complete somersault before it stopped rolling and lay still.

Another casualty a few feet away from me was Captain Iván Folimónov of our Guard Battery—the same man who had succeeded me in the command of its reserve section at Pávlovsk (p. 77) and whose gunfire had been decisive in putting down the attempted Bolshevik uprising against the Kerensky government in July, 1917, at Petrográd (p. 100). He had now been serving as a volunteer infantry private, and stopped for a second as he passed our gun car. At that moment a bullet hit him. He cried out, but at first I did not think it was serious because he was able to pull himself up to our platform from the tracks before anyone could help him. But his face quickly turned to an ashen gray as he lay stretched out behind our gun—he had been hit in the stomach and died two days later in a hospital.

The action before Dolzhánsk confirmed what the battle of Púlkovo had already shown three months earlier: The Red Guard detachments of volunteer workmen could put up an excellent fight, and there was no chance of beating them in the field when they had a definite numerical superiority. This they did have for the next few weeks, and the tactics of our side from then on took the character of purely delaying actions.

From Dolzhánsk we retreated through Prchlye back to Goúkovo, blowing up a couple of bridge culverts along the way. There we received reinforcements, but so did the Reds—they got a real armored train with field guns mounted in revolving steel turrets which could fire at almost any angle from the direction of the railroad track. Our makeshift mounting of field guns on open freight cars did not permit us to attempt a duel with that train over open sights. So we tried shooting at it from tracks behind some railroad sheds of the Goúkovo station, our fire being directed by Lieutenant Krassnóv by telephone from the top of the water tower. But, before we could inflict any damage, a Red shrapnel, apparently by chance, burst just to the right of my car where the field telephone operators were sitting,

killed them all, smashed the phone and, in addition, killed the trail
gunner of my team.

Shortly afterwards came the news that Likháya had been abandoned by our forces and that they were about to give up Zvyérevo as
well under Red pressure from the north. To avoid being cut off, we
had to steam rapidly back eastward to Zvyérevo and join the guerrilla
forces there in a further gradual retreat to the south.

We took two-day leaves, by turn, for a short rest at Novocherkássk. During my stay there I borrowed a civilian overcoat from
the Oupórnikovs, went to the *tolkúchka* ("flea" market), and bought
there a dilapidated soldier's overcoat, a soldier's blouse and an equally
shabby-looking fur cap. After thoroughly disinfecting my acquisi-
tions, I returned to the "front" wearing them and leaving my fur
coat and other officer's clothing with the Oupórnikovs.

We were in constant danger of being cut off, surrounded and captured, so I saw no point in wearing conspicuous officer's clothing when
I was actually performing the duties of a private. As an additional
precaution, I obtained from a medical doctor on a hospital train at
one of the stations a fake certificate that I was a hospital orderly in
his outfit. Regrettably, it was not long before all this proved quite
useful.

The overwhelming numerical superiority of the Reds before us
could easily have permitted them to surround us at night—and it was
only the reluctance of their untrained troops to fight in the darkness
that saved us for a while. We continued gradually retreating southwards with more fighting at Zapovyédnaya and at Kamenolómnya-
Shákhty. A howitzer high-explosive shell landed there on one of our
cars, killing all horses and three men who were in it. We had other
losses too.

About that time came the news of Atamán Kaledín's suicide (January 29/February 11, 1918). He had been terribly depressed by the
wholesale defection of the regular frontline Cossack troops, not a
single unit of which had agreed to fight the Reds under his command
although he had been elected to it. The heavy losses suffered by the
young volunteers who had rallied to his call made the situation look
quite hopeless and broke his spirit—the fine old soldier shot himself
through the heart (page 40 of Ref. 11, Vol. 1).

He was succeeded in the post of Don Atamán by General Nazárov.
One of his first acts was to promote to the next rank all officers who

were actually fighting the Reds at that moment—this is when I became a *Khoroúnzhi,* or Second Lieutenant.

Another quite spectacular action by Atamán Nazárov was to assemble at the Novocherkássk Officers' Club ("Sobrániye") a number of the "arm-chair" officers who had sat out the war there in various administrative offices. He then lined them up and had them marched off under escort to the railroad station from where they were shipped directly to the "front"—they were not even allowed to call at their homes.

This is how I got by way of a replacement for my dead trail gunner a middleaged supply colonel who in all his life had never before been under fire. Like others of his kind he proved quite a nuisance, as I learned in the next action.

The city of Rostóv to the south-west of us was still held by General Kornílov's volunteers, whereas we had already been pressed back close to Persiánovka, the first station north of Novocherkássk. A counterattack was ordered to slow down the Reds. It was carried out by one of the foot *sótnyas* (squadrons) of Colonel Semilyétov's Cossack partizáns, with our artillery support.

Our trains moved to within sight of a village close to the next station, which I believe was Kamenolómnya. It was held by the Reds.

Our infantry disentrained, deployed and advanced ahead of us over the deep snow in three or four successive lines on both sides of the railway. Soon after, fountains of snow and of frozen earth began spouting skywards among them from Red high explosive shells, which, judging by their size, came from at least 4.8-inch and possibly even 6-inch diameter howitzers.

Suddenly, we saw their flashes. They had the temerity to fire from an "open" position. Perhaps lack of field telephones had forced them to do so. Anyway, I could clearly see through my optical sights their two howitzers, side-by-side, as they kept up a continuous fire on our advancing infantry.

For some reason, which I do not now remember, our second gun could not fire that day. We were under two additional disadvantages: *first,* we had run out of high explosive shells and had only anti-personnel shrapnel, the lead bullets of which could not pierce the protective steel shields of the howitzers; *second,* the enemy guns were located some distance along a left bend of the railroad, which slowed down our rate of fire considerably because of our primitive

gun-mounting arrangement. The spade of our gun trail, which was
normally pressed into the ground and transmitted to it the force of
recoil after a shot, now rested against a wooden railroad tie which
was laid across the open freight car and was fixed to its surface. This
worked very well so long as we fired straight ahead but, if we had to
fire at an angle sideways, only the edge of the steel spade of the gun
trail would touch the wooden tie so that the recoil produced a couple
of forces—that is, a rotational movement around a vertical axis—
which made the wheels of the gun slip sideways, compelling a complete readjustment of the sighting after each shot.

Captain Konkóv estimated the range and the fuze: range 110,
*trúbka* (fuze) 110.* This first shot was a short, but the two howitzers
silhouetted against the smoke of the second, fired at a range 120,
fuze 120. It burst behind them, but uncomfortably close, and the
Reds immediately transferred their fire from our infantry to us.
Konkóv halved the bracket: "115, fuze 115." It was a short. "118,
fuze 118"—again a short. Konkóv lengthened the fuze—"118, fuze
119,"—thereby making the shrapnel burst almost at ground level
quite close to the howitzer shields. Once more it was a short, but
he had pinpointed them by the fifth shot, *"Byégly Ogón!* (Rapid
Fire!)," yelled the Captain.

But after each shot the wheels of our gun slid sideways almost a
foot on the open freight car, which was covered with ice. We all had
to grab both wheels and on my repeated count, "One, two, *three!,"*
would pull at them sideways simultaneously. It took three or four
such jerks to get the heavy 3-inch field piece back into approximate
position. Further rough adjustment would then be done by the supply
Colonel, who pushed a metal tube attached to the end of the trail in
the direction and by the approximate amount indicated by my right
arm and hand stretched out behind me as I peered through the optical
sights. Further fine adjustment of direction was done by me using a
hand-operated small wheel on the gun carriage.

Unfortunately, this unavoidable procedure slowed us down so much
that the Reds soon were able to bracket us with their shells.

A train similar to ours, which had been organized by Colonel

---

* The fuze settings in the Russian artillery corresponded to the range setting
of the sight elevation, thereby eliminating the need for conversion tables,—this
was quite an advantage (see p. 247). Each range setting corresponded to a distance of 20 *sajen,* or 140 feet. Thus our range of 120 corresponded to 5,600
yards in American units.

Nikolái Oupórnikov, tried to help us by steaming ahead on the right track,—we were on the left one,—but a shell blew off the corner of his ammunition car's roof just as it passed alongside our platform. Oupórnikov had to move back in great haste.

It was no fun to come out from behind the cover of our shield and tug at the gun with the sound of approaching shells and their explosions around us continuously in our ears. But all my crew performed wonderfully.

Then, just as we had dashed back to our posts around the gun after one of our tugging actions, a howitzer shell exploded with a terrific bang in the ditch at the bottom of the low railroad embankment just opposite us, showering us with snow and chunks of frozen earth. After that there was no response to my adjustment signal and, as I looked back, I saw the supply Colonel lying huddled up on the platform, his hands covering his head and a look of abject terror on his face.

I knew he had not been wounded and yelled at him to get back to his post—this made no impression. So I kicked his backside, and when that did not help, seized a pickax which lay on the platform and used it as a lever, its sharp point pressing him upwards. That made him sit up, but I had to hold my automatic at his temple and threaten to blow his brains out before he got up and resumed his duties at the back of the trail of my gun.

We must have fired only ten rounds or so after getting the exact range of the Red howitzers, their shells coming at us all the time and exploding all around. Miraculously, no one was hit, although the wood of our gun car and of the adjoining cars was covered with shell-splinter holes. Then I suddenly realized that the sound of approaching shells had ceased. Looking through my sights I could see black dots on the snow behind the howitzers—the Red gunners were running away. Captain Konkóv saw them too through his field glasses and increased the range slightly to speed them on their way. Then he ordered us to cease firing. No cigarette I ever inhaled before or after tasted so good as the one I then lit.

Our infantry was rapidly advancing and soon occupied the village on the edge of which stood the two abandoned howitzers. When Red reinforcements came up and forced them to retire, our men removed and brought back with them the optical sights and the breech locks of these guns.

Many a frontline lieutenant must have dreamed of kicking a sup-

ply colonel, but I was not happy after having actually done this. He
sat dejectedly in a corner of our car as we steamed back to Persiánovka, apparently thoroughly ashamed of himself, although not a
word was said by anyone about the incident. He went out at the
Persiánovka station and did not come back; we never saw him
again, but did not report his desertion.

On February 9/22, 1918, the large industrial and harbor city of
Rostóv-on-the-Don had to be abandoned by General Kornílov's White
Volunteers under strong Red pressure from the west and the southeast. The White Volunteers retreated northwards to the railroad station Aksái, about halfway to Novocherkássk. There they were to be
joined by our White Don Cossack detachments and were to leave the
railroad and head eastwards into the open steppe country (see Map
E, p. 142).

The general strategy of this move was to try and wait things out
in the steppes, as far away from railroads as possible, where the Red
Guards would have difficulty in following us. It was hoped that the
Cossacks would soon rebel against inevitable forced Red requisitions
of food and grain and would then join the Whites. Subsequent events
proved this strategy to be correct.

Meanwhile our detachment of about one hundred men and two
field guns was to delay the Reds for as long as possible at Persiánovka, just north of Novocherkássk.

In the morning of either February 12/25 or 13/26 the Reds
started advancing against Persiánovka under cover of artillery fire
from an armored train. They soon outflanked our infantry and forced
us to retreat to the station at Persiánovka. A telephone call from
there to notify Headquarters at Novocherkássk got no answer. Phone
calls over the city line to friends confirmed our fears—the town
seemed to have been already abandoned.

The Colonel in command of our detachment then ordered our train
to steam back full speed to Novocherkássk, only stopping to blow up
two bridge culverts along the way. On arriving at Novocherkássk
we found that it *was* empty of all our troops—due to some error, the
order to retreat several hours earlier had not reached us.

We did not know it at the time, but the Don Atamán, General
Nazárov, had refused to leave his post and stayed behind in the city
without attempting to hide. He was executed there by the Reds soon
after.

Telephone calls to Aksái also did not get through. Our Colonel feared that all our troops must have already left it and that it was about to be occupied by the Reds from Rostóv to the south. So he assembled the entire detachment on the tracks near our train and explained the situation. He had just received further bad news— Krivyánskaya, a large Cossack *stanítza* (township) to the east of us, had been occupied by a big detachment of Red Cossack cavalry under the command of the turncoat, Colonel Gólubov—the same man who had defeated and captured Chernetzóv (see p. 160). Since then, his men had not actually taken part in combat against us, but had been continuously menacing our right flank. We were now completely surrounded.

Our Colonel declared the detachment disbanded. In his opinion there was no chance for us to break out of encirclement as a unit, but individuals might seep through to the steppes, or succeed in hiding in the town. He left the decision to us as to which of these two alternatives had a better chance of success for any one of us—from then on it was to be every man for himself.

Captain Konkóv, Lieutenant Zinóvy Krassnóv and I decided to stick together and to head for the steppes. With us went our field telephone operator, a young schoolboy who came from one of the Cossack *stanítzas* east of Krivyánka and who offered to serve as a guide until we reached his home.

### 4. *Capture and Escape*

We first threw the optical sights and the breech locks of our guns into a cut in the ice of a small stream which flowed near the station. Then we headed eastwards on foot. We did not take any rifles with us, so that our arms silhouetted against the snow would not draw attention to us.

It was a gray foggy day. We decided to avoid the main road to Krivyánka, along which we could see people leaving the town on foot and in horse-drawn carriages. However, we were soon intercepted by a mounted patrol of some eight or ten of Gólubov's pro-Red Cossacks. I had to give up my automatic, this time for good. Then we were escorted into Krivyánka and into a large house where Gólubov held court.

Gólubov ordered us placed in an adjoining back room, while he received a delegation of "city fathers" which had just arrived. They implored him to enter the town with his pro-Red Cossacks before the Red Guards and sailors did so from the north. Colonel Gólubov willingly obliged and immediately left with all his entourage, forgetting us—either by accident or by design—in the back room.

The three of us, all officers, found ourselves alone in the house with its owners. Our schoolboy guide had managed to "evaporate" (as one used to say in those days) in the courtyard as we were led through a milling crowd into the house. Some months later I met him accidentally on the street. He told me that he had cut with his telephone knife the hitching thong of one of the horses which were tied up in the yard, led it unobtrusively away and then galloped all the way to his home village.

The owner of the house, an old and prosperous-looking Cossack, was thoroughly scared. He asked us to leave, fearing that he might get shot together with us should the Red Guards come and find us in his house. Since I was the only one not in officer's uniform, it was decided that I would go out and reconnoiter.

Just as I came out onto the village street, I found myself almost face to face with a horseman who was rounding the corner of the house and who pulled up sharply. He wore a long cloth-covered overcoat with a fur collar but no shoulder straps, a fur *papákha* (cap); the scabbard of his sword was silver inlaid, Caucasian style, but his saddle was not of the Cossack type—it was of the kind used by officers of the Regular Army. He had a thin, energetic, intellectual face, and his voice sounded like that of an officer used to giving orders when he asked me sharply: "Partizán?" As he said this, I realized that my knapsack had given me away. It was of an outdated model from some old surplus Army equipment stores in Novocherkássk which was used only by the White guerrillas. So I said, "Yes. And who are you?" "I am the Commissar from the *Shtab* (Headquarters) of the Moscow Military District, Pougachévsky."

This name was obviously not his real one, but a *nom de guerre*. Pougachóv had been a notorious Don Cossack who led an anti-landlord insurrection of peasants along the Vólga River in the reign of Catherine II, some 140 years earlier. I therefore assumed that the man before me was a former Imperial Army officer who had been forced by some circumstance or other temporarily to join the Reds, but who was not really one of them since he tried to conceal his true name. So, in turn, I introduced myself in what was intended to be an amiable manner: *Óchen Priyátno!* (Very pleasant!) I am Khoroúnzhi (Second Lieutenant) Chebotarióv, former officer of His Majesty's Don Cossack Guard Battery."

The moment I said this, I realized that I had completely misjudged the situation. Instead of suggesting that we each go our own respective way, as I expected him to do, the horseman froze into strained immobility in his saddle. Both his gloved hands had been on his reins when we met, and now he clutched them tensely; his eyes were fixed on my overcoat pockets in which I had deeply buried my gloveless hands to protect them from the cold. His expression suggested that he fully expected me to whip out a revolver and shoot him the instant he reached for his own pistol holster at his belt or for his sword. Since I had no weapons whatsoever on me, I was careful not to disillusion him by withdrawing my hands from my pockets. Instead, I tried to make them bulge somewhat, even though they were empty.

We eyed each other for a minute or so, then Pougachévsky took the initiative to break the silence by asking me with what unit I had now served. I told him, adding that I had served as pointer of one of the guns. "In what actions did you take part?" he continued. "Dolzhánsk, Goúkovo, Zapovyédnaya, Shákhty, Kamenolómnya, Persiánovka," I replied.

"Very interesting," he said. "I was in command at the first two. We smashed one of your guns at Goúkovo, didn't we?"

"No, you did not, you merely killed two and wounded one of my gunners. The gun itself was not damaged. Did you see what happened to your two howitzers at Kamenolómnya?"

"Was it you who fired at them?"

"Yes."

*"Prekrásno strelyáli!* (Excellent shooting!)," he remarked in a tone of genuine professional appreciation.

Shortly after that exchange a young man, dressed and equipped very much like Pougachévsky, and who seemed to be his aide, rode up followed by an escort of some twenty Don Cossacks from Colonel Gólubov's pro-Red detachment. They drew up behind him.

"Well, young man, now surrender your weapons!" ordered Pougachévsky. His face was quite a study when I turned my overcoat pockets inside out, showing that they were empty. Its expression reflected such a comic mixture of surprise and of anger at himself for having let me bluff him until then, that I could not help but grin at him. That did not make him any happier.

"Who else is in that house you came out of?" he roared. I said there was no one there and continued to affirm this until he told me: "Go inside, look in the cupboards and under the beds, and if you see anyone tell them that I will follow you in a minute and will shoot on the spot anyone I find, unless they come out themselves right now!"

There was nothing left for me to do but to go in and tell Konkóv and Krassnóv what a fool I had made of myself. They came out.

Pougachévsky cursed and swore at them, claiming that he had seen Konkóv in Moscow after the November 1917 fighting there. This was not so; Konkóv had not been there. Just then Pougachévsky's attention was diverted from them by a Cossack Army Captain, who had been stopped by a patrol of Gólubov's detachment. Pougachévsky rode his horse at him, knocking the Captain down and hurting his leg—he limped after he got up. This slowed down the two mounted Cossacks who were assigned to escort him.

Noticing that they were falling behind, Pougachévsky gave an order to hit anyone who did not keep up with the flat of a sword over the head to make them move faster. I told him that if anyone touched me, I would lie down and they could finish me off right then and there. "No, this order does not concern you, you are a *boyevóy protívnik* (a combat opponent)," he announced quite courteously. Our brief previous exchange had obviously impressed him. This gave me my cue.

Pougachévsky and his aide rode ahead of their Cossack escort and of the other prisoners, with myself walking alongside of them as we moved back along the road to Novocherkássk through the fog which was getting denser. The aide seemed quite interested in chatting to me, remarking that this was the first White Guard prisoner their sailors had let him see alive—gone was the comparative joviality of the Gátchino days (p. 127) at the start of the Civil War, and the "escalation" of brutalities had led to wholesale shootings of prisoners by both sides. But now we talked about the recent battles, national and international politics, and so forth. I tried to hold my ground firmly, but politely.

Suddenly, a burst of cheering was heard ahead where our road passed under the railway which could not yet be seen through the fog. "*Bodrítyess* (perk up), young man, the sailors have arrived!" remarked Pougachévsky. We went on ahead in silence. Somehow I did not believe that this was going to be the end, but nevertheless I was quite relieved when it turned out to be only pro-Bolshevik railroad workmen who were welcoming Gólubov's Cossacks as they entered the town—the sailors apparently had not yet been able to repair the bridge culverts which we had blown up that morning.

Our escort dropped behind to pick up cigarettes offered by the welcoming railwaymen, and the three of us were soon out of their sight in the fog as we moved up the steeply rising street away from the station and towards the center of the town. I felt that this was my last chance and decided to try and gamble on the obvious annoyance with himself displayed by Pougachévsky when he discovered that I was unarmed.

So I accused him with having tried to cheat me by waiting to show his hand until his escort rode up after we had exchanged introductions. He countered that I would never have dared introduce myself had I really known anything about him. Only three persons so far had come out of his hands alive,* he claimed, and, anyway, he could see that I was a convinced counterrevolutionary who would start fighting again if he let me go. I told him that this was so, but had nothing to do with my point, since I knew perfectly well who he was † and for that very reason considered that when two former "combat opponents" (here I used his own characterization) met after the fighting was over, I could safely introduce myself and expect a chivalrous reaction, but apparently I was naive.

* I recall that one name he quoted was that of the girl who had been in command of Kerensky's women's battalion which had attempted to defend the Winter Palace at Petrográd (see p. 109).

† I must confess that here I lied unashamedly—I am still not sure that I heard his name right on the windy street of Krivyánka. Sometimes I think that it may have been Toukhachévsky, whose name was unknown to me at the time, but which has a similar sound. He was a man who later became a Marshal of the Red Army, executed by Stalin in the 1930s. However, two of my friends to whom I told this story claimed later to have seen the name of Pougachévsky in print.

The first one told me of seeing it in 1918 or 1919 in a Red newspaper found in a village recaptured by his White detachment. It gave an account of how a Soviet Army Commander, Mouravióv, the same man who had been their Commander at Gátchino (see p. 126) had attempted to cross to the side of the Kolchák White Siberian armies in the Urál area, but had been unmasked and executed by the "valiant comrade Pougachévsky."

The second friend told me of reading in a German newspaper in the 1930s a list of names of high-ranking Red Army officers purged by Stalin. It was supposed to include the name of the Chief of Staff of the Army of the Caucasus, Pougachévsky.

But I have never been able to get any fully reliable data about the man, to whom, after all, I do owe my life. Maybe, before too long, the Soviet Government will open some of the Red Army archives to answer inquiries of this kind.

That did it. Pougachévsky abruptly pulled up his horse, peered at me for a moment, then stretched out his arm towards the steppe in a somewhat theatrical gesture and said: "Maybe we will meet again on the battlefield! *A tepyér, ouderyóte—váshe schástye; popadyótyess—penyáyte na sebyá. Proscháyte!* (And now, if you get away—your luck. If you get caught—blame yourself. Good-bye!)." He spurred his horse and galloped up the slope, followed by his aide who waved to me with a cheerful grin.

I remained standing for a moment, rather shaken up by what had happened and wondering what to do next. There was nowhere to hide. The street was deserted, all gates and doors were closed, and the windows were shuttered. Dusk was falling, but there was not a light anywhere.

The thought struck me that I must first of all get rid of my partizán knapsack, which had given me away once already, but, just as I took it off and headed for a high fence over which I intended to toss it, there was a clatter of hoofs behind me and I was challenged to stop by one of the Cossacks of the pro-Red escort who had been accepting cigarettes at the underpass and who was now trying to catch up with his Commissar.

I told him that Pougachévsky had let me go. The Cossack turned out to be a real Bolshevik and laughed derisively—he would believe it when he heard it from the Commissar himself. He unslung his rifle and threatened to shoot me, unless I came along with him. Another Cossack and the limping Captain emerged out of the fog and the four of us continued up the street. On the right was the second Cossack, then the limping Captain between him and the first Cossack, then myself. I managed to get rid of my telltale knapsack by informing my captor of its contents—an extra pair of boots, lard, etc.—and offering it to him since I would have no further use for it and was too tired to carry it. He grabbed it and hung it on the pommel of his saddle.

I had decided to make a dash for it at the first opportunity, but none presented itself—the frightened townfolk had boarded themselves up in their houses. Not a door was open, nor was there a single fence low enough for me to jump over.

We arrived at the top of the hill where stood the impressive Eastern Orthodox Cathedral (Fig. 31). We then turned to the left along the right lane of a boulevard in the general direction in which the photo, Fig. 32 was taken later.

About a block away was the main Army Guard and Arrest House and I felt that if we reached it, this would be the end for me.* But still there was no chance for me to run without being immediately shot down. Then luck smiled again.

We heard the sound of an approaching brass band. Round the corner of the next street and on to our side of the boulevard, with the orchestra at its head, swept a cheering crowd of pro-Bolshevik workmen of the city Water Plant on their way to greet the arriving Reds at the railroad station. I edged closer to the horse of my Cossack escort so as not to give him an inkling of what I was about to do. Then, as the band and the first three or four rows of workmen behind it passed us, I dashed into the crowd cheering and waving my fur cap together with them. I blended easily with the mob, where many were wearing soldier overcoats similar to mine.

The shouts of my escort were drowned out by the uproar all around us; he was unable to maneuver his horse in the dense throng; he unslung his rifle, but could not take aim—I was careful not to expose myself to it and dodged it by moving back and forth behind men in the crowd. As some people started turning their heads in all directions to see who it was that the mounted Cossack was trying to get in his sights, I did the same thing, pretending to search for the culprit. However, quite soon we had swept on out of his sight and into the fog—I did not have a chance to notice what had happened to the limping Captain.

For some distance I went along with the crowd, then I backtracked along side streets and knocked at the door of the Oupórnikovs' house, only a block away from the scene of my escape. It was quite dark by then and no street lights were burning.

They immediately let me in and arranged for a place for me to hide in their house should it be searched. Then I told them my adventures.

I was quite worried about Konkóv and Zinóvy Krassnóv, considering that it was my blunder which led to their capture too. However, Zinóvy turned up soon afterwards. Their two Cossack escorts had deliberately slowed down their pace, then took them into a side street of the town and told them to "evaporate." Konkóv had gone to the home of some relatives and Zinóvy, having none at Novocherkássk, came to the same house of our former battery commander as I did.

* My feeling was correct—all White prisoners brought there were subsequently executed.

The Colonel himself and his brother had managed to leave a day or two earlier for the steppes. His womenfolk, however, discovered that one of his civilian suits fortunately fitted Zinóvy and he quickly changed into it. My own attire was appraised as a disguise that could not be improved on. After much discussion they suggested that it would be too dangerous for us to stay at their house, which was bound to be searched repeatedly. But the biggest danger lay in gossipy servants. For instance, one of the two girls who worked for them by day might pick up a boy friend among the Red Guards. This danger would not exist at the small two-room wooden house of their old nurse, which they had bought for her on the outskirts of the town. She was devoted to them and readily agreed to help when one of the Oupórnikov women went to query her. So, we were stealthily taken there at about four in the morning, when there was no one about in the streets, and we went to sleep on the floor of one of her two rooms.

We were awakened by shouting and rifle shots outside. A White partizán had been found hiding in the adjoining house by a Red Guard patrol, was dragged out into the street and shot, his body remaining there in the snow in sight of our windows.

We quickly put on our boots and coats. In the process of tidying up, Zinóvy discovered that he did not know how to tie his necktie, which had been done for him the previous evening. Neither did I. I had not been abroad since my sailor-suit days and had always worn uniforms of one kind or another since then. So, we both settled down in front of an old-fashioned chair with a high pointed back and systematically worked at trying to find a way to make the tie look presentable on the chair. We finally solved the problem and I repeated the operation around Zinóvy's neck.

This helped take our minds off the Red Guard patrols who were searching many houses on our street. None entered our house however—all of the neighbors apparently sincerely believing that the old nurse lived there alone. No one had seen us come in the previous night.

We did not emerge from the little house for a few days. The second or third day we were there happened to be my nineteenth birthday, which I spent wondering whether it was going to be my last.

Then, I began sallying forth after dark, first cautiously peering through cracks in the fence to assure myself that there was no one on the street who would see me open the gate. In the town, Red patrols stopped me several times, but my fake pass of an orderly from a hospital train (p. 166) satisfied them. My general appearance was studiedly "super-proletarian"—I stopped shaving, so that my face was covered with a stubby beard; the ear flaps of my fur cap were not tied together over its top, but were allowed to protrude at crazy angles from its sides; I wore no belt around my overcoat which hung on me like a loose sack. In addition, I developed a slouching, shuffling gait; learned how to do without a handkerchief by bending over sideways, pressing peasant-fashion one thumb on a nostril and blowing air sharply through the other; also I continuously cracked sunflower seeds on the street, spitting out the husks in all directions, and cultivated a speech consisting of monosyllables and oaths.

All this seemed to work beautifully and I began getting cockier. Even people who knew me passed me in daylight on the street without recognizing me. Then, one day I barely missed being captured— my desire to take a bath almost proved to be my undoing.

Novocherkássk, like all Russian towns and most villages, had public baths. A *bánya* operates on a principle similar to the Finnish *sauna* or a Turkish steam bath. The surface of a low brick oven protrudes from one of the corners of a large room; it is fueled and serviced from the adjoining room. A large barrel is built into it to provide hot water; small wooden buckets are given to individual bathers in the entrance hall where they leave their clothes—they can then soap themselves, increase the amount of steam in the common bathroom by splashing water over the hot bricks of the oven and douse themselves with hot water to wash the soap off. Slatted wooden seats are built like steps along one of the longer sides of the room right up to the ceiling where it is hottest—one can then choose the elevation and hence the temperature at which one wants to relax. A barrel of cold water is also provided—a dousing by a bucket of it after one is well steamed up seems to have the same stimulating effect as does the more drastic Finnish custom of rolling naked in the snow and then dashing back into the steam again.

Separate hours were set aside for men and for women. In addition to a public room of the type just described, the bánya I went to also had a few private rooms with a western type of bathtub in each. The entrances to the two types of accommodation were separate, but the doors were side-by-side and the two hallways were partitioned only by the booth of the cashier, who had to service both. Naturally, I went to the private bath entrance, where I had to stand in line before the ticket office. Just as it was my turn to get a ticket, the tramp of heavy boots was heard outside and a group of some twenty men entered the public part of the building, stamping the snow off their feet and talking loudly. I thought I heard some voices which sounded familiar; then the face of one of Podtiólkov's henchmen in our former Guard Battery appeared in the small cashier's window opposite mine.

Fortunately, I saw him first and swung away from the cashier's opening in a fit of choked coughing which was not entirely simulated. I could hear them debating the crowded condition of the public bathroom and then deciding to try out the *bourzhóui* bathtubs in the private rooms.* So they all tramped out onto the street and back into our hallway. As I heard them coming, I pulled my fur cap as far down over my face as I could, dropped my earflaps down, raised my coat collar and stood in a hunched pose pretending to read a newspaper which I had just bought and now opened, holding it close to my face the way a short-sighted man would.

The Cossacks who were now pushing all around me were the Red "hard-core" of our Guard Battery who, after its dissolution as a unit, had remained with Podtiólkov and the Don Military Revolutionary Committee which he still headed. One of my arch-enemies, Ponomarióv (see p. 150), was among them and even jostled me as he tried to get by. They would probably have broken my neck then and there had I been recognized. So I edged my way to the street door, got out and kept going, having lost all interest in physical cleanliness.

Novocherkássk was getting to be most uncomfortable. I felt that my luck could not last there forever and that sooner or later I was bound to be recognized. Yet there seemed to be no way to get out of the town. Such sparse news as reached us from the outside indicated that the White volunteer detachments had retreated into the most inaccessible areas of the steppes and that it would be impossible to get to them past the numerous Red units all around. My fake certificate of a hospital train orderly was insufficient for travel away from the town. I racked my brains for some plan of action, but could think of none that would be likely to work.

Every three or four days in the evening I dropped in on the Oupórnikovs to chat and learn the latest rumors. On one of my

---

* They must have been disappointed—the Russian steam bánya is far superior to a bathtub, especially when there is much accumulated dirt to wash off, which then floats around one in the latter. The much more hygienic western spray shower was used only infrequently in those days.

periodic visits, I found them quite excited. Several Cossacks of our former Guard Battery had been there the day before. This was not the first time groups of our men, now pro-Red, had visited their house—something seemed to draw them to the home of their former commander. They never attempted to search the house and were courteous to the women there.

One of the men had specifically asked about me on the day before and was assured that I was somewhere in the steppes. However, that afternoon the same Cossack came back alone and said that he was not going to ask again where I was, but, if by some chance they should happen to see me, would they please pass on to me the folded sheet of paper he gave them—I might find it useful, and would they remember to tell me that it was Kouznetzóv who had brought it? He made them repeat his name, turned around and left. They all thought it was a trap—I did not.

The paper was a printed certificate form of the Don Military Revolutionary Committee. It was dated that day, but had no number in the space reserved for that purpose, and the first two lines following the printed words: THE BEARER OF THIS were left blank. On the third line was the name of one of the Cossacks of our former Guard Battery which was written in the same handwriting as the signature of the Chairman—Podtiólkov—below. The fourth and fifth lines were also left blank; at the bottom was the signature of the secretary whose name I do not recall and the official seal of the Revolutionary Committee.

About a year later I met Kouznetzóv on a station platform while waiting for a train at a railroad junction in the Don—like most other Cossacks he was back on the White side then. He told me that a slight hesitation of the Oupórnikovs in their answer to his query about me made him guess that I must be somewhere nearby. So he went to Podtiólkov and asked for a blank but signed and stamped certificate. Podtiólkov refused to give it to him, unless he first told him for whom it was intended and what it was for. Kouznetzóv knew that one of their group was going to desert that day and go home, so he gave his name, saying that he needed it urgently but had not said why. They finally compromised by Podtiólkov writing that name in the third line and leaving the first, second, fourth and fifth lines blank for him to fill in.

I guessed at that time that something like that must have happened. I could not believe that Kouznetzóv with whom I had so many friendly discussions about Yogi philosophy and other matters (see pp. 97 and 153) was capable of treachery. I was right. He never even tried to get in touch with me later to capitalize on the good turn he did me, apparently simply because he liked me.

So I wrote in after THE BEARER OF THIS, the words: *A citizen of the town of Pávlovsk, Petrográd Goubérniya (District)*, which filled the first and second lines, and then, after the name of the Cossack in the third line, which name I have now forgotten, added: *is permitted to travel without hindrance to the place of his permanent residence.* I also added a fictitious number, which gave the certificate an official appearance.

The next evening, armed with that document and carrying only a sack with some food slung over my shoulder, I went to the railroad station where a passenger train from Rostóv to Moscow was expected.

Its arrival was held up in part by a special train which was waiting at the ramp in front of the station building. It consisted of a sleeping car, of a passenger car already occupied by an armed bodyguard, and two open freight cars with two automobiles lashed down to them. A locomotive under steam was already coupled to these few cars in readiness to start north for Moscow as soon as the important Commissar arrived for whom this special train was waiting.

Soon after I got there, Red Guards began clearing and keeping open a path through the nondescript crowd which filled the waiting room. The outer door was held open and in strutted Pougachévsky followed by a suite of Red officers. He rapidly walked past, so close that I could have tapped him on the shoulder by making a step forward past the men in front of me and by stretching out my arm.

The crazy idea to do just that and to ask for a lift to Moscow crossed my mind, but something warned me not to tempt luck that much. So I simply watched from a distance as he boarded his sleeper, whereupon his special train immediately pulled out of the station.

An hour or so later the regular passenger train came in from Rostóv and, together with part of the waiting crowd, I managed to push, shove, kick and elbow my way in till I got a secure foothold on the steps of one of the passenger cars as it steamed north, leaving many other would-be travelers behind.

# 6 Bolshevik-Held Petrográd in Spring and Summer 1918

## 1. *Travel North*

The trip to Moscow took two or three days, much longer than usual. At each station the train was besieged by crowds trying to get on board. No one bothered to buy tickets, nor did the completely powerless railway personnel attempt to stop this.

At one of the stations I managed to push my way into the interior of the car. Then, during the general rearrangement of the tightly packed passengers when some of them left the train, I was somehow squeezed into the large toilet compartment where I joined its two already established occupants in defending it against all would-be newcomers.

We would let only one person in at a time, making sure that he—or she—left before anyone else was admitted. This gave us much more space than in the car outside and at times we even managed to relax somewhat in spite of the unpleasant odors and sounds inherent to the location, which at least was warm, its windows being unbroken.

My two companions were day-laborers from some village just south of Moscow—a middleaged man and his nephew. They were typical village proletarians who had volunteered for service with the Red Guards and who, after the fighting was over, were returning home, bringing their rifles back with them. The older man was violently pro-Bolshevik, but this caused no conflict between us because our mutual interest in keeping the toilet compartment we had occupied as much as possible to ourselves, and our successful joint efforts to that end, soon established friendly relations. We even shared some of the food we had with us. I was however careful not to engage in conversations which might give me away, and only emitted short grunts and oaths worthy of a village idiot.

For as long as I could I resisted the urge to use the toilet myself since this would reveal my only garment which did not fit the rest of my disguise: I had kept my trousers which had a red silk permanent cummerbund-type attachment at the top, a kind worn only by officers. This was normally well covered by my dilapidated soldier's blouse which I had considered sufficient protection, never imagining the predicament I was now in.

Finally I was compelled to throw caution to the winds and yield
to the demands of nature. My older Red Guard companion immediately spotted an edge of the red silk and wanted to know where I got
the trousers. My reply that they had belonged to an officer did
not satisfy him and he continued to peer at me intently. Finally, it
dawned on him who I was. An amused grin of understanding spread
over his face and he gave me a great big wink, but said nothing. In
the course of the subsequent journey he repeatedly made cracks about
the need to shoot all former officers, patting his rifle, but always
accompanied his bloodthirsty utterances with a good-natured wink.
He obviously wanted me to know that I had not fooled him, but that
he intended no personal harm. At some station near Moscow he got
out, wishing me a happy journey. The rest of the trip to Moscow
was uneventful.

This was the first time I had been in Moscow and I looked with
interest at its buildings, the walls of many of which had been pockmarked by rifle bullets and shell splinters during the November 1917
street fighting four months earlier when the Bolsheviks had seized
power there.

I took an electric streetcar to an apartment house where Mrs. Foli-
mónova lived—the wife of Captain Ivan Folimónov of our Guard
Battery who had been mortally wounded at Dolzhánsk (p. 165).
It was my unpleasant task to inform her that she was a widow.

As I swung into the vestibule of the house, my ragged appearance
so enraged the old doorman that, in spite of several months of Bolshevik rule, he leapt up, swearing, and ordered me to go up *"s chyór-
nago khóda* (by the 'black' or rear entrance)." This I did, covering
my retreat by appropriate curses, but feeling pleasantly reassured as
to the effectiveness of my disguise.

My sad mission accomplished, I took the train to Petrográd. To
do this I had to buy a ticket. In general, complete order had been
restored on that railway line.

## 2. *Life at Tsárskoye Seló*

My Podtiólkov-signed fake certificate (p. 181) had
served me well until then, getting me past all document controls.
But I could not reappear at home under a false name. So on the train
from Petrográd to Tsárskoye Seló I tore the fake certificate into little
bits and let them go one by one down a toilet drain.

On the next day, at home, I donned some of my officer clothes which I had left there, removing first the gold-braid shoulder straps, and presented myself at the local Soviet with a concocted story that I had just returned directly from the German front and had been robbed by a pickpocket of all my documents at the Petrográd railroad station. Since I was well-known in town, I received a certificate discharging me from military service. Thus I resumed life as a civilian under my true name.

On the day before that I had gotten home after dark and stayed up late telling Mother all about my adventures,—I enjoyed talking about them, once they were over.

In the morning I was awakened by a knock on the door of my bedroom and at first thought that I was having a nightmare—the man who came in wore the unmistakable overcoat of the Cossacks of our Guard Battery,* just like the one I had last seen under somewhat nerve-racking circumstances on Podtiólkov's pro-Red bodyguard at Novocherkássk (p. 180). But the man now before me stood to attention and was grinning amiably.

It turned out that he was a Corporal who had been left behind at the Pávlovsk barracks, after the Reserve battery of the Guard Horse Artillery there had been disbanded, to protect the furniture and other belongings of the officers of our Guard Cossack Battery stored in their pre-1914 barrack apartments.

He was a conservatively minded well-to-do Cossack from one of the rich southern *stanítzas* and had now displayed remarkable strength of character, intelligent ability and devotion to duty. For over three months he had remained alone at his post, although he was the only Cossack in the Red-occupied town, where the Bolshevik newspapers were full of stories about the Red successes in the Don. Every week or so he walked from Pávlovsk to Tsárskoye Seló to inquire if Mother had any news of me and of our battery. She had none, except a letter from me saying that we were back in the Don.

He now reported that a critical moment was approaching. The Reds were gradually taking over the empty barracks at Pávlovsk for their own new formations, whereas up to that time they had permitted the former officers of the Reserve battery, including its commander, Count Rehbinder (pp. 75, 76, 113, 118) to remain in their old

---

* At the start of the War in 1914 the Grand Duke Andréy Vladímirovitch, former battery commander (p. 75), had bought and personally paid for cloth-covered fur coats presented by him as a gift to every Cossack in the Battery. They were of a similar type to the one I am wearing in the photograph, Fig. 19, but were shorter and of a special snappy cut.

apartments. Now these officers were all ordered to leave, but were allowed to transport their personal furniture with them. The moving was to take place in a couple of days. Our Corporal, whose name I have forgotten, was certain that he would never be permitted to remove the furniture of absentee Cossack officers, but believed that this could be done surreptitiously at the same time as the authorized move.

He had made friends with some rich farmers of German origin in the vicinity who were strongly anti-Bolshevik. They had agreed to provide three extra horse-drawn carts, in addition to the ones they were hired to supply for the authorized move, and to take the furniture of our officers to an empty shed belonging to a food merchant who had been a supplier of our battery in peacetime, and who had now agreed to store it there secretly.

The Corporal was obviously and rightly pleased with himself. Nevertheless he inquired whether I approved of the arrangements he had made. If I did, would I, please, take over command of the operation? He could easily get me some peasant clothing from the farmers and I could then pose as one of the cart drivers.

After my Novocherkássk ordeal, penetrating in disguise into Red Guard barracks was about the last thing I felt like doing at that moment. It was however impossible to disappoint this splendid man —so I agreed, commending him for his resourcefulness and the completeness of his arrangements, which I could not improve upon.

Everything went off quite well. However, the sly fellow had not told me the whole story at first. As we carried out to the carts a large Ottoman sofa, I was surprised by its unusual weight. Questioning revealed that the Corporal had kept hidden in its interior three infantry rifles with several hundred rounds of ammunition which he had managed to purloin from a careless Red unit next door, hoping to use them if there was an anti-Bolshevik uprising. "You may get a chance to use them that way yet," he whispered.

He left for the Don on the next day, but I never heard of him again.

I cannot establish the exact dates, but all this was taking place about the middle of March, 1918.

Some of our friends had managed to leave town and many were planning to do so. Everyone was very tense, since there were numerous searches of houses, after which former members of "society" were frequently arrested and clapped into jail for no reason at all.

Professor and Mrs. Gregory P. Tschebotarioff in the garden of their Princeton home, May, 1964. (PHOTO BY WILLARD STARKS.)

*Figure b.* The author in 1918 (see p. 187).

By contrast, we were not molested in any way and not once was our apartment searched. I kept wondering what would happen if it was, since I had a whole collection of arms and trophies arranged as a panoply on a wall of my father's study. In the center was a painted cast-iron Austro-Hungarian frontier plate with the relief of the dual monarchy's double-headed eagle crest, which my father had removed and sent me when his brigade marched into Galicia at the start of the war. Above it was a spiked German helmet and swords; on the sides were hung several types of rifles—Austrian, German, and even a couple of old flintlocks of Albanian mountaineers which Father had brought back with him from his 1913 trip to the Balkans (p. 11). They were flanked on each side by two Russian light tubular steel cavalry lances of a discarded model. An Austro-Hungarian heavy machinegun belt formed a border to the entire collection; it was packed with cartridges, including some with explosive bullets.*

One day, as I walked past the studio of the former Imperial Court photographer, Hahn, I noticed that it was still functioning. It occurred to me that I had no professional close-up photograph of myself in officer's uniform. So I walked in and asked old Hahn if he would take a picture of me. He said he would, if I managed to reach him alive. This I did by wearing civilian trousers, shoes, hat and a light coat over one of my officer's blouses which I had left at home in November, 1917. But only the latter appears on the photo, Fig. b. The one star on my Guard Horse Artillery shoulder strap denotes the rank of *práporschik* (third lieutenant), although I was already entitled to the two stars of a *khoroúnzhi* (see p. 167).

Mother continued her work at the hospital part time for a while. Once, when she mentioned her worries about her home, a wounded soldier, a local man, assured her that she had nothing to worry about, since we had a powerful protector at the local Soviet. He then told an amazing story, which we checked and found to be correct.

In the preceding years, when off hospital duty, my mother used to read fairy tales to my little sister, who was then about seven years old. In good summer weather she did this sitting on a bench under

---

* These bullets emitted a puff of smoke after hitting an obstacle. Allegedly, they were intended to facilitate getting the right range. However, when they hit human beings, as some of them inevitably did, they inflicted horrible wounds, much worse than those caused by any bullets of the dumdum type. I carefully cut one open and satisfied myself that it had an explosive charge inside. Their manufacture and use by the Austro-Hungarians was a direct violation of International Red Cross conventions.

some lilac bushes in our garden, at the corner of a fence between it, an adjoining garden and the street. Children of various domestic help in the vicinity gathered to listen. At first they were shy and stayed on the other side of the fence; then some of the bolder ones climbed onto and sat on the fence; finally, seeing that Mother did not object, they ceased being bashful and used to gather around the bench in our garden. Mother liked having this crowd of urchins sitting on the ground and listening intently to her—she spoke of them jokingly as *moyá bosonógaya kománda* (my barefoot gang).

We did not know it, but among them were three children of the *dvórnik* * of an adjoining house who turned out to be an ardent Bolshevik. He never said anything to us before or after the Revolution, but had apparently noted with gratitude Mother's kindness to his kids. At any rate, when he became a leading member of the local Soviet, he told his comrades about this—also about Mother's uninterrupted volunteer hospital work during the entire three and a half years of the war. He then obtained a decision that we were not to be bothered in any way.

Many of our friends were however subjected to all kinds of annoyance. In a way this was ironic, because most of them held rightwing views and hence belonged to a group which—contrary to popular misconceptions abroad—was the least active in an anti-Bolshevik sense. The extreme view among them was expressed by the slogan, borrowed from Lenin's earlier days, *chyém khoúje—tyém loúchshe* (the worse —the better), meaning that the quicker things got into a complete mess all over the country (what was assumed to happen if the Bolsheviks were allowed to run it) the sooner it would turn back to the monarchy.

It was almost exclusively the moderate middle-of-the-roaders who did anything to carry on the anti-Red struggle. I got a whiff of what was going on below the surface when one evening in June, 1918, a man in the greasy black leather jacket, trousers and cap of a military automobile mechanic came to our house—I had to peer closely at him to recognize the artillery captain Novogrebélsky, by then a Colonel, who had been so kind to me when I was a boy (p. 36). He asked me to put him up for the night, which I naturally did. He confided that he was a member of an underground anti-Red officer group which was sabotaging Bolshevik efforts to build up their armed forces. For

* Meaning literally "yardman," a servant who usually combined the functions of a handyman and of a doorkeeper.

the past couple of months he had been working at a central depot for armored cars at Petrográd, making sure that no complete set of spare parts ever reached the same units, misdirecting them whenever possible. The Reds started an investigation and he had to "evaporate" in a hurry.

Before leaving in the morning, Colonel Novogrebélsky asked me if I wanted to take an active part in the organization he belonged to. Something very big was about to happen in a couple of weeks, he said —it would have a decisive influence on the entire course of the Russian Civil War, which by then was in full swing. It would mean very hard fighting for a while, but we would soon get active help from the Western Allies. He was not at liberty to tell me more at that time, but if I wanted to join, he would tell me how to get instructions as to where to proceed.

Some sixth sense warned me not to do this and I declined. About two weeks after that conversation came the news of the White uprising in the ancient town of Yaroslávl (see Map A, p. 44). The Reds did not print much about it in their papers at the time and it was only a year later, when I served at the Don Army Headquarters (Chapter 8), that I learned what had actually been involved.

At Yaroslávl and in its vicinity were located the biggest Army ammunition stores in all of Russia, and the Reds would have inevitably lost the Civil War had they been deprived of them. In secret agreement with British and French agents, some 2,000 anti-Red former Russian Army officers inconspicuously seeped into Yaroslávl and seized the town in the name of the Constituent Assembly.* They were soon besieged by large Red forces, but expected to be relieved by an Allied column from Archangel, about 400 miles to the north which was, they thought, already in Western hands.

The White volunteer officers fought gallantly to the last man for over two weeks (July 6 to 21, 1918; new style). I never heard of Colonel Novogrébelsky again; he must have perished at Yaroslávl also. The only thing the abortive uprising achieved was the provision of a convincing argument to those who claimed that perfidy was something inherent in Western attitudes towards Russia. Many more such arguments were to be provided later by short-sighted and contradictory Western actions.

We did not know all this at Tsárskoye Seló at the time. Life was

* Dissolved by the Bolsheviks on January 6/19, 1918.

a constant struggle for food which was rationed and getting very scarce. No money could be withdrawn from the banks. Mother's higher rations because of her parttime continued work as a hospital sister of mercy were a great help, but they were insufficient for a family of five—my maternal grandmother, Doubiágsky, and my sister's French governess were still living with us. Like most of our friends we were compelled gradually to barter away to peasants paintings and furniture in exchange for food. I remember a very large two-tier oak cupboard covered with carved scenes of Mexico's conquest by Cortez being carted away from our diningroom by a farmer from a nearby village in exchange for one sack of flour. I have no idea what he was going to do with it—it seemed much too big to be reassembled in a peasant cottage.

Occasionally I ventured out into the now deserted vast Tsárskoye Seló park, concealing a small-caliber light rifle of French make—a Francotte—under my civilian overcoat. Now and then I succeeded in shooting a crow. Grandmother flatly refused even to taste what she considered to be a filthy bird. So we soaked a carcass of one of them for two days in vinegar, which tenderized somewhat its tough meat. Then we served it to Grandmother, assuring her it was a pigeon; she loved it.

### 3. *Letters from Tobólsk*

Just before Easter, 1918, we received an unusual treat—an excellent ham sent to Mother by the Empress Alexándra Fyódorovna from her Siberian exile at Tobólsk. It arrived by parcel post and must have been the package referred to by the Empress in her letter of February 3/18, 1918, a photocopy of part of which is given by Fig. 28.

At this point, a brief review of the fate of the Imperial family since the Revolution may be of interest—in a way this will be a continuation of Chapter 2, pp. 52–62, where some of the personalities now referred to have been described. To do this I first have to go back a year in time.

Things were made no easier for the Tsar's family at the moment of the February/March 1917 Revolution, which brought the Provisional Government to power, by the homely fact that three of the children were then sick with measles at the Tsárskoye Seló palace, where they were kept under arrest.

On page 148 for April 3[*16, 1917*] of Mother's journal, Ref. 6a, I find:

"El[*izavéta*] Nik[*oláyevna*] Coúriss repeated the words of the priest, Father Afanásy, from the Znám[*enya*] church, that the Gosudár [*Tsar*] now frequently weeps during the service, but she is cold and inscrutable—'the *gordýnya* [*pride touched with arrogance*] is the same.' "

On page 151 Mother continues under the date of 12/25 April:

"An interesting letter today from T[*atiána*] N[*ikoláyevna*]—she pines without work . . . 'It is so strange to sit in the morning at home, to be in good health and not to go to the change of bandages!' She inquires about everything— . . . 'O[*lga*] and M[*aríya*] are still in bed, I walk with papa and work in the garden' . . ."

On the same page 151, but under the next day's date of April 13/26, 1917, Mother adds:

"Today I went to the Palace Commandant Korovichénko—to inquire whether this correspondence is fully permitted, or whether it is allowed only *a contre-coeur* [*i.e., grudgingly*] . . ."

and on page 152:

"He read my letter—'It will certainly be transmitted, and, in general, one can exchange messages with the children, but I have to request better not to write to Alex[*ándra*] Fyód[*orovna*].' Something hard flitted across his face as he said this—in general an interesting clever face, but very tired, a Lieutenant Colonel, apparently of infantry, with a badge, I believe, of the Law Academy. Kerensky recommended him as his friend (somewhere at a meeting of radical parties) . . ."

Speaking of Kerensky's visit to the City Hall on the next day and his repudiation of demands for the transfer of the Imperial Family to the Peter and Paul Fortress at Petrográd, Mother continued on pages 1 and 2 of the second volume of her journal, Reference 6b:

"This is what appeared on the next day in the newspaper where it was reported that after that Korovichénko spoke in defense of correspondence with the children: 'They were workingwomen; they labored like real sisters [*of mercy*]—how can one deprive them at Easter of the joy of exchanging greetings with their former wounded or their comrades in work. All letters pass through me, absolutely innocent. Sister Khitrovó, and other sisters write frequently—such letters I transmit. But I have a boxful of letters from the Románov family—such correspondence is not permitted.' "

Further, on page 2, Mother notes:

"The priest, Father Afanásy, says that they [*The Imperial Family*] are clean like children of all charges of treason leveled at them—they do not understand the position they are in."

On page 9, April 25/May 8, 1917:

"Our cryptic sentences of greetings have not been understood—apparently the general aloofness is taken very hard. Tatiána writes to Ríta [*Margaríta Khitrovó*]: 'Why is that that Var-[*vára*] Af[*anásievna Vilchkóvskaya*], Val[*entína*] Iv[*ánovna Chebotarióva*], Véra Ig[*nátievna Gedróitz*] do not write to the "shef" * [*the Empress*] directly. Are they afraid?' I pity the poor things, but I would not be able to write to her—after all she is the terribly responsible guilty one, even if not voluntarily."

On page 15, May 15[*28, 1917*]:

". . . to be honest, is there anyone among us who would want a return of the old in its entirety—of the influence of A[*lexándra*] F[*yódorovna, the Empress*]—when one had to live through the days of 'government crises.' And with all the new misfortunes which are striking Russia, it is so painful to realize that it is she who is the one who is mainly guilty for it all—had it not been for her, had it not been for the fateful meddling in politics, had it not been for Gríshka [*Raspútin*] and those fatal appointments of Shtúrmer, Protopópov, Golítzin—in view of the softness of the Gosudár [*Tsar*] it would have been possible to have a responsible council of ministers, commanding confidence, and broad social reforms too. But the Army and the form of government would have been kept intact."

* That is, honorary head.

On August 6/19, 1917, page 19:

"On July 28[August *10, 1917*] I first learned that the entire family of the Tsar will be taken away in the night of August 1[*14, 1917*]. . . . On the 30th * [*July/August 12*] I congratulated Tatiánochka on the birthday child and ended: '. . . and you, my dear child [*rodnáya dyétka*] permit the old V[*alentína*] I[*vánovna*], who loves you greatly, to bless [*perekrestít*] and firmly kiss you.' I received an answer both from her and from her mother—already after their departure. . . . I greatly regret that I was unable to kiss Tatiána and take leave of her personally—but kindness from [*illegible, apparently A.F., the Empress*] I find difficult to bear. I feel terribly sorry for her and yet it is all so painful that I cannot find the warm feelings of old, after all she is the awful cause of all the misfortunes of our land, she ruined her entire family, the unfortunate—sick of soul, sick with mysticism and arrogant pride. . . ."

On page 21:

"When the train started, there were few who saluted . . . thus ended that act of tragedy, the last episode of the Tsárskoye Seló period. What will await them at Tobólsk?" †

and on page 22:

"The attitude of simple people—of soldiers, is ironical and hostile. In the morning I entered the 7th ward, all those who were capable of walking were hurriedly dressing—where to? 'We hear they will be taking away Nikóloushkou—dourachká [*the poor fool*] today, we want to go and watch.' To my remark that it is a sin to kick someone who is down, came the answer: 'And what has he done to us, what is Russia living through because of him. . . .' . . . But the monarchists are convinced that the people are for him. Never, they [*the monarchists*] are the blind ones, they are the enemies of the country and of them [*meaning the Imperial family*]. . . ."

Mother describes some foolishly unprepared attempts to "rescue" the Tsar, which almost ended in tragedy and certainly made things worse for him.

---

* The birthday of the Grand Duchess Tatiána's young brother Alexéy.
† A city in Siberia, some 150 miles east of the Urál Mountains.

On page 23 Mother notes a conversation she had with Geringer, an old lady who was entrusted, together with Benkendorff, to seal up the personal belongings of the Tsar's family which they had left behind at the Alexándrovsky Palace where they were under arrest. The two dogs were taken to Siberia with them, but:

"There was a drama with the cats. The kitchen was closed—there was nothing to feed them with—there was not a soul in the palace. On the very first day that Gerin[ger] arrived the unfortunate hungry animals dashed towards her . . . a dismal impression, a dead, empty palace, all exits are locked and only 3 cats flit about like shadows. . . ."

Homes were found for the unfortunate cats. They were apparently taken out through a "tunnel (?)" which, according to Mrs. Geringer, permitted her and Benkendorff access to the Palace. Mother had placed a question mark after the word "tunnel"—it seems that the very existence of this underground passage was kept secret even by the Revolutionary authorities of Kerensky's government who must have been aware of it to permit its use by Mrs. Geringer and her escort. The entrance to it was supposed to be located in one of the private houses adjoining the park, but which one was not revealed.

On page 87, December 17/30, Mother wrote:

". . . today our officers' section was finally closed—by a curious coincidence the beloved creation of the Tobólsk dwellers ended its existence on the anniversary of the death of Gr[igóry Raspútin]! It will not be possible to carry out their request to preserve and store everything in the big palace. . . . . . I worked for three years and four months. I will continue going for an hour or so to the soldiers' section until my pupils Khramtzóv and Lemyákin leave—they study so well; they have mastered fractions to perfection and solve very well problems on rates of interest. . . ."

The last entry in Mother's journal is under the date of January 5/18, 1918. She had just received my letter of December 16/29, 1917, from Kámenskaya in the Don which we had reached after a twelve-day trip from the front.

The correspondence with Tobólsk went on openly through the mails. Fig. 27 reproduces the beginning and the end of a letter, dated December 9/22, 1917, from Tatiána Nikoláyevna—it is interesting not only because of her firm, energetic handwriting but also because its contents reflect the nature which endeared her so much to my mother. The English translation of the part of the letter shown on Fig. 27 follows:

"Tobólsk

Former Governor's H.[*ouse*]

9 December

1917

"My dear Valentína Ivánovna,

Have you received my letter of the 29th? Be kind enough to transmit this letter to our prince. You are probably now missing L.F.? * But it is nevertheless good that they are together. I pity poor Filátov that he cannot get well so long. He was at the hospital when we were still there. Can it be that the same wound bothers him, or is it something else? And our Baron how [*several lines omitted*] . . . frost recently. It reached 24 degrees. When there is wind, it strongly cuts the face. Today is calmer. The sun shines every day. At Ts[*árskoye*] S[*eló*] this never happened at this time of the year. Well, good wishes, my dear dove, Valentína Ivánovna. Christ be with you. If anyone wishes to write us, let them write directly. I kiss you firmly, as I love, Alyúsha † too and O.P. [?] Good wishes.

Your

*Tatiána*"

Apparently the Empress sent Mother a food package some time in January, for which Mother felt she had to thank her directly. The beginning and the end of the subsequent eight-page letter by the Empress, dated February 3/16, 1918, is reproduced by Fig. 28. I give its translation in full, because I think that it clearly reflects the mystic detachment from life of that tragic woman.

3 February/1918. T[*obólsk*]

"Dear Valentína Iv[*ánovna*]

I am so glad you were pleased by the parcel that I am sending you [*one*] again. It is hard to think of you all and to know how

* Lýdia Fyódorovna, wife of General Piótr Krassnóv.
† Author's sister.

difficult will be your life. Here it is easier to get anything, although [end of first page] prices continue to rise and there is a
card system—these committees spoil everything.

So you had to give lessons too, in any case our senior sister
is a *bolshói molodétz* [*i.e., very fine girl*] and your husband can
be proud of you.—Where is your son? It is painful to reminisce
how pleasant everything was and how terribly everyone lives
now. But the Lord God knows why it was necessary to send such
trials and He will give strength to bear everything to all who
address themselves to Him with faith, and there will be a reward
for everything and everything there will be clear and understandable for us. One should only bravely look forward, He is *not*
without mercy, and when it seems that there is no salvation, He
will appear in His splendor. One feels a light behind the clouds—
one knows that the sun is there and that she * will again shine
to us; one should suffer a little more without murmur, accept
everything from His hands, only pray, have strength, and not
weaken in faith and in hope. He sent His son to suffer for our
salvation—so the entire Earth suffers and will be rescued because of His unending love for us sinful mortals. Everything
seems terrible—and so it is, but for the purification of sinful life.
I am writing you in a dull way, my dear, forgive me. We are
living passably. The soul is calm, feels the proximity of God.
Lessons as before—they are playing on the hill. T[*atiána*] is
writing to you what else they do. I believe today is the 15th, but
for us it is still the 3rd, hence we had a small service yesterday
(again they would not let us go to the church), we have not yet
been to one this year. What impression do the young [*names
illegible*] make on you? There is much sun here, which is good.
We make embroideries for the local church, knit stockings! Ríta
[*Margaríta Khitrovó*] is still at Odessa. Sýrov [?] at Vladiv-
[*ostók*], he studies the English language—he had an appendicitis
operation there early in December. Bogdánov is in Moscow, is
starving at a hospital, gets only bread with admixtures at four
o'clock and hot water. [*start of last page*] Write to me, to your
bandage-room sister—otherwise it is sad. May God protect you.
I firmly kiss you, the Countess, the Baroness!!! Hearty greet-

* One of several minor Russian grammatical errors.

ings to the Baron, to Iv. St. Koup [?]. Greetings to your Sónya *
and a kiss to your daughter.

Your old
*Sister"*

In April-May 1918, the Tsar's family was transferred from Tobólsk
in Siberia to Ekateríninburg (present-day Sverdlóvsk) on the European side of the Urál Mountain chain (see Map A, p. 44).

The last letter received by my mother from Tobólsk was from
Tatiána Nikoláyevna, dated May 1/14, 1918 † and, in English
translation, reads in part:

". . . How did you spend the [*Easter*] holidays? They were sad
for us, since we were without Father and Mother. You have
probably already heard that they were taken away from us [*one
word is illegible*]. It was so sad to separate ourselves from them.
You are sure to understand. Maria [*3rd daughter of the Tsar*]
went with them and we stayed with my brother, who is sick.
Of course we were not told where to and for what purpose they
were being taken—neither did they know anything. Almost a
week after their departure we learned that they had arrived at
Ekateríninburg. We receive letters from them. It is such a joy for
us—Mother's heart is hurting very much as a consequence of the
awful road to Tyumén [*a Siberian town*]—they had to travel
over 200 *versts* [*140 miles*] by horses [*that is, by horse-drawn
vehicles*] along a horrible road. They spent nights in villages.
Now they live in three rooms. Before their windows is a huge
fence, so one sees only the top of a church. We are now expecting
to leave shortly, as soon as brother fully recovers. . . ."

We did not receive any letters from Ekateríninburg. As the Civil
War spread and the possibility arose of their liberation by the Siberian White armies, the entire family of the Tsar was brutally murdered there on July 17, 1918, by order of the Soviet rulers. The
details are generally known and will not be recapitulated here.

In my opinion, published data indicates that no one could have
escaped, and I therefore think that the woman who claims to be the

---

* *Diminutive of Baroness Sophie von Medem.*
† The new calendar (p. 3), introduced by the Soviet Government, was beginning to be accepted, at first alongside the old one.

Grand Duchess Anastasía, the fourth and youngest daughter of the Tsar, must be an impostor.

## 4. *My Engineering Studies*

I had never intended to become a career army officer and decided on my return to Tsárskoye Seló to follow in the footsteps of my grandfather Grigóriy Chebotarióv (p. 5) and become an engineer. However, mining did not particularly appeal to me, whereas construction did.

There were many excellent engineering schools of higher learning, called "Institutes," in Imperial Russia, and at least six of them were located at Petrográd—namely, the mining, the technological, the polytechnic, the electrotechnical and the engineering construction institutes. I decided to try for the oldest of them all, the Institut Inzhenérov Putéy Soobschéniya (Institute of Engineers of Ways of Communication), which was an excellent school, a diploma from which carried a great deal of prestige. The Institute had been founded in 1810, during the reign of the Tsar Alexander I, and bore the name of that Emperor. The photograph Fig. 58 shows the relevant inscription over its main entrance, as it looked before the Revolution. By the time I joined it, the name of the Emperor and the crowns over the eagles had been removed from the façade.

In 1809 French engineers and professors had been called in to get it started, so it was originally patterned after the famous Paris École des Ponts et Chaussées. At first it concentrated on canals and roads, bridges being of course included. Railroads and their rolling stock were added later.

As in all Imperial Russian engineering schools, admission was on a purely competitive basis which was particularly severe at the Institute of Ways of Communication. An applicant, just to be admitted to the written examinations, had to have completed his general education with specified minimum grades in mathematics, physics and in the Russian language. In practice this meant that only students in the upper 10 percent of their classes in schools for general education could take part in written exams, which consisted of theoretical derivations of equations, the solution of tricky problems in algebra, geometry, trigonometry and physics, and a Russian language composition on a given theme. In spite of the selective restrictions imposed, usually up to seven candidates for every vacancy took the exams.

My grades at the classes for general education of the Imperial Law School qualified me for participation in the competitive examination. However, I took no chances, and spent about three months, together with a dozen other hopefuls, working with an alumnus of the Institute, Sikórsky,* an engineer who specialized in preparing students for the exams. He made us work terribly hard, but it certainly gave us excellent refresher training, which was very much worth the time and effort expended on it.

The exams were given in the summer, I believe in June or July, and I felt that I had done pretty well. Nevertheless, it was with considerable anxiety that I approached the bulletin board in the entrance hall of the Institute where the lists of the several hundred students admitted were posted in the order of their standing a couple of weeks later. I was delighted to find my name halfway down the list.

At once I donned the light green cap of military style, with dark green border, worn by our students. A crossed axe and anchor of silver—the emblem of the Institute and of railway and canal personnel in general as well—was fixed to the dark green velvet band of the cap (see Fig. c).

*Figure c.* Silver plated badge worn on their caps by students of the Institute of Engineers of Ways of Communication at Petrográd (see p. 372).

Studies began almost immediately, but I had time to complete only one topographic drawing before the developing Civil War compelled me and others to drop out. The Institute itself closed down for a while soon after. Nevertheless, I am considered to be a member of the class—*priyóm*, that is, admission, of 1918 (see p. 343), which was the last year that old-style competition examinations were held.

* Not a relative of the famous helicopter designer.

## 5. *Travel South to the Don via the Ukraine*

Only fragmentary news reached us as to what was happening in the South. By reading between the lines of Bolshevik newspapers it was evident that the entire Ukraine had been occupied by the Germans and that anti-Red uprisings had taken place in the Don and in Siberia where severe fighting was going on.

The first direct news which reached me from the Don could have easily been my undoing. One day the postman delivered a registered letter, mailed to my name and Tsárskoye Seló address directly from the German-occupied city of Kíev, capital of the Ukraine. It was sent by a friend of my childhood, the daughter of a Don Cossack general, and read something like this: "Dear Grísha, You must have heard that Piótr Nikoláyevich Krassnóv has been elected Atamán of the Grand Army of the Don. We had dinner with him the other day and he asked us to let you know, should we have the chance to do so, that you can choose between a post in the armed forces or in the diplomatic service of the Don on your arrival there. . . ." I nearly jumped out of my skin when I read this and expected to be arrested by the Reds at any moment. But, by some miracle, the letter apparently had not been opened by the as yet poorly organized Bolshevik censorship, and nothing happened.

Soon after, we received further news which was sent in a more circumspect manner. General Krassnóv had established fairly friendly cooperation with the German Army which had occupied the Ukraine (p. 209), as a result of which all Don Cossack prisoners-of-war were being returned from Germany to the Don. At Krassnóv's personal request my father was one of the first to be repatriated and was already back at his birthplace, Novocherkássk, the Don Cossack capital, arriving there June 26, 1918. Through the Don embassy to the Ukraine at Kíev, which was headed by his old friend and classmate General Cheriachóukin, Father had arranged for a passage from Petrográd to Kíev for Mother, my sister and myself on one of the so-called Hétman's trains.

These trains were part of a most peculiar hush-hush arrangement between the Hétman Skoropádsky, the German puppet-ruler of the Ukraine, and the Soviet Government. In some ways it was a precursor of the Castro-United States Christmas 1962 deal for the release of the prisoners captured by the pro-Castro Cuban forces during the ill-fated Bay of Pigs attempt to invade that island.

In 1918 there were not enough officials available who were capable or willing to staff the various administrations and ministries set up by Hétman Skoropádsky's puppet government of the Ukraine. So, with the help of German mediators, he made a secret deal with the Soviet Government in Moscow, whereby in exchange for a specified number of trainloads of Ukrainian wheat, the Bolsheviks would permit the departure from Petrográd to Kíev of several passenger trains filled with persons selected at the sole discretion of the Hétman's Ministries. These trains were to enjoy extra-territorial privileges, were to be protected on Soviet territory by two armed detachments—one Bolshevik and the other Ukrainian—and the Reds were to permit anyone arriving at the Petrográd railroad station to freely board them unmolested and without searching their belongings. The only check of credentials was to be made by the commandant of the Ukrainian train.

We decided to go. Grandmother's two daughters by her first marriage, the sisters Tikhomírov (p. 9), agreed to take care of her, so she moved to their Petrográd apartment. My sister's French governess was expecting to be momentarily repatriated to France, so she was the only one to remain for a while at our Tsárskoye Seló house. The bare minimum of essential furniture was left in her room and the rest from the entire house was quickly sold.

An exception was the furniture of my study and a painting or two that we valued for sentimental reasons, which we stored in the attic of our friends, the Coúrisses, across the street from us. We still believed then that I would soon be able to return to Petrográd to continue my engineering studies. But it was not until forty-one years later that I saw the city again (Chapter 10). In the same mistaken expectation, my old canine friend, the French bulldog Búlka (Fig. 15) was found a temporary home. In the years which followed, when famine in Petrográd grew worse and worse, I frequently reproached myself for not having put him to sleep before we left.

Just before our departure, the Soviet Government proclaimed a general mobilization of former army officers, and on the eve of our departure we learned that during the night there had been mass arrests in Petrográd of officers likely to be hostile. Mother became very anxious and insisted that we leave Tsárskoye Seló immediately and spend the one remaining night at my paternal uncle's Petrográd apartment. It was lucky she had her way against my pooh-poohs—her presentiment saved my life. On the next morning my sister's French governess arrived from Tsárskoye Seló to warn us that there had been numerous arrests there that night and that armed Red patrols had come twice to our house to take me away. They were most surprised and annoyed to find the house completely deserted, except for herself, with all rooms empty and only a panoply of arms still adorning a wall of my father's former study.

Most of the officers arrested at Petrográd and in its suburbs at that time were placed on barges which were towed into the Finnish Gulf where they were sunk with everyone on board. Apparently this was done for purposes of intimidation of the remaining officers to insure their compliance with the draft. Organized Red terror was beginning in earnest.

We boarded the Hétman's train that afternoon without any difficulty. For reasons of their own inner politics the Soviet rulers had not disclosed its real nature and had vaguely labeled it "a train of Ukrainian railroad workers." But we heard Red sentries grumbling that the train was filled with the most unproletarian-looking railwaymen and families they had ever seen. Actually, the cream of the old Petrográd society was on board, with or without former ties to the Ukraine, and I seem to have been the only person there who had even a remote connection to railroads—my Ways of Communications student cap (p. 199) proved a great help shortly afterwards.

The women and small children were given "soft," that is upholstered, first- and second-class carriages, so my mother and sister had a two-berth compartment to themselves. I traveled in one of the "hard" third class carriages, the type of accommodation assigned to the men.

The journey proceeded smoothly until Vítebsk, the last big town before the Ukrainian border (Map A, p. 44 and Map G, p. 354). A crowd which filled the station tried to force its way into our train there, but was beaten back by the joint efforts of the Bolshevik and Ukrainian detachments which were assigned to protect it—they had to roll out their heavy machine guns onto the platform and threaten to use them before the crowd gave up its attempts.

As our train left Vítebsk, the Ukrainian and the Bolshevik officers and soldiers on board arranged a joint victory celebration of their success, in the course of which they all got gloriously drunk by the time we reached the border station of Órsha.

The passenger station there was occupied by the Reds but the railway yards and sheds—just a few hundred feet away from the platform alongside which we had to pull up—were held by the Germans. Shortly before our arrival there had been a peasant revolt in the vicinity against Soviet food requisitions, and a sizeable detachment of newly formed Red Army troops was on hand at the station. They were commanded by a stern-faced man who must have been a former Imperial Army officer, and a distinguished one at that, since he still wore the white-enameled officer's St. George Cross on his tunic. This was the most highly prized combat decoration of the old Army, which was awarded only for battlefield valor.

The tipsy Ukrainian train commandant staggered out onto the platform towards him. The Red officer said that he had orders to walk quickly through the train—the inspection would be a mere formality, after which we could proceed. But the Ukrainian, swaying from his drunken bout, announced: "Your foot won't be on board of my train!" and blurted out instructions to steam to the German side immediately.

The Red commander responded by snapping several curt orders. Armed Red soldiers rushed out of the station building, seized and disarmed the drunken Ukrainian commander and his men, locking them up in their carriage, and removed from the train their own equally drunken escort. Heavy machine guns were rolled out onto the platform with orders to riddle the locomotive and all carriages with bullets if the engine driver made any attempt to dash across the border. The train was then shunted to a reserve track, the locomotive was taken away, armed sentries were placed at each of the four doors of all carriages, forbidding anyone to leave or to communicate with other carriages, and a search began which lasted almost two days. The stupid behavior of our commandant had apparently convinced the local Red command that there was important contraband on board.

Actually nearly everybody had taken along with them their most valued souvenirs of the old Imperial days, in the belief that we would be immune from search. So had we. I bluffed my way out of an examination of my hand baggage when the soldiers who were conducting the search noticed the crossed axe and anchor on my cap (Fig. c, p. 199) and greeted me with joyous surprise as "comrade railroader" —the first one they had seen on the train which was supposed to be full of them. Mother simply thrust several hundred roubles into the hand of the leader of the search group of their car and he took all his men away from her compartment without looking at any of her hand baggage. Not all were as lucky—a woman who started arguing and cursing the Reds had the soles and heels of her elegant shoes ripped off to see if anything was hidden there.

When the search of the cars was over, the passengers were permitted to walk to and around the station building, get hot water there and so forth. Then the examination of the luggage van started and the passengers had to unlock their trunks which had been laid out on the tracks alongside the van. I experienced a tense moment when one of the Red commissars held up a bundle of notebooks—which contained my write-up of the battle of Púlkovo and of the fighting in the Don—remarking that they had better take this along to the local Soviet for examination. But another commissar knocked them out of his hands back into the trunk, saying that there was too much of such —— there already.

As soon as the passengers had a chance to communicate with each other, they chose a very energetic Caucasian prince, whose name I have forgotten, to act as their representative and spokesman, since the Ukrainian commandant was obviously useless. The prince immediately dispatched two young men to make separate attempts at a surreptitious crossing of the border to inform the Hétman Skoropádsky, who had personal relatives on board our train, as to what had happened to it. Both succeeded in doing this.

As we learned later, this produced immediate action—all exchange trains carrying food for the Soviets were stopped in the Ukraine and other reprisals were taken. The results were soon felt. Two or three days later the message was circulated among the passengers that the Moscow authorities had ordered the local Reds to let our train go through, but that the latter were going to check first at their places of origin the status of all men of military age. Anyone who felt that such a check might end badly for him should see our princely leader immediately.

My status at Tsárskoye Seló certainly could not stand any checking, since the Reds there had tried to arrest me the night after we left. So I went to the prince, who had a plan ready for such cases, of which there were several: he promised to remove my name from the list of passengers if I undertook to *isparítsya* (to evaporate)—that is, attempt to cross the border on my own and give my word of honor not to reveal my connection with the train if the Reds caught me in the process. I agreed, since by staying I could not be of any use to my mother and sister and might only endanger them too.

Fortunately, I had taken the precaution of getting an official certificate from the Institute of Ways of Communication before I left Petrográd, which stated that I was a student of the Institute and was traveling to Mogilióv—the nearest large town on the Ukrainian side of the border. With this document I proceeded to the Executive Committee of the local Soviet, explained that I wanted to barter at Mogilióv some food supplies for my family at Petrográd and was issued a *própusk* (a pass) to Mogilióv in the "occupied territories"—an apt description of the status of the Ukraine at that time. I still have it— it bears the date of August 19, 1918.

The Red sentries let me through the gate in their barbed-wire fence without any trouble. As I crossed the hundred-foot or so wide strip of no-man's land, I pocketed the Red pass, took out my Ukrainian pass and approached with it the gate in the barbed wire fence which was held by an armed German infantry patrol. My document was written both in Ukrainian and in German on the printed letterhead of the Ukrainian Ministry of Foreign Affairs, was issued at Kíev on July 24, 1918, and had three signatures for the Minister, the Department Head and the Director of the Consular Section, and was stamped with the official seal of the Ministry. This too is still in my possession. Nevertheless, the German Lieutenant to whom I presented it, speaking to him in German, arrogantly refused to pay any attention to it— he did not care what the so-and-so Ukrainians wrote and would not let me through unless I had a document from the German military command.*

It was obviously useless to argue with that fellow, so I decided to wait between the two lines of barbed wire until some other officer relieved him at the gate. I cannot say that I felt at ease, since I could not help wondering when the Red sentries would notice my predicament and would haul me back for questioning. I tried again when there was a change of guard at the "Ukrainian" gate.

The German Lieutenant I had to deal with now proved much more amiable. He was aware of the existence and plight of the Hétman's train held up by the Reds a few hundred yards away and that it had a blanket clearance from the German command for everyone on board.

---

* A vivid illustration of the degree and nature of the so-called Ukrainian independence (see p. 360).

But could I prove that I actually came from it?—the Ukrainian pass was insufficient. He had strict orders not to let any individual former Russian army officers through, since they might be heading for the Kornílov-Deníkin Volunteer Army in the Northern Caucasus, which was strongly anti-German. Only if one of the Ukrainian border-guard officers vouched for me could he make an exception.

I asked for the names of the local Ukrainian officers. The second in command was a man by the name of Nikoláyev—which is about as common, especially in North Russia, as that of Smith in England or in the United States. Nevertheless, I announced that I knew him and wrote him a note, in Russian, explaining who I was and saying that I did not expect he was my former Imperial Law School classmate, but nevertheless hoped that he would help me out.

Shortly after this, a Ukrainian officer came hurrying along—it was Nikoláyev, who, by a thousand to one chance, turned out to be a cousin of my former classmate. The Germans immediately let me through their barbed wire fence into Nikoláyev's custody.

My worries however ended only a day or two later when the Reds finally let the Hétman's train go through and I rejoined my mother and sister on board—they had not been molested in any way. Some twenty other young men had to "evaporate" from it, as I did, and the majority got through by various means and now boarded the train. But several were missing—some of them were known to have paid a large sum of money to local smugglers to get them across the border, but the scoundrels seem to have handed them over to the Bolsheviks instead.

We spent several days at Kíev, headquarters of the occupying German Army. We stayed with the family of General Cheriachóukin, who was Don Ambassador there, while we obtained various German and Ukrainian documents required for our travel across the Ukraine eastward to the Don. The German part went smoothly and efficiently, but the situation at the various Ukrainian offices could have been patterned after some musical comedy. Most of the officials there could speak and write only Russian and very few knew any Ukrainian at all. It had always been debated whether Ukrainian is a separate language or merely a local dialect referred to in the past as "Little Russian" (see p. xxi). But orders now were to carry on all correspondence only in Ukrainian. This caused considerable delays where permits like ours, involving several departments, were concerned. The first official contacted would write out a letter in Russian; then we would have to

wait until it was transcribed into Ukrainian and at the receiving end
we would have to wait again until it was translated back into Russian
before any action could be taken by persons with power of decision.
They were mainly rightwing Russians whose attitude could be expressed by the slogan: "With the devil, if he is against the Bolsheviks."

Finally we got under way, traveling in comparative comfort. It was
painful to see uniformed German officers and troops guarding bridges,
occupying all railroad stations along our route and acting like people
who owned the place, which they obviously did at the time. Considerable numbers of German troops were in evidence, since there had
been many uprisings of Ukrainian peasants against forced requisitions
of food for shipment to Germany.

This state of affairs ended at Taganróg, a town on the Azóv Sea.
The station was jointly occupied by German and Don Cossack troops
—from then on only Don Cossacks were in evidence, both officers and
men wearing exactly the same uniforms and shoulder straps as they
had done in the Imperial Russian Army. Perfect order was maintained
everywhere.

We changed trains at Rostóv-on-the-Don for Novocherkássk where
Father was waiting for us on the station platform. There was a joyful
reunion, after a three-year separation.

# 7

## The Don Under the Atamán General Krassnóv

### 1. Anti-Red Uprising in the Don, Spring, 1918

I will now give a brief outline of what happened in the Don during the five-and-a-half months of my absence.

The general strategy of the White units which had retreated into the inaccessible parts of the steppes (p. 170) had been vindicated. As expected, most of the Cossacks soon rebelled against requisitions of food and other high-handed acts of the Reds and gave support to the White units which began returning from the steppes. Uprisings started in earnest during the month of April when the Bolsheviks in the Don area were weakened by the menace to their rear from the west, where German troops were rapidly advancing eastward through the Ukraine.

During the peace negotiations at Brest-Litóvsk (December, 1917–March, 1918) the Germans pressed for the "independence" of the Ukraine since they hoped to obtain there foodstuffs without which the blockaded Central Powers could no longer continue their war against England, France and the United States. To that end, on February 9, 1918, Germany signed a peace treaty with a delegation of the Ukrainian socialistic *Ráda*.* To give it a semblance of legality, on January 9/22, 1918, that is four days after the Bolsheviks forcibly disbanded the All-Róssiyan † Constituent Assembly in Petrográd, the Ukrainian socialist Ráda proclaimed at Kíev the "independence" of the Ukraine. It should be noted that there never had been any general vote of the population in the Ukraine for the election of the Central Ráda as national representatives, nor had there ever been any general vote for the proclamation of "independence."

This proclamation by the Ráda was typical of a number of similar actions throughout Russia at the time when the All-Róssiyan Constituent Assembly, where the Bolsheviks had only some 25 percent of

---

* Ukrainian word meaning Council, or Soviet.

† The delegates to the Assembly were elected from all parts of the former Russian Empire. I therefore use here the word "Róssiyan" in the sense of its meaning defined on p. xxiv.

the seats, was forcibly disbanded by them. It then became evident that there no longer was any legal means by which local needs and aspirations could receive orderly recognition. The spread of Bolshevism inevitably resulted in a period of complete dislocation of the usual order of things; the ensuing bloody anarchy threatened all moderate groups. Under the circumstances various separatist movements which had been promoted by the Germans for the general purpose of permanently weakening Russia (pp. 39–40, 49, 360) received some support. However, this support represented a temporary anti-Bolshevik attitude, rather than a permanent anti-Russian one.

At the time the Ukrainian socialistic Ráda was proclaiming Ukrainian "independence" at Kíev, it had only some 3,000 troops at its command there, and fighting against local Bolsheviks and the pro-Soviet Ukrainian Government at Khárkov (see Map A, p. 44) was in progress everywhere. The Central Ráda had to abandon Kíev to the Reds on the same day, February 9, 1918, that its representatives were signing a peace treaty with Germany. Answering the Ráda's call for help, the German troops marched into Kíev on March 1, 1918, and completed their occupation of the entire Ukraine two months later. Then, on April 30, 1918, they deposed the socialistic Ráda which had invited them in the first place. The German military command installed instead as their puppet ruler General Pável Petróvich Skoropádsky * who was proclaimed Hétman of the Ukraine by a Conference of well-to-do farmers and landowners. I have already sketched on pp. 205, 206 what this meant in practice—the Germans were the factual rulers.

In the Don area, however, the expulsion of the Reds was carried out by the Cossacks themselves after some severe fighting. A number of dramatic episodes occurred in the process, of which I shall mention two.

The first episode concerned one of the former sub-lieutenants in our Guard Cossack Battery, Podtiólkov, who had become a pro-Red leader (pp. 99, 149–153, 160). At the end of May, 1918, he was captured and executed by his former friend of our Guard Battery, Lieutenant Spiridónov (pp. 82, 83). The fact itself is dramatic enough, showing the extent of the cleavage in all social stratas which the Civil War was bringing about. But there were elements of an

---

* A former General of the Imperial Russian Army, one of whose ancestors had been an ally of Peter the Great, replacing Mazépa as Hétman of the Ukraine (see pp. 17, 361).

ancient saga about the way Podtiólkov's capture took place, as nar-
rated to me the following summer by two young Cossacks of the 2nd
Don Cossack Battery I then served with (pp. 239–252). These men
came from the same village where Lieutenant Spiridónov had lived.

He was the only officer in the vicinity there and the Cossacks of
his village were quite proud of him and of his promotion from the
ranks. The news of the formation of an anti-Red Don Cossack government in the Novocherkássk area and of its orders for the capture and
execution of Podtiólkov had already reached them when a horseman
from a neighboring village to the south galloped in one evening to
warn them that Podtiólkov with a small band of followers had stopped
there for the night. He was trying to make his way to the north, away
from the anti-Red uprising. The tocsin was immediately sounded by
the bells of the church, bringing all Cossacks to a meeting in the
square nearby, armed and ready for action.

The village elders were in favor of a sudden surprise attack that
same night, but Spiridónov flatly refused to take his former friend
unawares. Since Spiridónov had been elected local Atamán, his will
prevailed, and a messenger was sent to tell Podtiólkov to meet Spiridónov at dawn—alone—at the top of a *kurgán* * about midway between the two villages.

As the young Cossacks told me the story, they were in Spiridónov's
detachment which stopped short of the kurgán and dismounted. They
could see through the dim light of dawn a similar group of men some
distance away from the kurgán, from which group a horseman detached himself and rode to the kurgán's top to meet Spiridónov.

It must have been quite a sight as the first rays of the rising sun
bathed the huge figures of these two former Guardsmen and friends,
facing each other for a while on their motionless steeds, talking, while
the burial place of an ancient ruler of the steppes was still cloaked in
semidarkness beneath them.

Then they turned around and rode back to their men. A short en-
gagement followed in which Podtiólkov's demoralized detachment was
defeated and captured.

From then on the story, as told to me, generally agrees with the
grisly description of Podtiólkov's hanging given by the Soviet writer
Shólokhov on pages 720–750 of his *And Quiet Flows the Don,* Ref. 56.

* A prehistoric burial mound of Scythian or other ancient nomadic kings,
usually some thirty feet high. It was placed at high points of ridges, serving in
the past as an observation post for lookout sentries.

But Shólokhov's version of Podtiólkov's capture has none of the romantic flavor of the one I have given above and which I believe to be correct. Some time later (in 1919) I met Spiridónov (p. 254) who by then was a captain and commanded a battery. I asked him what he had talked to Podtiólkov about on the kurgán. His face clouded as he replied: *"O próshlom* (about the past)"—and would say nothing more. Thus he indirectly confirmed the kurgán episode I had heard of.

The second dramatic episode which I want to mention took place at the town of Novocherkássk, which had been freed from the Reds on April 23, 1918, by the Cossacks of the neighboring stanítzas. The Bolsheviks however received reinforcements, regrouped, and on April 24 started offensive operations again. The Cossacks were hard pressed and for a while it looked as if they would again have to abandon their capital city. Then, at a critical moment, suddenly arrived the news that a sizable force of White volunteers * under the command of a Colonel Drozdóvsky had appeared, seemingly out of nowhere, in the west on the flank of the Reds, ensuring thereby the complete rout of the latter. I have often heard this story in the Don—it has been written up on pages 192–200 of Ref. 50, by Gen. I. A. Polyakóv, former chief of staff of the Don Army.

This detachment had been formed in Rumania after the Russian troops there had disintegrated under Kerensky's Government. Colonel Drozdóvsky gathered around him officers and men who had heard of the formation of an anti-Red Volunteer Army in the Don and who had decided to make their way across the Ukraine. Railroads no longer functioned, but Drozdóvsky's detachment managed to cover the 600 miles by road through a countryside in the throes of anarchy, bringing artillery and an armored car with them, which proved decisive in defeating the Reds before Novocherkássk.

General Polyakóv describes in Ref. 50 how the Don Cossack commanders learned from Drozdóvsky of the appearance of German troops on the borders of the Don. A difficult decision as to basic policy towards them had to be made. It was impossible to continue fighting the Germans while fighting the Bolsheviks at the same time. For that reason the Don Cossack commanders established friendly contact and cooperation with the new German neighbors on their western border.

Shortly afterwards (May 1 to 5, 1918) a Cossack "Krug Spaséniya

---

* The nucleus of what soon became the famous Drozdóvsky division of the Volunteer Army.

Dóna" (Assembly for the Salvation of the Don) met and restored to the region its seventeenth-century name of "Vsevelíkoye Vóysko Donskóye" (Grand Army of the Don). The Krug elected Gen. Piótr Nikoláyevich Krassnóv to be the Don Atamán. He continued and developed the policies of the previous local commanders by cooperating with the German occupiers of the Ukraine, since a struggle against them would have been futile.

Both sides adapted themselves to the realities of the situation. The German military command saw that the Cossacks were perfectly capable of keeping the Reds out of their own territory and that the presence of German units in the Don would only cause friction between them and the Cossacks. So the German command withdrew their troops back into the Ukraine from the Cossack border areas they had at first occupied. They also supplied Atamán Krassnóv's government with arms and ammunition in exchange for foodstuffs. The Don government was formally recognized on June 5 by the German Military Command in Kíev. The German Ukrainian puppet, Hétman Skoropádsky followed suit on July 29, 1918 (Refs. 35 and 50).

## 2. *Our Life at Novocherkássk*

In retrospect, Atamán Krassnóv had no choice but to do what he did. At the time, however, I felt differently, as did a great number of other young Russian officers—collaboration with the German Army for any reason whatsoever seemed inexcusable. I therefore made use of a technicality to avoid serving in troops which were fighting other Russians in alliance with Germany. The Don government had decreed exemption from military service to anyone who wanted to complete his education; in addition, former *partizáns* (guerrillas) of the epic days of Atamán Kaledín were to be given special privileges, including admission, ahead of any other candidates, to any school they chose.

I promptly applied for and immediately received admission to the Engineering Construction Department of the Don Polytechnic Institute at Novocherkássk. My paternal grandmother Ríkovsky tried to influence me to enter instead the Mining Department by offering to deed me some of her remaining as yet undeveloped coal-bearing lands if I did so—apparently she hoped to see me follow in the footsteps of her late husband, my namesake and grandfather Grigóriy Chebotarióv (pp. 5, 6). But I resisted the temptation, largely because I did not believe that private ownership of mineral wealth would ever be restored in Russia. So I decided to follow the field of civil engineering which I had started on at Petrográd and which interested me most.

Grandmother Ríkovsky did not take this badly and tried to make amends for the past (p. 10) by buying for father a two-story stone house at Novocherkássk. Mother was at first quite busy refurnishing it, which was something of a problem in those days.

However, Mother was soon back at hospital work—this time at a higher level of authority. Atamán Krassnóv asked her to assume the role of a roving inspector of military hospitals in the area, with the aim of improving their functioning. Mother plunged into this work.

Father was at first given the post of chairman of the Technical Committee of the Artillery Administration of the Don Army. Then, on November 27, 1918, he was appointed Director of the Don Cadet Corps, the same school from which he had graduated in its first class (p. 7). Fig. 33 shows him with some of his officers and the graduating class of the Corps in the spring of 1919. A few of the cadets in that picture can be seen wearing combat decorations which they had won as volunteer partizáns in White guerrilla detachments before being returned to school.

### 3. *General Krassnóv's Personality and Attitudes*

As a young officer of the Leib-Guard Atamánsky Regiment—the second of the two regiments of Cossack Guards at St. Petersburg—P. N. Krassnóv took part in the Abyssinian expedition of 1898 (pp. 14–16). On his return he wrote a short novel *Lyubóv Abissínki* (*The Love of an Abyssinian Girl*) which scandalized many dowagers of the nation's Capital, thereby drawing the attention of society to him. This first effort seems to have impressed on him the publicity value of eroticism in literature. His later novels—such as *From Double Eagle to the Red Flag*—were not exactly reticent in featuring sex, so that some of his critics charged him with what they called, in the parlance of the day, a "boulevard" style of writing.

During the Russo-Japanese War of 1904–1905 he was in Manchuria as a correspondent for the official newspaper of the Imperial Russian Army, *Rússky Invalíd,* and continued to write there later under the nom-de-plume of "Gr. A.D."

The War Ministry at St. Petersburg appears to have held him in high esteem. Sometimes it used his articles to launch trial balloons to get reactions concerning debatable innovations. So there was considerable curiosity as to who the author was, most people believing that "Gr." was an abbreviation for *Graf* (Count), but wondering who "A.D." was. Actually *Grad*, meaning "Hail," was the name of his favorite old horse.

He met his wife, Lýdia Fyódorovna, at the St. Petersburg Art Academy while attending some courses there. She was then married to a painter, Bákmanson—the same man whom my father commissioned later to do a painting for him in Bulgaria (p. 14). She divorced him after meeting Krassnóv. A talented singer, she then had to give up the stage because of the convention that wives of Guards officers should not perform professionally, but frequently appeared at amateur society concerts or benefits. They had no children.

Krassnóv was an excellent horseman and for a while—around 1910—held the post of Senior Instructor at the Officer's Cavalry School where captains went for advanced refresher training. Figure 29 shows him in 1918, at the time he was Don Atamán. He is wearing an officer's St. George Cross won at the head of the 10th Don Cossack Regiment shortly after the start of the war in 1914. He then successively commanded a brigade, a division, and finally the IIIrd Cavalry Corps —I have described in Chapter 4 the tragic last stages of his command of that unit.

He had a good sense of humor. His favorite drawing, which hung over his desk, was a colored cartoon of himself—I believe by the Russian battle-painter Samokísh who may have also been a 1904–1905 war correspondent in Manchuria. It depicted Krassnóv in his Atamánsky Regiment uniform flying over the Japanese lines astride a large artillery shell, holding at-the-ready under his arm a quill pen instead of a lance—a parody on one of the stories by the famous German prize-liar Baron von Munchausen.

Krassnóv never held against me my desire not to serve under him while he was militarily allied to the German Army in occupation of the Ukraine, and seemed to fully understand my feelings—at any rate his later praise of some of my other actions was unstinted, as shown by the photocopies, Figs. 26 and 30 and their English translations.

An excellent orator, he spoke in a straightforward, understandable but at the same time flowery manner which found its way to Cossack hearts. On pp. 125–127 I cited an example of his ability as an actor in a critically tense situation. Soon after our arrival at Novocherkássk

I witnessed several events which testified to his skill in staging things on a much grander scale.

By that time most of the Don had been freed from the Reds, and Atamán Krassnóv called for elections (among Cossacks only) to the Bolshói Voyskovói Kroug (Big Army Circle, that is, General Assembly). It met on August 15/28, 1918, and the photographs, Figs. 31 and 32 illustrate the opening ceremonies before the Novocherkássk Eastern Orthodox Cathedral. Fig. 32 was taken from its steps and shows in the background the mass of the delegates of the Kroug moving towards the cathedral past a dismounted Don Cossack unit which is presenting arms. They are preceded by Cossack officers carrying velvet cushions with regalia of the Don—mainly decorations bestowed on the Don Army as a whole by Russian Emperors of the past. The fourth man from the left is Colonel Nikolái Oupórnikov under whom I had served in the Don Cossack Guard Battery in 1917.

Fig. 31 shows the beginning of the march of the troops past the delegates of the Kroug after the end of the service. The officer closest to the camera is General Krassnóv's aide-de-camp, Captain Koulgávov, to whom I referred on pp. 122–124 in connection with Kerensky's escape from the Gátchino Palace in November, 1917.

But the most impressive ceremony I saw at that time took place on August 26/September 8, 1918, at Persiánovka where General Krassnóv presented to the Kroug the so-called young army he had created. These were units commanded by picked Cossack officers, sergeants and corporals of the old Imperial Army, the privates however being newly recruited nineteen- and twenty-year-olds who had not served previously and who hence had not been subjected to Bolshevik propaganda in the days of the Kerensky Government.

Only a few hundred yards away from the spot where six months earlier our dilapidated handful of White partizáns had made its last effort to stem the Red tide as it was rushing on towards Novocherkássk, some 15,000 splendidly outfitted and trained crack White troops were now lined up on parade. The entire proceedings reminded me of similar past functions at the Krásnoye Seló camp of the Imperial Guards.

About a quarter of a mile away from the spectator stands and facing them, units of infantry, cavalry and artillery formed a continuous line along the front of which Atamán Krassnóv galloped with a half dozen officers and a flag bearer behind him. Each unit, as he approached it, presented arms, the band played, the men answered in rhythmic cadence Krassnóv's greetings, making it sound as if they had a single gigantic voice, and then cheered—the continuing rolling *"hurr-a-a-ah"* of the old Russian Army—and kept cheering until he passed the end of the entire line. It was a beautiful and stirring picture—the flashes of swords and of bayonets in the sunlight as the Atamán approached each unit and their answering roar which was heard over the uninterrupted fluctuating background flow of cheering and of martial music.

At this point Krassnóv departed from the usual procedure of an Imperial parade. Instead of riding over to take the march past in front of the spectator stands, General Krassnóv arranged for the 300 or so delegates of the Kroug to stand there at the place usually reserved for a reviewing sovereign. Then he himself led on horseback the march past, saluting the members of the Kroug as he passed them with the ceremonial mace of the Don Atamáns.

The political symbolism of this act underscored the sovereign powers of the Kroug. The point was not lost on them, since the majority were former veterans, and they showed their appreciation both of this act and of the evidence of successful military reorganization they had just seen. The Kroug promoted the Atamán on the spot to the rank of a full General-of-the-Cavalry (Ref. 50, page 290), skipping one grade—Krassnóv had been only a Major-General in the Imperial Army.

Contrary to the assertions of present-day anti-Russian propaganda in the United States, General Krassnóv certainly was not a separatist of the recently invented "Cossackian" type (p. 360). According to his memoirs published in 1922, Ref. 34, pages 100–101, as early as the summer of 1917, when addressing the Cossacks of the 1st Kubán Division, he spoke of:

". . . the geographical impossibility of creating an independent Cossack republic . . . the majority leaned towards seeing Russia a constitutional monarchy or a republic, the Cossacks being given wide autonomy."

After his election to the post of Don Atamán, he confirmed this general approach. Announcing his election in a letter to foreign governments, dated May 23/June 5, 1918, Krassnóv stated (see Ref. 11, Vol. III, page 328, Document No. 4):

"Until the creation, in one form or another, of a United Russia (Edínoy Rossíi), the Don Army is to be a democratic republic, headed by myself."

However, democratic rights were extended to Cossacks only. The overall result was the rule of an armed minority, a substantial one, it is true (pp. 4, 144), which settled problems of its own by parliamentary methods but delegated, as in the days of yore, temporary semidictatorial powers to a wartime executive—the Atamán.

It is incorrect that this procedure had any antisemitic basis—not only Jews, but all other non-Cossacks, including Great-Russians and Ukrainians, were deprived of equal representation at the Kroug. There were no pogroms or other similar anti-Jewish acts in the Don under Krassnóv's rule—there were very few Jews there anyway—most of the commerce being dominated by Armenians and Greeks. General Krassnóv did develop a strongly antisemitic attitude later, but this happened largely under the influence of persons and events he came in contact with in the 1920s in Germany (p. 302).

Although following in practice a policy of "The Don for the Don Cossacks," in the final analysis General Krassnóv never thought of the Don or of himself as anything but an integral part of Russia. He frequently expressed views and feelings to that effect (pp. 110, 301–308). Personally, he favored a monarchy for Russia. In the past, Tsar Nicholas II had known of his writings and had received him in personal audience. The Empress and the Grand Duchesses also knew of him and had met his wife through my mother—Tatiána Nikoláyevna refers to her, for instance, in her letter, Fig. 27, also see p. 195.

After the murder of the Tsar's family, Atamán Krassnóv officially ordered a ceremonial church funeral service dedicated to their memory, although this increased opportunities for criticisms of him (Ref. 35, page 215).

Thus General Krassnóv was a very strong and complex personality, a man of great personal courage and an able organizer who had to cope with an extremely difficult, novel and rapidly changing situation. He had to improvise new solutions continuously and rapidly implement them, one action often being in basic contradiction with another. Accordingly, he was accused later, with considerable justification, of being an opportunist. Also, he was charged with being intolerant of people who criticized him, which is only partially true. In the abstract, these characteristics may be considered negative. But without them he could not have continued to walk the tightrope of constructive leadership in the midst of world-shaking revolutionary turmoil for as long as he actually did in South Russia.* His actions were motivated above all by a strong sense of duty, and not by mere vanity, as sometimes charged.

## 4. *The Don Between the German and the Volunteer Armies*

In the spring and early summer of 1918 the Volunteer Army, which had been organized by the generals Kornílov, Alexéyev and Deníkin, was only beginning to recover from the rigors of their epic *Ledyanóy Pokhód* (Icy March) through the steppes after they had been forced by the Reds to abandon Rostóv in February, 1918. The few survivors of this march were awarded a decoration which consisted of a silver crown of thorns pierced by a sword. It was worn on an orange-and-black striped ribbon—the colors of the St. George Cross, traditionally awarded for military valor only.

The crown of thorns may seem pretentious, but it truly symbolized what that nucleus of the Volunteer Army had been through. Moving across the icy and sparsely populated steppes, they were constantly harassed by pro-Red detachments, especially in the vicinity of railways, suffering numerous casualties in continuous engagements. The wounded could not be left behind since they were certain to be murdered. As a result, by the month of May, 1918, the Volunteer Army had lost much of its mobility and capacity for offensive action, its remaining combat units being largely used for the protection of a huge transport of wounded. The Kubán Cossacks, in whose territory the Volunteer Army had been mainly moving, were slower than the Don Cossacks in rising and in taking determined action against their local largely pro-Red non-Cossack majorities.

The difficulties of the Volunteer Army are frequently dismissed abroad by flippantly saying that they were just "Tsarists," as if this catch-all term represented real issues at the time. Most of the Volunteers were former Imperial Army officers, it is true, but very few of them were monarchists, in part for reasons given by me on pp. 188–189.

The top leaders of the Volunteer Army were of humble origin. Thus General Kornílov was "the son of a Cossack and of a *krestiánka*

* See pp. 301–308 concerning his activities between the two world wars and his tragic end.

(peasant woman)" as he said in some of his speeches. One may add that his mother came from one of the native Siberian tribes, which accounts for the partly Mongolian features of Kornílov. General Deníkin was the grandson of a liberated serf.

A great many officers in the ranks were not career men at all, but had joined the Imperial Army in wartime only. Socially most of them belonged to the intelligentsia, so that at the time they were often jokingly referred to as *"raskáivshyisy intelligénty"* (repentent intellectuals)—because of their horror and revulsion at what the "freedoms and liberties" they had always believed in had done to the Army and to Russia when permitted by the Kerensky regime to reach limits which were utterly absurd in wartime. Their main motivating emotion was anger at the Bolsheviks for having abused these freedoms and for destroying the Russian Army by their propaganda, thereby placing Russia at the mercy of Germany.

Unswerving loyalty to the wartime Western Allies as true friends of Russia, the slogan *"Rossíya, Edínaya i Nedelímaya"* (Rossíya,* One and Undivided), support of the idea of a Constituent Assembly to solve all political problems, and implacable anti-Germanism were what sustained the majority of them during the terrible trials of their Icy March. One can therefore imagine their indignation when they found their present neighbors to the northwest, the Don Cossacks, cooperating under Atamán Krassnóv with the German Army which had occupied the Ukraine. Their feelings were similar to but much more violent than my own which had prompted me at first to stay out of service for the Don government of General Krassnóv (p. 212).

However, General Krassnóv at that time was not actually pro-German in his feelings—that came later (p. 302). He was merely being realistic. Turkey, allied to Germany, still blocked the Dardanelles and the Bosporus to England and France interdicting communications between them and anti-Red forces in South Russia. There were no ammunition or armament stores in the Don and combat supplies had to be captured from the enemy—sudden night attacks and encirclements constantly had to be used to achieve this. At the same time the Germans had found in the Ukraine large stores of the old Russian Army and were willing to trade them in exchange for foodstuffs. In addition, Krassnóv's cooperation with the German Army in the Ukraine kept it out of the Don and yet assured the Cos-

* See p. xxiv for explanation of term.

sacks a safely protected left flank permitting thereby the release of all of their armed forces to fight the external and the internal Reds.

In some ways Atamán Krassnóv may have gone too far to establish good relations with the German High Command. Thus he sent two personal friendly messages to Kaiser Wilhelm and dispatched a Cossack military mission to Berlin which even visited the battle lines in France, viewing them from the German side. He also supported the formation in non-Cossack areas—freed from the Reds by the Don Army—of a German-financed so-called Yúzhnaya (Southern) Army which was in direct competition with the pro-Allied Volunteer Army. All this produced storms of indignation in the Volunteer Army and among some Cossack intellectuals as well.

In this connection it should be remembered that, not having any common border with the German Army—the Don Cossacks being in between,—the Volunteer Army was not confronted with the same dilemma which Atamán Krassnóv had to face. It was therefore easy for them to criticize him, although he realized the need of helping the Volunteer Army and actually did so by sharing with them the military supplies which he obtained from the German Command in the Ukraine. This gave a strong talking point to Atamán Krassnóv and to his aides in the acrimonious exchanges, some of them public, concerning his dealings with the Germans.

Emphasizing that the Volunteer Army had no roots in the territories it moved through and hence did not have the same responsibilities as did the Don Cossack government, the Don Army Commander, General Deníssov, on one occasion not too tactfully referred to them as "wandering musicians." On another occasion, learning of a charge which came from Volunteer Army Headquarters that "the Don Army is a prostitute which sells itself to whoever pays it," the same General Deníssov retaliated in kind by answering: "If the Don Army is a prostitute, then the Volunteer Army is a pimp which uses her earnings and is kept by her" (page 205 of Ref. 35).

Atamán Krassnóv himself used more literary but no less sarcastic language. Thus (on page 207 of Ref. 35) to quote him:

". . . already during the session of the August [*1918*] Kroug, the Atamán, answering attacks for his dealings with the Germans and hearing that the dovelike purity of the Volunteer Army, which on its banners carried unshakable fidelity to the Allies, was being pointed out to him as an example, exclaimed:

" 'Yes, yes, gentlemen! The Volunteer Army is pure and faultless. But it is I, the Don Atamán, who with his dirty hands takes German shells and cartridges, who washes them in the waves of the Quiet Don and who hands them over, clean, to the Volunteer Army! The entire odium for this action lies upon me!'

"A storm of applause covered the words of the Atamán. Attacks of the 'German orientation' ceased."

Krassnóv's wisecrack about washing German shells in the river Don for Deníkin became very popular among Cossacks and I recall hearing it often at the time.

But the pro-Volunteer Army and pro-Allied feelings among the Cossack delegates to the Kroug were very strong and centered around Gen. Afrikán Petróvich Bogáyevsky who was then chairman of the Council of Ministers of the Grand Army of the Don. When Bogáyevsky made an anti-German speech before the Kroug, the representative of the German High Command at Rostóv, Major von Kochenhausen, who served as a liaison officer with the Don Government, reacted to it on September 4/17, 1918, by writing to Atamán Krassnóv a letter (pages 216–217, of Ref. 35) which ended by the sentence: ". . . I am afraid that the High Command will draw its conclusions and will stop the supply of armaments."

This letter formalized previous oral communications to Krassnóv in the same vein. Atamán Krassnóv had no choice but to do all he could to placate the German High Command, and it should be remembered that the latter encouraged policies which would promote the dismemberment of Russia.

It is in this atmosphere that the *Bolshói Voyskovói Kroug* (The Big Army Circle; that is, General Assembly) promulgated on September 2/15, 1918, the *Osnovnýe Zakóny* (The Basic Laws) for the Don. Its first article reads: "The Grand Army of the Don is an independent State, based on the principles of rule by the people" (Ref. 11, Vol. I, page 301, Document No. 1). There was no reference to a United Russia, such as had been spontaneously made by Atamán Krassnóv earlier on his election in May of that year (pp. 216, 217).

In evaluating the long-range significance of the above unqualified statement concerning the independence of the Don in its Basic Laws of September 1918, one should remember all that has been said above concerning the dependence of the Don Army on military supplies delivered to it by the German High Command and the latter's policies aimed at the dismemberment of Russia. As soon as German influences were removed a couple of months later, these separatist aims were no longer pressed.

Secondly, it should also be remembered that the Kroug was elected in the midst of a raging Civil War by Cossacks only; that is, by an armed minority of the population of their region.

The non-Cossack majority was not trusted to fight the Reds and was not mobilized to do so.

On page 221 of Ref. 35, General Krassnóv writes:

". . . At that time the Don was split into two camps—the Cossacks and the peasants. With few exceptions the peasants were Bolsheviks. Uprisings against the Cossacks did not cease in places where there were peasant villages. The entire north of the Don Army, where peasants predominated over the Cossacks, the cities of Rostóv and of Taganróg, the Batáisk settlement, were soaked with Cossack blood in their struggle against the peasants and the workmen. Attempts to draft peasants into the ranks of Don regiments ended in disaster. The peasants betrayed the Cossacks and defected to the Bolsheviks, forcibly taking along with them their Don officers to torture and to death. . . ."

Faced with this situation, with the pro-Volunteer Army sentiments of many Cossack intellectuals and with the opposite pro-separatist pressures from the German Army Command, Krassnóv attempted to bolster the morale of the Don Cossacks by emphasizing at that time the differences between them and the rest of Russia and by stressing that: "The Cossacks defended their Cossack rights against the Russians" (page 221 of Ref. 35). He frequently reminded the Cossacks of the good old days of yore when they were semi-independent frontiersmen and the only inhabitants of their area, then a border region. At his insistence, the Kroug voted to restore to it the seventeenth-century name of *Vsevelíkoye Vóysko Donskóye* (Grand Army * of the Don), as well as its ancient official seal with the image of a stag pierced by an arrow and with the inscription: *A stag may be swift, but a Cossack arrow overtakes him* (see Fig. 34 and p. 268).

But memories of past links with the Russian Imperial Crown were also carefully preserved. I have already mentioned on p. 215 the

---

* Some authors, for instance in Refs. 53 and 72, translate the word *vóysko* as "host." I use the word "army" instead since in Russian the word *vóysko* designates only an *armed* multitude of people.

parading at the opening of the Kroug of regalia granted by the Tsars (Fig. 32). Another example is the continued wearing of the emblem A III on their shoulder straps by the officers and cadets of the Don Cadet Corps (Fig. 33) in memory of the Tsar Alexander III in whose reign the Corps had been founded. A document I have bears the seal of the Corps with the inscription, *Don Cadet Corps of the Emperor Alexander III* around the same image of a stag pierced by an arrow which appears on Fig. 34. There was no contradiction in this—the Cossack claims to a special status, including land reserves and other privileges, were legally based on Imperial edicts of past years.

The real attitude of the Don Cossack Kroug towards Russia and its people was expressed five days after the promulgation of the Basic Laws in its decree (*Ukáz*) of September 7/20, 1918, containing a message of friendship for the Russian peasants of the Bolshevik-held Vorónezh district, which adjoined the Don region on the north. A part of that message reads:

"We remember very well that we are flesh of the flesh and bone of the bone of the Russian people. We do not forget for a minute that the fate of the Don Cossacks is closely interwoven with the fate of the Russian people and of the Russian State." (See Ref. 11, Vol. III, page 351, Document No. 17.)

The *Ukáz* continued on page 350: "The Army Kroug has frequently stated that until reunification with Russia, after the reestablishment of lawful rule there, Cossacks wish only one thing: to safeguard the borders of the Army by occupying essential railway junctions and to establish firm order in its area."

Certainly the above could not be the sentiments of anti-Russian separatists.*

Two months later the military organization of the Central Powers collapsed and on November 11, 1918, they were compelled to sign an armistice with the Western Allies. The German troops which were

---

* Similar attitudes prevailed in the Kubán Cossack area, but were expressed more firmly. Thus the Kubán Constitution, promulgated December 5/18, 1918 (see Ref. 32), spoke about federation with Russia of which the Kubán considered itself an inseparable part. Ref. 32 can be examined—courtesy of the Kubán Atamán, Lt. Col. Boris J. Tkatschéw—by bona-fide scholars at the Museum of the Kubán Cossack Army which was evacuated abroad at the end of the Russian Civil War and which is now located in a house owned by the Kubán Cossacks, No. 30-83, Thirty-first Street, Astoria, New York.

occupying the Ukraine rapidly disintegrated, elected their own Soviets and ceased obeying their officers, just as had happened eighteen months earlier in the Russian Army. They no longer exercised a stabilizing influence in the Ukraine, their sole concern being to get back to Germany as quickly as possible.

Uprisings against the German puppet, the Hétman Skoropádsky, took place everywhere in the Ukraine, which was plunged into a state of complete anarchy. In its eastern part, especially in the Donétz coal mining basin, pro-Bolshevik groups predominated from the very start. In the southcentral part, bandit detachments of a self-styled "anarchist" and violent anti-Semite, Makhnó, dominated and plundered the countryside and the towns alike. In the west, the Hétman Skoropádsky tried to hold out in Kíev for a while, but soon gave up and was secretly spirited out of town by departing German officers.

On December 1/14, 1918, Kíev was occupied by Ukrainian separatist troops of a so-called Direktóriya—the name of a nationalist Ukrainian government formed by the same leftwing groups, headed by one Petliúra, which had invited the German Army into the Ukraine a year earlier, only to be deposed by them two months later (p. 209). A substantial part of its troops were Austro-Galicians (see area "A" on Map F, p. 353).

The Direktóriya was however unable to enforce its rule over the rest of the Ukraine and by January, 1919, most of it was in the hands of local Bolsheviks who prepared the way for advancing Soviet troops, spearheaded by divisions composed of Ukrainian pro-Red refugees from the past rule of the German Army and of their Hétman Skoropádsky.

On January 23/February 6, 1919, the Direktóriya fled westward from Kíev itself, abandoning it to the Red Army. This separatist group had been there for less than two months and from then on was continuously on the move to escape pursuing Reds—hence its nickname of "A Government on Wheels."

The entire left flank of the Don Cossack Army along the Ukrainian border, which previously had been unmanned since it was protected by German troops, was now exposed to envelopment by the Reds.

## 5. *Interpreting English for the Atamán after November, 1918*

On November 25/December 8, 1918, the first representatives of England and of France arrived at Novocherkássk. They were naval officers who had landed at Marioúpol—some 80 miles west of Taganróg—on the Azóv Sea (Map E, p. 142) to reconnoiter the situation after Turkey's surrender which permitted the Allied fleets to enter the Black Sea through the Dardanelles and the Bosporus. Atamán Krassnóv sent his personal special train to meet them there and then arranged a ceremonial reception for them at Novocherkássk.

During the state dinner in their honor, General Krassnóv proposed the toast: "For the great, united and undivided Russia! Hurrah!" The toast was followed by the playing of the national anthem of old Imperial Russia * (page 273 of Ref. 35).

Thus, as soon as the German Army left the Ukraine, separatist tendencies ceased to be evident in the Don.

The first Anglo-French mission remained for a few days only and left to make its report. Shortly after that a regular exchange of letters began with the British mission, headed by Maj. Gen. F. C. Poole, which was attached to General Deníkin's Headquarters at Ekaterinodár in the Kubán.

General Krassnóv started calling me in to translate English messages as soon as they were received. I also translated into English his replies—both the Russian original and its translation were then sent on to General Poole.

I did this on an informal basis, continuing my engineering studies and wearing civilian clothes. On several occasions a uniformed orderly appeared in a draftingroom of the Polytechnic Institute, where I worked, and reported that the Atamán requested me to proceed immediately to his palace. This naturally intrigued my fellow students, especially the co-eds, all the more so since I enjoyed creating an air of mystery about it by refusing to say what I did in such exalted company.

As a result of this preliminary correspondence a meeting was ar-

---

* During a similar reception at General Deníkin's Volunteer Army Headquarters, the old anthem "God Save the Tsar" was *not* played. This reflected the republican middle-of-the-road attitudes of the majority of that Army, about which I wrote on p. 218.

ranged between the British General Poole and the Atamán Krassnóv.
Both men were accompanied by several staff officers—General Poole
by the British Lieut. Col. T. H. Keyes (who spoke good Russian), by
General Dragomírov (of General Deníkin's staff), and by Colonel
Zveguíntzev, who served as his interpreter. The Atamán had with
him his Army Commander, General Deníssov, and several other officers. I went along, still wearing civilian clothes, to act as Krassnóv's
interpreter.

The meeting took place on December 13/26, 1918, at Kouschóvka
the railway station at the border of the Don and of the Kubán areas

At first it looked as if it would never get started. General Dragomírov of the Volunteer Army tried to create a petty conflict right
away by insisting during the preliminary exchange of courtesy calls
that both the formal conference and the luncheon be held in their
train. He did this in a very rude and challenging manner—Atamán
Krassnóv reciprocated in kind. When General Poole tried to put an
end to this by remarking that one should stop behaving like a baby
General Krassnóv replied that he agreed with this completely—there
was no point in debating with *groudnýie mladéntzi* (breast-sucking
infants), after which remark he left for his train. I was quite happy
not to be wearing my lieutenant's uniform while translating such exchanges between a group of high-ranking generals.

A few minutes after the Atamán returned to his specially outfitted
conference car, Lieutenant Colonel Keyes came to call on him personally. I was the only other person present, but did not have to
interpret since Keyes could keep the conversation going in Russian

His attitude was one of backing Dragomírov, although he did at
first try to avoid unnecessary exacerbation of relations. Thus, at one
point during our preceding call on General Poole, I translated as
"astonished" Krassnóv's remark that he was *oudivlyón* by something
that had been said. Keyes immediately and correctly softened this by
interrupting me and saying, "surprised—*not* astonished."

Now however he rubbed Krassnóv the wrong way. When the
Atamán saw fit to retrench himself behind the argument that after
all he was the head of an independent state and as such had the duty
to rebuff offensive attitudes such as had been exhibited by Dragomírov, Keyes coolly remarked that none of them would have come
to the meeting had they realized that the Don was independent. That
"blew the fuse"—although, knowing Krassnóv, I feel that much of
his outburst was just one of his displays of magnificent acting.

The Atamán banged his fist on the table and roared, *"Yésli tak— von! Von otsiúda!* (If that is so—get out! Get out of here!)." He jumped up, pointing towards the door and stamping his spurred boots as he continued yelling, *"Von! Von!"* Keyes stood up too and for a moment it looked as if he was going to yell right back. But I stepped up, obviously ready to intervene physically, if need be, and Keyes left without saying a word.

A few minutes later a locomotive was brought out of the railway depot and was coupled to the head of the Volunteer Army train. Krassnóv ordered that the same be done with ours. Then the locomotive of the Volunteers gave two toots, as if it was about to leave— Krassnóv ordered ours to give three.

After that nothing happened for a few minutes until we suddenly saw General Poole walking briskly along the station platform past the windows of our cars, looking straight ahead and paying no attention to General Dragomírov and Lieutenant Colonel Keyes who were trying to keep up with him on either side. Both were speaking to him vehemently, as if they were trying to dissuade him from doing something that he had decided to do.

Krassnóv correctly interpreted this as a conciliatory gesture and immediately sent me to bring in General Poole's interpreter, Colonel Zveguíntzev, who was walking behind the trio I have just described, wearing the cap and shoulder straps of the old Chevaliers Gardes Regiment.

In a sudden change of tactics very typical of him, General Krassnóv now dropped all talk about the "independence" of the Don and said instead that, painful as it was for him to see an officer in the uniform of a famous old Russian regiment serving foreigners, nevertheless he requested Colonel Zveguíntzev to tell General Poole that, for the sake of Russia, he, Atamán Krassnóv, was willing to hold the conference as well as the luncheon anywhere General Poole wanted to.

I watched through the window as Zveguíntzev came up and spoke to General Poole who immediately walked towards our car and entered it. There he remarked that it looked just the right place for our conference—from then on he and the Atamán got on beautifully, but Keyes and Dragomírov sulked for a while.

Other officers from both sides were called in. Colonel Zveguíntzev came up to me while I was standing next to the Commander of the Don Army, General Deníssov, and said that he hoped I would not object to his doing the interpreting at the conference since General

Poole was used to him. Deníssov was pretty much the same type of petty scrapper (p. 226) as was Dragomírov from the other side. So he immediately objected, saying that while Zveguíntzev could translate what General Poole said, I *had* to translate what the Atamán said. I took advantage of my temporarily independent civilian status and told the Army Commander that such a "duet" would not work —let the Colonel do the translating and if he slipped up in anything I would correct him.

The conference lasted for about three hours and towards its end Zveguíntzev naturally got tired and did slip up when translating a few essential points—so I corrected him as I had said I would. This seemed to annoy him considerably and at the end of the meeting he came up to me and, not knowing my background, angrily told me it was insolence on my part to interrupt him. But his attitude changed completely when I replied: *"Brósstye, Polkóvnik!* (Drop it, Colonel!) Better tell me whether you have any news about your nephew, Sásha, whose family lived across the Zakharzhévskaya Street from us at Tsárskoye Seló." *

The luncheon which followed the formal conference was held in a dining car at the rear end of the Volunteer Army train. It had a large window across almost the entire width of its back wall through which one could see the rear car and the full length of the Don Army train on the adjoining track. Everything went smoothly and many speeches were made—I was kept busy interpreting some of them, alternating at it with Colonel Zveguíntzev—and many toasts were drunk. Towards the end of the luncheon General Poole noticed through the large window a procession of orderlies carrying baskets from our train towards the one of the Volunteers we now were in—so he inquired what was in them. It turned out that the Volunteer Army train had run out of wine and that their mess officer had to borrow several cases from ours. General Poole could not help grinning broadly, as did all the Don Cossack officers present—to have this happen after all the fuss General Dragomírov had raised to compel us to lunch in his train! Nothing was said about it then by anyone, but Dragomírov's expression forecast trouble for his improvident mess officer.

---

* Five years later I met the Colonel at the Paris home of my Tsárskoye Seló friends and reminisced with him about Kouschóvka where we had been "on opposite sides of the fence" for a while. Incidentally, his nephew, Sásha Zveguíntzev, married an American girl and has been living in Philadelphia for years.

Most of the Kouschióvka conference discussion had revolved around two alternate strategic plans for the coming military operations. General Dragomírov presented the plan of the Volunteer Army. Its first phase called for the complete elimination of all centers of Red resistance in the Kubán area, in the northern foothills of the Caucasus and in the adjoining non-Cossack Stavrópol area (Map A, p. 44 and Map E, p. 142), which was inhabited mainly by Russian peasants. Only after its rear was fully secured by the completion of this phase of operations, would the Volunteer Army send north into the Don area any of its own units or any units of the Kubán Cossacks which were under its strategic command. Then all White forces in the southeast of Russia, including the Don Cossacks, under the Supreme Command of General Deníkin, would concentrate on driving the Bolsheviks out of the Ukraine to their west, subsequently joining up with the French, who had landed two divisions of their troops at Odéssa a few days before the conference—on December 4/17, 1918.

General Krassnóv countered that now, when his left flank had been exposed by the German withdrawal from the Ukraine, his Don Cossack Army could not possibly hold out alone until General Deníkin's forces had finished fully securing their own rear; that he could not subordinate his forces to General Deníkin, even strategically, until the troops of the Volunteer Army were actually fighting side-by-side with the Don Cossacks; that help was needed urgently since otherwise a large part of the Don Cossack area would have to be abandoned to the Reds who would devastate the Cossack settlements there. As regards future operations, General Krassnóv felt that a westward thrust into the Ukraine would be a mistake because of the strength of pro-Bolshevik sentiment there. Instead he favored a northward thrust along the Volga River * in order to join there and form a common front with the Siberian White forces of Admiral Kolchák—then march with them eastwards directly on Moscow, thus striking at the center first and bothering about the peripheries afterwards.

General Poole personally supported the views of Atamán Krassnóv. However, since he was under orders to bring about the latter's military subordination to General Deníkin and actually succeeded in

---

* This is the area where a mythical independent state called Idél-Urál was supposed to have been located at the time, according to our "Captive Nations" United States Public Law 86–90 (see pp. 365–366 and Ref. 78). Yet I never heard anything about Idél-Urál until that law was voted by the United States Congress in 1959.

achieving this, naturally it was Deníkin's strategic plan which was put into effect. It failed.

First, the Don Cossack Army was greatly weakened by the irreparable losses which the Don suffered while attempting alone to stem the Red onslaught from the north, just as Krassnóv had predicted; second, the French landing in Odéssa proved a complete failure (see p. 232); finally, last but not least, by the time Deníkin's Volunteer Army forces had succeeded in driving the Reds out of the Ukraine late in 1919, the Red Army had defeated Kolchák first on the Volga, then in the Uráls and in Siberia. It was therefore able to concentrate later all of its forces against Deníkin and crush him.*

Would things have have been any different if the strategic plan of Atamán Krassnóv had been adopted instead? No one can tell, but at the time it seemed and it seems to me now in retrospect that it was much sounder than the one which had been put into effect.

After the Kouschióvka conference Anglo-French pressure on Atamán Krassnóv to subordinate himself to General Deníkin continued unabated. Finally, a compromise agreement was reached on December 26, 1918/January 9, 1919, during a personal meeting of the Generals Deníkin and Krassnóv at the railway station Torgóvaya, an agreement by which the Don Army recognized the Supreme Command of Deníkin, but only in operational military matters.

Significantly, two days later the British General Poole made his first official visit to the Don and arrived in Novocherkássk on December 28, 1918/January 11, 1919. With him came Lieutenant Colonel Keyes and several junior British Army officers, also Captain Fouquet, the Head of the French Mission, and French Army Lieutenant Erlich who had grown up in Moscow and spoke faultless Russian. All wore their respective uniforms. The kilt of a Highlander produced a sensation among the local urchins who followed him in droves whenever he appeared on the streets.

There was a ceremonial reception and dinner for the foreign guests at the Atamán's Palace, and I was again busy interpreting. One episode stands out in my memory concerning the day which the Anglo-French mission spent in Novocherkássk. During a visit to the Don Army Museum, General Poole noticed two old guns with British lions on their barrels flanking the entrance to the museum and wanted to know where they came from. "The British gunboat *Jasper*," replied

---

* A good chronological tabulation of relevant dates is given in Ref. 14.

the Atamán. "Who took them?" My grandfather," said Krassnóv,"
not without a touch of understandable pride.* Poole only grunted
something unintelligible and went inside.

After spending a day in Novocherkássk, the Anglo-French mission
left for an inspection trip to the front in the Atamán's train. Krassnóv personally accompanied them and took me along as his intepreter.

I was surprised to find that there was considerable ill-feeling between the allied British and French officers. Thus, at the start of the
first meal in our diningcar, the Atamán stood at the head of the table
and invited General Poole to sit on his right, Lieutenant Colonel
Keyes to sit on his left, and Captain Fouquet to take the second
seat on his right. The French Captain, however, apparently considered that it was not his rank but his status of chief of mission which
mattered. So he pushed Keyes almost bodily aside and took the chair
on the Atamán's left. Whatever the merits of the case from a point
of view of formal protocol, Fouquet's action made a very bad impression on everyone present.

Heavy old Chios wine from Greece, of which the Atamán's Palace
happened to have an ample supply in its cellars, flowed freely at our
"lieutenants' end" of the table and loosened tongues. The French
Army Lieutenant Erlich was aspiring to become a member of the
Chambre des Deputés in Paris. He was an excellent speaker and delivered a long speech in perfect Russian, embellishing it however with
various Gallic oratorical tricks and gestures of an experienced poli-
tician. This did not go down well with the young British officers. As
his speech went on and on, they took up in unison a steady chant in
muffled voices: "Sit down!—Sit down!—Sit down!" The kilted Lieutenant who sat across the table from him punctuated the chant by
rhythmically swinging his fist at his own teeth. General Poole and
Lieutenant Colonel Keyes, who had good reason to be annoyed with
Erlich's boss, Captain Fouquet, pretended not to notice what their
subalterns were doing. Finally, Erlich did sit down, glaring at the
Highlander.

* The Atamán's grandfather, Nikolái Ivánovich Krassnóv, then a Práporschik
(Third Lieutenant) of the Don Cossack Guard Gattery, was transferred as a
Sótnik (First Lieutenant) to Taganróg during the 1855–1856 Crimean War to
organize the harbor town's defenses. The British gunboat went aground nearby
in the shallow Azóv Sea after an exchange of fire with Krassnóv's shore battery
and an unsuccessful landing attempt. Krassnóv assembled a group of armed
Cossack volunteers and, after dark, with muffled oarlocks rowed up and boarded
it, only to find that it had been abandoned by its crew. He withdrew, taking
the guns with him (page 46 of Ref. 4).

Soon I began to share the feelings of the Britishers after repeat
edly hearing Erlich and other Frenchmen sing *"La Madelon de la
Victoire"*:

> "Nous avons gagné la guerre,
> Joffre, Foch et Clemenceau."

Nobody else but these three unquestionably important French
leaders appeared to have had a share in winning the war against the
Central Powers.

I found the attitude of our French guests towards the Russian
Civil War particularly irritating. They seemed to pooh-pooh our problems and difficulties and implied that the arrival of a couple of French
infantry battalions would solve everything.*

Most railway stations where our train stopped were crowded with
Cossacks traveling to or from the frontlines, and Lieutenant Erlich
enjoyed making fiery speeches to them in Russian from the window
of one of our cars. He was more tactful then, speaking about the
great debt France owed to Russia, but saying that this debt would
soon be repaid since French troops were on their way to fight shoulder to shoulder with the Cossacks to help them restore law and order
in the entire country. This, of course, had an electrifying effect on the
Cossack morale—but for a very short while only, since no French
troops did arrive.

The trip to the front made a very favorable impression on General Poole. He visited several frontline positions, satisfying himself
of the good care and maintenance the guns were being given there
and seeing for himself the sturdy spirit of the Cossacks which was
kept up in spite of the extreme hardships they had to endure in
the frozen windswept steppes.

The local guard of honor which presented arms at the last railway
station before the front on the Likháya-Tsarítzyn line, where our
party detrained, provided a vivid illustration of the magnitude of the
war effort of the three and one half million Don Cossacks. The guard

---

* The two war-weary French divisions which had been landed at Odéssa
rapidly disintegrated there under the influence of Red propaganda. Three months
later (March 26/April 8, 1919) they had to be evacuated under the pressure of
armed bands of local Ukrainian Reds—before any of the Red Army troops got
there—abandoning large quantities of supplies and artillery. This was a bad
blow to the White cause, but many White officers who, like myself, had come
into contact with patronizing attitudes of members of French missions, could
not help chuckling about it.

consisted of three squads, each representing a different generation.
On the left flank stood the sons—beardless boys aged sixteen to
twenty—who had not seen active service before. In the center stood
the fathers—veterans of the World War and of the Japanese War of
1905. On the right flank stood the white-haired grandfathers, many
of them wearing medals and decorations won in the Turkish War of
1877.

General Poole studied the entire situation at the front and realized
that Krassnóv was right and that irreparable losses would be suffered
by the Don Cossacks and hence by the entire anti-Red cause unless
armed help arrived immediately. A considerable number of British
troops had been landed at Batoum—the Black Sea terminal for the
Caspian oil exports from Bakou (Map A, p. 44) which the British
also occupied. More were available in the Constantinople area. On
January 6/19, 1919, General Poole left the Don for London, promising Krassnóv before he left that he would arrange for the dispatch
to the Don of a battalion of British troops within five days and of a
brigade within two weeks.* He did not succeed in having this done
and was himself kept in England instead. Another British General
replaced him as Head of Mission at Deníkin's Headquarters, and his
politician-aide, Lt. Col. Terence H. Keyes was promoted to Brigadier
General and made "Acting High Commissioner to South Russia"—
whatever this was supposed to mean.

Thus England did manage to find troops to occupy what at the
time were Russia's main oil wells. They were located in what was
then the Turkish-sponsored Azerbeidján Tartar Republic, it is true,
and their Black Sea export harbor, Batoum, was in the Georgian Republic, but this did not change the substance of the matter. These
republics could exist only so long as the Volunteer Army and the
Kubán and Don Cossacks kept the Red Army at bay to the north of
the Caucasus mountain range. The decisive fighting was there, but no
British troops were sent there to fight alongside their embattled
friends and Allies—they were used to secure Britain's hold on oil
exports instead. This produced charges of perfidy and great indignation among all Russian anti-Reds.

This anti-Western indignation increased still further among persons who were aware of the attempt by Captain Fouquet, the Head
of the French Mission, to force Atamán Krassnóv to guarantee on

* See page 298 of Ref. 35. My personal recollections are in complete agreement
with what General Krassnóv writes here.

behalf of the Don Cossacks the payment, with interest, of all losses suffered by French industrialists during the revolution in southeastern Russia and in the adjoining Donétz mining basin. This was made a prerequisite for any help from France. Krassnóv flatly rejected this (pages 307–310 of Ref. 35) and was fully backed by General Deníkin in this matter (pages 74–76 of Ref. 9).

When by mid-January no French or British troops appeared in the Don, in spite of the promises made by Lieutenant Erlich in his speeches, Red propagandists seized on this to spread rumors among the Cossacks that the Allied Mission was a fake and that it had consisted of Russian officers dressed up in French and British uniforms. As proof of this contention they cited the speeches of Erlich which so many Cossacks had heard during the mission's trip to the front— how could a real Frenchman speak such faultless Russian?!

Just as Atamán Krassnóv was pondering what to do about these intelligence reports, he was confronted by a further development of the same problem in the person of a British Army captain, Cazalet. He was a tank expert who arrived to inspect the suitability of the terrain around Tsarítzyn * for the operation of tanks—no tanks had been used in Russia before that by either side.

It was essential to let Cazalet go to Tsarítzyn—the Reds had succeeded in holding it, their rear being protected by the wide Volga River and their front by several rows of barbed wire entanglements. Thus there was no room there for maneuver, at which the Cossacks excelled. Nor did we have any heavy artillery to demolish the entanglements. Several months earlier an attempt had been made to cut a path through the barbed wire by continuous bombardment with 3-inch field pieces. However, the path was so narrow and took so long to cut, that the Reds had the time to mass opposite it over one hundred of their field guns almost hub-to-hub behind the crest of the next ridge closeby—their hurricane fire met and stopped the units of the 2nd Don Cossack Division which charged through the cut in the barbed wire when it was completed.†

It was now hoped that tanks could quickly open up paths through the barbed wire for our troops at several unexpected locations. Ob-

---

* Later renamed Stalingrád, and recently Volgográd.

† Stalin had been there at the time and is supposed to have been responsible for this massing of artillery—hence the change of name from Tsarítzyn to Stalingrád.

viously Captain Cazalet's trip to Tsarítzyn therefore was of the greatest importance, but—he spoke no less faultless Russian * than had Lieutenant Erlich before him. To let him do this now would play into the hands of Red propagandists and would convince many Cossacks that all Allied officers must be fakes as was claimed by the Reds.

Atamán Krassnóv solved the problem by explaining it to Captain Cazalet and requesting him to speak only English on this trip, using me as an interpreter.

The matter was so urgent that we took off in a special train consisting of a locomotive and just one sleeping car, its sole occupants being the two of us, plus an orderly who also acted as our cook. We first had to travel in a southeasterly direction via Rostóv, Kouschóvka and Tikhorétzkaya, then northwards toward Tsarítzyn, and then we detrained at Sarépta, which was then a small village of German colonists on the banks of the Volga River just to the south of Tsarítzyn.

Everything along the way went well. Crowds gathered on the platforms at every stop, attracted by the unusual sight of Cazalet's British uniform. There were many amusing incidents when men around us, hearing me interpret for Cazalet and therefore thinking that he knew no Russian, uninhibitedly discussed among themselves his appearance and made various personal remarks about him. Fortunately none were offensive. We managed to keep straight faces through it all but laughed ourselves out when we got back to our car.

Then, at Sarépta, a real "snafu" occurred. One of Cazalet's kneecaps had been shot away during the fighting in France, so he could not ride. Only one automobile—a model-T Ford—was available. An armed guide sat next to its driver and one of the two rear seats had to be taken by a Don Cossack artillery captain who was familiar with the local course of the preceding military operations. So Cazalet took the remaining seat, and the model-T Ford drove off immediately —the terrain inspection had to be completed before darkness fell. Our train had arrived somewhat late, so the Ford driver was in a hurry.

Unfortunately, the stirrups on the saddle of the horse assigned to me were much too long and had to be adjusted. By the time I and a Cossack orderly were able to gallop off after the Ford car, it had

* His father had been a British businessman in Petrográd or in Moscow, so he had received his secondary education there in Russian schools.

already disappeared out of sight round the bend of a ravine along
which the dirt road ran. As we galloped along, we found that many
other dirt roads branched off. We did not know which one to take
since their surface was frozen hard and the Ford tires had left no
marks on it—the snow had melted away during a preceding thaw.
My Cossack orderly had no idea where the Ford had headed to.

So, after riding around for over an hour in the bitterly cold wind
and meeting no one in the deserted steppe who could give us directions, we gave up and returned to the train. I was feeling quite de-
jected at having failed to be present at the most important point of
my mission.

However, no harm was done, since Cazalet managed to muddle
through without me. When he realized that we had lost their trail,
he decided to take the Cossack Captain into his confidence and spoke
in a low voice into his ear in Russian. The Captain quickly recovered
from his surprise and got into the spirit of the thing. They agreed to
step aside—out of anyone else's earshot—whenever Cazalet had to
ask him questions. Meanwhile, Cazalet gave him the answers to
questions most frequently asked about tanks and the Captain tried
to memorize them. So, when at one of the battery positions the Cossack gunners crowded around them and bombarded them with questions, the Captain, who knew some French, supposedly translated
them by voicing any French words he could think of. Cazalet replied
by declaiming English verses from Shakespeare, after which the Cossack Captain answered the questions in Russian to the best of his
own ability and imagination. No one seemed to catch on as to what
was actually happening.

The trip accomplished its purpose—Cazalet pronounced his tanks
eminently suited to roll up to and through the barbed-wire entanglements at the locations shown to him.

However, before any tanks arrived, the Don Army was already in
full retreat, and it was not until five months later that Tsarítzyn was
again under White attack, its capture being achieved mainly by Kubán Cossack divisions under Baron Wrangell's command.

I was then at another sector of the front, so I have no direct
knowledge as to what happened before Tsarítzyn. But I have heard
stories that Cazalet's tanks played an important role in flattening
the barbed wire, that Cazalet was wounded in the process when he
got out of one of his machines to inspect a damaged tread, and that
Red agents attempted to poison him when he was being evacuated

from the front. But I did not have the opportunity to check the accuracy of these rumors.

On pp. 85–88 of his Memoirs, Ref. 77, General Wrangel mentions the role which tanks had played in breaking through the barbed wire before Tsarítzyn, but gives no further details.

## 6. *The Resignation of Atamán Krassnóv*

The menace to the exposed left flank of the Don Army, which was posed by Red troops and Bolshevik volunteer formations in the Ukraine and in the Donétz mining basin, compelled the Don commanders to shorten their front by slowly abandoning the northern and the central parts of the Don area. This withdrawal was accompanied by great losses which created anxiety and discontent among the rank-and-file Cossacks.

The Volunteer Army had meanwhile completed most of the cleaning-up operations in its own rear and it was known that several Kubán Cossack divisions were ready to be entrained to the Don. But for some reason their departure was being delayed.

The impression grew that this was done for the purpose of bringing political pressures to force Atamán Krassnóv's resignation. Although he had formally accepted General Deníkin's supreme command, Krassnóv was much too strong and independent a personality to be palatable to the Volunteer Army leaders.

The Don Army Kroug (Parliament) was meeting then at Novocherkássk. Krassnóv was much too popular with the Don Cossacks to be attacked directly, so this was done indirectly. His opponents at the Kroug used the discontent created by the general retreat to bring about a vote of non-confidence in the Don Army commander, General Deníssov and in his Chief of Staff, General Polyakóv.

Krassnóv correctly interpreted this vote as being aimed at himself. So, on February 2/15, 1919, he resigned from his post of Atamán of the Grand Army of the Don and four days later left the Don area on his way abroad (Ref. 35).

The Kroug elected the Don Cossack, General Afrikán Petróvich Bogáyevsky, to succeed him in the post of Atamán. He had made the Icy March (p. 218) in the ranks of the original nucleus of the Volunteer Army and had maintained since then good personal relations with Deníkin and his staff.

The new Atamán had been a classmate of my father's in the first class to graduate from the Don Cadet Corps. He now transmitted to me through my father an offer to stay on as his personal interpreter and, in addition, to put on my uniform again and serve as his personal aide-de-camp.

This I declined, although all student exemptions from service had been abolished because of the critical situation at the front. I felt that Krassnóv had been treated unfairly and hence did not wish to continue serving in the same capacity as I had under him. Instead I decided to go back into the ranks of combat units.

# 8  In the Ranks of the Grand Army of the Don, 1919–1920

### 1. *Northward Advance with the 2nd Don Cossack Battery*

At the time I joined it, the 1st Division of the "Young Army" was held in reserve not far from Novocherkássk. It consisted of four regiments, the 1st, 2nd, 3rd and 4th, and of two batteries, the 1st and the 2nd.

The 1st and the 2nd regiments became known—at first informally and then officially—as the "Brigade of Guards." This was because in the 1st Regiment all the officers, sergeants and most of the corporals had previously served in the old Imperial Russian Leib-Guard Cossack Regiment, while the 2nd Regiment had veterans of the old Imperial Leib-Guard Atamánsky Regiment for its backbone. The privates were young nineteen- and twenty-year-old Cossack recruits.

Only about one half of each regiment was mounted—the remaining squadrons served on foot because of a shortage of good horses.

The Division was commanded by General Fyódor Fyódorovich Abrámov who had begun his service in our Guard's Battery together with my father. The artillery of the Division was in charge of Colonel Nikolái Nikoláyevich Oupórnikov who had been my commander on the German front in the Guard's Battery. Now there was a vacancy in his 2nd Battery and I took it.

A few days after I put on my uniform, the Brigade of Guards and both batteries were urgently ordered to the front which now was only some 50 miles away from Novocherkássk. Large numbers of Red troops had crossed the still frozen Donétz River to the northeast and were attempting a daring thrust directly at the Don Cossack capital —our orders were to throw them back. A sudden thaw, however, mired our guns in the deep mud, but the two young Guard regiments, under the personal command of General Abrámov, did not wait for us to catch up with them and went straight on to their battle christening and to an important victory.

The decisive action took place February 19/March 4, 1919, when the Brigade of Cossack Guards met head-on and defeated units of the 23rd Soviet Division, completely annihilating their 199th infantry regiment by skillful maneuvers in which both the foot and the mounted squadrons played their part. A spectacular cavalry charge of two squadrons of the Leib-Guard Cossack Regiment broke the enemy resistance at a crucial moment in the battle.

The last commander of the Leib-Guard Cossack Regiment, General Ópritz, describes this charge in pages 154–155 of Ref. 46, as follows:

"Having passed a rise in the terrain, the Leib-Cossacks saw infantry lines, machine guns and field pieces of the Reds and, to the left, about a squadron of cavalry—in all about 1,500 men. The enemy opened rapid fire.

"Although the squadrons had only slightly over 200 sabres, their *láva* * continued to move forward. . . .

"Sabre blades flashed in the air, the *ourrah* resounded through the frosty air and the láva changed to a career, hoofs beating on the even frozen steppe as on a wooden pavement. Killed and wounded men and horses began falling. The impetus was, however, so strong that Cossacks who had lost their horses continued to run after the láva with their rifles and sabres.

"The láva reached the Red lines. Some of the horsemen dashed through to the reserves and the field pieces. Lances and sabres went to work.

"In the 1st *sótnia* [*squadron*] a squad commander, Lieutenant Doubéntzov, attacked a machinegun squad of the opponents and had almost reached it when he shouted—'Corporal Zolotarióv, command, I am wounded'—and fell dead.

"Captain Pashkóv and Lieutenant Liákhov were cutting down some gunners when a Red army man killed Captain Pashkóv by a shot fired point blank from behind the cover provided by the shield of his field piece, blood spattering Lieutenant Liákhov. A Cossack who was dashing by picked off with his lance the skull of the Red who had killed Captain Pashkóv.

"Not a single unused cartridge was left after the charge in the revolvers of the squadron commanders, Captain Krassnóv and Captain Vorónin.

"Lieutenant Rótov, who with his squad was in the reserve of the 6th *sótnia* [*squadron*], attacked a half-squadron of the Reds, cut down 12 horsemen and put the rest to flight.

* The name of a deployed battle formation of the Cossacks who traditionally did not charge in closed ranks. This was possible only because of their high quality as individual fighters.

"In that charge Lieutenant Rótov's horse was killed under him. Pinned down under his steed Lieutenant Rotóv had four ribs and his collar bone broken.

"According to the testimony of the commander of the 1st *sótnia,* Captain Krassnóv, sub-Lieutenant Migoulin and Sergeant Bodroúkhin particularly distinguished themselves in the attack.

"The Reds could not withstand the blow and fled. Their gunners abandoned their field pieces, cutting the traces. The Cossacks continued to sabre the fleeing enemy. . . ."

The official on-the-spot report concerning that charge was brief and read:

"To the Commander, 1st Don division, *khoútor* [village] Semímayáchny.

"19th February, 11 hours. South of khoútor Mechiótny—5 *versts* [*3 miles*]. At 10 hours attacked the Reds by the squadrons of Captain Krassnóv and Captain Vorónin 5 *versts* to the south of khoútor Mechiótny. Our trophies: 3 field pieces with caissons and one team of horses, 7 machineguns, many machinegun belts and cartridges, 150 shells, 130 rifles, 2 field kitchens, 15 carts with horses, 38 prisoners. About 400 corpses and many as yet not assembled weapons remain on the battlefield.

"Our losses: killed: Captain Pashkóv, Lieutenant Dubéntzov, 2 Cossacks and 10 horses. Wounded: 13, Cossacks and 13 horses.

[Signed] *Colonel Farafónov."*

One, or at most two days later I rode over that battlefield as our battery passed closeby—the thaw had ended on the day before the charge of February 19/March 4 as suddenly as it had begun, permitting the artillery to catch up.

According to page 158 of Ref. 46, two guns of our 2nd Battery and another 8 guns from the 1st, 6th and 27th Don batteries had arrived with other reinforcements on February 20 and 21/March 5 and 6.

Although not more than two days had thus elapsed since the action, all the corpses had already been stripped of their clothing by the inhabitants of neighboring villages—such was the shortage of cloth and footwear all over Russia at that time. It was a grey foggy day and the naked white bodies which lay around in grotesque poses presented an unforgettably gruesome sight. The wounds on many of them bore eloquent testimony to the terrific force of the sabre blows which had brought them down. Most of these blows had been dealt by nineteen- and twenty-year-olds who were in action for the first time. The fact that they were led by picked veterans had a great deal to do with the successful charge, of course.

This success had an enormous effect on the morale of other Don Cossack units who up to then had been continuously retreating during several weeks. The engagements with the Cossack "Young Guard" on February 19/March 4 completely shattered the 23rd Soviet Division, which retreated to the left bank of the Donétz River.

Our battery took part in the action three days later (February 22/March 7) against the 16th Soviet Division, which adjoined the 23rd to the north. The Reds managed to hold their ground during that day, but suffered such heavy losses in the process that during the night the 16th Division also retreated to the left bank of the Donétz River.

Thus the bridgehead which had been established on the right bank of the Donétz by the IXth Soviet Army was completely eliminated and with it disappeared the threat which it had posed to Novocherkássk. The spring breakup of the ice on the rivers came soon after that and the flooded Donétz presented an unsurmountable obstacle to any further immediate attempts of the Reds to cross it.

The Soviet High Command began shifting its troops westward along the left bank of that river, in preparation for a new thrust at the Don through the Donétz coal mining basin which is located in the upper reaches of the Donétz River.

This took them quite a while and gave a much needed breathing spell to the Don Cossack Command, permitting it to regroup its forces to meet the new threat. Our 1st Division was also sent westwards to meet it. This time we were assigned a holding action over a fairly wide sector of the front.

During the next six weeks we took part in indecisive seesaw fighting. The Reds always outnumbered us and were continuously receiving reinforcements which were fresh, if not well trained. They usually attempted daylight advances and frequently forced us to retreat, only to be thrown back again at night.

Our daylight cavalry charges were successful when the distance to be covered in the open was comparatively short and when the enemy was more or less taken by surprise and panicked as a result. But I saw one of our mounted attacks start from too long a distance and turn back in the face of a sustained withering fire. Similarly, our own fire not infrequently turned even infantry back—I remember one occasion when this was followed by our counterattack which I accompanied as forward artillery observer. I then saw at a close distance the havoc wrought by a direct hit of one of our 3-inch high-explosive shells on a heavy enemy machine gun—it literally made hash out of the Reds who had been manning it.

On another occasion we learned of the arrival that day of a fresh full-strength (some 1,000 rifles) Red infantry battalion which had taken up quarters in a village about 4 miles from a hamlet which we held with only some 200 men.

A preventive attack that same night was decided upon, whereby the frontal assault was to be delivered by . . . my field gun! The plan was to have our scouts silently crawl up to the Red outposts and sentries and "eliminate" them before they could raise an alarm. Then, an hour or so before daybreak, my 3-inch gun was to be silently wheeled forward by hand to within a couple of hundred yards of the Red-held village—all of its metal parts which could clank against each other were to be wrapped in rags.

Meanwhile all of our infantry was to take up positions on both sides of the village—which lay in a hollow—and start raking it with rifle and machinegun fire the moment my field piece fired its first shell. Our cavalry—some fifty men—were to take up positions in the rear of the village to pick up any Reds who would attempt to flee.

Surprisingly, everything went off without a hitch and as planned. We had not heard a sound when returning scouts reported that all of the Red outposts had been taken care of. So we started slowly rolling our gun through the pitch-dark night towards the village until we reached the place which had been designated for our position. It was a weird feeling, silently waiting in the darkness alone with only a dozen Cossack gunners and knowing that there, just ahead of us an entire Red battalion was sleeping—if only a couple of dozen of their infantrymen made a dash for us, we too would be "eliminated" right away!

Finally, just as the sky in the east began turning grey, the luminous hands on my wristwatch indicated that the time had come to start action. Shell after shell in rapid succession hurtled through the darkness and exploded nearby, starting fires in the village, which facilitated the aim of our infantrymen and of their machine guns. The

Red outfit had not been in action before and the manner of their sudden awakening amidst a frightful din made them panic. Some tried to flee in the direction from where no firing was heard only to be intercepted there one by one by our horsemen; others tried to hide in cellars and sheds, from where they were flushed out as full daylight came. Virtually the entire Red force in the village was wiped out with minimal losses on our side.

But small as our losses were in most engagements, their cumulative effect was considerable. Our ranks were further decimated by sickness which was advanced by poor nourishment. There were practically no local foodstuffs in this mining area and for days we had to subsist on black bread only, which was baked somewhere in the rear and often froze at night on its way, so that ice crystals glistened in its cavities when a loaf was cut open. The rare occasions when we managed to get some potatoes and fry them in sunflower oil were considered to be a real festival.

Most of the local men and even some entire families had managed to move out of this part of the mining district into the Red-occupied zone. Nevertheless, the housing conditions were very poor, overcrowded and unsanitary. It was too cold to camp out and officers and men had to sleep closely packed together on the floors of small cottages. This facilitated the transmission of lice and of the typhus infection which many of these insects carried.


Under the new administration in Novocherkássk Mother continued the volunteer hospital work which she had begun there at the request of Atamán Krassnóv (p. 213). In the course of this work she too was infected with typhus and died within a short time. I was given leave from the front to attend her funeral (on April 23/May 6), but arrived too late.

As I am writing these lines a faded blue silk ribbon lies before me. I took it with me from her grave just before having to leave Novocherkássk for good eight months later. On it is printed in large silver letters:

ОТ ПОПЕЧИТЕЛЬСТВА И
ВОЙСКОВЫХЪ ЛАЗАРЕТОВЪ
НЕЗАБВЕННОЙ В. И. ЧЕБОТАРЕВОЙ
ОТДАВШЕЙ ЖИЗНЬ «ЗА ДРУГИ СВОЯ»

In English this means:

FROM THE TRUSTEES AND
THE ARMY HOSPITALS
TO THE UNFORGETTABLE V. I. CHEBOTARIÓVA
WHO GAVE HER LIFE "FOR HER FRIENDS"

The Red pressure on the Don Army was relieved somewhat during that time by Kolchák, who launched an offensive from the Uráls on February 28/March 13, 1919. This compelled the Soviet command to divert many of their new army formations against his Siberian White armies.

Meanwhile, Deníkin's Volunteer Army had successfully completed their operations in the northern Caucasus and in the Kubán and Stavrópol areas. This finally permitted them to transfer most of their own and of the Kubán Cossack troops to the Don. When this concentration was completed, a multipronged offensive was begun on May 6/19 which resulted in a rapid advance and general rollback of the Reds along the entire front of the Southern White armies.

Our 1st Don Division had suffered such heavy losses during the preceding ten weeks of continuous successful holding operations that it was not called upon to participate in the first stages of the rapid big push. Instead we moved at a leisurely pace northwards along the main railroad which led from Rostóv towards Vorónezh. We made frequent stops at railway stations, received Cossack recruits to replace our casualties and went through training exercises for them. These recruits were of about the same age as I was, but I no longer felt uncertain of myself as I did when I first joined the Guard Battery two years earlier (pp. 81, 83)—the experience gained during that time took care of that.

The British government started sending in large quantities of their supplies (which became surplus after the collapse of the Central Powers and the end of World War I) a couple of months before that, and now we too began receiving them. The British army clothing we got had obviously been worn, but had been cleaned and neatly packaged. It was very welcome, especially the excellent heavy boots, even though they had to be worn with puttees, to which we were not accustomed.

The British also sent in entire batteries of their light 18-pounder field guns, complete with mule teams. At first they created quite a sensation, since mules were practically unknown in Russia then. Our four-gun battery received two such guns to experiment with and I immediately volunteered to serve in the squad to which they had been assigned. However, they proved a complete disappointment and a couple of weeks later I obtained a transfer back to the other squad of our battery which was still equipped with the old 3-inch guns of the Imperial Russian Army—these were vastly superior to the British 18-pounders in a war of movement.

First, our Russian horse-drawn gun teams had a harness (Fig. 4 and p. 71) which made them much more maneuverable than the British mule-drawn teams. The latter were at best suited to support infantry only and were much too slow to permit participation in a rapidly developing cavalry action.

Second, their gun sights were much more cumbersome in use than were ours when firing from a "closed" (that is, invisible to the enemy) position. The Russian sights had the circle divided into 6,000 parts, which was close to $1,000 \times 2\pi = 6,280$. The French and the German armies had a similar arrangement. Thus, a change of angle by one division would shift the shell bursts laterally by one thousandth of the range one was firing at—to the right, if the dial setting was increased, and to the left if it was decreased. This was easy to remember and to figure out quickly in one's head.

The British however had the circle divided into degrees and minutes and, to make computations still more complicated, the dial read from 0° to 180° on one half of the circle, which was of a light color on the dial, and then again from 0° to 180° on the other half, which was dark colored. Gun direction settings became an infernal nuisance to figure out, especially when one was in a hurry and under enemy fire. At first we thought some civilian surveyor must have designed this masterpiece and it was only many years later, here at Princeton, that I heard a plausible explanation of its peculiarities. The Navy is the Senior Service in England and Navy Ordinance men were probably responsible for the division of the circle into two separate halves —one for starboard and the other for portside. This made sense on a ship, but not in a rapid action on land. I can only swear when I think what a nuisance it was!

When supporting cavalry it would often be suicidal to fire over open sights if the enemy's artillery was invisible—one had to take up "closed" positions too. As soon as our advancing squadrons disappeared over a ridge which limited the vision of the artillery observer from his old post, it became necessary to dash forward after them, the guns following close behind. A new position would have to be selected for them at a glance behind the ridge ahead—a gesture to one of the field telephone operators and he would drop off his horse at that spot, holding onto the end of a wire which would unwind from a revolving spool attached to the saddle of another telephone orderly who followed his officer at a gallop. The commander would then quickly ride along the ridge until he was approximately in line between his guns and the first target he selected; he would then stop there, with his drawn sword extended straight over his head as he tried to stay as motionless as possible in his saddle. The gunner would point his piece straight at him and fix the direction on the horizontal dial of his sights with reference to a distant tree or some other object on his side of the ridge—the commander would then dash aside to a less conspicuous observation point and order by telephone corrective changes of the horizontal dial setting after the first shot was fired in the direction he had staked out in person. All this could be done in a couple of minutes with Russian guns—not so with the British ones.

Finally, the British fuse settings were graduated in seconds, so one had to waste time looking at a table to find the reading corresponding to a given range. And if one lost the table . . .– ? The Russian fuse settings, on the other hand, had graduations which corresponded to the range setting—this did not require any tables or any figuring, which speeded things up quite a bit (p. 168).

In the wake of the advancing White armies we continued our leisurely movement northwards and soon crossed the border of the Don region into non-Cossack territory. After crossing the Don River at Pávlovsk and a brisk action there, for a while (in July, 1919) we were stationed in an area southeast of Líski (Map E, p. 142) and went through intensive training of the replacement recruits we had received.

Our division commander, Gen. F. F. Abrámov, took special precautions to see that the local inhabitants were not molested in any way by his Cossacks. To this end every cottage in the area was assigned to some unit of his division, even if no one was quartered in it. The entire unit was to be held collectively responsible for anything that happened in its area. We learned the hard way that he really meant it.

One morning it was discovered that some men with a "sweet tooth" had carried off a couple of beehives belonging to a peasant within the area assigned to our battery. They had killed the bees over a smoke fire and made off with the honey. Since the culprits could not be found—quite likely they were from another unit—General Abrámov ordered our entire battery, officers and men, to bivouac out in the steppe where he kept all of us for three days. Unfortunately for us, it started raining and, since we had no tents, everyone was thoroughly soaked and feeling miserable. As a result, when we were allowed to return to the village, our Cossacks supplemented the regular official patrols by volunteer ones to make sure that nothing happened in their area again.

The peasants of that district had very fine heavy horses due to the presence of a government stud farm nearby. The breed was known as *bityugí* which, when crossed with lighter horses, was excellently fitted for service in gun-carriage teams.

Our own horses, not receiving enough grain fodder and being constantly on the move, were in rather poor shape. A favorite joke was for the Sergeant, when asked about the state of the horses, to reply that they were reading newspapers—a crack about the mass of printed White propaganda which reached us from the rear and the lack of essential fodder.

Requisitions of replacements were officially permitted, but—in contrast to the practices of the Red Army which took what it needed without many formalities—we had to perform this ceremoniously in the presence of the village mayor (*stárosta*) by selection from among all the assembled horses of the village. Monetary inflation was developing at the time and the price paid for a requisitioned horse was insignificant. To reduce discontent, we informally supplemented it by giving the peasant one of our very tired and skinny horses which the peasant by good care could restore to a normal state within a couple of months—officially we then reported the horse as having been killed in action.

However, no horses that were any good were ever voluntarily brought to the public requisitions. A couple of such functions ended in complete failure and our commanders were at a loss what to do— it was impossible to thoroughly search the entire large sprawling villages and woods nearby. Then, one of our Cossack corporals hit on a scheme which worked beautifully.

He would leisurely stroll about among the peasants while they were waiting with their horses in the village square for the inspection to start and would make a mental note of a couple of the better horses (even though they were not good enough for us) provided their peasant owner did not seem to be a particularly tough character. That Corporal seems to have had a really good knowledge of men— his judgment in this respect seems to have been unerring. He was quite a good actor too.

I saw him in action on some such expeditions which it was my turn to command. At first various lame and scraggly looking critters were led one by one past the table behind which I and the village mayor sat. The Corporal waved them all on until his selected victim turned up. Without once looking at the peasant the Corporal put on a most convincing show of a man who had grave doubts at first about the quality of the horse before him, but gradually became persuaded that it had real merit. He started by sadly looking at it and slightly shaking his head; then, as he inspected its teeth and repeatedly felt the muscles of its legs, back and shoulders his face gradually bright-ened up until he stepped aside, saluted and happily reported that the horse would do for service in the battery. He would then be ordered to take it aside. As soon as they were out of earshot of the *stárosta* at my table, the peasant owner of the horse thus selected would be drawn into a long dialogue with the wily Corporal at the end of which he usually confided that there were much better horses hidden in the village. He would then strike a deal with the Corporal that his horse would be unobtrusively released under some pretext if a really good horse were found on the strength of his revelations.

By this procedure we usually got a couple of good horses in every village to replace the ones who had been tired out by the rigors of the preceding campaign. After canvassing all the neighboring settlements it became necessary to go farther and farther afield eastwards and even penetrate into an area which at that time was practically a no-man's-land, where both Red and White cavalry patrols were roam-ing about.

On one occasion, when it was my turn to command such a requi-sitioning party, I arrived with five of our battery Cossacks at the village designated to me, only to find that the orders (which had been sent the day before) to have the horses assembled in the square had not been carried out. The village *stárosta* and his aides were profuse in their apologies and offered many but not too convincing explanations as to why they had been unable to carry out the orders. They assured me that the horses would all be there for inspection on the next morning, including some excellent steeds. They then sug-gested that I and my men would be well entertained if we stayed overnight in the village. I sensed something phony about the manner of these fellows, and became convinced that a trap to cut our throats during the night was being prepared when I found that all my men were assigned to separate cottages and that I was to be quartered alone at the schoolhouse, next to the apartment of the female school-teacher, who tried hard to look seductive.

I pretended to like the general arrangements, and the *stárosta* and his aides departed, apparently very well pleased with themselves. As soon as they were out of sight, I told the girl teacher that I would take a stroll to see how our men were set up. To allay suspicions I unbuckled my sword and left it on her table—I had an automatic in my pocket. Before that I had the Corporal inconspicuously pass the word around to my men not to unsaddle their horses, but just to loosen the girths and spend the time rubbing down their steeds until they got my signal. As soon as I reached my orderly, I mounted my horse, quickly gathered my other men, collected my sword from the apartment of the now thoroughly frightened schoolteacher and gal-loped away with an unpleasant feeling that perhaps I was making a fool of myself. However, my doubts on this point were soon set at rest by several rifle shots fired after us from the village outskirts.

On the next day a half squadron of our cavalry was sent into that village. Of course the *stárosta,* his aides and the schoolteacher had all "evaporated"—it turned out that they were all Bolsheviks and were active members of the village Soviet when the Reds were in occupation.

This sort of thing happened in many villages—the same persons remained in authority both under the Reds and under the Whites— only the titles of their posts changed. It was however unusual that they exhibited active pro-Red sympathies. The general attitude of the vast majority of the peasants was a desire to be left in peace to do their work and a strong feeling of annoyance at the various requi-sitions of food, fodder, horses, carts and men to which they were subjected by both sides. "A plague on both your houses!" is the way one might sum up their attitude towards both belligerents in the Russian Civil War.

In its extreme form this attitude led to the formation of so-called Green guerrilla detachments—the name being derived from the fact that they hid in the green forests which provided them with cover. They opposed both Reds and Whites—whoever occupied their terri-tory at the moment. The open steppes did not provide any effective hideouts and for this reason there were comparatively few active Green groups in the Ukraine, most of which is located in open steppe country. There were plenty in the wooded foothills of the North Caucasus, however.

I first learned of the existence of the "Greens" at the time I am now describing when we were in the Vorónezh province on the southern borders of the forested regions. There were several "Green" detachments operating to the north of us in a very large and dense forest. They were under the general command of a former army Colonel and even had some artillery of their own. They did not bother us—their main idea at the time was to keep themselves from being drafted into the Red Army (we took only volunteers) and, when possible, to protect their neighboring home villages from too drastic and oppressive requisitions.

Later, in the 1920s, these and other "Green" detachments formed the nucleus of a largescale anti-Bolshevik peasant uprising in the adjoining wooded province of Tambóv, some 150 miles to the northeast. The Red Army had a lot of trouble suppressing it. The area was inhabited almost exclusively by Great Russians (p. xxi) and for that reason this and other similar anti-Soviet uprisings are hardly ever mentioned by anti-Russian propagandists in the West who try to present the Russian Civil War as a clash of nationalities, whereas in reality it was mainly a social and class struggle (p. 365).

Some time in August, 1919, our division was moved eastward to a large village called Boutourlínovka (Map E, p. 142) which was located in fairly open country suitable for cavalry action. It was close to the eastern edge of the large forest I have just mentioned.

What at the time was referred to as a *koulák* (fist) * of some 15- to 20,000 cavalry—the IVth Don Corps—was being concentrated there under the command of the Cossack General Mámontov for the purpose of a deep raid behind the Red lines. Our division was assigned the task of rolling back the Reds on Mámontov's left flank, when he started his breakthrough, to prevent them from harassing him. The Red Command learned of what was coming and attempted to disrupt Mámontov's concentration by a sudden punch of their own—however, they missed Mámontov's "fist" by 10 miles or so, hit our division instead, and penetrated its lines. Our reserves counterattacked and, for a day or two what was then known as a "layered pie" resulted—

---

* The word "koulák" was also used to designate a rich peasant, meaning one who held the others in his fist.

Red and White lines followed one another in a disorderly sequence. At one stage I recall a squadron or two of our own division's 3rd Kalmúck Regiment charging by mistake a two-gun section of our battery. Fortunately its commander, Captain Nefiódov, recognized his attackers through his field glasses and held his fire. The embarrassed Kalmúcks pulled up in front of him, having realized their mistake.

In this action our division was badly mauled, but the overall result was excellent—Mámontov's IVth Don Corps had no trouble punching past the Red concentration which was attacking us. His group then headed north as a compact body. The realization that a large mass of Cossack cavalry was in their rear made the Reds around us retreat in haste.

General Mámontov headed to the northeast, still keeping his mass of cavalry in a compact group, and reached Tambóv, some 140 miles away from Boutourlínovka, where he had first broken through the Red lines. He then turned westward and moved in that general direction along a zigzag route, dodging big Red troop concentrations for well over a hundred miles before turning back south and rejoining the main lines of the White armies.

In the course of his raid Mámontov completely disrupted the rear of a wide sector of the Red front—he burned their army stores and depots, blew up bridges, destroyed locomotives and rolling stock, executed captured Bolshevik commissars, sent home peasants they had mobilized, but permitted only a few selected volunteers to join his forces.* The South Russian newspapers emphasized at the time that there had not been anything even remotely like it since the cavalry raids during the American Civil War half a century earlier.

After the Mámontov raid was started, our division was moved some 40 miles westward and took part in the capture of the railroad junction Líski, 50 miles south of Vorónezh. While this operation was in progress, I was suddenly called to Division Headquarters where its Commander, Gen. F. F. Abrámov, an old friend of my father's, showed me a telegram he had received ordering him to detach me for service at the Headquarters of the Don Army, and asked me if I wanted to go. I did not, as I liked my service with the 2nd Battery, its commander Colonel Afanássiev, the other officers, and the men.

---

* Among them was Járov, a church choir leader from Central Russia, who was accepted as one of them by the Cossacks of the famous Goúndorovsky Regiment, and who later became world-known as the leader of an *emigré* Don Cossack choir abroad.

So the General sent a reply that he could not spare me because of a shortage of officers.

The next day he summoned me again, greeting me with the words: "Well, Grísha," (he knew me since childhood) "there is nothing I can do about this!" The telegram he showed me was signed by the Commander of the Don Army, General Sidórin, and ordered him to send me immediately to his Army Headquarters, authorizing him to select any artillery officer of the Don Army he might wish to have to replace me.

So I left, wondering what was behind this sudden interest in me.

### 2. *Aide-de-Camp*
### *to Inspector of Artillery*

It turned out that a new post of Inspector of Artillery of the Don Army had been created and that General Baron Máydell had been appointed to it—the Don Atamán A. Bogáyevsky had known him in service previously and thought highly of him.

But Cossacks never liked having non-Cossacks for commanders and were certain not to take kindly to a Baron of German origin. So, as a start for his campaign to win Cossack sympathies, Máydell decided he should have a Don Cossack officer for his aide-de-camp. However, to facilitate mutual understanding and promote congenial relations, this officer should have belonged to St. Petersburg society. It turned out that the only young artillery officer in the entire Don Army who had these qualifications was myself—hence my orders.

My staff duties consisted mainly in tabulating the weekly reports from Corps and Divisional Headquarters on guns and ammunition used up, lost or captured, and thus keeping track of the artillery and ammunition resources available on different sections of the Don Army front. A surprising number of trophies were still being continuously taken from the Reds—the figures reported were not exaggerated and, on the contrary, probably often were too low since local commanders usually preferred to downgrade the supplies they had captured, especially those of shells and of cartridges, in order to be able to ask for more from depots in the rear.

At first I was afraid that this kind of office work would prove intolerably dull, but I was soon relieved to find that General Máydell made frequent inspection trips to various sections of the front, taking me along with him. At times things even became too lively for my liking because the Baron—knowing how Cossacks respected and admired personal courage, especially in their commanders—did all sorts of rash things to win popularity among them. I remember one occasion when we followed on foot the advance of our infantry, stopping part way down a slope to the village which they went on to capture at bayonet point. From there we watched at close range a sudden counterattack of Red Kubán Cossack Cavalry which made our infantry panic and retreat through the village and past us in disorder. The General rushed about trying to stop and rally them, but unsuccessfully. He then sat down on the edge of a furrow and calmly watched through his field glasses the shell bursts in the village just in front of us fired by three of our batteries he had come to inspect, never once turning around to see that our infantry had retreated past us to the top of the ridge and now was twice as far from us as were the Reds. I pointed this out to him, remonstrating that any Red cavalry patrol could now dash out from the village and pick us off without any trouble at all, since I had only an automatic pistol with me and the Baron did not have even that—just a swagger-stick type of riding whip! The General however calmly told me that I was welcome to go back and join the infantry, if I felt like it. So I had to stay with him, mentally cursing him all the time since I did not feel like taking personal risks just to give him a chance to "show-off."

After a while, when the Baron could be sure that his behavior must have been duly noted from all three of our artillery observation points, he got up and slowly walked back with me, stopping at times to take another look at the Reds through his field glasses as if still reluctant to retreat.

This performance seemed to achieve its purpose—at any rate the particularly snappy salutes he got from the Cossack gunners and the friendly grins on their faces showed that telephones from the observation points had conveyed the news that he was what Americans would call a "real guy" and not just an arm-chair general after all.

One of these three batteries was commanded by Spiridónov, by then a Captain—the former sub-Lieutenant of our Guard Battery (p. 82). It was then that I questioned him about his conversation with Podtiólkov on the *kurgán* (p. 210) before the latter's capture and execution.

The armored trains were under the jurisdiction of the Inspector of the Artillery. Just about the time that post was created, we began receiving at Army Headquarters reports of a number of our advancing armored trains being put out of action by some mysterious new type of mine which the Reds had begun using.

Two types of mines had been used by both sides until then—both were concealed in the ballast under the railway ties. The first type was a contact mine which exploded the moment the first axle of a train passed over it. To meet this danger, two or three low open freight cars with spare rails and ties were placed at the head of an armored train which moved very slowly when advancing into enemy-held territory. Not much harm could be done then since only the expendable front car would be damaged and derailed—it would then be simply pushed off the railway bed, the tracks would be quickly repaired and the train would go on.

The second type of mine was exploded electrically under the locomotive by remote control. This was prevented by having cavalry patrols precede the train into enemy-held territory on both sides of the tracks where they would watch like hawks for any sign of disturbance of the ground which would indicate that wires had been laid.

But now Red mines started exploding right under our scarce locomotives without any traces of wires being found afterwards—in those days wireless had not yet been developed to the point where it could be used for such purposes.

The riddle was solved by our Army intelligence only after the White troops occupied Vorónezh which had large railroad repair shops. Some observant mechanic there, while watching rails deflect under each axle of a passing train, had realized by sheer intuition that this elastic deflection and rebound was due to the compression of the ballast and soil immediately beneath the tie, but that the soil deeper down did not contribute much to the movement at the surface. In modern soil mechanics terms (p. 289) one would say that the "seat of settlement was shallow." So this bright fellow designed a large mine which would be buried three feet or so below a railway tie. A steel rod, pressed upwards by a spring against the bottom surface of the tie, was protected by a loose pipe around it from friction against the surrounding soil and at its lower end rested on a ratchet wheel connected to the mine. Every train axle which passed over that tie would depress the rod slightly so that it would move one tooth of the ratchet down before being pushed back upwards by the spring when it latched onto the next ratchet tooth. If one had noted beforehand the number of axles of a given armored train from its head to the middle of its locomotive, one only had to set the mine to explode after the same number of ratchet tooth movements.

These mines were essentially a weapon for use during retreats and the Reds did not take advantage of it for long since our advance was not to last much longer.

To the east of our Don Army, the White Kubán Cossacks under General Baron Wrangell had captured Tsarítzyn (Stalingrád) in June, 1919, had continued their northward advance along the west bank of the Vólga River, but were stopped in the area of Kamýshin.

To our west, the Volunteer Army made rapid progress in the Ukraine, picking up many new adherents there as it went. The large cities of Khárkov and Yekaterinosláv (present-day Dniepropetróvsk) in its eastern part were taken during the month of June and Kíev and Odéssa in its western part during August, 1919. Except for the Reds, the only serious opposition encountered there by the White Volunteer Army came from a self-styled "anarchist" Makhnó, who at first sided with the Reds, but then acted on his own against every-one else. The Ukrainian nationalists did not make themselves con-spicuous anywhere except to the west of Kíev where their detach-ments consisted largely of Ukrainians from Galicia, who were former soldiers and officers of the old Austro-Hungarian armies (see Map F, p. 353).

In September, after driving the Soviets out of the Ukraine, the White Volunteer Army continued its advance northward deep into territories inhabited by Great Russians (p. xxi), and reached on October 1/14, 1919, the city of Orél, only 240 miles from Moscow (see Map A, p. 44).

But here the tide turned. By that time the Reds had finished mopping up most of Kolchák's White Siberian armies which had been defeated by them during June in the Vólga and Urál regions. An advance in September by General Yudénich and a small body of his White Volunteers from Estonia against Petrográd did not succeed in drawing away any sizable number of Red troops, the bulk of which could now be concentrated against Deníkin.

On October 7/20, 1919, the Reds retook Orél. From then on the retreat of Deníkin's overextended White forces was continuous, and by mid-December they were compelled to abandon to the Red Army practically all of the Ukraine and all the gains which had been made to the east of it.

The reasons for this disaster were analyzed in a lecture which I heard as it was delivered to the officers of the Don Army Headquar-ters by a Colonel B., a graduate of the old Imperial General Staff Academy who had just returned from a secret mission in the course of which he spent incognito several months behind the Red lines. His lecture was entitled "The Causes of the Red Successes and of Our Failures" and, in my opinion, gave a succinct and entirely correct explanation thereof.

First in order Colonel B. placed the simply expressed and definite political program of the Bolsheviks, their political unity and party discipline. The White leadership left all outstanding political questions—such as the redistribution of land—for a future decision by an All-Russian Constituent Assembly which was to be convened after the final defeat of the Bolsheviks. The Reds, on the other hand, using the simple slogan *grab nagráblennoye* (rob what you have been robbed of) proclaimed the immediate redistribution of land, thereby getting the support of poor peasants and of workmen who were persuaded by the Bolsheviks that the Constituent Assembly would cheat them, since it would be controlled by the rich.* The Reds had only one single political program and only one party whereas the Whites had dozens of both, most of them in conflict with each other.

Second, Colonel B. emphasized a similar difference in the military field—a single unified command in a central location on the Red side, as contrasted with a number of disconnected White armies on the peripheries with separate commands and no coordination of their operations.

This was all true, but there was nothing anyone could do about it then.

It should however be noted here that the High Command of the Red Army had a number of General Staff officers of the old Imperial Russian Army to help with the strategic planning of its operations. They included General Broussílov, of the 1916 "Broussílov Breakthrough" fame (p. 50). Many of them did this out of a sincere conviction that in the presence of a foreign menace above all their

---

* Conservative elements on the White side emphasized at the time that a redistribution of land would prevent the industrialization of Russia which even then was widely recognized as essential for the continued independence of the country. Small landowners are apt to use for themselves most of their produce (so ran the argument for the agricultural status quo); only large domains produce enough surplus for export to pay for machinery from abroad. The Reds learned this fact of economic life the hard way during the 1920s and this is probably one of the main reasons why they had to introduce the large collective and state farms. But I think that many of their leaders did not fully realize this in 1917–1920 and that at the time they had not deliberately cheated the peasants by promises of peasant land ownership after its redistribution.

duty was towards the people of their country and whatever central government it had.*

Some time early in December or late in November, 1919, I received two weeks' leave and spent it at home in Novocherkássk with my father, at his apartment as Director of the Don Cadet Corps. The wife of a cousin of his, Mrs. Danílova, with her seventeen-year-old daughter Lyólia and her fourteen-year-old son had stopped there for a rest on their way from Kíev to rejoin her husband at Batoum, on the Black Sea in Georgia. He had gotten into some trouble with the German Army of Occupation in the Ukraine and had to "evaporate" in a hurry from Kíev in the summer of 1918, leaving his family stranded there through the successive German and Red occupations of that city, until General Deníkin's Volunteer Army drove the Reds out.

It was while I was at home that I came down with typhus. The incubation period after infection by that disease—if I remember correctly—is fourteen days. Looking back on what had happened that number of days before I fell sick, I came to the conclusion that it must have been, literally speaking, a "Red louse" that got me—lice transmit typhus in very much the same way that mosquitoes transmit malaria after having stung a sick person. I was then accompanying General Baron Máydell on one of his field inspection trips when we went along with some of our counterattacking troops who were attempting to retake an isolated village in the steppe. In winter weather such engagements were fought by both sides with particular tenacity since whoever ended by controlling the village did not have to trudge through the bitter cold to the warmth of the next inhabited place, which could be 5 or more miles away. So it was only towards the evening that we finally entered that village and the cottage assigned to us. By then we were so tired that we did not bother to change the straw which covered the floor and on which Red soldiers had been sleeping the night before—one of them must have already been infected with typhus.

I was lucky to have come down with it while I was at home, because

* Typical in this respect are the pros and cons for a decision by Colonel Count Ignátiev, a former Chevaliers-Gardes officer and the Military Attaché of Imperial Russia to France, not to resign his post after the Tsar's abdication. These pros and cons were written down at the time during a sleepless night and then reproduced on pages 282–284, Ref. 23. He later handed over to the Soviet government all the funds at his disposal in Paris and subsequently returned to the Soviet Union.

I got excellent treatment in the ward for infectious diseases of the Don Cadet Corps Hospital, which was located in the same large building as my father's apartment. My pretty young cousin was allowed to visit me occasionally, but most of the time I was only semiconscious because of high fever. Then, as is usual in typhus cases, came the so-called crisis, when the fever suddenly dropped off, leaving one weak and limp.

I learned then that things had gone so badly at the front meanwhile that Novocherkássk was in the process of being hurriedly evacuated. To convalesce I should have stayed in bed for another ten days or so, but this news brought me to my feet and out of the hospital in a hurry three days after the drop of my fever.

The Don Cadet Corps was leaving in a day or two after that—on foot—since the large railway junction of Rostóv-on-the-Don to the southwest of us was so jammed with trains which were converging on it from the north and from the west that there was little hope of getting through it by rail. So the Cadet Corps was to bypass Rostóv, taking a direct dirt road through the steppes to the railway station of Kouschóvka on the Kubán border. Officers of the Corps had to leave their families behind, so Father, having a mass of service matters to attend to, asked me to find a place in the town where the Danílov family could hide. My eleven-year-old sister Álya was to stay with them.

At first I considered placing them on board our railway sleeping car which formed the office base for the Inspector of the Artillery and which happened to be at the Novocherkássk railway yards at that moment. But I decided that the odds were too great against it getting past the Rostóv bottleneck to the south. Actually, that car did get through, but was riddled by bullets in the process—local Rostóv Reds staged an uprising to help the advance guard of the Red Army as it approached the city. A book recently published in this country *Last Train Over Rostóv Bridge* (Ref. 1), gives, on pages 250–283, a vivid description illustrating what I know had occurred at Rostóv then.

So I quickly located and rented a small inconspicuous apartment in Novocherkássk for the Danílovs and my sister and moved them into it with a few of our belongings which we wanted to try and save. But when I called on them the next morning to say goodbye, I found my aunt in a state of near-hysterics. She had spent a sleepless night thinking of all the awful things they had lived through under the

Red rule in Kíev and implored me to get them out no matter what risks would be involved during the journey across the wintry steppes.

So I decided to try, the role of a rescuer of my pretty cousin being difficult to resist. I had at least a couple of weeks' leave due to me for convalescence, counting from the "crisis" of my typhus, and until that was used up I could do what I pleased. So I employed the usual technique of going to one of the main streets along which retreating baggage trains were passing through Novocherkássk and then waiting there for something to come along which could be used to get a lift. Usually something like that did happen and this day was no exception.

After waiting for a couple of hours I saw the baggage train of the Leib-Guard Atamánsky Regiment file past, including two carts which were empty. The rear was brought up by the officer in charge of the baggage train, whom I knew personally. I explained my problem to him and asked for the loan of one of the two empty carts since he was not using them anyway. He said he would need both the next day in Stáro-cherkásskaya, some 10 miles away, but would let me have one cart until then if I promised to return it there. I said I would. *"Chéstnoye Slóvo?* (Word of Honor)" *"Chéstnoye Slóvo,"* I replied. Nothing further was needed between oldline officers, and I got my cart.

Suitcases with a few of our most valuable belongings were piled on it and we set out of Novocherkássk. My aunt, my cousin Lyólia and my sister Álya sat on the suitcases while the cart driver, my boy cousin and I trudged alongside and behind it on foot. The rutted dirt road surface was frozen hard and the going was not easy. A long line of various other vehicles with people fleeing Novocherkássk stretched as far as the eye could reach both ahead and behind us.

When we were an hour or so out of the city a two-horse carriage overtook us—in it was the Commander of the 2nd Don Division which had been already pulled farther back. He had begun his service under my father in the Guard Battery at Pávlovsk—I believe his name was Popóv, but I am not sure now. His wife was with him. They recognized me, stopped and offered to take my sister into their carriage till Stáro-cherkásskaya where they were going to spend the night and where I could pick her up. I was anxious to relieve the load on our cart and to shorten the time my sister had to be out in the bitter cold, so I let her go with the friendly couple.

However, it was already dark when we reached Stáro-cherkásskaya, a large sprawling Cossack *stanítza* which was more of a village than a town. There was no street lighting and we slowly made our way through the darkness while I asked every figure I bumped into where were the Headquarters of the 2nd Division. Nobody seemed to know. Then someone told me it was *na khoutorákh*, meaning somewhere on one of a string of outlying farms, several miles away. This made me sit down on the ground, close to despair. I was absolutely exhausted and could not possibly walk even one mile more—and yet I had to return our only cart right here. Pulling myself together I continued my inquiries, trying to find out at least on which of the farms the Headquarters of the 2nd Division was located, but I had no luck. Then, a match lighting a cigarette gave me a glimpse of the number of a regiment of the 2nd Division on the shoulder straps of a Cossack nearby. It turned out that he was attached to its divisional headquarters, which were just around the corner.

Minutes later we were all reunited with my sister Álya in a warm room. All our luggage was unloaded from the cart—I then let it go to find its baggage train of the Atamánsky Regiment.

On the next morning I used the same old technique of waiting by the roadside until something came by. I was optimistic that something eventually would do so; nevertheless, I could not quite believe my eyes when I saw an approaching baggage train of some thirty *empty* carts! Important supplies were being abandoned in Novocherkássk and at other railway stations, yet through some administrative snafu this particular group of carts had not been given any assignment to pick anything up. As the train commander told me, his orders were only to proceed to Kouschóvka. Since I was heading there too, he willingly agreed to let me have two of his carts.

In the late afternoon of the same day we passed through a village where I saw familiar faces—Cossacks of the 2nd Don Battery with which I had served a few months before—they had been pulled back from the front. Its commander, Colonel Afanássiev and the other officers of the battery gave me and my party a cordial welcome, a good supper and put us up for the night. We learned that my father with his Don Cadet Corps had passed on foot through that village only a few hours ahead of us—we were rapidly catching up with them.

On the next day the Colonel offered me the loan of his own carriage, drawn by two horses, so that my aunt, my cousin Lyólia and my sister could travel in comfort till Kouschóvka. We continued at a forced pace that day and by nightfall reached the village where the Don Cadet Corps had stopped.

My father's surprised reaction at suddenly seeing us was one of mixed pleasure and embarrassment—after all no other officer of the Corps had his family with him. But I took the position that the family was not with Father, but with me, that I was not under his orders, that in the midst of the general debacle I was entitled to use my sick leave in whatever way I saw fit and that I would bring the family to Kouschóvka and put them there on a train for the harbor of Novorossísk (on the Black Sea) without any help whatsoever from my father or anyone else in his Cadet Corps. There was nothing here that Father could formally object to, so he said nothing—and I had a feeling that in his heart he was not displeased at the way things had worked out. So I continued following the Cadet Corps with my carriage and two carts.

On the last day before reaching Kouschóvka the spokes in a wheel of one of my carts broke as we were passing through a peasant village, so I sent the carriage and the other cart on to follow the Corps and stayed behind with the damaged cart. Since it belonged to a military baggage train, a replacement wheel could be requisitioned from anyone in the village, but its inhabitants were well aware that this was a frequent occurrence when troops passed by—all the carts in the yards of the neighboring cottages had their wheels removed and hidden somewhere.

However, the driver of my cart was a peasant himself. He had made the retreat all the way from somewhere near Vorónezh, where he had been drafted into non-combatant transportation service. Knowing well the village tricks, he immediately started prodding a haystack nearby with a long stick and soon found a wheel. Just as he was triumphantly pulling it out of the hay an angry roar was heard and the owner of the wheel (who had apparently been watching things through a window) emerged from his cottage and went at us with a hatchet in his hand. The expression on his face clearly indicated that he was going to use it, so I drew my revolver and took aim at the upper part of his shoulder, wondering if I could avoid splintering a bone and whether my shot through muscles only would stop him and make him drop the hatchet. But, apparently my face conveyed to him that I was about to press the trigger and this stopped him a few feet away from me; he then retreated to his cottage, cursing all the way.

We left our wheel with its broken spokes on his doorstep, and I laid some money under it—it should not have taken him too long to get it back into use.

*Figures 1 & 2. Top, left and right:* The author's parents, ca. 1908. *See p. 8.* *Figure 3. Bottom:* The author's maternal grandparents with other relatives and friends, ca. 1900. *See p. 8.*

*Figure 4. Top:* The Don Cossack Guard Battery on parade before the Palace in St. Petersburg, ca. 1902. *See p. 9.* *Figure 5. Bottom:* The of the Don Cossack Guard Battery reports directly to Tsar Nicholas II, r *p. 9.* (from Ref. 4.)

*igure 6.* Painting of the Don Cossack Guard Battery's march to outflank Turkish
3alkan positions at Právetz, 1877. *See p. 13.* (from Ref. 4.)

PHOTOS OF GUARD BATTERY DON COSSACKS (from Ref. 4.)

*Figure 7. Top, left:* Lieutenant Avédikoff, former sergeant, 1878. *See p. 14.* *Figure 8. Top, right:* Corporal Schedróff, 1898. *See p. 15.* *Figure 9. Bottom* Instructors sent to the Far Eastern army, 1905. *See p. 17.*

Figure 10. *Bottom:* The Leib-Guard Don Cossack Regiment entering Paris in 1814
ead of the Allied monarchs and their armies. *See p. 18.* (Courtesy of General Ilyá
ritz.)     *Figure 11. Top:* A French cartoon of the period. *See p. 18.* (Courtesy
General Ilyá Ópritz.)

*Figure 12.* Etching of horseman of the Leib-Guard Don Cossack Regiment, 1881, by famous French painter, Edouard Detaille. *See p. 18.* (from Ref. 10.)

*Figure 13. Bottom:* Fires in the besieged Austro-Hungarian fortress, Peremýshl, 1914. *See p. 47.*     *Figure 14. Top:* Author's father at the Carpathian Ouzhók Pass, Spring, 1915. *See p. 47.*

*Figure 15. Top:* Author mother and sister. Tsársk Seló, 1915. *See p. 52.*

*Key to Fig. 16. Middle.*

1. Gosoudárynya
   (The Empress)
2. Olga Nikoláyevna
3. Tatiána Nikoláyevna
4. A. A. Víroubova
5. Pr. Gedróitz
6. V. A. Vilchkóvskaya
7. S. I. Dobrovólskaya
8. U. F. Lvóva
9. ... I.

Fig. 16. *Bottom:* Grou Tsárskoye Seló Palace Hospital, 1914, and notes author's mother on back photo. *See p. 53.*

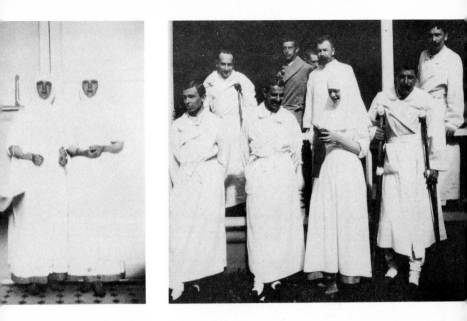

Figures 17 & 18. *Above:* The two elder daughters of the Tsar at the Palace Hospital, 1915. *See p. 60.* Figure 19. *Bottom, Right:* The author, with the Reserve Battery of Guard Horse Artillery at Pávlovsk, January, 1917. *See p. 76.* Figure 20. *Bottom, Left:* Note from the Tsar's elder daughter to author's mother. *See p. 78.*

# LA CRISE
## DE
# L'ARMEE RUSSE

« La Russie, malgré ses défaillances, aura au moins rendu aux Alliés un immense serv
de leur montrer les funestes conséquences pour la vie des Etats des théories international
leur faire faire l'économie d'une révolution. Notre pays, c'est l'ilote ivre, qu'il faut mo
nations de l'Entente pour leur donner l'horreur du désordre, de l'anarchie, de l'indiscipline,
patriotisme, de toutes les théories qui amènent à grands pas la désagrégation de l'un des p
empires du monde. »
DÉCLARATION D'UN RUSSE, DIRECTEUR D'INDUSTRIE, A UN CORRESPONDANT DE « L'INFOR

Soldats fuyant à travers un village, après avoir jeté leurs armes, dans une panique qu'un provocateur avait fait naître en criant
« La cavalerie allemande a percé ! »

Soldat russe de la vieille école se servant de son fusil pour arrêter deux fuyards.

## UN EXEMPLE DES EFFETS DE L'INDISCIPLINE DANS UNE ARMÉE

Le photographe anglais, M. G. H. Mewes, correspondant du Daily Mirror, auteur de ces clichés, se trouvait avec les automobiles blindées britanniques juste derrière les lig
à la fin de juillet quand il fut témoin de ce grave incident, qui ne devait, hélas ! pas être isolé.

*Figure 21. Left page:* Demoralization of troops under Kerensky after the Revolution in July, 1917. *See p. 88.* (from Ref. 25.)    *Figures 22 & 23. Above:* Groups of officers of the Don Cossack Guard Battery with their orderlies on the Stohód River positions, May, 1917. *See pp. 91, 97.*

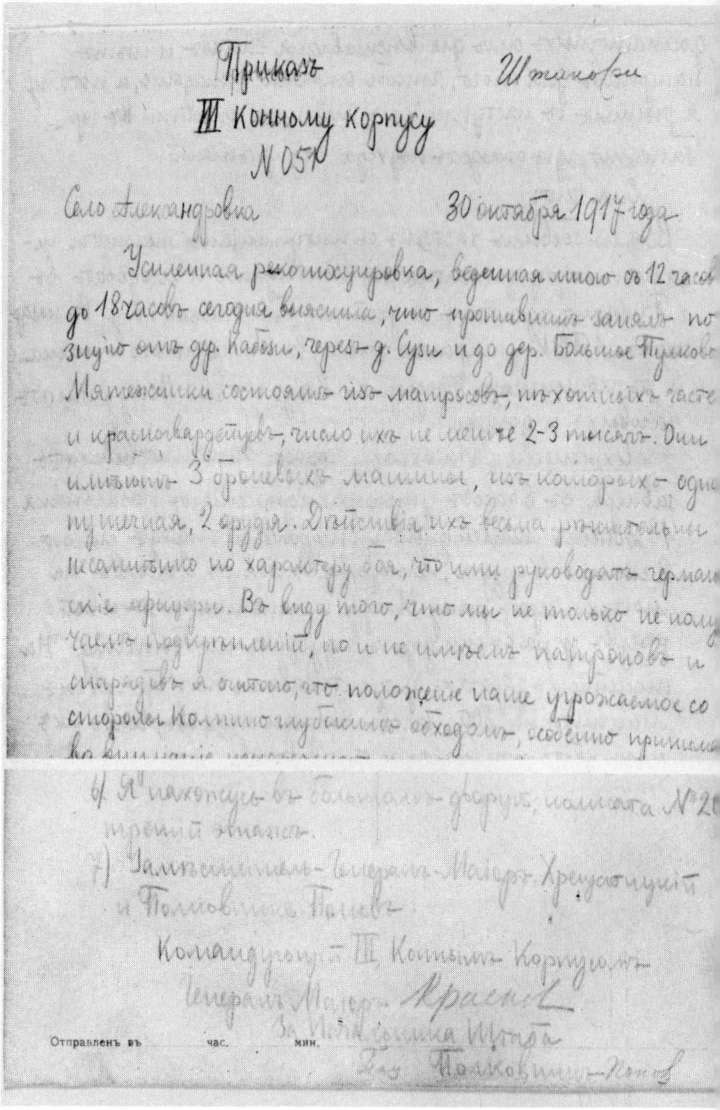

Приказъ Штакорп

III Конному корпусу

N 051

Село Александровка 30 октября 1917 года

Усиленная рекогносцировка, веденная мною съ 12 часовъ до 18 часовъ сегодня выяснила, что противникъ занялъ позицію отъ др. Кабози, черезъ д. Сузи и до дер. Большое Пулково. Мятежники состоятъ изъ матросовъ, изъ хотинскихъ частей и красногвардейцевъ, число ихъ не менѣе 2-3 тысячъ. Они имѣютъ 3 броневыхъ машины, изъ которыхъ одна пушечная, 2 орудія. Дѣйствія ихъ весьма рѣшительны и замѣтно по характеру боя, что ими руководятъ германскіе офицеры. Въ виду того, что мы не только не получаемъ подкрѣпленій, но и не имѣемъ патроновъ и снарядовъ я считаю, что положеніе наше угрожаемое со стороны Колпино глубокимъ обходомъ, особенно принимая во вниманіе ...

6/ Я нахожусь въ большомъ дворцѣ, комната №20 третій этажъ.

7) Заместитель — Генералъ-Маіоръ Хрещатицкій и Полковникъ Поповъ

Командующій III Коннымъ Корпусомъ
Генералъ Маіоръ Красновъ

За Начальника Штаба
Полковникъ Поповъ

Отправленъ въ час. мин.

*Figure 24.* Beginning and end of three-page Orders by General Piótr Krassn to retreat to Gátchino after first field action of Russian Civil War. (Dictated author under Red fire, one mile north of Tsárskoye Seló.) *See p. 118.*

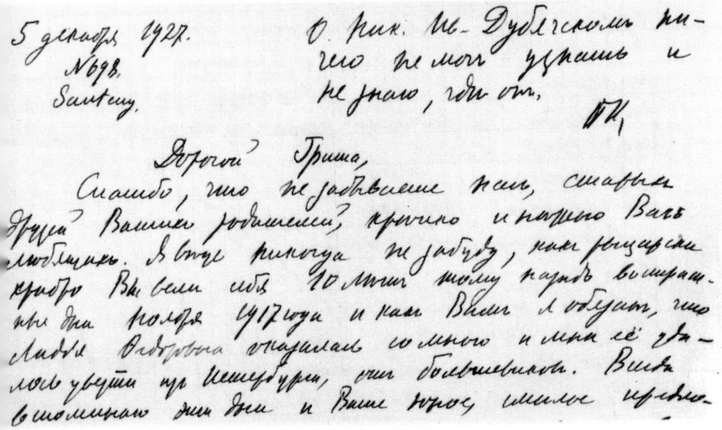

5 декабря 1927.
№ 698.
Santeny.

О рик. М.-Дублянском ни-
чего не могу узнать и
не знаю, где он.

ПК

Дорогой Гриша,

Спасибо, что не забываете нас, старых
друзей Вашей родители; приятно и нужно Вас
любящих. Я Вас никогда не забуду, как рыцарски
храбро Вы вели себя 10 лет тому назад в страш-
ные дни полдня 917 года и как Ваша любовь, что
Лидия Федоровна оказала со мною и мне её ста-
лось убыть при Петербурге, они большевики. Вас
вспоминаю эти дни и Ваше горю, милое пре-

*Figure 25. Bottom:* The door to the room at the Smólny Institute where the author
as issued his return pass to Gátchino by the Council of People's Commissars. *See*
*131.* (from Ref. 52.)      *Figure 26. Top:* Relevant reference at beginning of
ter letter from General Piótr Krassnóv to the author. *See p. 136.*

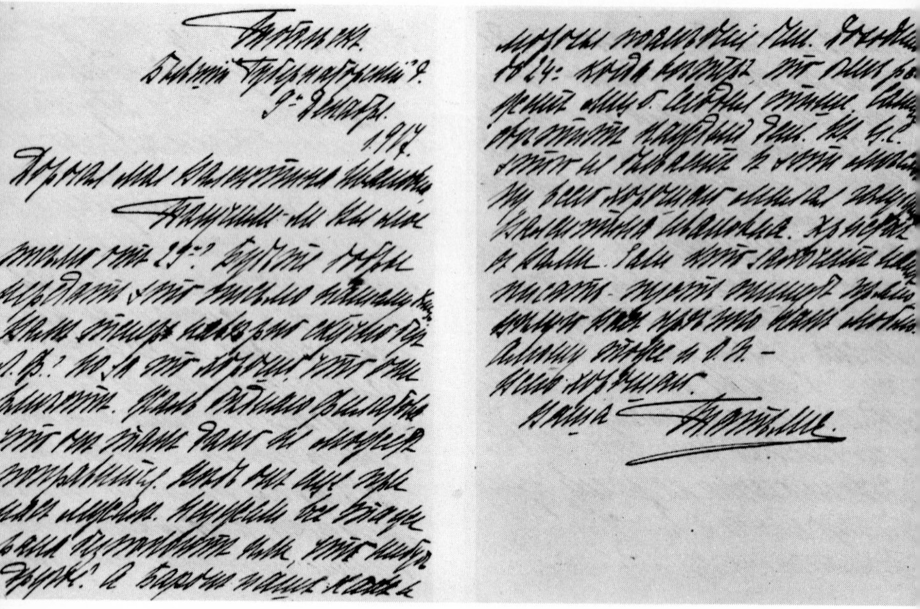

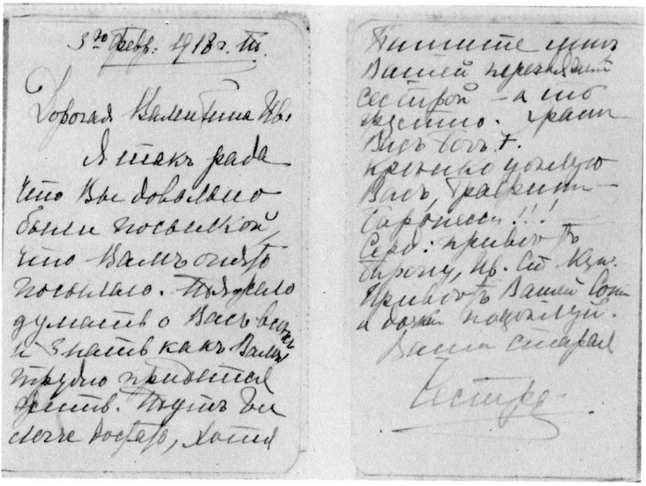

*Figure 27. Top:* Beginning and end of letter to author's mother mailed by second daughter of Tsar from their Siberian exile. *See p. 195.*     *Figure 28. Bottom:* The first and last pages of an eight-page letter to author's mother mailed by the Empress from her Siberian exile. *See p. 195.*

*Figure 29. Bottom:* Atamán of the Grand Army of the Don, General Piótr Krassnóv, Fall, 1918. *See p. 214.* *Figure 30. Top:* Inscription on reprint of later article (Ref. 35) describing fighting in the Don. *See p. 214. Translation from Russian of Fig. 30:* To the valiant defender of the Quiet Don, first Don partizán and young friend, Grísha Chebotariov, in unforgettable memory of our graves. P. Krassnóv 31 July 1922, Castle Seeon

*Figures 31 & 32.* Opening ceremonies of the Bolshói Voyskovói Kroug (Big Army Circle, that is, Parliament) at the capital of the Don Cossacks, Novocherkássk, 1918. *See p. 215.*

УДОСТОВѢРЕНIЕ.

Предъявитель сего есть
дѣйствительно Хорунжій ЧЕБОТА-
РЕВЪ /Григорій Порфирьевичъ/,
прикомандированный къ Донскому
Кадетскому Корпусу въ качествѣ
переводчика англійскаго языка
для сопровожденія Корпуса при
его эвакуаціи за границу, что
подписью и приложеніемъ печати
удостовѣряется.

Генералъ-Лейтенантъ

*Figure 33. Bottom:* The graduating class of the Don Cadet Corps at Novocherkássk, Spring, 1919. *See p. 213.* *Figure 34. Top:* Orders to the author to proceed abroad. *See p. 268.*

*Figures 35 & 36.* The author and his sister at the Don Cadet Corps camp on the banks of the Suez Canal. Ismailia, Spring, 1921. *See p. 279.*

*Figure 37.* The author with The Reverend and Mrs. Arthur A. Simmons, of the American Y.M.C.A., and two other Russian engineering students at Berlin, Fall, 1921. *See p. 285.*

*Figures 38 & 39.* Cossacks in Hitler's army. *See p. 300.* (From an unfinished Nazi World War II film. Courtesy of Mr. Friedrich Hammerstaedt, West Berlin.)

*Figure 40. Top:* Members of Soviet foundation engineering exchange delegation in New York—June, 1959. *See p. 323.* (Photo by author.)     *Figure 41. Bottom:* A light moment during U.S.A.-U.S.S.R. engineering seminar at University of Illinois —June, 1959. *Left to right:* Prof. R. Peck; author; Soviet Engineer, Mikhail M. Lévkin. *See p. 325.* (Photo by Mr. Toshinobu Akagi.)

*Figure 42.* American E
neers and their Soviet h
lunching at the House
Scientists, Moscow, Sept
ber, 1959. *See p. 328.* (Ph
by author.)

*Figure 43.* View across N
River of the Peter and P
Fortress, from window
House of Scientists at L
ingrád, September, 19
*See p. 328.* (Photo by
thor.)

*Figure 44.* Prof. N. A. T
tóvich introduces one of
Aspirants for higher degr
*See p. 329.*

*e 45.* Another Aspirant
ers questions, Septem-
959. *See p. 329.* (Photo
uthor.)

*e 46.* Prof. D. I. Pól-
discusses some of his
rch with American
s at the Institute of
dations and Under-
d Structures, Moscow,
:mber, 1959. *See p. 329.*
to by author.)

*e 47.* Part of exhibit
ged for American Dele-
n by the Ukrainian
emy of Construction
Architecture at Kíev
:rning research work
r its jurisdiction, Sep-
er, 1959. *See p. 329.*
to by author.)

*Figure 48.* Crossing Vólga River along the then under construc above Stalingrád, Sep ber, 1959. *See p. 335.* (P by author.)

*Figure 49.* Group of S construction workmen ing to author at the St grád dam. *See p. 335.*

*Figure 50.* Novel type vibratory sheet pile d at work on constructio a Vólga River pier b Stalingrád, September, 1 *See p. 338.* (Photo by thor.)

Figure 51. Erection of prefabricated and post-stressed reinforced concrete bridge units on new highway near Moscow, September, 1959. See p. 338. (Photo by author).

Figure 52. Moscow architect, V. P. Lagouténko, explains his design of prefabricated reinforced concrete housing units, September, 1959. See p. 338. (Photo by author.)

Figure 53. A factory-assembled bathroom unit with fixtures is set into place by crane, September, 1959. See p. 339. (Photo by author.)

*Figure 54. Top:* The Red Square at Moscow, September, 1959. *See p. 339.* (Photo by author.)    *Figure 55. Bottom, left:* Moscow University. The silhouette of the new "tall houses" is similar to that of the ancient but much lower Kremlin towers—*see above. See p. 339.*    *Figure 56. Bottom, Right:* The white-enameled rhombus of the university alumnus emblem is very similar to the one of pre-Revolutionary days, *see p. 341.* (Photo by author, September, 1959.)

*re 57.* The St. Isaacs ᵤre at Leningrád looked ᵣ much as the author re-ᵤbered it some forty ᵤs earlier when the city called St. Petersburg ᵣr called Petrográd). *See* ᵤ1.

ᵤre 58. The Institute of ᵤineers of Ways of Com-ᵤications, where the au-ᵣ began his engineering ᵤies in Petrográd, as it ᵤed before the Revolu-ᵤ. *See p. 343.*

*ᵤre 59.* The same build-ᵤ as it looks now after the ᵤition of two stories, Sep-ᵤber, 1959. *See p. 343.* ᵤoto by author.)

*Figure 60.* The buildin[...] Tsárskoye Seló—now ca[...] Poúshkino—where the [...] thor first went to a g[...] *názia* (high school). Se[...] *345.* (Photo, Septem[...] 1959.)

*Figure 61.* The Grand [...] cal Palace at Pávlovsk, S[...] tember, 1959. *See p. [...]* (Photo by author.)

*Figure 62.* Large colo[...] signboard at entrance [...] avenue in picture abo[...] Gives plan of the Pávlo[...] Park and invites visitor[...] the "palace museum," S[...] tember, 1959. *See p. [...]* (Photo by author.)

*e 63.* The walls of a fort built on top of old works recaptured in from the Swedes at ovsk, the author's birth- . *See p. 346.* (Photo, ember, 1959.)

*e 64.* The author be- the old Chougoúnnye ta (Cast-Iron Gates) Pávlovsk, September, . The original crown the eagle was knocked 1917. *See p. 348.*

*e 65.* The Palace at dvorétz was restored original crowns over ouble-headed eagles on wer. In foreground, our , Soviet architect, B. ravióv, September, 1959. *p. 348.* (Photo by au- )

*Figure 66.* The central tion of the Palace at Pe dvorétz as the retrea Nazis left it in 1944. *p. 348.*

*Figure 67.* The same after restoration, Sept ber, 1959. *See p. 348.* (Ph by author.)

*Figure 68.* The restored widened Khrestchátik, street of Kíev, the cap of the Ukraine, Septem 1959. *See p. 350.* (Phot author.)

*Figure 69. Top:* Statue in Kíev to the famous Ukrainian poet, Tarás Shevchénko.
*See p. 352.* (Photo by author, September, 1959.)     *Figure 70. Bottom:* Nine-
centuries-old Byzantine-style mosaic in the ancient St. Sophia Cathedral at Kíev,
September, 1959. *See p. 350.* (Photo by author.)

Figure 71. *Top:* Statue to St. Vladímir still stands at Kíev overlooking spot whe Christian baptism was first brought by him to Russia from Byzance almost a tho sand years ago. *See p. 350.*    Figure 72. *Bottom, left:* Statue at Kíev to th Hétman Bogdán Khmelnítzky who led the 1648 Ukrainian Revolution against Poli rule, which culminated in the reunification with Russia in 1654. *See p. 351.*    Fi ure 73. *Bottom, right:* Marble plaque on an outer wall of the St. Sophia Cathedr in Kíev, September, 1959. The inscription is in Ukrainian.

"At this Cathedral
on 17—19 (27—29) January 1654,
Kíevans unanimously approved
the historic decision of the
PEREYASLÁVSKAYA RÁDA [Congress]
on the reunification of the
UKRAÍNA with ROSSÍYA,
and took the oath of
allegiance to Rossíya."

See p. 351. (Photo by author.)

The railway station and the village of Kouschóvka lay on the other (southeastern) side of a dammed-up small river which had to be crossed over a narrow causeway. Several baggage trains had been converging towards it so that it became a bottleneck for them. I found that the several (less than a dozen) carts of the Don Cadet Corps and my carriage and other cart were lined up along the edge of the pond, waiting for a chance to get into the traffic line which was streaming at right angles past them. Father was with them—he had ordered all his officers and cadets to cross the causeway on foot to the warm school building which had been assigned to them for the night, but had stayed with the carts to get them across. He was used only to the orderly procedures of the old Imperial Army and was now at a loss as to how to cope with the disorderly mob before him. Having been a prisoner of war in Germany since 1915 (p. 48), he had missed the period of the disintegration of the Army after the Revolution.

Personnel of baggage trains were never renowned for discipline and the mob now before us certainly had none. Someone had spread the false rumor that Budiónny's Red Cavalry had broken through and was nearby—this created a near panic. No order of arrival was observed—it was just a wild scramble among the several converging columns as to which would force its way first into the single file which passed us and then went onto the causeway.

I proposed a plan of action to which Father agreed—luckily I had a flashlight with me. So I picked up a loaded rifle from among the several which lay on one of the carts of the Corps and waited until darkness fell. Then, remembering the demonstrations of practical psychology I got from our 2nd Don Battery Corporal (p. 248), I walked down the approaching single line of carts, flashing my light at the drivers until I saw one who looked like somewhat of a weakling. I moved along with him in the darkness until his horse was just about to pass the lead cart of the Corps. Then I suddenly stepped in front of him, stuck my rifle muzzle into his body and ordered him to stop his cart or be killed. He stopped, and the carts of the Cadet Corps immediately began moving into the gap which was thus formed in the advancing single file. I brought up their rear. My sister tells me that she still remembers that night, mainly because of the shock at hearing me use the elaborately profane language I apparently employed.

We all got safely across and when everyone was installed in the village, Father came up to me and said only one word: *"Spasíbo!*

(Thank you)"—but I shall never forget the look on his face as he shook my hand. It remains one of the happiest memories of my life.

On the next day I installed the Danílovs and my sister with all our luggage on a train bound for the Black Sea port of Novorossísk, where the Cadet Corps was also going. I then dismissed the two carts, said goodbye to Father and headed back in the two-horse carriage of my former commander in the 2nd Don Battery, which I duly returned to him.

It was a clear frosty day as we drove back just before Christmas. As the sun was setting in the west, white puffs of shrapnel bursts were silhouetted in the distance against the reddish-colored edge of the sky, indicating that our frontlines had been again pulled still farther back.

I returned to the Headquarters of the Don Army three days before the expiration of my "sick leave" and spent them in bed in a compartment of our sleeping car.

Soon after that Baron Máydell was off again for his on-the-spot checks of artillery at the front. We went along with a detachment which made an unsuccessful attempt to recapture Novocherkássk by a sudden pre-dawn thrust. Then we spent several days inspecting armored trains along the Batáisk-Azóv line which follows the left bank of the Don River to its estuary. Rostóv, which is located on the right bank opposite Batáisk, had been abandoned to the Reds on December 26, 1919/January 8, 1920.

One episode of that inspection trip stands out in my memory. We had left Batáisk on a foggy day in a light armored train and drove to a small railway stop in the open steppe where we got out to look at a 6-inch naval gun of French make, "Canet," which was mounted on a large railway flat car. It was commanded by a formerly retired Cossack sergeant who, as it turned out, had served under my father in the Guard Battery. He had two of his sons with him, so I lingered behind near their platform, chatting with them, while General Máydell, in the company of its commander, walked back towards the light armored train a couple of hundred feet away.

Suddenly, yells of "ourrah" were heard and out of the fog, their sabres drawn, dashed some twenty Red cavalrymen. A quick glance back at my General showed that he was sprinting towards the light armored train, which fortunately he had almost reached, at a pace which no short-distance champion runner could have exceeded. So I tried to do the same, but in the opposite direction, since the 6-inch gun was closest to me,—I barely made it. As helping hands pulled me on board, one of the Red horsemen came close to slashing through one of my ankles, but someone on the flat car brought him down just in time by a well-aimed revolver shot.

The locomotive of the 6-inch gun open freight car then slowly moved it away while our light armored train, with the General safely on board, steamed off in the opposite direction, its machine guns blazing—our car had none.

The attacking group of Reds was only one of the advance scout parties for a large body of Red cavalry which had suddenly crossed the frozen Don River over the ice. Just then gusts of wind cleared most of the fog away and we witnessed a remarkable sight. On the river side of some four or five farm cottages, where they had apparently been quartered, about a hundred or so infantrymen were forming a line to face wave after wave of Red cavalry which were coming at them. It was an all-Officer company of the famous Drozdóvsky Division of the Volunteer Army (p. 211). Two field pieces, flanked by machine guns, were in the center. A single line of infantrymen, standing motionless almost shoulder to shoulder, were on each side. It all looked as if they were on parade.

In front of them, coming at a brisk trot over the light snow cover of the steppe were about five consecutive waves of Red cavalry, some 100 feet apart, the horsemen in each wave being at approximately 20-foot intervals. When the front wave was only a couple of hundred feet away from the Drozdóvsky company, the latter opened fire, the individual riflemen shooting from the shoulder in volleys which, together with the booming of the field pieces, punctuated the continuous rattle of the machine guns. In less than a minute the entire center of the frontlines of the attacking Reds was down and the rest withdrew back across the Don in complete disorder.

Some of the armored trains on the Batáisk-Azóv line belonged to the Volunteer Army from which they continued to get directly their supplies of ammunition; but operationally they were subordinated on that section of the front to the Don Army Command and were therefore subject to inspection by General Máydell. In the course of that visit the Baron was surprised to find that the Volunteer Army trains were obviously getting more shells per gun than were allotted by the same Volunteer Army Supply Services for the Don Army armored trains. Baron Máydell began therefore suspecting that these Services had not been giving him the true figures of the ammunition supplies

which they received from the British for all of South Russia. So he
sent me to Novorossísk to do a bit of confidential checking around
the harbor.

Luckily, I soon ran into a Major of the British Army who had
been one of my tutors at the classes for general education of the Imperial Law School at St. Petersburg (p. 24)—I believe his name
was Stanton. I formally identified myself and my official position and
then frankly explained to him the nature of my mission. He and his
superiors cooperated fully and within a couple of days I was able to
return and report to my General figures which clearly proved that his
suspicions were correct and that the Volunteer Army Supply Services
had been consistently cheating the Don Army by giving a preferential
status to their own units in disregard of existing agreements.

But it was too late to do anything about it; the general retreat
was gradually turning into a major disaster and recriminations between the various commanders—Cossack and non-Cossack—as to
responsibilities for it were increasing in intensity.

The mood of the Reds must have been jubilant. Their airplanes
dropped leaflets calling for general surrender. I recall one, which
consisted of only three short-rhymed lines:

| | | | |
|---|---|---|---|
| *Soldátiki* | *—k nam;* | Soldiers | —[come] to us; |
| *Dobrovóltzi* | *—po domám;* | Volunteers | —[go] to your homes; |
| *Ofitzériki* | *—po grobám.* | Officers | —[go] to your graves. |

This is just about what their policies were with respect to prisoners,
even though the words "soldiers" and "officers" in the above message
were given in a kindly diminutive form, obviously meant to be offen-
sively ironical towards the latter.

The Reds had learned the hard way from our Cossack General
Mámontov the value of breakthroughs by cavalry concentrations
(p. 251) and now imitated him. Their largest cavalry "fist" was
under the command of Budiónny, a former Sergeant of the Imperial
Russian Army and a future Marshal of the Soviet Union.

In mid-February Budiónny with a Corps of some 20,000 Red
cavalry rapidly advanced southwest along the railway line which ran
from Tsarítzyn (Stalingrád) to Tikhorétskaya (Map E, p. 142).
From there he would be in a position to penetrate deep into the Kubán
area, splitting the White lines, outflanking and threatening the rear
of large sections of the White front.

This sudden Red move had not been expected and it took several days to get together a concentration of White cavalry to intercept Budiónny.

In some areas they had to move for three days in bitter cold through virtually uninhabited steppes where there was no food or shelter for themselves or for their horses. Frostbite and sickness took a heavy toll, so that out of some 20,000 White cavalry who had started out towards their point of concentration only some 12,000 reached it in a state fit for combat. Budiónny's 20,000 men were, however, virtually intact because he hugged the railway line, along which many settlements were located.

Baron Máydell of course knew what was going on and was intent on taking part in what he correctly predicted would be the last action in history fought by massed cavalry. He could get there in time by air only—so he tried to get two planes, one to transport him and the other for myself. He got only one * and took off, leaving me behind.

Judging by what I heard later from Máydell himself and from other White participants, the cavalry clash which then developed was really something quite fantastic. The steppe in the area where it was fought was absolutely flat, so the horse artillery batteries of both sides had to fire over their open sights, taking a heavy toll of each other and of the masses of cavalry (both Red and White) which charged mainly in closed formations since their commanders feared that otherwise they might lose control over them in the rapidly developing battle of maneuver.

The weight of numbers however proved decisive and Budiónny's Reds won the action.

### 3. *Orders to Proceed Abroad*

The day after Baron Máydell's departure was February 15/28, 1920—my twenty-first birthday. As usual in his absence, I received and opened telegrams addressed to him. I still have one of them, which reads in English translation:

"In view of the imminent departure of the Corps I request to urgently send to Novorossísk as interpreter of the Corps, Lieutenant Chebotarióv. 15 February 1/3. Director of the Corps, General Cheriachoúkin."

* I believe he got it from a British volunteer squadron, in which Captain Marion Aten was apparently flying—the author of Ref. 1, who it is claimed was the only American to see combat service in the South Russian campaign. Appropriately, he was the son of a Texas Ranger.

I knew that Cheriachóukin, the former Don Ambassador to the Ukraine (p. 206), had been without a job since the collapse of the Central Powers and of their Ukrainian puppets. Since he now signed as Director of the Corps, this could only mean that something had happened to my father.

In the absence of General Máydell, I went to General Sidórin, the Commander of the Don Army, whose office was located in the same train, showed him Cheriachóukin's telegram and asked for instructions as to what I was to do about it. Sidórin told me that in half an hour he was scheduled to have a teletype conversation with the Don Atamán, General Bogáyevsky; I was to come back in an hour.

When I did this, General Sidórin solemnly told me that I had been right in my premonitions—my father had died of typhus five days ago. The Don Atamán ordered me to proceed immediately to Novo-rossísk, as requested by Cheriachóukin, but to stop to see him at Ekaterinodár * on the way.

This I did, reporting to General Bogáyevsky two days later. He received me in a compartment of his train, looking terribly tired and depressed. He gave me then the certificate ordering me abroad (Fig. 34), which reads in English translation:

DON ATAMÁN
of the
Grand Army
of the Don

_____

17 February
1920
No. 610

_____

City of
Ekaterinodár

## CERTIFICATE

The bearer of this is truly the Khoroúnzhi †
CHEBOTARIÓV (Grigóriy Porphyrievich) which is attached to the Don Cadet Corps as English language
interpreter to accompany the Corps in its evacuation abroad, which is certified by signature and
application of seal.

*Lieutenant General* [*signed*] *Bogáyevsky*

INSCRIPTION ON SEAL:

Don Atamán
*A stag can be swift*
*But a Cossack arrow overtakes him*

---

* Present-day Krasnodár.
† Second Lieutenant.

It took me about two more days to get to Novorossísk—the Don Cadet Corps was already in the process of boarding the Russian steamer *Sarátov*. I found that my father, when he came down with typhus, had sent my sister with the Danílovs by ship to rejoin his cousin Danílov at Batoum in Georgia—that was all I knew, not even their address at Batoum. But all our personal suitcases, filled mainly with various mementos and documents, were intact and I placed them on the *Sarátov*.

Father had been buried in a military cemetery on a hillside which overlooked the harbor and the sea. I filled one of the pockets of my tunic with earth from his grave and I have kept some of it to this day—according to Russian custom I want it buried with me when I die far away from my homeland.

The British evacuation permit issued to me for the *Sarátov* at Novorossísk has the date 3.6.20 on it—that is, February 21/March 6, 1920. Just before sailing the Don Cadet Corps was lined up on the quay alongside the *Sarátov* for inspection by the British Acting High Commissioner to South Russia. I stood on the flank of the Corps.

Keyes, now a General, slowly walked along the front of the Corps. He had never before seen me in uniform but nevertheless immediately recognized me, obviously remembering my presence during his personal discomfiture by General Krassnóv at Kouschóvka (p. 226) over a year before that. At any rate he stopped abruptly and asked in a far from friendly tone: "What are *you* doing here?" I told him. "On what authority?" he continued. I had a feeling he would have liked to prevent my leaving. I told him that I was going on the strength of personal written orders signed by the Don Atamán, General Bogáyevsky, which were in my pocket together with an evacuation permit signed and stamped at his own British High Commissioner's Office. Keyes stood looking at me for a moment, then moved on without saying another word but with an expression which in a civilian would have amounted to a shrug of the shoulders.

Immediately after this inspection we all boarded the *Sarátov* and sailed for Constantinople and an uncertain future abroad.

### 4. *End of White Resistance in the Crimea—and Its Aftermath*

Three weeks after we sailed on the *Sarátov* the Red Army occupied Novorossísk—on March 14/27, 1920.

There had been a great dearth of shipping there—the vessels available were used mainly to transport White combat units to the Crimea where a last stand was to be made. But Deníkin's command evacuated first the troops of the Volunteer Army, leaving behind most of the Cossack units which were covering the retreat to the harbor and the embarkation there.

Baron Máydell witnessed this and told me later abroad that, had he been in the place of the Cossacks who were left behind, he would have turned not just plain Red, but *pountzóvy* (crimson). Some of them did just that. Others fought their way out to the southeast along the coast where White ships, returning from their first evacuation shuttle, managed to pick some of them up and take them, too, to the Crimea.

But bitter feelings at this discrimination against them in a moment of supreme peril naturally persisted in the hearts of many of these Cossacks. This is one of the very important reasons why some of them succumbed later to anti-Russian propaganda for the creation of a mythical nation of "Cossackia," the very name of which was "discovered" in and promoted from Central Europe just before the start of World War II (pp. 298–308, 360).

A great number of civilian refugees were also abandoned at Novorossísk—some of the tragic scenes which took place there on the quays are well described on pages 324–335 of Ref. 1 and correspond to what I have myself heard from a few survivors I talked to.*

The narrow Perekóp isthmus which joins the Crimean peninsula to the mainland in the north facilitated its defense and gave a breathing spell to the White troops which had been concentrated in the Crimea.

On March 22/April 4, 1920, General Deníkin relinquished his command and was succeeded by Baron Wrangell. The British had stopped all active help to the White armies, but the French started giving some since this would indirectly benefit Poland, whom they were backing. The Polish Army had advanced into the Ukraine and occupied Kíev on April 23/May 6. But the Reds started a counter-

---

* At first I thought that a woman Kubán Cossack officer mentioned in Ref. 1 must have been a fictional character invented to create romantic interest. But I checked with Lt. Col. Borís Ivánovitch Tkatschéw, the present Atamán of the Kubán Cossacks in exile (p. 223), and he tells me that they did have a girl who was given the rank of *khorounzhi* (second lieutenant) for valor which she had displayed in combat.

offensive and drove them back. To help the Poles, Baron Wrangell's troops emerged from the Crimea on May 24/June 6 and advanced towards the Dníepr River, inflicting there near Kakhóvka a serious defeat on the Red troops of the Southern Ukraine. Nevertheless, the Poles were driven back by the Reds almost to the gates of Warsaw and only on August 4/17, 1920 were they able to strike again under the general guidance of Maréchal Weygand of France.

Peace negotiations were begun on September 8/21 and a Provisional Peace Treaty between Poland and the Bolshevik government was signed on September 30/October 12, 1920, leaving General Baron Wrangell's White troops to fare for themselves. This permitted the Reds to concentrate large forces against Wrangell and start a major attack against him less than two weeks after Poland had signed the peace treaty.

The Reds broke through the Perekóp isthmus and on November 1/14, 1920, the remnants of Wrangell's White troops were evacuated by ship to camps at Gallipoli and the island of Lemnos in the Aegean Sea where they were virtually interned. The Russian Civil War was over.

Again, the Russian armies had been left in the lurch after having served as a catspaw for foreign interests. This, coming as it did after the less than halfhearted and mainly material support previously given by the British, who at the same time were able to find troops to occupy the oil wells of the Caucasus (p. 233), and after the selfish mercantile pressures of the French as a precondition for their help (p. 233), produced a wave of lasting feeling against the Western Allies. The general distrust took various forms of expression.

Some, like Gen. Piótr Krassnóv (pp. 298–308), developed an increasingly pro-German attitude, considering that the Germans, although our former enemies, at least were people whom one could trust when they were on your side—something that, he held, could not be said about the Western Allies.

Others, like General Slastchióv, considered that Russia's future would be decided within its own borders by the people there and that *émigrés* could have no effect on developments—so they returned to the Soviet Union to meet whatever fate awaited them there.

Much has been written about how the Allied intervention on the White side is responsible for Russian distrust of the West because this intervention was directed against the Revolution. This is only

partially correct. No less important in this respect are the feelings of
deep distrust engendered in Russian hearts by the way the West was
unwilling to make any real sacrifices in the struggle and the way it
repeatedly let down the Russian Whites who had put their trust in
their Western "Allies"—something very well known to the Russian
Reds.

# Part III    EMIGRATION AND "FORTY YEARS AFTER"

# 9    Life in Emigration Abroad

## 1. *Interpreter to the Don Cadet Corps in Egypt*

The steamer *Sarátov* had at least three times as many people on board as it was designed for. The Cadet Corps was the last to embark so that most of the officers and boys had to sleep on the floors of the upper cargo holds without any bedding or blankets, without undressing, just wrapping our overcoats around us. Only our General and his family were given a cabin.

The crowded and unsanitary conditions favored an outbreak of several epidemics—first came cases of typhus among people of all ages who had been infected ashore; then scarlet fever and chickenpox broke out among the numerous children.

By the time we reached Constantinople (now Istanbul) the ship had to be virtually quarantined and only our General and myself, as his interpreter, were allowed ashore. But we were unable to learn there what our destination was going to be—apparently it had not been decided upon by the British authorities who were in charge of the evacuation. To gain time for them we were ordered to steam out of the Bosporus into a remote bay of the Marmara Sea where we anchored for several days.

Then we left via the Dardanelles strait for Cyprus. Fortunately, the weather was good, the sea was calm and the Greek islands rising out of the blue sea looked beautiful, although barren, as we passed them in the Aegean. Reaching Cyprus, we anchored at Famagusta, a harbor at the eastern end of the island. But we were not allowed to land there either, because the epidemic on board had reached alarming proportions and the local British authorities felt that they did not have the hospital and quarantine facilities to cope with the infectious diseases among the people on board. Several more days were spent in idle waiting in the harbor, the nerves of the anxious civilian female refugees getting more and more strained. Several outbreaks of hysterics occurred.

Someone at the British Headquarters finally recalled the existence of a quarantine-type hospital camp for Moslem pilgrims traveling to Mecca via Sidi-Bishr—a suburb of Alexandria in Egypt. Its barracks were capable of accommodating up to 8,000 people at once and were empty at the time. So we were ordered there and disembarked at Alexandria after over three weeks on board the *Sarátov*.

The British ran the Sidi-Bishr hospital camp very efficiently on an "assembly line" basis. People, their clothing, and their other belongings were moved separately through one disinfection compound after another and were then reunited. I do not think that a single louse survived the operation; these typhus-transmitters were all exterminated. The balmy weather helped, since it was possible to move around in the open clad only in long white hospital shirts while the disinfection was going on. But leather articles were ruined unless separated from the rest of the clothing which underwent steam treatment. I was too busy interpreting to take good care of my own belongings, and as a result my fur coat went through the "assembly line" and emerged shrunk to a size fit only for a midget, the leather having become brittle and crumbly. I had to throw it away.

The sick were left at the Sidi-Bishr hospital while the rest of the *Sarátov* refugees were moved in several trains to Tel el Kebir, an Arab village on the eastern edge of the Nile delta, near which was located in a desert a large empty hospital camp just vacated by Turkish prisoners of war. Our Cadet Corps was given a compound there separate from the civilian refugees.

Near us was a camp of a Lancer Regiment of the Indian Army. The Colonel in command of that regiment paid a formal call on our director, General Cheriachoúkin, and invited him and myself to dinner at their officers' mess. Nearly all the officers were English. After dinner we rode out with the Colonel to the 1882 battlefield nearby where a small British force, after unexpectedly landing in the Suez Canal, surprised and defeated the Egyptian Commander, Arabi Pasha. The outlines of some of the old field earthwork fortifications were still visible then, and the Colonel explained to us the details of that historic action.

Shortly after that we were visited and were formally inspected by British Lieut. Gen. Sir Walter Norris Congreve, V.C., Commander of the EEF—the Egyptian Expeditionary Force, as the British Army in Egypt was then called. He appeared to be favorably impressed by the general appearance and discipline of our Cadets and promptly decided to separate us from the demoralized civilian refugees nearby and to move us to a special new camp at Ismailia, a little town on the banks of the Suez Canal, halfway between Port Said and Suez. As he told our General through me, there were some very nice French families living there who were "bored to tears" from not having anything to do and who would surely "make quite a fuss" over all of us.

We found that the kindly old Englishman had not exaggerated. The main Administration of the Suez Canal Company was located at Ismailia—a small garden city with an artificially irrigated park planted half a century earlier in the days of De Lesseps, the French builder of the canal. The British had acquired a controlling interest of the shares of the Canal since then, but had wisely left its administration in French hands. Ismailia had retained its original flavor of a cozy French colonial town, and was known as the "Emerald of the Desert" because all its streets were lined with shade trees and the numerous villas had luxurious subtropical gardens.

We were all housed under canvas in a tent camp which was located on an open stretch of desert sand near the edge of a large lake through which passed the Canal. A nice sandy beach was within close walking distance, and our boys had the opportunity for frequent bathing and swimming across the Canal to its other side and back.

As General Congreve had predicted, we were very well received by the French colony of the town who hospitably invited our officers to many functions. General Cheriachoúkin appointed me Adjutant of the Corps, a post which he newly created to help me cope with the many new problems which arose. One of them required maintaining social relations with the French colony, which was not too easy since the town was a couple of miles from our camp and each prominent French family made it a point to have a different formal "at home" day. We had no cars and there was no other transportation available, so practically every day I had to tramp on foot to some reception in the afternoon heat still wearing a heavy Russian uniform. Except for this inconvenience, I enjoyed the friendly atmosphere of these visits. I was given the courtesy of the Club of the Suez Canal Company and spent many evenings in the library there going over the wartime issues of the Paris *l'Illustration* which we could no longer receive at home after the outbreak of hostilities in 1914.

Ironically, none of the officers of the British Army camps in the vicinity enjoyed the same Canal Club privileges at that time—they used to have them, but they were withdrawn by the French about a year earlier after some Australians imbibed more Scotch than was good for them at the bar, started a brawl and wrecked the whole place.

The Britishers did not seem to resent in any way the special favors the French accorded us and I formed several friendships with English officers. One of them, a Major, commanded a squadron of the Royal Air Force which was stationed on the other side of Ismailia and offered to have his several planes take up some thirty of our boys, our General and myself for a flight over the Canal area.

We accepted with pleasure, but requested that the actual flight be postponed until about six weeks after we had announced it—only the best behaved boys from all classes were to be selected for it. Never before or after that did we have such perfect behavior in the camp as we did during those six weeks!

I took part in the academic instruction of the Cadets by giving lessons in English. All teachers had to start under considerable handicaps since no text, notebooks or any other accessories were at first available at the camp. However, one of our officers had discovered several huge rolls of newsprint in one of the cargo holds of the *Sarátov* and had persuaded the Captain of the ship to let us take them with us when we disembarked. These rolls were then cut up into notebooks for the boys, pencils were donated by the French, and large sheets of the same newsprint were used instead of blackboards, with pieces of charcoal from the camp kitchen replacing chalk.

Gradually, with help from many sources, we managed to replace these primitive appliances with conventional ones, received British khaki summer uniforms, and generally settled down.

Towards midsummer of the year 1920 it became evident that the British would soon have to abandon Batoum since the Red armies were moving through the Caucasus towards it and the oil wells of Bakou. I decided to make an attempt to get my twelve-year-old sister out of there and obtained leave to do so from General Cheriachoúkin. The British authorities in Egypt were also most sympathetic and cooperative and even arranged a free first-class passage for me from Port Said to Constantinople as an "Allied Officer on leave" on board a British military transport.

But when I landed at Constantinople I found a completely different atmosphere. There had been comparatively few Russian refugees in Egypt, so that we were not really a burden to anyone. Constantinople however was overcrowded by such a mass of people evacuated from South Russia that the British and French authorities could not cope with the situation and many *émigrés* were left in dire distress. This enraged some evacuated convalescent White Russian officers who felt that the Western Allies owed a great debt of gratitude to Russia * which they should have now tried partially to repay. It was rumored that some felt so strongly about what they considered a betrayal that they made their way via Batoum to the Turkish troops of Kemal-Ataturk to fight with them against their former Allies. The natural countermove of the British was to prevent any Russian officer from sailing to Batoum if he did not happen to be on official business.

So I found myself stranded at Constantinople. Soon after my arrival I ran into my old Tsárskoye Seló friend Níka Coúriss who had rented an old dilapidated house, which was abandoned because it was uninhabitable in winter. In the summer it was quite nice, however, since it was located at the top of a hill overlooking the Bosporus at Arnaout-Keoy with a beautiful view from its windows. I joined him there and subsisted by gradually selling off my father's gold watch, his decorations and various family gold trinkets.

One day I met by chance a former officer of our Guard Horse Artillery, Prince Kozlóvsky, who luckily happened to be then the Aide-de-Camp of General Wrangell's Batoum representative and who was sailing there the next day to bring his family back. By sheer good luck they happened to live in Batoum practically next door to the Danílovs, with whom my sister was staying, and knew them—I could not have possibly found them otherwise without going there myself since I had no idea what their address was! I immediately gave him a written authorization to bring my sister back with him, which he did. Soon after I returned with her to Egypt.

At the Ismailia camp I was first given for myself and my sister a large tent located in the married officers' compound (Figs. 35 and 36). Nevertheless, this presented a number of problems and my French friends soon arranged for the admission of my sister to board at the local French school run by nuns of the St. Vincent de Paul order.

An important change in the general administration of our camp took place after my return. It was an indirect result of the anomalous

* See pp. 42–45, 50–52.

situation we were all in. Outwardly, we were an independent Allied military unit. The old Russian national flag—white, blue and red horizontal stripes—flew from a flagstaff, and a row of stacked rifles was guarded by an armed senior Cadet sentry near the camp entrance. We received British Army rations of food, clothing and blankets which were issued through a British liaison Lieutenant who lived with us in our camp. But only three persons in the Cadet Corps were formally considered part of the camp personnel and received any pay—the medical doctor, the hospital nurse and the interpreter (myself). None of the other officers nor any of the cadets received any pay; so they lacked any pocket money whatsoever, since Russian currency brought with us had by that time lost all value.

This and the monotonous diet of British Army rations made some of our boys easy victims of Arab peddlers who lurked around the camp offering dates, figs and other tempting delicacies in exchange for articles of clothing. The boys did not realize that these articles could not be replaced by the time winter came when they would badly need them.

When requests for local police action did not improve the situation, our General Cheriachoúkin decided to take action himself. He sallied forth with an armed patrol of our older Cadets, rounded up the Arab peddlers in the vicinity, confiscated any Corps property found on them, beat them up and had their hand-pushed carts with the dates and other illicit exchange wares thrown into the Canal.

This sort of action could have been taken under the conditions of the Russian Civil War we had just left behind us. Many of the conservative local Frenchmen applauded this, feeling that it was the right way to handle obstreperous native peddlers, but at the British Army Headquarters, who were formally responsible for us, it produced shudders of horror. The incident came at a time when their relations with the Egyptians were very strained and delicate. What would this "wild Cossack" do next? And how could the British G.H.Q. control him?

General Congreve did not want to withdraw his recognition of the Corps as an Allied unit and hence could not subordinate our General to any British officer of lesser rank on the spot. I was told that he therefore welcomed as a gift from Heaven the sudden arrival on the scene of an Anglican clergyman, Roland H. Cragg.*

---

* He later became the Canon of Gibraltar.

Mr. Cragg had long been interested in things Russian and had even been a member of a British ecclesiastical delegation to St. Petersburg just before the war, which was sent there to explore possibilities of a closer union between the Russian Orthodox Church and the Church of England. He now appeared at the Sidi-Bishr refugee camp near Alexandria as the Commissioner for Egypt of the British-Russian Red Cross, which was under the patronage of Princess Mary.

General Congreve persuaded the Reverend Mr. Cragg to establish his office at our camp instead of at Sidi-Bishr, renaming our place "The Russian School Camp," and naming Mr. Cragg its Superintendent. He was made responsible for all external relations and for anything that happened outside of the limits of the camp proper. However, he was not to interfere in any way with the inner administration of the Don Cadet Corps itself.

Thus the demarcation lines of authority between Cragg and Cheriachoúkin were rather nebulous and considerable friction and ill-feeling gradually developed between the two. When they started using me as a go-between, each expecting me to persuade the other to yield, I found that any compromises I suggested were never accepted. In order to be in a position to decline any further hopeless missions of this kind, I finally resigned my post as Adjutant of the Corps on June 9, 1921, but kept the ones of teacher of English and of interpreter both of the Corps and of the Camp. From then on I declined to do anything more than translate what the two had to say to each other and my work became much more bearable.

Complications, but of a different kind, arose also in connection with the arrival of an American Y.M.C.A. secretary, the Reverend Mr. Arthur A. Simmons, a Congregational minister. He and his wife were exceptionally nice and kind people who did a lot for our boys. They arranged for the delivery to our Camp of a very large recreation tent of the circus "flat-top" type with pingpong tables, boxing gloves, chess and checker sets and other recreational facilities. This made the Simmons husband-and-wife team very popular with everybody in the Corps, but not so with the British who felt that they were stealing their thunder in the sense that the much more costly main necessities of life provided by the British—the tents for housing, the food, clothing and hospital care—were getting much less appreciation than the entertainment efforts of the American Y.M.C.A. couple. After a few sour remarks about this by Mr. Cragg, Mr.

Simmons and his wife decided to return to America, but left with us the recreational Y.M.C.A. tent with all that it contained.

Shortly before their departure they unwittingly caused an incident which illustrates the problems of an interpreter who tries, as I did, to prevent ill-will between the groups for whom he serves as a channel of communication. Mr. Simmons periodically arranged through the American Y.M.C.A. in Cairo for lecturers on varied topics to come and address our Cadets, with myself doing the translating. One day he told me that he was somewhat worried by the personality of the next speaker selected by the Cairo Y.M.C.A.—he was a Baptist preacher of the "fire-and-brimstone" type who was just back from many years of missionary work in China. Mr. Simmons feared that he might say something that would offend our Russian Eastern Orthodox priest, with whom Simmons was on good terms, as well as others. Would I soften things in my translation if the missionary became tactlessly overzealous? I promised that I would.

Things started off quietly in the recreation tent before an overflow audience. Our General, other officers, our priest, Mr. Cragg and Mr. Simmons sat in the front rows. However, apart from myself, only one other person in the audience knew both English and Russian—he was Colonel Pável Richárdovich Neviadómsky, a Roman Catholic Pole who had been my 1916 battery commander at the Miháilovsky Artillery School in Petrográd.

As the preacher made some cautiously probing but rather tactless remarks, I took the sting out of them in my translation, as I had promised to do. But this had an effect we had not anticipated. The missionary's eyes kept scanning the faces of the audience before him for any signs of resentment. Seeing none, he grew bolder and bolder so that I found it increasingly difficult to soften anything. Soon a "point of no return" was reached and the only thing left for me to do was to translate the reverse of what the Baptist actually said. From then on everything was simple.

For example, the speaker told of a Russian girl who had renounced her Eastern Orthodox faith after coming into contact with Baptists. Mr. Simmons, with a stern expression on his face, started to rise to stop him, but was held down by Colonel Neviadómsky who had been sitting next to him, shaking with silent laughter at the comedy which was developing. The Colonel whispered something in his ear as I translated—in reverse—that the speaker knew of a Russian girl who had resisted all blandishments of missionaries and never once wavered in her original Orthodox faith. Mr. Simmons looked at me with an air of worried incredulity but appeared calmed by the grin and wink I gave him. A glance at our priest, who was obviously pleased by what he was hearing, appeared to finally reassure him.

The meeting ended in an ovation after the preacher had thundered in English: "Abandon the ways of your Fathers and join us!"— echoed by me in Russian as: "Never forsake the faith of your Fathers!"

I immediately took him and Mr. Simmons aside and explained what I had done to save all of us from considerable embarrassment— our General would have otherwise surely stopped the meeting and ordered me to march the preacher under armed guard out of the camp. At that the latter started to sputter with indignation, but Mr. Simmons stopped him short by solemnly shaking hands with me, saying: "On behalf of the American Y.M.C.A., I thank you for what you have done!" I never saw a man change so quickly from a state of great exhilaration to one of complete dejection. The preacher silently slunk away and I could not help feeling sorry for him.

I soon encountered another case of overzealous proselytizing which gave me much food for thought concerning the sectarian foolishness of some missionaries who undid the good they were doing by making efforts to combat other branches of the Christian church in the chauvinistic belief that theirs, and theirs only, was the true faith. The nuns at the French convent school where my sister was boarding were all sincere, very kind and dedicated persons, but I was shocked to discover that they had given her a book to read about a Russian girl who had become a Roman Catholic nun. They were doing other things to influence her in the same direction. I felt that this was an unfair way to take advantage of our plight and decided to remove my sister from the convent school at the first opportunity.

One solution would have been to take her with me to Yugoslavia, where the Don Cadet Corps was to be transferred shortly. King Alexander had not forgotten the help his country had received from Russia during its liberation from the Turks (pp. 13, 14). He now welcomed educated Russian refugees, who assisted him in staffing the new administration of the former Austro-Hungarian provinces which were inhabited by kindred branches of the Southern Slavs. As part of this general program two other Russian cadet corps, including all their officers and cadets, had already been incorporated in the Royal Yugoslav Army. The Serbian and the Russian languages are so similar that no difficulty was anticipated in making a gradual transfer of teaching from Russian to Serbian as older officers retired, Cadets were promoted into the Army and new officers and Cadets of local origin were admitted to the vacancies thus formed. I understand that all this was done eventually.

But I had not intended to become a regular peacetime Army officer even in old Russia and now wanted to continue and complete my engineering studies. So I wrote several letters to explore possibilities in that direction, including one to Mr. Simmons in the United States.

I was quite surprised to get a reply from Berlin where Mr. Simmons had been sent after his return home. I also got a letter from Mr. A. A. Ebersole, Secretary, Student Relief of The International Committee of Y.M.C.A.s there, offering to help me enter one of the German engineering schools and promising support for the first semester—they could not commit themselves beyond that.

Within a few days of the receipt of these letters early in September, 1921, I got another one from the Baroness Sophie von Medem who was my sister's godmother. She and her husband were Russian-Baltic Germans who had managed to leave Petrográd via Finland after the Bolshevik revolution and were now living in Lübeck in northern Germany. She wrote that she had heard of American organizations in Berlin who were helping Russian refugee students study there and offered to take care of my sister if I saw my way to continue my studies on my own.

It did not take me long to make up my mind. I obtained a written certificate of discharge from General Cheriachoúkin, various travel documents from the British Headquarters and ten days later I was with my sister on board a P. & O. liner, sailing for London.

## 2. *Engineering Studies and Work on Three Continents*

For the purpose of encouraging refugees to leave their camps, the British Government bought steamer tickets for anyone who was going to do so. There were as yet no direct sailings for any German harbors from Egypt at that time, so I had to content myself with passages for my sister and myself to London, paying my own way from there on. I had saved very little from my interpreter's pay at Ismailia, since both the medical doctor and myself—the camp plutocrats—felt obligated to help out our penniless brother officers at parties and on similar occasions. Also I had to outfit myself with civilian clothes. So, after leaving my sister at Lübeck with the von Medems, I reached Berlin with only ten shillings (two dollars and fifty cents) in my pocket.

I arrived just in time for the last academic screening before the start of the fall semester. It was arranged by the American Y.M.C.A. and consisted of a conversation with two of their top men and three German professors for the purpose of checking credentials submitted. The Germans were well aware of the high standards for admission to the Petrográd Institute of Engineers of Ways of Communication (pp. 198, 199) from which I had a certificate. So, after questioning me for about ten minutes in Russian, German, English and French, they offered to admit me to any school of my choosing. I selected the Berlin Technische Hochschule * in the borough of Charlottenburg and hopefully started studies there at the Department of Civil Engineering (see Fig. 37).

However, within a few months the American Y.M.C.A. decided to discontinue their Russian student relief work in Germany. Apparently they had rather indiscriminately agreed to help a lot of men from various refugee and former prisoner-of-war camps who subsequently were found not to be qualified for study. So they went to the other extreme and decided to close down altogether. However, feeling that mine was a special case, they made an offer to send me to a World Christian Student Conference which was to be held at Peking, where I was to represent Russia. After that they would send me for two years to an American college if I agreed subsequently to become a Y.M.C.A. secretary.

This I declined since I could not picture myself in such a role any more than I had been able to contemplate my sister as a future Roman Catholic nun. Nor did I feel that I had any right to take upon myself the representation of Russia as had been suggested to me. I said so to Mr. Ebersole.

Mr. Simmons was very disappointed since he had apparently hoped to see me follow in his footsteps—but we parted friends.

Things then became really tough for me. My only income was from a few lessons of English I had managed to get and that was barely enough for a semi-starvation diet. I had to live in a tiny unheated space adjoining a kitchen and often woke up in the night

---

* That is the Polytechnic Institute—the German word *Hochschule* refers to any specialized institution of higher learning and is *not* the equivalent of the American term "high school."

dreaming I was back on a sunny beach at Ismailia. I also developed a bad case of sciatica, which the doctors attributed to the effects of the cold I was being exposed to after a hot summer in Egypt. Surgeons however now tell me that it must have been a slipped disk all along. This could well have been the case since when I moved I carried all my belongings in heavy suitcases suspended from leather belts slung across my shoulders. But the slipped disks were discovered to be a source of sciatica only some ten years later (in the 1930s) so it is not surprising that the anti-rheumatic treatments I was given then for a while produced no results. At times I was barely able to move about with the help of two canes.

Suddenly, when things were beginning to look quite hopeless, I received most welcome news from Mr. Cragg. Just before I left Egypt, an American, Mr. Thomas Whittemore, had visited our camp and I had shown him around. He had now returned for a visit to Ismailia in his capacity of Director of the American Committee for the Education of Russian Youth in Exile which he had organized. He wanted to select some Cadets for fellowships permitting higher education in various European countries and, on hearing of my plight, offered one such stipend to me.

Soon his representative, Mrs. Sómova, a kindly old Russian lady, arrived in Berlin, followed by several students he had selected to study there. We each received a stipend of fifteen dollars a month which was paid out in one dollar bills. This was a most fortunate detail since inflation was developing at a progressively increasing pace. We managed to get along and continue studying by changing our dollars, a few at a time, but at the very moment a big drop in the value of the mark was announced. We then immediately bought food supplies before the shops had time to raise their prices.

During one of his first visits to Berlin, in July, 1922, Mr. Whittemore assembled the Russian students his Committee was helping there and announced that he was assigning each one of us to an individual American supporter of his Committee—on the letters we would write to them would depend the continuation of their interest in the work of his Committee and hence in ourselves as well.

The list he left with Mrs. Sómova had several Russian students assigned to each American donor except for myself—my name was the only one appearing opposite that of Mr. J. P. Morgan, 23 Wall Street, New York City. As suggested, I wrote him a personal letter of thanks and received a very courteous reply from Mr. J. Axten, the personal secretary of Mr. Morgan. I continued to write at Christmas every year, giving an account of the progress I had made. It was Mr. Axten who replied, always graciously—sometimes from New York and sometimes from England, wherever Mr. Morgan happened to be.

Twenty years later, in 1942, after I had become an American citizen, I received a personal letter of congratulations from Mr. Morgan himself who very kindly wrote that I was ". . . the most outstanding success of the people [he] was privileged to help get an education after the last war."

When the German mark was stabilized in 1923, things became much more difficult for our group. Personally, I managed to get along by giving English lessons, but the majority of my Russian fellow students had no such special knowledge to capitalize upon and could not obtain any paid work to supplement their small stipend—the German labor unions prevented this because of considerable unemployment in the country. Mr. Whittemore than started looking for some solution and decided to move everybody to France. The incident that finally made him take this step was being rudely shoved and called a *verfluchter Ausländer* (accursed foreigner) by a German who heard him speaking English on the street.

Most of the students who were transferred to France in 1924 had only a year or two of studies in Germany. On the other hand I had already two and a half years behind me there and could expect to complete my work at Berlin in another year and a half. I did not want to start all over again in France, leaving my sister behind with the Medems, and therefore flatly refused to be transferred there. Mr. Whittemore at first threatened to withdraw my stipend but then relented on condition that I spend the summer vacation in the "fresh air of France." I was only too glad to do so, having spent a previous vacation wielding a sledge hammer in a team of hand-riveters on construction work in Polish Upper Silesia. I did not find that my sciatica made the work any easier.

In Paris I was pleasantly surprised to find that Mr. Whittemore's local representative was my former Tsárskoye Seló classmate, Solomón (p. 23), whom I had erroneously believed killed with Chernetzóv (pp. 159, 160). Fortunately, he was very much alive and, with the help of letters of introduction which I typed in French and which he signed, I got a job of "calculator-draftsman" in the famous consulting engineering offices of Pelnard-Considère and A. Caquot, specialists in reinforced concrete design. I formed some lasting friendships there.

Returning to Berlin in the fall of 1924 I resumed my studies with an increased stipend from Mr. Whittemore's Committee and got my degree of "Diplom-Ingenieur" in December, 1925.

For about two months I vainly searched for work. In view of the considerable unemployment in Germany, I was lucky to get then a job as engineer in the Berlin office of Dr. Kirchhoff who reviewed plans of old steel bridges and designed their strengthening for the German State railways which was about to introduce heavier locomotives. Then, late in 1926, I moved to a better paid job in Bremen with a construction firm, Paul Kossel & Co., where I worked on reinforced concrete design problems.

A friend of our chief engineer was looking for a young reinforced-concrete specialist with some knowledge of French or of English for a branch of their firm just starting in Egypt. I seemed to be just the man for this and from the middle of 1927 till the spring of 1929 I worked in Cairo as a designer of the Austrian Building Company's office there.

Financially, this branch office was very far from being a success and soon closed. My contract with the Austrian Building Company provided for a paid return passage to Germany and I made use of that clause.

On my return to Berlin I obtained a field job with the Haberman & Guckes-Liebold A.G. on the construction of a lock on the river Weser at Hameln, of Pied Piper fame. Robert Browning was guilty of some poetic exaggeration when he wrote of "the river Weser, deep and wide," but the job was nevertheless an interesting and pleasant one.

By the end of 1929 signs of the coming big depression began to multiply. The city of Berlin stopped all new subway construction on which most of the engineers of our company had been employed. It was evident that I would be discharged before long to make room for some of these men who were on the permanent staff of the company.

Just as I was getting more and more worried, I received a letter from Cairo informing me that I could have a job at the Ministry of Public Works since I had been placed at the top of the list of the engineers who nine months earlier took a competitive examination for a vacancy there—I had taken it just before leaving Egypt. Now I accepted the offer with alacrity, thinking that I would go there for a year or two, until things improved in Europe—instead I was to remain in Cairo for seven years.

I was assigned to the Technical Office of the State Buildings Department and at first worked on reinforced concrete designs. The very poor soil conditions—soft clays and silts—of the Nile delta presented special problems for the foundations of structures. Just about that time new engineering approaches to such problems began to develop, largely as a result of the research work of an Austrian engineer, Karl Terzaghi. A new term "soil mechanics" appeared which was based on his research studies. It did not refer to agricultural tractor drivers, as some people at first believed, but to the behavior of soils as a supporting material for foundations or as a construction material for earth dams, roadbeds and so forth. This new field became a specialty of mine after I had the opportunity to study for the Egyptian Government several cases of troublesome foundation failures.

In 1933 I spent three months of my leave in Austria and Germany, studying at my own expense the organization of soil engineering laboratories there—first with Professor F. Koegler at Freiberg in Saxony, then with the Prussian Waterways Experiment Station at Berlin and with Professor Terzaghi in Vienna.

On my return to Cairo I was transferred to the Egyptian University to organize there a Foundation Soils Research Laboratory under an Egyptian head, Dr. William Selim Hanna. This I did, and in 1935 spent another three months' leave working at the same laboratories in Austria and Germany which I had visited earlier.

In June 1936, as part of the tercentenary celebrations of Harvard University, the first International Conference on Soil Mechanics and Foundation Engineering was held there with Professor Terzaghi serving as its President. Dr. Hanna and I were sent to that conference by the Egyptian University and presented papers on the research we had carried out. This was my first visit to the United States.

Dr. Terzaghi knew that I was far from being happy with my position in Egypt and passed the word around. During an excursion to the Quabbin Dike reservoir construction site near Boston, Mr. Lazarus White, a prominent New York City foundation engineer of Spencer, White & Prentis, Inc., came up to me and asked if it was true that I would welcome an offer of a job in America? If so, how would

I like to go to Princeton University? I must confess that my reply was: "Where is Princeton?" but I immediately realized that it must be a good place when I heard that Professor George E. Beggs headed the Civil Engineering Department there—I had heard before of his pioneer work in structural model testing. Professor Beggs was a friend of Lazarus White and had asked him to find an engineer at the International Conference who would be willing to come to Princeton and organize there a Soils Laboratory and courses on Foundation Engineering, none of which the University had at the time.

Mr. White drove me to Princeton to meet Professor Beggs and Dean Arthur M. Greene. Since I was in America as an official delegate from the Egyptian University, I had to return to Cairo. However, after receiving there a cabled confirming call from Princeton, I made use of a three-month notice clause in my contract with the Egyptian Government, resigned my post and in January, 1937, landed in New York for permanent residence in the country.

As I built up over the years the laboratory work and the teaching of Soil Mechanics and Foundation Engineering at Princeton, I successively moved up the academic ladder from lecturer to assistant,—associate,—and then full professor of Civil Engineering. There were many opportunities for interesting consulting work and for research projects in my field, some of which I carried out for the Civil Aeronautics Administration and for the Bureau of Yards & Docks of the United States Navy. However, because of my Russian origin, I deliberately steered away from classified subjects.

My research work brought me in 1952 an earned degree of "Doktor-Ingenieur" from the Technische Hochschule at Aachen in West Germany and, in 1959, a degree of "Docteur honoris causa" from the Université Libre de Bruxelles in Belgium, which I received at the one hundred and twenty-fifth anniversary celebrations.

In 1955 I persuaded President Dodds to try out what I facetiously called the "New Princeton Progressive Retirement Plan—Old Professors Never Die—they slowly Fade Away into Consulting." So I officially went on halftime pay and duty, keeping my rank and tenure, but limiting my work at Princeton to one graduate course per term. This permitted me to join as an associate King & Gavaris, the New York firm of civil engineering consultants.

I met my wife in 1938 and we became engaged two weeks after meeting. Financial problems delayed our wedding until we had saved up enough money for it by the spring of 1939. My sister came to the wedding from Germany and my wife's brother from California. Soon they too were engaged and married.

### 3. *Some Socio-Political Observations During My Wanderings*

As I left Ismailia and Egypt in 1921, I had some apprehensions about the relationships I would have with Germans. However, as things turned out, my fears of any personal difficulties were unfounded. Common misfortunes seemed to attract German sympathies towards Russian refugees and formed an invisible bond between them—both countries had lost the war and both were suffering from its aftermath. Also numerous German refugees remembered with nostalgia their life in old Imperial Russia and the simple and easy ways of its peoples—I frequently heard many of them reminisce on the subject.

A large number of my fellow students at Berlin had been officers in the German and Austro-Hungarian armies and showed me special courtesy when they heard that I was a Don Cossack—they had learned on the battlefields to respect Cossacks. I found it easy to discuss any controversial topics with them without arousing ill feelings. A frequent subject of argument was what had caused World War I. Naturally, they maintained that Germany had not wanted it, but I was pleased to find that they had no answer when I pointed out that Germany had happened to declare war at the moment when its rearmament program was completed and Russia's was only getting started (pp. 40, 41).

I enjoyed these frank exchanges and only on one occasion did I feel that I should abstain from revealing all of my thoughts. One of my fellow civil engineering students, by the name of Azzola, came from the Austro-Hungarian province of Transylvania, which now is part of Romania. In spite of his name, Azzola considered himself a German and referred to his home province as Siebenbuergen. He was a former Austro-Hungarian artillery officer and, when he gave a birthday party, he invited to it several other former Austrian artillery officers, as well as myself. During an exchange of war reminiscences it turned out that one of the guests had been stationed opposite us in 1917 at the same location on the Stohód River where I had been. He remarked that it could have been quite a pleasant place, had it not been for a *"verfluchte Kosakenbatterie* (an accursed Cossack battery)."* At first I cheerfully identified myself as having belonged to that unit. But then he went on to describe, from his point of view, the episode I wrote about on pp. 94–95.

The commander of the Austrian infantry regiment, which held the frontlines opposite us, had decided to throw a party in the parklike garden of an abandoned landowner's house a short distance behind his front trenches. Everything had been quiet there for weeks with hardly a shot fired on some days, so he invited to his party not only officers of adjoining batteries and other Austro-Hungarian supporting units, but a number of nurses from their field hospitals as well. They were all sitting around tables set up under the shade trees laughing and enjoying themselves, when, suddenly, Russian artillery shells started exploding in their midst. "If only that so-and-so Cossack officer had fired just one shell to check the range!" remarked my new acquaintance. He saved himself, as he told me, by tipping over backwards, chair and all, into one of the communication trenches which crisscrossed the park and which happened to be behind his table. He did this the moment his trained ear heard the sound of our first approaching shells, but one of his best friends was less agile and was killed. Another high explosive shell hit smack into a table under which some nurses had sought refuge, killing them all.

I could not bring myself to tell him that it was I who had directed our fire that day and merely remarked that people who arranged wartime picnics within the limits of frontline trenches should not have expected anything different from what happened.

Germans of all classes whom I met on trains and elsewhere usually brought the conversation around to a possible repetition of past partitions of Poland between Germany and Russia. Of all their setbacks the inclusion in a newly independent Poland of the Polish provinces which they had tried so hard to Germanize (p. 40), seemed to rankle most of all with them at the time.

Although most Germans of the period professed to look forward to a renewal of past Russo-German cooperation, some groups were still working hard at a continuation of the plans for the dismemberment of Russia which had failed so completely in 1918. Thus, two students in the drafting room I used were refugees from the Russian Ukraine. We got along well and frequently discussed details of our engineering studies until one day (in 1922 or 1923) they suddenly started answering me in German when I spoke to them in Russian. I retaliated by declining to help them in their work, although I had been doing so before that. They then confessed that they were compelled to act the way they did because they had accepted stipends from a German-sponsored Ukrainian separatist organization and might lose the financial help they needed if anyone overheard them speaking Russian and reported them—they would however be glad to talk to me in Russian if there was no one else around!

Liberal and democratic trends in Germany were dealt a mortal blow by the inflation which I witnessed at Berlin during the first two years of my studies there. As a result of the unreasonably harsh economic terms of the Versailles Treaty the value of the German mark dropped at a progressively increasing speed, and before the mark was stabilized in 1923 an American dollar could be exchanged literally for millions of worthless paper marks. In order not to starve, middleclass Germans had to sell for a pittance their belongings, including their houses. I know of cases in which five- and six-story brick city houses were sold for the equivalent of some fifty to sixty dollars each—practically all of the privately owned Berlin real estate changed hands in this manner at the time. It was mainly foreigners, many of whom were Polish and Russian Jews, who became the new owners, thus laying the foundation among the dispossessed native Germans for the advent of Nazism with its virulent anti-Semitism. I rented a room at the time in an apartment owned by a middleclass Jewish family and found that they were extremely apprehensive about the future because of the widespread bitterness aroused all around them by the economic disaster of the inflation.

I have kept some letters I received from Professor Thomas Whittemore,* the Director of the American Committee for the Education of Russian Youth in Exile. The views he expressed are quite remarkable because of the nature of their practical idealism.

I received the following mimeographed circular letter which at Christmas 1926 he sent to all past or present students supported by his Committee:

"My dear Mr. Tchebotarév,

A merry Christmas and a happy New Year!

I have just returned from America and bring you the affection-

---

* By profession he was an archaeologist, so that some unkind people wisecracked that he was specializing in digging up Egyptian mummies and Russian students. But his main interest lay in the field of Byzantine studies in which he made an important contribution by organizing the restoration of the ancient Christian mosaics in the St. Sophia mosque at Constantinople. I believe he was Roman Catholic.

ate greeting of friends. They continue to hear with deep interest of you in the pursuit of your study.

I am bidden to offer congratulations to those who with such surprising distinction have already taken diploma or certificate and are availing themselves of the immediate, albeit temporary, practice of their professions in the countries in which they have studied.

Your friends are glad that the danger of success and of denationalization which presents itself to young Russians in America is among you avoided. Nevertheless in America, we have occasional glimpses of Ostróvsky's Dimítri Glúmov—*Enough Stupidity in Every Wise Man.*\*

To be trained in America is to be trained into America.

You are Russians. Your seed can fertilize only if put back into the creative elements to which you are native and endued.

The only agreeable offering which you can make to life is the offering of your education to Russia.

Stick to your profession and let politics alone in all shades and degrees.

Fishes do not marvel at water: they are too busy swimming in it.

Keep faith with Russia. Do not let your mind become detached, for your heart will soon follow.

Do not cease the ardent pursuit of your return.

A new synthesis calls you.

I hope that you will not long be spectators.

Cast out the fear of your elders; in this, there is no sacrifice from which you will not draw more joy than it cost you pain to make up your mind to do it.

As vessels prepared for the service of the Holy Liturgy put to other use are contaminated, so you cannot use yourselves outside of Russia without profanation.

> Ever faithfully yours,
> (Signed) *Mr. Thomas Whittemore*
> Director"

Only seven years had elapsed since I had been engaged in open combat against the Bolsheviks, so the idea of returning to a Russi

---

\* A Russian play, written in 1868, which satirized the superficial culture of th new bourgeoisie.

ruled by them appeared preposterous to me and to all of my friends.
I wrote to Mr. Whittemore in that sense. The main part of his reply
of April 11, 1927, read as follows:

". . . I like the spirit in which you have written. We are both
very ignorant of Russia. Only Russia can teach us about herself.
Of this I am sure."

At the time I bristled at the suggestion that I too was very ignorant
of Russia, but the magnificent performance of most of the peoples of
Russia in its defense during World War II made me change my
mind. Whittemore's words, "Only Russia can teach us about herself,"
have often been recalled by me and I have had to admit that in this
respect at least he was a very wise man after all.

The seven years I spent in the Egyptian Government service taught
me a number of things, one of which was the very important difference in the attitudes of Englishmen and of Russians towards Eastern
races, a difference which is not usually realized in the West.

In Cairo I lived in a pension owned by a Russian couple and
inhabited mainly by English people among whom I made many real
friends. I was however amazed at the strict line they drew as a group
against any continued social contacts with local Arabs, and at the
many taboos which resulted. For instance, I know of two cases when
English girls married Egyptians and were subsequently ostracized by
most of their former countrymen. Nothing of the kind existed at any
level between Russians and, for instance, the various Mongol minorities of the multinational Russian Empire, nor have I seen any indications that anything like it exists now within the Soviet Union. This
fact is crucially important, but it is left out of consideration by some
people in this country who speak of the former British colonialism
as if it corresponded to the past and present relations between the
various nationalities of Russia and of the Soviet Union. The less
racially tolerant British attitudes may in part be explained by the
greater differences between the White and the Black races, as compared to the differences between the White and the Yellow races.
But this cannot be the sole reason.

During my stay in Cairo I frequently had the opportunity to see
and hear things which eloquently testified to the strong sympathies
for Russia and for the Russians among various Near Eastern races.

For instance, I was once invited in my capacity of a foundation engineer to inspect the local Greek (Eastern Orthodox) Cathedral, which had developed some cracks in its walls. During my visit * I went over the entire structure from cellar to its roomy attic, where I found neatly stacked away huge portraits of the Russian Tsars Nicholas I, Alexander II, Alexander III and Nicholas II, as well as of their Empresses. During the reign of Nicholas I Imperial Russia had forced Turkey to grant Greece its independence (in 1829). Since then, until the 1917 Revolution, the portrait of the reigning Russian Tsar and of his Tsarina had adorned the main reception hall of the Greek bishops in Cairo. No other foreign nation was so honored.

On another occasion I met an old Bulgarian who had served as a young officer of the Bulgarian Army in the 1880s. As a result of the Russo-Turkish war of 1877–1878, Bulgaria obtained its independence, but pressures of the Western powers at the Berlin Congress forced the new country to take a German prince for king who at first adopted an anti-Russian attitude. The feelings of the country and the realities of Balkan events however soon forced him to change, but Alexander III refused to consider any rapprochement until all neglected graves of Russian soldiers who had fallen for Bulgaria's freedom on her soil had been restored and had received military honors. This was done and my Cairo acquaintance spent part of a summer with one of several companies of the Bulgarian Army assigned to the job. They marched from one restored Russian grave to another in the Balkan mountains, firing a volley in salute and dipping their colors before each. According to my acquaintance, all his fellow Bulgarians felt that there was no humiliation whatsoever for them in all this—but only for their German ruler—since they were only paying to the memory of their Russian liberators from Turkish oppression honors which were long overdue.

Thus, most of the Eastern Orthodox Christians of the Near East looked on old Imperial Russia as their natural and proven defender. A chance meeting I had however showed that the Moslems of the Russian Empire were nevertheless given fair treatment. I already knew this from my St. Petersburg days since so many Moslem officers—Tartars and others (p. 34)—had attained high positions

* Reported in the May 23, 1936 issue of the Cairo Greek language newspaper, ΕΦΗΜΕΡΙΣ (*Ephimeris*), page 1.

in the capital that the Tsar Nicholas II had a beautiful mosque built there for them, personally contributing most of the funds for its construction (see also p. 342). But while in Cairo I got an interesting sidelight on the problems of Moslem administration in old Russia. Since I was then stateless, in order to travel abroad I had to obtain an Egyptian *Laisser-Passer* as a substitute for a passport. Such matters were administered by a special Russian Bureau of the Egyptian Ministry of the Interior which had for secretary a Moslem Tartar from the Crimea. As I waited in his office one day while his messenger was collecting various signatures of approval for my trip abroad from his superiors, he told me how he happened to come to Egypt. He had been an official of a branch of the Russian Ministry of the Interior at St. Petersburg which dealt with Moslem affairs. According to him, the Imperial Russian Government scrupulously tried to leave all decisions on internal Moslem quarrels to their own religious courts which ruled on the basis of the Koran, the sacred book of the Mohammedans. But the local religious courts of various Moslem minority enclaves in the Crimea, on the Volga and in Central Asia frequently disagreed with each other on the proper interpretation of some of the Koran laws and then appealed to the Russian Government to resolve their differences. Not wishing to make arbitrary decisions on matters they knew little about, the Ministry of the Interior at St. Petersburg sent this man to Cairo for two years of study at the famous ancient University of Al-Azhar, the fountainhead of Islamic religious thought, where he was to submit some particularly troublesome case problems for consideration by its luminaries. This is where he was at the start of World War I which left him stranded in Egypt.

At the time when I was seriously considering leaving Egypt (in 1936) for the United States, I had some politically significant conversations with some of my friends among German engineers. Professor Koegler, under whom I had first formally studied soil mechanics in 1933 at Freiberg in Saxony, had become the chairman of the board of consultants in that field to the famous German engineer Todt who headed a construction organization of the Nazi Government which at that time was building the *Reichsautobahnen*—the first modern express highways with no level crossings. Later the same group carried out most of Nazi Germany's military fortification work. They paid special attention to the new science of "soil mechanics" (p.

289), but could not fill all their vacancies because of a lack of specialists in this new field. Professor Koegler mentioned my name to Todt, who instructed him to make me an offer.

A member of the official German delegation to the 1936 First International Conference on Soil Mechanics and Foundation Engineering held at Harvard University, Regierungsbaurat (State Construction Counselor) Ehrenberg, of the Prussian Waterways Experiment Station, whom I had met there in 1933 and in 1935, made an attempt to persuade me to accept that offer. We sat side by side on the train from New York to Boston and talked in German all the way. I pointed out that, from what I knew of contemporary German attitudes, war was inevitable and that Nazi Germany would soon attack the Soviet Union not just as an anti-Communist move, but as an anti-Russian one. Ehrenberg did not deny this, remarking that *"Gewisse territoriale Zugestaendnisse werden selbstverstaendlich erforderlich sein* (Certain territorial concessions will naturally be necessary)," but that I did not have to worry about any restrictions against Russians in national-socialist Germany since I was a Cossack and hence of a different race.

This was the first time that I personally came into contact with the ludicrous concept of "Cossackia," the recent acceptance of which by our United States Congress has placed it and this country in such an embarrassing position (pp. 360, 365).

Naturally I declined Ehrenberg's overtures.

### 4. *Cossack* Émigré *Politics before and during World War II*

After the end of the Russian Civil War in 1921, the Don, the Kubán and the Térek Cossacks who had fought on the White side in South Russia found themselves scattered all over Europe. Some eventually made their way to North and to South America but, prior to World War II, the largest numbers of *émigré* Cossacks were to be found in Yugoslavia, in France and in Bulgaria.

Within the Soviet Union all features of the past Cossack way of life were abolished since Cossacks were considered there to be primarily members of a former privileged class for which there could be no place within the framework of a proletarian society.

Abroad, although widely scattered, the Cossack *émigrés* attempted to maintain contacts with each other in the hope of a better future and an eventual return to the lands of their forefathers. The majority recognized the authority of their last Civil War Atamáns and, when one of them died, held elections of their successors by mail.

Among the Kubán and Térek Cossacks these elections went fairly smoothly, but a bitter strife erupted among the Don Cossack *émigrés* after the death of the Atamán A. P. Bogáyevsky. No general agreement could be reached as to who should be his successors and in recent years two rival contenders have each claimed to be the lawful Don Atamán, thereby earning the derisive nickname of "half-Atamáns."

One group of Don Cossack *émigrés* represented the rightwing monarchist elements who were led by former friends and associates of Gen. P. N. Krassnóv. The other consisted of middle-of-the-road former supporters of Gen. A. P. Bogáyevsky, who had succeeded P. N. Krassnóv in the post of Don Atamán. Personally, I always maintained friendly relations with both groups, refusing to be drawn into their internal squabbles.

Among the rightwing Don Cossacks abroad the remnants of the Leib-Guard Cossack Regiment deserve special mention because of the exceptionally sturdy spirit they displayed in the face of adversity. Several officers of our Guard Don Cossack Battery were with them. After the collapse of Baron Wrangell's White Army in the Crimea they were all evacuated abroad with the remnants of his troops and spent some time in Yugoslavia on border guard duty and on road construction work in the mountains along the Albanian frontier. Then they moved as a body to France. A couple of hundred officers and men worked there side by side as a unit—all ranks doing the same heavy manual labor unloading railway cars at the Gare du Nord in Paris.

Nevertheless in off-duty hours they still voluntarily maintained three separate messes for officers, sergeants and privates, as well as the customary military discipline of the unit—a testimony to the moral authority of the officers. This was well described by a famous World War I French battle painter, Georges Scott, in an article entitled *"Les Chevaliers Mendiants"* ("The Beggar Knights"), Ref. 26. I visited them when on summer leave from Egypt a few months after this article appeared in 1928 and I can testify that it does not exaggerate the remarkably strong *esprit de corps* which they displayed.

As regards later years, I am glad to note that, with one or two exceptions, the former members of this famous Imperial Russian regiment remained aloof from cooperation with the Nazis during their occupation of France and did not respond to their recruiting efforts.

Some Cossack groups however did cooperate with the invading armies of Hitler. Most of them consisted of men who had remained in the Soviet Union or who had returned there after the Civil War of 1917–1920 and who spontaneously started local guerrilla operations against the Communists when the German armies again approached the main Cossack regions during World War II. Some of these small detachments were consolidated by the Nazi command into a cavalry corps of some 15,000 men under a German, Gen. Hellmuth von Pannwitz. However, it was not trusted by the Nazis in Russia and was sent by them to fight Tito's Red guerrillas in Yugoslavia.

Figs. 38 and 39 show Cossacks incorporated into the Nazi Army. The officer in Fig. 38 and the men in the second row of Fig. 39 definitely do not come from the Don but are either Kubán or Térek Cossacks since they wear the Caucasian *cherkesska* (p. 12). The officer in Fig. 38 must have been a private in World War I because he wore the soldier's St. George Cross. The uniforms and the insignia are those of old Imperial Russia, but superimposed on all of them is clearly visible the emblem of Hitler's Wehrmacht—the eagle with spread wings which somewhat resembles an airman's badge.

This incongruous combination is representative of the confusion in the minds of these men. Most of them appear to have still thought in terms of a return to their old free, easy and privileged way of life before the 1917 Revolution. They did not realize that Nazi Germany would use them only as tools for her own ends which were inimical not only to everything Russian, but to all branches of the Slavic race as well.

To forestall any such realization by the mass of the Cossacks, the Nazi propaganda machine attempted to promote a ludicrous concept of "Cossackia," according to which the Cossacks were not Russians at all, but were the descendants of the Scythians, an ancient non-Slavic race.[*] The very term "Cossackia" had not been even heard of in South Russia during the 1917–1920 Civil War but was used in Central Europe between the two world wars as part of an

---

[*] Attempts are now made to justify this by quotations which show that the Scythians were called "Kazáks" in ancient Persian and their land "Kazakía." This is just a phonetic similarity, since the Scythians were annihilated by successive waves of invaders from Asia, starting with the Huns in the fifth and ending with the Tartars in the thirteenth centuries, see Ref. 65e.

overall plan for the dismemberment not only of the Soviet Union but of its predominantly Great Russian territories as well.

In December, 1927, there began appearing in Prague, Czechoslovakia, a bi-lingual (Russian and Ukrainian) bi-weekly paper called *Volne Kozactvo*. Some four years later that paper printed a "Project of a Constitution for Cossackia" (Ref. 74). It was explained in a preface that the name "Cossackia" was to designate a union of seven "units"—the Don, Kubán, Térek, Astrakhán, Urál, Orenbúrg (all six being the regions of former Cossack armies of these names), and the Kalmuk district.

Special thanks for help in the preparation of the constitution were expressed to a Professor of the Ukrainian University in Prague, O. O. Eichelmann. No other names were mentioned in this connection. Thus the Ukrainian *émigré* separatists—who later foisted the "Cossackia" hoax on the United States Congress—definitely had a hand in its original creation.

The extent of Nazi participation in the invention of "Cossackia" to my knowledge has not yet been established. The facts that the constitution of that mythical country was published in 1932 (Ref. 74), that is a year before Hitler came to power, and that this publication was done at Prague, are inconclusive. It should be remembered that the Nazis started preparing their ideological program for the conquest and the partition of the lands of Eastern Europe long before they became the rulers of Germany, and that many of the Sudeten-Germans of Czechoslovakia were among their early supporters. But the later efforts of the Nazi Government to promote the "Cossackia" concept are on record, even though they failed to make any impression on the vast majority of the Cossacks (Ref. 17). Vice versa, there are also published reports concerning the praise and promises of support which some "Cossackian" leaders (now residing in the United States) lavished on Hitler when he attacked the Soviet Union in 1941 (Ref. 51).

Some of the present-day anti-Russian propaganda in the West attempts to present General Piótr Krassnóv as the spiritual ancestor and supporter of the "Cossackian" separatists. This is completely in error. I have already described on pp. 213–218 the real attitudes of P. N. Krassnóv in 1918–1919 when he was the Atamán of the Grand Army of the Don. In view of the importance which his past actions have acquired since the 1959 recognition of the mythical "Cossackia" and of its separatism by the United States Congress (p. 365) I shall now set down what I know about his later attitudes from per-

sonal contacts and correspondence with him. He most certainly did
not change heart and become anti-Russian.

General Krassnóv and his wife were living in Germany during the
time I was there. We did not meet often, since they were staying at a
Castle Seeon some distance away from Berlin—in Bavaria if I remember correctly—but we corresponded often. The General seemed to
have the friendliest of feelings for me as evidenced by the autographed
inscription on a reprint of his 1922 account concerning his leadership
of the fighting in the Don (Fig. 30) and by a personal letter written
in 1927 (Fig. 26).

However, his rightwing German friends who put him up as their
guest at the Castle Seeon, and the misery of the inflation years in
Germany (p. 293) strongly affected his thinking in what seemed
to me an irrational direction. When he sent me one of his novels
written at the time and asked for my opinion I could not help reply-
ing that certainly there were many Jews among our Russian revolutionaries, but that I thought it a great mistake to blame the Jews for
all the misfortunes which had befallen Russia—this inevitably cur-
tailed the self-criticism necessary for the understanding and the correction of our own errors. The General's answer was vitriolic—
"Acquaintance and friendship with the American Y.M.C.A. seldom
leaves a person unscathed," he wrote. "You repeat like a gramophone
record what they have been whispering to you!" The General did not
know that I had parted ways with the Y.M.C.A. some time before
that (p. 285). My sciatica happened to be quite painful at the time
and my temper was correspondingly short. So I responded in kind
by saying that the General's writings reminded me of the refrain to
an old ribald song *: "*Kto vinovát?* (Who's fault is it?)—*Paulína,
dzim-boum!*" He had used the word Jews instead of Paulína.

After that, there was a prolonged and pained gap in our correspondence. When some mutual friends let me know that the old man was
still quite upset and unhappy about my reply, I wrote him an apology
for having lost my temper.

I got back a very revealing postcard which, unfortunately, I have
lost. In it the General did not refer to the incident between us but
wrote: "How I envy the knowledge you are acquiring. No one now
needs my knowledge—war and everything related to it." His point
was reinforced by the nature of the painting shown on the reverse

---

* Each verse of that song described all kinds of impossible situations supposedly caused by a girl called Paulína.

side of the postcard—it depicted a dreary autumn day and an empty muddy country road the ruts of which faded away in the fog of the distance.

In the late 1920s General Krassnóv and his wife moved from Germany to France where he became the personal advisor on Cossack Affairs to the Grand Duke Nikolái Nikoláyevitch, the former Commander in Chief of the Imperial Russian armies at the start of World War I, who was then the titular head of the Románov dynasty in exile. The Krassnóvs spent about ten years living on a farm at Santeny, near Paris, a few hundred yards away from a mansion occupied by the Grand Duke. During that period the General issued several pro-monarchist and anti-separatist messages addressed to Cossacks —obviously, he would not have done that had he been in sympathy with anything resembling present-day "Cossackian" propaganda abroad.

In addition to his 1927 letter from Santeny (Fig. 26) I have preserved letters written by him to me in 1934, 1935 and 1936 while he still was at Santeny, none of which contain any "separatist" sentiments—quite on the contrary, he wrote above all about Russia.

Thus on January 18, 1934, he wrote to me in Cairo:

". . . we learned about the successes of your sister and about your difficult position among foreign people who are foreign to you. It seems to me that living as you do away from Russian *émigrés,* you do not realize how hard it is for Russians to live in foreign lands. You cannot imagine how hard it is for us and for Russians around us. One must realize fully the terrible misfortune which has overtaken Russia and the horror which developed as a result of the forced abandonment by Russians of the struggle for Russia. . . .

"It seems to me that if you could now move to Germany and find work there, then you would feel easier. . . ."

He repeated this advice to me to leave Egypt, where I had a very hard time, and return to Germany when I visited him at Santeny in August, 1936, on my way back to Egypt from my first visit to the United States (p. 289). General Krassnóv expounded to me then his hopes that Hitler's Germany would be led by rightwing elements, among whom he had many friends, and that they would revert to a policy of friendly cooperation with Russia which would be even closer than the one during and before Bismarck's administration. I argued that this was out of the question, representing wishful thinking on his part, and that the racial anti-Russian and anti-Slavic ideas of the Nazis would carry the day in Germany. We parted on personally friendly terms, having "agreed to disagree" on things political. Unfortunately for him, subsequent events developed as I had expected.

We resumed an exchange of personal letters after my sister came to Princeton for my wedding in April of 1939 and stayed there, later marrying my brother-in-law, Edward C. Bill. The childless Krassnóvs had seen much of her and had grown very fond of her when they moved from France to Berlin after the death of the Grand Duke Nikolái Nikoláyevich. (My sister had studied at Berlin University and had obtained her doctorate there.)

Between the start of World War II in the fall of 1939 and America's entry into the war in December, 1941, it was possible to send food parcels to persons in Germany. We sent some to the Krassnóvs who seemed to be deeply touched by this and wrote me some very nice letters. The following excerpts may help visualize the General's thinking:

In a letter of August 17, 1940, he wrote:

". . . We are glad that at last, after such stormy and at times wearying wanderings, you have reached a quiet haven and have found happiness. May the Lord make it eternal, as mine with Lýdia Fyódorovna. I am also very happy that, having become an American and having earned there, a foreign country with developed technology, a well-known name, you do not forget the country of your birth which is now in the midst of misfortunes and that you defend it whenever you read vicious calumnies about it in the American press.* Russia will never forget this about you and it is so important that *truth* about Russia be heard in a country where there are so many lies about her. . . .

". . . I am happy that the name of a Russian, and of a Don Cossack at that, will adorn the lists of books in America. . . ." †

* He was referring to my protest against a *Life* magazine article which was printed in the New York rightwing Russian-language daily *Rossíya* on June 27, 1939 (see p. 88).

† I had then started writing my book on foundation engineering which, however, was not published until 1951 (see p. xviii).

And on November 27, 1940, he continued:

". . . How is your scientific work coming along? We are always proud when we hear that Russians, and COSSACKS at that, lead in science in the learned and industrial America. How your father and mother would have been proud of you. . . . How I wish I could see your home and look at how you have settled in America which is so strange—at least to my heart—and to see how you live, how you work and how you pass the short hours of your leisure. We have nothing to write you about ourselves. After a long and difficult, varied and spotty life, which encountered prisons and palaces, the glory of victories and the shame of defeats we no longer live, but are ending our lives with colorful but at times frightening reminiscences. At present life here, as well as in almost all of Europe, has stopped. And our future depends on how soon it will be started again. Personally I live by reminiscences. Having served in a now defunct branch of armed forces * and knowing it and only it, I particularly feel that I have outlived myself and am no longer needed. . . . Both of us still cannot get used to American names and are afraid to refer to your wife as 'F.D.' † I beg you to kiss for me the hands of your spouse. . . ."

General Krassnóv's last letter, of July 19, 1941, passing as all his letters did then through the German censorship and bearing their check marks on its envelope, did not directly refer to the Nazi attack on the Soviet Union a month earlier, but contained the following:

". . . the main thing that we find difficult is our almost complete loneliness. Except for the Medems we have no one who is close to us here . . . we reminisce about the many good and cordial things we saw from your father and mother at Tsárskoye, when you were a youth, at Pávlovsk, when you were quite small, and finally in Petersburg and in the Don, when you so manfully helped save Lýdia Fyódorovna. These are things which can never be forgotten. . . . We were very heartened to hear that you plan to settle firmly in your town which has given you what the country of your birth took away from you and how we would

* Cavalry.
† The nickname of my wife, Florence Dorothy.

like to see at least the photograph of your house when it is
built. . . ."

General Krassnóv went on to write of:

". . . these anxious and tense days when the fate of our Mother-
land is being decided and with it our own fates.
"We spent eight weeks at Nauheim. The cure strengthened both
of us considerably but, on my return, I became involved in such
important and tense work that I fear my weak health of an old
man has been overstrained. . . ."

In none of the above letters was there a trace of the anti-Russian
separatism now attributed to him. On the contrary, he repeatedly
linked the terms "Russian" and "Cossack."

I have been told that at one of the later stages of World War II
General Krassnóv made a speech to Cossacks who had joined the Nazi
Army during which he extolled the ancient freedoms of the Cossacks.
Somebody interrupted him by shouting: "And what about Russia?"
He is supposed to have replied, "Where *is* Russia now? Show her to
me, and I will answer you!" Knowing General Krassnóv as I do,
all this is not in the least indicative to me of any change of heart on
his part in favor of Cossack separatism, but rather of his opportunism,
prior examples of which I have already given on pp. 122–124 and
213–218. Illustrative of this are also his views given on page 90 of
Ref. 41.

He certainly could not have been happy at Hitler's policies in
Russia which were so contrary to the hopes he had expressed to me
at Santeny in 1936. But, having thrown in his lot with Nazi Germany,
he had no choice but to make the best he could out of a bad situation.
Characteristic of his feelings, however, is the fact that he never once
went to the Don during the entire period when its area was under
Nazi occupation. He joined the Cossack units in the field only when
Hitler's final debacle was already under way and the Cossacks who
had been in Yugoslavia assembled in southern Austria together with
various other of their units and refugee groups.

I have seen a photograph of him taken at the time, but I have not
attempted to get it for reproduction here since it was only a sad
shadow of the remarkable man I had known. On the right side of the
photo was a Don Cossack who was presenting arms with his sabre,
Krassnóv was in the center holding the bridle of a horse on the left,

but the cane which hung over his arm instead of a riding whip showed that the group was unrealistically posed. His haggard and aged face and, above all, the look of utter despair in his eyes bore no resemblance to what he had been in better days.

The Cossack camp was surrounded by British troops and laid down their arms at their behest. The officers, including General Krassnóv, were invited to come to what they were told would be a conference at British Headquarters. Instead, British cars drove them straight into a Soviet Army compound and handed them over to the Reds.

The remaining rank and file, deprived of their commanders and of their arms, with many civilian refugees and their families among them, knelt around an Eastern Orthodox priest who conducted an open air service which was however broken up by British tank supported troops. This happened on June 1, 1945, near Lienz and is represented by a well-known painting by Korolkóv (see Ref. 41). The Lienz tragedy is commemorated annually by Russian and Cossack *émigrés* the world over. Many Cossack men and women committed suicide and killed their children at Lienz; a few managed to escape and hide out in the neighboring woods, but the majority were herded into trucks and were handed over to the Soviet troops in accordance with the Yalta agreement (p. xiv).

Details of the Lienz tragedy have been given in a great many Russian-language books and articles. I know of only one English translation of any of these books, namely Ref. 33, which was written by N. N. Krassnóv, Jr., the great nephew of General Piótr Krassnóv who accompanied his uncle from Lienz to Moscow and stayed with him until his trial and execution there for lending help to enemy armies.

Mrs. Krassnóva died a year or so later in an old persons home in Bavaria without having been told of her husband's fate.

Several other top-ranking Cossack officers were executed by hanging at the same time as General Krassnóv, as well as the German General Helmuth von Pannwitz who had commanded a Cossack Corps of Hitler's Army. It should be noted to the credit of von Pannwitz that he chose to remain with his men until the very end, although he could have avoided extradition.

The younger Cossacks were sentenced to various terms at hard labor, after having served which, those of them who were citizens of foreign countries were allowed to leave the Soviet Union. (It should be noted that this was done after Stalin had died.) Young Krassnóv was a Yugoslav citizen and was therefore released in the late 1950s after serving a ten-year sentence in a Siberian camp. He then made his way to Argentina.

To me the most interesting thing about his book (Ref. 33) is what his uncle told him the last time they saw each other as he was helping the old man soap himself in a Moscow prison shower bath. It included the following advice:

". . . Whatever happens, never dare hate Russia. It is not Russia or the Russian people who are to blame for this widespread suffering. . . . Russia has existed and will exist . . . the resurrection of Russia will be gradual. It will not happen all at once. Such an enormous body cannot recover its health suddenly. It is a pity I shall not live to see it. . . ."

This was the real Piótr Krassnóv speaking, as I have known him. He could then freely speak his mind, since he knew that he was about to face his Maker.

### 5. My First Contacts with Soviet Engineering Colleagues

During the first forty years after the Revolution my personal contacts with Soviet engineers were few and far between. To be precise, they happened to be spaced at almost exactly ten-year intervals—1927, 1936, 1946 and 1957. Their nature reflected to a certain extent the healing effect which time had on the attitudes of both sides. The biggest change, however, took place after World War II.

The first confrontation took place at Bremen in 1927. In addition to local construction, Paul Kossel & Co. (p. 288), were doing foreign work as well—in Ireland and in the Soviet Union, where they had started a joint venture with the Soviet Government, founding a firm in Moscow called Russgerstróy, (an abbreviation for Russo-German Construction Co.). I had applied for a job with the parent firm for work in Ireland, in answer to a coded advertisement, but, when I was hired by old Kossel I found that he hoped to persuade me to go and work for them in Moscow where they were putting up multistoried houses with walls made of light-weight pumice concrete. This I firmly refused, but agreed to translate for them into German at their Bremen main office the Soviet reinforced concrete regulations then in force.

One day Paul Kossel told me that the Chairman of the Board of Russgerstróy, a man by the name of Beloússov, was coming from Moscow for a conference at Bremen and that he wanted me to meet him. I agreed to do so, but declined any responsibility for the consequences. A row did develop, but I must say that it was I who, figuratively, "fired the first shot."

When I was called in by Kossel's younger brother, Max, to translate into Russian for Beloússov the minutes of the Board's meeting drafted in German by Paul Kossel in the adjoining room, I loudly remarked so that it could be heard by them through the open door that I did not know how to translate the word "Herr" before Beloússov's name—no equivalent of "Mr." was used by the Bolsheviks. Should I translate it as "comrade"?—and I laughed derisively. Max Kossel shushed me, telling me to call Beloússov "chairman" in the Russian translation. This I wrote out in the old orthography * just to annoy Beloússov, although in general I had already changed to the new one. A number of acid exchanges took place as a result when I was introduced to Beloússov who was a former village school teacher and an "Old Guard" Bolshevik who had become prominent because of his personal friendship with Lenin. I later learned that he demanded my immediate dismissal, but old Kossel told him that he was not in Moscow and had nothing to say about the composition of the personnel of the parent firm in Bremen.

However, when the Chief Engineer of Russgerstróy, an old-time Professor Mikháilov, arrived in Bremen a few months later, Paul Kossel did not want to have us meet. But Mikháilov insisted and, when we did, his attitude was markedly and even exaggeratedly different from that of Beloússov.

At our first conference everyone but the Soviet guest and Paul Kossel were standing around a table. Mikháilov jumped up, saying that he felt uncomfortable sitting down while I stood. So I had to

---

* The Imperial Russian Academy of Sciences had been working for years and had completed just before the Revolution a simplification of the alphabet which consisted of the abolition of a couple of letters which had the same sound as letters which were retained. The Bolsheviks actually proclaimed this reform. At first most *émigrés* refused to accept this perfectly reasonable measure just because it was the Bolsheviks who had announced it. Now, with the exception of a few rightwing groups, most *émigré* newspapers abroad use the new spelling—so do I, in my personal letters.

take a chair, while our Chief Engineer and my other German bosses remained standing.

Mikháilov had brought his wife along with him. She did not speak any German, so he requested that I be invited to a formal dinner which Paul Kossel was giving in their honor at his Bremen villa. I sat opposite Mikháilov and next to his wife at the center of the long dining table around which were gathered some of the most prominent merchants and industrialists of that ancient Hanseatic city interested in furthering trade relations with the Soviets. They made one toast after another to "Russgerstróy," to Soviet-German relations and so forth. I translated, but left my glass untouched.

When Mikháilov's turn came to reply, he looked at me and said: "And what shall I wish *you?* Please translate what I shall say." We both got up and he continued: "I raise my glass to the day when circumstances shall take such a turn (*slózhatsya tak*) that it will be possible for you to return to your Homeland (*Ródina*). May that day come soon, for it will then be better for all of us!" As I finished translating, I stood to attention, drained my champagne glass in one breath and then held it in old Russian Army fashion turned over my head to show that not a single drop had been left. After all, Mikháilov's toast amounted to the expression of hope for a complete reversal of Communist policies!

Our host and his German guests were literally dumbfounded by this action of a Russian engineer, who happened to be an official Soviet representative. Things were somewhat damped after that, since they did not seem to know what to make of it all.

A possible explanation for it came to me on the next day when we were driving in a car and Mikháilov asked me some leading questions about the financial status of the Kossel Company, which, at the time, was quite precarious. But he did not seem to resent my "know nothing" response. It is quite possible that he had been permitted to try and make friends with me in order to get some inside information about the Kossel firm, but I am confident that the feelings of his dinner toast were spontaneous and genuine. I have given his real name since none of the Soviet engineers I met after World War II had heard of him, so I presume that he must have perished during the Stalin-instigated purges in the 1930s. He would have to be in his eighties if alive now, which therefore seems most unlikely.

My second encounter with people from "over there" took place nine years later, when I was returning on the *Queen Mary* from the 1936 International Foundation Engineering Conference at Harvard. The ship had just been put into service and I arrived early to take a look at the first-class accommodations. Leaving my luggage in my two-berth tourist-class cabin, I wandered about the ship, returning only when we were already at sea. Opening my cabin door I saw that a man was unpacking his luggage in the middle of the floor while two others—apparently his friends from another cabin nearby—were sitting on a sofa. He must have read my name on my luggage labels—which gave both my New York and my London addresses only as care of the American Express Company—for he asked me in Russian if I was Chebotariόv. There was something about the trio—difficult to describe but evident to a Russian—which indicated to me that they were Soviets. To make sure, I countered by asking how far they were going. "Back to the Union," * they replied, "and you?" "Back to Egypt." It was their turn to look surprised.

This sailing of the *Queen Mary* when she was going to try for the West-East transatlantic Blue Ribbon had been sold out for months in advance and there obviously was no chance to get moved to another cabin. So I sat down on my bunk, remarking that I wanted things to be clearly understood from the very start—I was an official of the Egyptian Government, a former Don Cossack artillery officer of the Imperial Guards and of the White armies, but I had nothing against continuing our conversation if they felt the same way about it.

There was a long silence—they must have had the same thoughts as I did about being stuck together for the rest of the crossing, by courtesy (intentional or accidental?) of the Cunard Line officials who had assigned us to the same cabin. Then one of them asked in a somewhat hesitant manner what languages were spoken in Egypt. We got along quite well from then on, although they avoided me on deck and declined to talk about life and conditions in the Soviet Union even when we were alone in our cabin.

They were part of a group of some thirty electrical engineers who were returning on the *Queen Mary* after having spent several months in the United States studying the operation of an entire radio factory which the Soviet Government had acquired.

An amusing episode involving another member of this group oc-

* I have never heard Soviet citizens, whether Russians or not, speak about going to "Russia," the way Americans constantly do.

curred when we landed at Southampton and our boat train reached London. I was met at the station there by my cousin Fyódor Ríkovsky * who wore in his lapel, apparently in my honor, a large enameled white-blue-red old Russian national flag with a gold double-headed eagle added in its center. I could not find my luggage under the letter "T" and, before telling my cousin about the Soviet engineers on the train, started looking for it elsewhere. Perceiving one of my suitcases, I quickly walked up to it, saying to my cousin in Russian: *"Vot odín, Derzhí yegó!* (Here is one, Hold him!)" † A man who was bending over an adjoining suitcase immediately swung around and found himself facing the Russian monarchist emblem in my husky six-footer cousin's lapel. He staggered back with an expression of utmost alarm which however changed to an embarrassed grin when he realized from my cousin's evident bewilderment that we were not referring to him.

Although I had refused to follow General Krassnóv's example in returning to Germany, since I felt that a Nazi attack on the Soviet Union was inevitable, I was convinced that it would collapse under the German onslaught. I therefore was opposed at the time to American help to the Reds believing that this would only get the United States into serious trouble later.

But, using Whittemore's words (p. 295) I was pleasantly surprised to find that "Russia taught me about herself." The turning point in my feelings came when I heard at a home of Princeton friends some records of new Red Army choir songs—they conveyed to me better than anything else could have done that the spirit of Russia was still alive. Many memories came back to me when I saw that the music for one of the most stirring songs had been written by a former classmate of mine (p. 23).

It was therefore with a much changed attitude and frame of mind that I accepted in 1946 an invitation from my good engineering friends Spencer, White and Prentis, Inc., of New York City to attend a technical film showing they were arranging at the Columbia Club

---

* He was the younger son of my father's half-sister. Once abroad, she had written me several nice letters, clearly indicating her desire to stop the old family feud (p. 10). I responded in kind, "burying the hatchet," and then visited her in London in 1928. Her elder son became later a Royal Air Force fighter pilot and was killed in the Battle of Britain.

† In Russian the word "him" is used instead of "it" when speaking of a *chemodán,* or suitcase.

for a visiting Soviet civil engineering delegation—they were still considered to be our Allies at the time.

The party had just assembled when I arrived, and Mr. Prentis introduced me, pronouncing my name, in one of the several erroneous versions practiced over here, as "Ts-chebotériof." I saw a puzzled look of incomprehension on the faces of the Soviet engineers and said, with a grin, "Chebotarióv." They understood and all grinned back. The ice was broken right there and I had pleasant chats with all members of their group during the cocktail party which followed the film showing. They made a very good impression on me.

I was interested to note that Professor D. P. Krýnine of Yale University was also present, but was not formally introduced to the group when he arrived shortly after I did and that only two men who were his former students at Moscow chatted with him later on. Here I first noticed something that seems to be pretty general—the difference in the attitude of most Soviet people towards former active Whites as compared to their own later defectors. Professor Krýnine was a so-called non-returner, having remained abroad when sent there on a technical mission by the Soviets in the 1920s. They seemed to have much more respect for their former open adversaries. Maybe time will soften this too.

During the cocktail party I asked the head of the mission, a civil engineer by the name of Novozhílov, whether they would like to visit Princeton if I obtained permission to show them the unclassified research I was doing there for the Bureau of Yards & Docks concerning lateral earth pressures against harbor retaining walls. He said that they would and gave me his card.

Thereupon on the next day I got the agreement of the Dean of our School of Engineering, telephoned the Navy officer in charge of our project in Washington, who had no objections, and then sent to Novozhílov an English-language letter of invitation with copies to everyone concerned. A week went by without any reply, so I telephoned him. The moment he heard my name over the wire, he audibly tensed up and his tone became quite different from the one when we first met. No, they would *not* come to Princeton, he said, adding: "Should this become possible later, I shall get in touch with you—but I doubt that this can happen soon." Someone must have vetoed the visit at their end.

I soon got a pretty transparent hint that my initiative had not been welcomed at our end either, when my wife and I were invited to a cocktail party at a house of some new arrivals to Princeton. As I was chatting there with a girl I knew, a man I had not met before came up and started telling us for no apparent reason how he had been employed by the United States Army during the war to check on possible Communist contacts of officer candidates. "And as to the Navy," he added, looking straight at me, "I hate to think what they would do to anyone who maintained Soviet connections." Having said this he moved on to an adjoining group. The girl did not get the significance of what had been said and started asking me questions about Russia. The would-be intimidator heard this and turned towards us, saying, "Talking about Russia? A subject which it is safer to stay away from!"

It was not for another eleven years that I happened to meet again any of my Soviet engineering colleagues, this time at the 1957 Fourth International Conference on Soil Mechanics and Foundation Engineering which was held in London. I had attended the first three—the first at Harvard in 1936, the second at Rotterdam in 1948 and the third at Zurich in 1953—but this was the first time any Soviet representatives attended such a meeting.

The Soviet delegation consisted of some fourteen engineers, many of whom I already knew by name through their technical publications, and they seemed to know my foundation engineering work too. There was no evidence of any of the political supervision over them about which I had been reading so much in the anti-Soviet press and I was pleasantly surprised to find that they did not hesitate to talk to me alone, which they were supposed to avoid according to the same press. It is true that they belonged to the top level technological Soviet élite in the field—Academy members, professors, winners of Stalin (now called Lenin) prizes.

They made a very good impression of poised, thoughtful persons who obviously had lived through many hardships but who had not been broken by them, and who had retained their dignity and courage. By contrast I found that many of my American colleagues were ill at ease when talking to anyone of the Soviet group.

Later, after my return to Princeton, I was asked to give a talk to our Engineering Faculty about the London Conference I had just attended. Someone asked me how the attitudes of Soviet delegates compared to those of the Americans. I replied: "Gentlemen, you will not like this, but I had the definite impression that on a man-to-man basis my Soviet colleagues have gotten over their fear of Stalinism to a much greater extent than my American friends have forgotten McCarthyism."

I definitely liked my new acquaintances and I think they sensed it—we had many friendly talks, largely on technical matters. However, about three different persons asked me in different ways but essentially the same question as to what impression their delegation made on me and "other foreigners."

There was not a trace of anxiety in the question, just straightforward intellectual curiosity, typical of the detachedly critical individual Russian mind, always interested in getting the objective truth. Yet, when I later mentioned that question in America, one of my colleagues exclaimed: "So, they still have not gotten over their inferiority complexes!" He did not quite believe me when I tried to explain to him that this had absolutely nothing to do with any feelings of inferiority and it was only natural for and to the credit of these Soviet engineers, who came for the first time into contact with their foreign counterparts, to be impartially curious as to how they measured up and to get an opinion thereon from someone who they knew was in a position to make the comparison and whom they trusted, feeling that he was sincere and friendly.

*Tempora mutantur et nos*
*mutamur in illes. . . .*

# 10    1959 Visit to Soviet Union with the United States Exchange Delegation

## 1. Reception in the United States of the Soviet Foundation Engineering Delegation

I was very favorably impressed by the technological competence of the Soviet engineers I had met at the 1957 Conference in London and by a number of novel developments in the Soviet Union which they described. Therefore, after the conclusion a year later (in 1958) of the Lacy-Zarúbin Agreement for a program of official cultural exchanges between the United States and the U.S.S.R., I suggested to Mr. Fred Burggraf, Director of the Highway Research Board in Washington, D.C., the possibility of arranging an exchange between American and Soviet engineers in the field of Soil Mechanics and Foundation Engineering (see published official report on the exchange, Ref. 57). As stated in that report: "The purpose of this exchange was to facilitate an interchange of knowledge in the field of soil engineering, including theoretical and applied research, laboratory and field testing of soils, and design and construction procedures."

With the authorization of Mr. Burggraf I informally explored the possibilities for this proposed exchange in personal correspondence with the Chairman of the Soviet National Association—a section of the International Society of Soil Mechanics and Foundation Engineering, Professor N. A. Tsytóvich, whom I had met a year earlier in London. My letters were in English, since copies went to the National Academy of Sciences in Washington. Those of Professor Tsytóvich were in Russian. The plan was to start the exchange by having a group of Soviet soil engineers present papers at the annual meeting of the Highway Research Board in January, 1959. Professor Tsytóvich expressed general agreement with that plan and Mr. Burggraf then officially requested the State Department to approve it.

After one meeting with me, the East-West Contacts staff of the

National Academy of Sciences decided to let the State Department's section of the same name handle the matter. This was done and a complete "snafu" resulted. They spent four months debating among themselves and with various Washington "experts" the details of the "reciprocity" which they wanted to be assured of in advance, then sent through the Soviet Embassy in Washington a vaguely worded formal invitation to discuss the proposal, leaving only about three months to do so before the scheduled date of the first exchange step. In addition, they changed the entire topic so that the proposal was forwarded to the wrong address.

Professor Tsytóvich wrote both to Mr. Burggraf and to myself that the official United States proposal was not in the field of soil engineering we had agreed on, but referred to an exchange of transportation experts. It had been therefore forwarded to the Soviet Highway Authorities who knew nothing about our preliminary informal agreements since they were independent of the Academy of Construction and Architecture of the U.S.S.R. which sponsored the Committee headed by Professor Tsytóvich. It had become impossible to straighten things out in time for them to come to the January, 1959, Annual Meeting of the Highway Research Board. But he expressed the hope that an exchange of delegations between our two countries could take place during 1959, emphasizing that it was to be in the field of soil mechanics and foundation engineering.

In his letter to me Professor Tsytóvich, when writing about the exchange of delegations, added "with your participation." A similar letter, expressing the hope to see me in Moscow, was received by me from the late Professor Borís Petróvich Popóv, whom I had met at the London Conference. I was sure that they were all very well informed as to my background, but I decided that I had better first "dot the i's and cross the t's" both in that respect and concerning my overall attitudes. So I replied by sending them a reprint from *Who's Who in Engineering*, on which I had marked the combat and staff positions I had held in the White armies. I also wrote:

". . . I want it to be clearly understood that forty years ago I fought in the ranks of the White armies and that I am not prepared to be apologetic about any of my past. However, at the present time I wish to do everything possible to improve relations and understanding between the countries of my birth and of my adoption."

In one of the several letters I received from Professor Tsytóvich concerning details of the proposed exchange, he mentioned about three months later that there were no objections at their end to my coming to the Soviet Union as a member of the United States delegation on "Soil Mechanics and Foundation Engineering" since my work in the field of "Soil Mechanics and Foundation Engineering," and especially my book in that field, were very much valued in the U.S.S.R.

Meanwhile Mr. Fred Burggraf had submitted the exchange proposal to the Executive Committee of the Highway Research Board, which voted to approve it, whereupon its Chairman appointed a committee of six professors from as many American universities, specialists in the field and members of the Soils and Geology Department of the Board, including myself, to work out the details of the plan.

The greatest difficulties we encountered were caused by lower- and middle-echelon members of the East-West Contacts Staff in Washington. Due to an obsession with "security," many of them seem to have been selected for their posts mainly on the strength of their militantly anti-Soviet backgrounds and attitudes; the remainder went along in the resulting atmosphere, their chief concern seemingly not to appear "soft-on-the-Reds" and lose their jobs or their promotions as a consequence.

I have the impression that this state of affairs was somewhat improved under the Kennedy administration; nevertheless, I will set down some of the things I witnessed, since in effect they sabotaged one of the main purposes of the exchanges—the encouragement of friendly feelings by presenting a true and good picture of America to the visitors.

Our first difficulties arose in connection with the general approach to the organization of the exchange. We began receiving advice from Washington containing such stereotyped cliches as "the time to bargain is now, before the Russians are here," and "we must firmly demand reciprocity," and so forth. This time my critical replies and questions could not be ignored since copies thereof went to senior officials of the Highway Research Board and to my committee colleagues at five other universities. It soon developed that the "experts" advising us had only very vague ideas as to what we were supposed to bargain about, and that one of the main practical suggestions they had as to what we were to "demand" not only fell entirely outside of the stated scope of the proposed exchange, but would have been certain to lead either to its complete breakdown or to a development of an atmosphere of suspicion and distrust.

After extensive correspondence and lengthy telephone conversations the general approach I was advocating was finally adopted—we would let our Soviet counterparts know in a general way what our interests and wishes were and then, once they had accepted them in principle, trust that they would arrange details at their end accordingly. But first we would do our best to show them at our end what they were interested in. This was done and the final results seem to have been satisfactory for the engineers of both sides.

However, in the process of developing our program we had to overcome numerous obstructions raised by the "closed area" rules of the State Department. The Soviet Union had forbidden foreigners to visit certain of its areas which it considered to have military importance. As a measure of retaliation and of pressure for the revocation by the Soviets of their security rules, our State Department closed off numerous areas of the United States which were arbitrarily selected and were scattered at random throughout the country. This totally ineffective spite measure of the Dulles era was revoked by the Kennedy administration,* possibly because Communist planners would not be upset if their citizens were not given here the best possible picture of America and because it only embarrassed the American hosts of the visitors.

We had many such embarrassments. For instance, we had to abandon a plan to take the visitors for a swim on Jones Beach which was "out of bounds." A formal request to let us do this was turned down and a couple of beaches in Queens were suggested to us instead. Since we knew that the water there was partially polluted at the time, we dropped the idea of a swim for our guests entirely. I was very sorry we had to do this, because the sandy beaches of the Atlantic seaboard are one of the beauties of America and contrast favorably with the Black Sea beaches which, like those of the French Riviera, are mostly pebbly.

Another example is the trouble we had to get agreement on a satisfactory route for the visitors' journey by car to Princeton. I received a mimeographed list of routes prescribed by the State Department,

---

* A letter by Harold Taylor, former President of Sarah Lawrence College, which was published by *The New York Times* on September 26, 1963, however indicates that this revocation, at best, was only partial.

according to which Soviet citizens had to follow U.S. Highway #1 if they traveled from New York to Princeton, but must follow the New Jersey Turnpike if they traveled to Rutgers University at New Brunswick. I got nowhere when I pointed out that normally one drives from New York to Princeton by the Turnpike, leaving it at the New Brunswick exit and then continuing along U.S. #1. The answer was a firm "no"—we had to follow the mimeographed directive to the letter, although it was obvious that the person who had drawn it up did not have the foggiest notion about highway travel in the area. I was told that we *had* to take U.S. #1 all the way from New York to New Brunswick, even though it was a dismal section of the route, lined with hotdog stands and the like, and in no way representative of modern American highways. Of course, I could have circumvented this by scheduling the first stop at Rutgers University instead of at Princeton, but I did not want to resort to this subterfuge and decided to fight the issue out. Dr. Goheen, President of Princeton University, had supported the idea of the exchange all along, so I asked his office for help. It was only after his assistant talked on the phone personally to Ambassador Lacy in Washington that the ruling of one of his aides forbidding us to use the New Jersey Turnpike while permitting Rutgers visitors to do so on the same stretch was rescinded.

I must confess that I won another similar argument by guile. After three days at Princeton we were to take our guests for a short visit to the Rutgers laboratories on their way back to New York. I wanted to drive them to New Brunswick, not along U.S. #1, but by a back road, to show them some of the New Jersey countryside with two brief stops on the way—one at Mettler's Woods, a stretch of primeval virgin forest, purchased and presented for preservation to Rutgers by the Carpenters Union; the other at a pre-Revolutionary farmhouse, still in the hands of the same family although most of the original farmland had been sold. I thought that this would illustrate to our Soviet guests some evolutionary features of American life which are little known abroad. But again my proposal was turned down. When I telephoned Washington to say that I had personally driven along the route in question and that there was absolutely nothing there except pleasant scenery, I happened to mention the name of my friends who owned the farmhouse. "What did you say their name was? The Alsops?" and the voice at the other end of the wire suddenly sounded interested. "Are they related to the columnists?" I had an inspiration—"Well, I seem to remember hearing them deny it once," I said, "but I am not really sure." The approval of my proposal came in the next mail.

After several months of hard and often frustrating efforts, the program for the three weeks' American visit of the Soviet delegation was finally worked out in every detail—almost hour by hour—and was typed up and officially approved at our end. The six-man delegation arrived in the evening of May thirtieth. They were met at Idlewild and driven in my car and another private car first to a New York hotel and then to Princeton on the next morning.

The State Department had assigned one of its East-West Staff interpreters to accompany and help the Soviet delegation. I will not give here his real name, but will call him Mr. E. W. West, since I will have some not entirely complimentary things to say about his attitudes which—I wish to emphasize—should in no way reflect on his personality but rather on the atmosphere to which he became used in Washington and which he at first reflected. Basically, he was quite a decent fellow and his questionable attitudes changed markedly towards the end of the Soviet delegation's visit. But, largely because of him, I did not have a dull moment during the trip, most of which I accompanied in an unofficial capacity and at my own expense to help smooth things out.

The program of the visit was organized around four centers—Princeton, M.I.T., the University of Illinois, and the University of California at Berkeley—where technical seminars and discussions were to be held under the auspices of local committees.

The three days at Princeton were to try out the general approach we had in mind. For that reason two professors, representatives of two of the three other university committees, came to see how things would work out. The very first evening we all held an informal conference with the Soviet group to explain and check with them the program we had prepared. They seemed satisfied with everything, but it turned out that their plane tickets to Chicago were booked from New York and not from Boston, as they should have been. The chairman of the Soviet delegation, Mr. I. M. Litvínov, an Active Member and Secretary of the Ukrainian Academy of Construction and Architecture at Kíev, then asked Mr. West if he could straighten this out for them. This was just the sort of thing Mr. West was supposed to do and the request for it was made in my presence and in a perfectly polite way. Nevertheless, Mr. West snapped back: *"Ya vam nye malchíshka na pobyegoúshkakh!* (I am not an errand boy for you!)." I sternly rebuked Mr. West right there, then took aside a young man who represented the East-West section of our Academy of Sciences and told him what had happened. "But, Sir!" he exclaimed in a tone of real shock, "we must present a united front!" "No, Sir," I replied, "certainly not when it is a matter of discourtesy to our guests, which I will not tolerate when I am in charge, as I am now!"

He and Mr. West took off to telephone to Washington—so did I, to talk to the Highway Research Board. When I was asked if I wanted Mr. West replaced, I answered in the negative since I thought somebody even worse might be sent instead of him. All I requested was that he be given no encouragement or support to continue his present line, and I thought I would then be able to make him behave.

The engineering seminars at Princeton were held in the large Hall of the Woodrow Wilson School for Public and International Affairs and were attended by over a hundred prominent American civil engineers invited to participate because of their special interest and competence in the field to be discussed. The late Vice Admiral W. Mack Angas, CEC, USN, retired, then the chairman of the Princeton Department of Civil Engineering, presided and introduced the chairman of the Soviet delegation, I. M. Litvínov, who introduced one by one the other five members of his delegation.

The morning session was devoted to construction on Permafrost.* A paper with lantern slides by Professor N. A. Tsytóvich, a specialist of world repute in that field, was followed by a panel discussion of four American specialists, one of them being a representative of the U.S. Army Corps of Engineers. Questions from the floor and answers followed. I translated, since a non-specialized interpreter like Mr. West, who could not be familiar with special technical terms, inevitably got into difficulties and many essential shades of meaning became lost.

The afternoon session dealt with novel methods of vibratory pile-driving developed in the Soviet Union. First, a Soviet film of its use on construction jobs was shown, then Professor R. A. Tokár, Director of the Moscow Institute of Foundations, presented an illustrated

---

* Permanently frozen ground in the Artic which presents special foundation problems since its upper layer melts and softens in the summer or if heat is transmitted to it from new structures.

paper which was discussed by a panel of four other American engineers and by questions from the audience.

Similar seminars on the same and on other foundation engineering topics were subsequently held at M.I.T., Illinois and California. All papers presented have been published in their English translation (Ref. 57).

The seminars, as well as other informal discussions, the visits to points of interest on the campus and so forth, all took place in an atmosphere of friendly cooperation.

After a brief visit to Rutgers University, the Soviet delegation spent two days in New York. An evening was devoted to a discussion during a meeting at the Engineer's Club, the rest of the time was spent sightseeing and visiting construction sites. The photo on Fig. 40 was taken during a visit to the caissons being sunk for the piers of the Throgs Neck Bridge. From right to left are: Academician I. M. Litvínov (the chairman), Director R. A. Tokár, Professor V. M. Bezrúk, and Professor N. A. Tsytóvich.

During the subsequent train journey from New York to Boston I chatted with three of the Soviet engineers, while Mr. West sat across the aisle, his feet resting on the opposite seat, eyes closed—apparently asleep. Our conversation ranged far and wide, and at one point they mentioned one of their friends who had agreed to have his illness treated on an experimental basis by an ancient Chinese method— that of controlled pin-pricks of certain nerve centers—at a Moscow clinic which was studying whether there was anything to that procedure. Then we went on to other subjects.

At some point one of the Soviet engineers got up to go to the men's room and a woman passenger promptly plumped into his seat. Apparently it had gotten around the car that there were Soviet visitors on board; so she, the devoted wife of a chiropractor, wanted to know what were the chances of introducing chiropractice into the Soviet Union. Mr. West woke up immediately. After she left us, not without some indirect encouragement by me, I was asked to explain just what chiropractice was. I turned to Mr. West and asked how would he do that? "Well," he replied, "it's just as big a fraud as that Chinese method you were . . ." here his voice trailed off and the consternation on his face showed that he had suddenly realized that he had revealed not having been asleep at all. But it also revealed that he had wanted us to think that he had been asleep. The three Soviet engineers only grinned broadly in silent amusement. I was speechless too, but from extreme annoyance. I relieved my feelings later, both at M.I.T. and at Illinois, by cursing at length about the incident in talks to my American friends there.

During the tour of the M.I.T. campus we were shown their "mechanized" interdenominational chapel—a cylindrical structure with no windows. The movable altars of the different denominations were kept in the basement when not being used for a service but were designed to be easily rolled onto a platform which could be rapidly raised to the main floor. The Soviet visitors were impressed by the listing of church services at the entrance which showed that Protestant services preceded and followed a Jewish service. "In the old days the Holy and Ruling Synod would have first spent a week sprinkling the place with holy water," remarked one of our guests—and I think he was right. Incidentally, only one of the six-man delegation was a Great Russian, and even he had been born in Central Asia—the rest were Ukrainians, Jewish and a Byelorussian. This was only one of the many illustrations I had as to how nonsensical is the clamor of some groups in this country about the alleged "oppression" of national minorities in the Soviet Union.

We visited several construction sites which were of interest from a foundation engineering point of view. A significant incident took place at one of them. A radio truck drove up to make a recording of a statement by the chairman of the Soviet delegation for later broadcasting on the local network. Since it was not to be of a technical nature, I thought that this would be a good occasion to let Mr. West do some work and translate what Mr. Litvínov was going to say. I invited him to do so. But the other members of the delegation took me aside and insisted that I do the translating since they feared that Mr. West would insert something into it which might be embarrassing for them. They refused to release the tape until it had been played back to me and I assured them that Mr. West had done an honest job of translating. I felt complimented by this display of confidence in my integrity.

From Boston we flew to Chicago (the flight change having been arranged by Mr. West) and, after a day of engineering sightseeing around that city, we went by train to Urbana for a visit at the University of Illinois. We left most of our luggage at a Chicago hotel since we were going to return there, but, on our arrival, it was discovered that there had been a mixup of suitcases so that a film needed for the seminar had been left by mistake in Chicago. Here I must give full credit to Mr. West for having risen to the occasion and done wonders to get the suitcase with the film delivered to Urbana just in the nick of time.

The seminar went off very well. The photo on Fig. 41 was taken by a Japanese graduate student just after I had finished translating a remark by M. M. Lévkin, Chief Engineer of the Moscow Department of Large Bridges, which he made at the end of his illustrated talk describing the vibratory sinking of cylindrical caissons for large piers. He had apologized for having run somewhat over his allotted time, saying that he could not help vibrating himself when he talked about his vibrators.

A real "whodunit" happened soon after which may have meant that Mr. West's earlier sins on the trip had caught up with him. As I got into the elevator when we returned to our hotel he rushed in after me in a state of great excitement, exclaiming: "This is the darnedest thing that ever happened to me—look at this!" It was a note from the hotel manager which he had found in his key box requesting him not to let uncaged live pigeons fly about his room. I followed him to see what it was all about. When he opened the door of his room we saw a live pigeon sitting on a newspaper spread out in the middle of the floor, a short string tying one of its legs to a foot of a chair placed nearby. The hotel manager's story was that a maid had found two pigeons fluttering about, had succeeded in capturing one and in tying it to a chair, but that the other had escaped through a broken wire screen which covered a wide ventilation opening. He speculated that it might be through that ventilation opening that the pigeons had entered the room in the first place.

Maybe—or was it a student prank? If so, what was the meaning of the joke? Was it intended to make fun of the Soviet peace symbol, the Picasso "dove of peace"? Or, as someone suggested, was it a reference to the slang term "stool pigeon" in connection with the episode involving Mr. West on the New York to Boston train about which I had told many people?

After a very instructive visit to a large test road project administered by the Highway Research Board in the vicinity, we were driven in private cars to a railway station and boarded a train for Chicago.

I did not go with them from there to California because there were some urgent matters in my consulting engineering practice which I

had to attend to. Also I knew that there were Russian-speaking civi
engineers at Berkeley who were competent effectively to translate a
the seminar.

But I rejoined the group for a closing session at the Academy c
Sciences in Washington, D.C. Mr. West had been mellowed so muc
by that time that he even invited them to make a short visit to hi
house nearby, which they did.

They left by air soon afterwards, I believe feeling quite pleased b
their visit and by the predominantly friendly reception everywher
They certainly tried to reciprocate fully during our return visit t
the Soviet Union.

### 2. Reception in the U.S.S.R.
### of the U.S. Exchange Delegation

The seven-man United States delegation was ap
pointed by Dr. D. W. Bronk, the President of the National Academ
of Sciences. It consisted of five university professors, including my
self, selected by the Highway Research Board, and of a consultin
engineer and a senior civilian engineer of the U.S. Corps of Enginee
proposed by the American Society of Civil Engineers. The cost c
the trip was paid by the National Science Foundation—the Sovi
Government had paid for the cost of the visit of their delegation t
this country. The Soviet visas on our passports were obtained for u
by the Highway Research Board.

We changed planes at Copenhagen and flew on to Moscow, land
ing at the Vnúkovo airport on September 14. A hearty receptic
awaited us there—a number of Soviet engineers welcomed us as w
left the plane and entered the airport building. We saw many fami
iar faces—nearly all our recent guests and several men we had me
at the 1957 London conference were there to greet us.

We were quickly cleared through the passport controls, our lugga
was waved through the custom house without any examination (n
was there any examination when we left three weeks later), and w
were driven to the Metropole Hotel in two Soviet-made ZIM limo
sines of the Academy of Construction and Architecture of the U.S.S.1
(our official hosts) and in three private cars. Professor Tsytóvic
the senior man of the welcoming group, had borrowed his son's pe
sonal car and a driver for it from the Academy. Two others—D
rector Tokár and Dr. Barkán, a specialist of world repute in the fie
of soil vibrations and a past Stalin-prize winner for technologic

achievements—drove their own Soviet cars, a smaller Vólga and a Moskvích.

I could not help feeling amused since all this was so different from what we had been led to believe during an extensive "briefing" just before we left New York. The "expert" on travel in the Soviet Union who spoke to us spent quite some time advising us how to obtain cars from the Intourist Agency; he brushed aside my remark that we would not have anything to do with that agency since we were going to be the official guests of an Academy; he ridiculed my assertion that some of our Soviet colleagues had told us they would drive us in their own cars, as we had driven them. That was impossible, he said. Our actual experiences during the entire trip proved he was several years behind the changing times.

On the morning after our arrival the President of the Academy of Construction and Architecture received us in his office where we were given copies of the proposed program for our visit and were asked for comments. The chairman of our delegation remarked that no visits to highway construction jobs had been included and that, although we were soil engineers, as representatives of the Highway Research Board we would like to see some actual highway construction work in progress. "The American is perfectly right," said the Academy President when I finished translating. "Why hasn't this been done?" It turned out that some officials of the Highway Administration, which was independent of the Academy, had cold-shouldered relevant suggestions. "Did you speak to . . ."—and he mentioned several names, apparently of higher officials. "No? Then do so." Turning to our chairman, the Academy President said that he would see to it that on our return to Moscow we would be shown construction work on the new ring highway circling that city—our itinerary was to be Moscow, Kíev, Leningrad, Stalingrád, Moscow (we flew all the way —in Soviet jets to Kíev and to Leningrád).

When the business part of the meeting was over, I asked for permission to make a personal request. According to our program, on the second Sunday of our visit we were to leave Leningrád around ten in the morning for Púshkino—the old Tsárskoye Seló. I explained that I had been born about two miles away in Pávlovsk—its old name had been restored to it. There was no point in taking our entire delegation there, but could I hire a taxi and leave Leningrád a couple of hours earlier to visit my birthplace? I would then rejoin the delegation at Púshkino. The Academy President readily agreed.

It was interesting to find the special privileges accorded to scientists in the Soviet Union. They were extended to all university professors, including those of technological institutes. Their salaries were higher than in industry—a situation which is the reverse of the one unfortunately prevailing in the United States.

In the major cities "Houses of Scientists"—which might be described as glorified clubs—were located in some of the best buildings available. Fig. 42 shows our luncheon at the Moscow House of Scientists which occupies what in the old days was the mansion of a very rich merchant. In Leningrád the former palace of the Grand Duke Vladímir Alexándrovich, with a beautiful view of the Nevá River through its windows (Fig. 43), was the House of the Scientists.

At our first luncheon we were very much impressed by what Professor Tsytóvich told us—in answer to our questions—about the education of civil engineers in the Soviet Union. Their high school preparation, as in most other European countries, was much more thorough than that in the United States, so that they had a comparative advantage at the very start of their university-level studies. Then, instead of the four years customary in this country, it took them five years to obtain their first degree, that of "Engineer," so that it really corresponded more closely to our degree of "Master," rather than to our "Bachelor," granted after completion of the four years of undergraduate study. Their thorough theoretical training was not divorced from practical realities—they did much design work and they were required to spend most summers on construction jobs where they were moved from work as simple craftsmen to that of foreman, and so on, in accordance with a planned and supervised program.

There were two higher degrees: that of "Candidate" and that of "Doctor" of technical sciences. Engineers preparing themselves for the first of the two were called "aspirants," and it took them at least two years of further study to earn the title of "Candidate." Thus it was approximately equal to the American Ph.D. degree.* The title of "Doctor" was much more difficult to earn and, accordingly, only a rather limited number of persons had it. A doctor's degree was however a prerequisite for the post of professor.

Professor Tsytóvich was asked if he could arrange a session for us

---

* For relevant other data on engineering education and impressions see the book, Ref. 60, which Professor Stephen Timoshénko of Stanford University wrote after his 1958 trip to the Soviet Union.

with some of his "aspirants" at the Moscow Civil Engineering Institute. He did this when we returned to Moscow. Each of the five aspirants he selected gave us ten- to fifteen-minute-long reports on their research—Figs. 44 and 45 *—and then readily answered questions which members of our group asked them. They made an excellent impression.

A number of exhibit-type conferences were specially arranged for us in several places (Figs. 46 and 47) when individual professors and engineers explained to us through Soviet engineer-interpreters the research in their charge and then answered our questions.

We gave three seminars—at Moscow University, at Leningrád Polytechnical Institute and at Kíev House of Architects. A combined total of some 700 persons attended these three meetings. I had written and read my paper in Russian, the others were translated. All were published in English in our official report on the exchange, Ref. 57. Our Soviet hosts had expressed the intention of publishing them in Russian too, but this was not done. I did not press for an explanation in 1961 when I met some of them at the Fifth International Conference on Soil Mechanics and Foundation Engineering in Paris, since I saw no point in embarrassing them—obviously someone had overruled them in this respect.

The overall impressions of our delegation were expressed as follows in a Summary on page 9 of our report, Ref. 57:

"The American delegation is of the unanimous opinion that the entire exchange was most productive and worthwhile, both in terms of the knowledge gained, as summarized in the remainder of the report, and in terms of potential long-term exchanges of information and experiences.

"The status of soil engineering in the USSR is well advanced in areas which, in the past, have been deemed of particular importance to the economic development of the country; these include the development of precast foundation units, vibratory driving of piles and hollow caissons, thermal stabilization of loess, construction on permafrost, etc. However, the delegation saw little evidence of any extensive studies of the shear strength of clays or the properties of compacted soils and field compaction

---

* Amateur photographers may be interested to know that these and other indoor pictures on the trip were taken by me without flashbulbs, using an old Leica camera, f:3 shutter setting, 1/20 second shutter speed, and a high-speed Kodak Ektachrome color film.

problems; work on cement, bitumen and chemical stabilization had apparently only recently been activated and modern equipment for undisturbed sampling of clays was not observed. As the economy expands, the scope of the Soviet effort probably will be broadened.

"Education in soil engineering at both undergraduate and graduate levels is of high quality. Fostered by a highly selective system and by large incentives for scholarly achievement, substantial numbers of highly motivated, dedicated, and competent soil engineers and researchers are being developed.

"In anticipation of a large civil works program, funds, facilities and personnel are being provided for long-term research on the performance of actual structures by teams of scientists, engineers and construction specialists. The magnitude of the effort expended on large-scale experimentation and subsequent evaluation appears to exceed that being done in the United States.

"Soviet soil and foundation engineers are better informed of work done in the United States than their American counterparts are of developments in the Soviet Union. The American delegation feels strongly that better methods for obtaining and disseminating Soviet technical knowledge in this field are urgently needed."

It is interesting to note that the Russian translation of this Summary was reprinted in full by the relevant Soviet technical periodical.* "It was a good and objective report," commented one of my Soviet colleagues at the 1961 Paris Conference.

In this connection I must say that at no time did I notice anything about the attitudes of Soviet engineers which would justify the frequent charges in the West of their alleged tendency to make exaggerated claims of superiority. During our trip I was asked by one of our hosts how their work compared with similar work in the West. When I truthfully answered that in some respects they were ahead and in others we were, the Soviet engineer remarked that this was fine, provided they were not behind in too many important respects. His attitude reflected just a straightforward competitive spirit and honest intellectual curiosity which unfortunately are all too often misunderstood in the West (see p. 315).

The opinions of the delegation were based on visits to and dis-

* *Osnováníya, Fundámenti, Mekhánika Gruntóv (Bases, Foundations, Soil Mechanics)*, 1961, No. 3, page 32, Moscow.

cussions at: one university, two polytechnic institutes, two civil engineering institutes, four research or design institutes, the Ukrainian Academy of Construction and Architecture in Kíev, the local branch of the Academy of Construction and Architecture U.S.S.R. in Leningrád, and the City Trust of Geological Engineering and Mapping in Moscow; two sites of highway pavement and construction work, including two grade separation bridges; the Stalingrád hydroelectric station which was nearing completion; two locks on the completed Volga-Don Canal; several sites where vibratory pile-and-sheet pile driving was being done; prefabrication plants for large reinforced concrete units—foundation footings and wall panels—and the subsequent assembly of such units at four apartment building construction sites.

Our official report was prepared and discussed in all of its parts by all seven members of the United States delegation. It states (on page 7 of Ref. 57):

"In its visits to the various academies, institutes, ministries, trusts and construction jobs, the delegation was accorded the greatest respect and cordiality by everyone it encountered. These favorable circumstances were undoubtedly facilitated by the relaxed climate of USSR-USA relations coincident with the visit to America of N. S. Khrushchév, Chairman of the Council of Ministers USSR, which took place during the delegation's stay in the Soviet Union. However, an important factor was the goodwill created by the friendly reception accorded the Soviet delegation during its visit to this country in June 1959."

Personally, I feel that the latter factor should not be underestimated. I had many impressions to confirm this. Thus, when I thanked one of our former guests who had gone out of his way to straighten out a difficulty which had arisen, he replied: "Grigóriy Porphyrievich, you know the Russian saying: '*Dolg platezhóm krásen* (A debt is good in its repayment)'—remember how we were received in America!"

On page 4 of Ref. 57 we continued:

"The Soviet Committee also served as hosts for entertainment features whenever time permitted. During the three-week stay members of the delegation attended three ballets, an ice show, two circuses, a puppet show and Cinerama; visited the Kremlin, several museums and art galleries, and were guests at a number of banquets."

Although we did meet the wives of some of our colleagues at theater performances and at restaurant dinners, we were not invited to any of their homes. This was in contrast to the reception of the Soviet delegation in the United States, when a large part of the entertaining was done by individual professors in their private homes.

Personally, I was shown the greatest courtesy and friendliness everywhere, in spite of my background, which everyone knew. For instance, in Leningrád each member of our group received local descriptive material in a zip-up type of briefcase which was made of fine pigskin embossed with the symbol of Leningrád—the equestrian statue of the Tsar Peter the Great. Mine was presented to me with a friendly smile and the remark: "Even a monarchist would not object to this!" I did not try to explain that I was not a monarchist.

The only thing that persistently "rubbed me the wrong way" on the entire trip was the behavior of some of my younger colleagues on the delegation. I had a hand in their selection and I still think that it was the right, proper and best possible one. Perhaps, surrounded as I was by nostalgic reminders of my youth, I was overly sensitive and too easily irritated by various silly jokes and displays of ignorance about "the old country" which an *émigré* to the United States is gradually compelled to get inured to over here. But some things did go much too far.

No one tried to dance the cake-walk around Stalin's tomb. The story somehow got around in this country that one of us actually did, but a not entirely dissimilar incident happened as follows:

On our first Sunday morning we visited the Kremlin. Part of it was temporarily closed off to the numerous Soviet tourists who were taken around by guides in large groups, but our hosts arranged for us to be shown that part too. In one of the ancient vaulted rooms the woman historian who explained things to us said that we were now in the oldest part of the Kremlin. Pointing to a large chair, all upholstered in faded red and gold brocade, she added that this was where the first Tsar of the Románov dynasty, Mikhaíl Fyódorovich, received his advisors after his election in 1613.

I translated this, then the woman historian, Professor Tsytóvich and I moved into the next room, but since no one followed us we turned back—and saw the following scene.

A full professor was sitting on the throne; another full professor was kneeling before him, one hand stretched out in a clowning gesture of supplication; and a third member of our American delegation, laughing, was taking a flashbulb color picture of him.* The incident happened in the morning, before lunch, so that everyone was stone sober.

No one among our Soviet hosts who were accompanying us said a word. I was utterly, but also silently, disgusted. Earlier I had remonstrated in private with my fellow delegates about some actions of theirs which were not quite as tactless as this one, but to no avail. It seemed to me that the only effective step I could now take would be to go to the American Embassy and request permission to return home immediately, unless drastic action were assured to prevent this sort of thing from continuing. But if this was not done and I did have to return home, this would damage rather than improve Soviet-American relations, thus running counter to all my previous efforts. So I decided to first find out how my Soviet colleagues felt about it, and, when we were crossing a courtyard, I took one of them aside. I had met him earlier and had the impression that he was a very intelligent and level-headed man. I told him that I would like to have his opinion; forty years' absence had made it difficult for me to judge whether he and his colleagues felt the same way about things as I did, for instance about the incident which had just taken place. If they did, I would take action. I did not tell him what I had in mind, but he seemed to sense that it would be something serious.

"Grigóriy Porphyrievich," he replied, *"please* do not do anything. We are *beginning* to get accustomed to American tourists. They act like big children, but at heart they are good people. And who was it who said—I forget who it was, but he was so right—there is a a lot in common between the average American and the average Soviet man. So we are not offended—please do not do anything."

My American colleagues were unaware of all this at the time and the younger set continued in the same vein as we went through several museum halls where groups of Soviet visitors respectfully listened to the explanations of their guides concerning the relics of Russia's past on exhibit before them. Everyone spoke in hushed voices. We stopped before a large glass case which contained some gorgeous ancient ecclesiastical vestments—of the sixteenth century if I remember correctly. As I translated our guide's remark that the weight of the pearls alone on a single vestment was over one hundred

---

* It came out quite well but, when we later exchanged various pictures we had taken on the trip, I refused a copy of what I termed an "incriminating document" for them.

pounds (I forget the exact figure she named, but it was quite large) one of our group slapped another on the back, loudly exclaiming: "Oh, no-o-o!" The woman historian had spoken only Russian until then, but here she turned on him and said in English: "Please *be* quiet!" Her eyes flashed as she said this.

The mood of the days when Paul Robeson was said to have been invited to sit on an Imperial throne and pose for propaganda photographs had vanished in the fires of the country's defense against Hitler's invasion. As one of our escorts remarked to me with pride when we were entering the Kremlin: "We are not passportless Iván's—we have a rich historical heritage!" This was particularly noteworthy since he seemed to be a devout Communist and was a Jew who lived in the Ukraine.

As to the behavior of my younger American colleagues, I must say that it went much further than some of the horseplay customary at United States conventions. But I do not blame them personally for this since I feel that it was a reflection of the moods which prevailed then in the United States and which unfortunately still do. It seemed to me that subconsciously they must have been overwhelmed by the cordiality of their reception and, especially, by the contrast it presented to the briefing they had received before leaving New York, which must have made them feel that they were going into hostile territory.

In the summer of 1962 I attended a seminar "Search for New Directions" organized in a Pocono camp by the American Friends' Service Committee. I asked a psychologist whom I met at this Quaker-sponsored meeting whether my above tentative explanation made any sense to him. He said that it did—that there even was a technical term, "regression," to designate childish behavior of people acutely embarrassed by an unresolved subconscious mental conflict. I am happy to say that our Soviet hosts did not seem to be at all annoyed by its manifestations—but I could not help resenting them, especially since they came from my associates.

### 3. *At the Stalingrád Dam across the Volga*

This dam, now completed, is part of a number of dams which form a series of lakes and regulate the flow along the entire course of this mighty river, which is the longest in Europe and over a mile wide at Stalingrád. It is a multipurpose dam, storing water for irrigation, assuring navigation and providing 2,563,000 kva electric power. In this latter respect it is the largest in the world,* followed in order by the Soviet Kúibyshev plant higher up on the Volga and the Grand Coulee in the United States. It has a number of technically interesting features which are outlined on pages 36–40 of our report, Ref. 57.

It was nearing completion when we visited it in 1959—Fig 48. We arrived at this site in a special bus and disembarked before the temporary administration building. As we waited for our passes to be cleared there, a workman heard me speaking both Russian and English and asked me who I was. I told him. Soon a group of construction workmen gathered around me (Fig. 49) and started asking questions. The ensuing conversation ran something like this:

"Are there any workmen in your delegation?"—"No, we are all engineers."—"How do workmen live in America?"—"Pretty well." —"What is the pay of a workman there?"—"That depends on his qualifications."—"Well, say that of a *slésar* (mechanic) like myself?"—"About three dollars an hour."—"What can one buy for that?"—"In the price of what are you interested?"—"Say, a suit."— "One like this would cost about seventy dollars," and I unbuttoned my Burberry raincoat pointing at the tweed suit I was wearing.— "No, I mean a good one." This stumped me for a moment. "A good one? What do you mean by that?"—"One made of Boston cloth."— "Boston is an American city, but I never heard of Boston cloth over there. What is it?" †—"This is Boston cloth," said the workman pointing at the raincoat of Dr. Ter-Stepanián, an English-speaking Armenian soils engineer who was traveling with us.—"We would call it gabardine," I replied.—"We too, gabardine or Boston cloth, it's the same."

When another workman ended a question by remarking that they knew a lot about American conditions, having read various pamphlets from the United States exhibition in Moscow, a voice quietly

---

\* Several dams now nearing completion on Siberian rivers, for instance the one at Bratsk, will have an even higher capacity.

† I told this as a joke to the people at Langrock's in Princeton and they were quite chagrined at the impression made on a Stalingrád workman by the tweed suit they had sold me. They too had never heard of Boston cloth, although Boston apparently had been an important textile town in the past. I suppose the expression had a similarly uncertain origin to that of "Russian" dressing on salads served in American restaurants—I have never seen anything like it in Russia either before or after the Revolution.

broke in: *"Yésli znáyesh—zachyém spráshivayesh?* (If thou knowest —why asketh?)." It was the Assistant Chief Engineer for the dam construction who had come up to the group with our approved passes. *"Khochoú znat, chto vrout oní íli nyet* (I want to know whether they lie, or not)," cheerfully answered the young workman.

As we walked across the dam (Fig. 48), I was favorably impressed by the apparent relationship between the Assistant Chief Engineer and his workmen. He was a big, quiet, middleaged man who at the peak of the construction work had several thousand workmen under his direction. This was the third or fourth dam he was building. He addressed his predominantly young charges in the old fashioned paternalistic way as "thou," but without any touch of condescension about it; their attitude towards him was respectful, but without any evidence of fear or servility. Thus a woman worker did not hesitate to call out to him as we passed: "Comrade Chief Engineer, from where is this delegation?" He answered her in a matter of fact way.

On the other (the eastern) bank of the Volga River was a new town, Volzhsk, which had been specially built for the construction force. It was a far cry from the filthy barracks I had become used to reading about during the Stalin days when most of the heavy construction had been done by slave labor. This was a well laid out permanent town of three-story concrete-block houses with a stadium of its own, a large hall for indoor sports with a swimming pool and a library. Many of the young couples who had been employed on the construction of the dam were staying in Volzhsk to work in new factories which were going up nearby to utilize the newly available electric power. Because of the youth of its inhabitants, the town was supposed to have the highest birth and the lowest mortality rates in the entire Soviet Union, and they seemed proud of this and of their soccer team having beaten the team of many times larger neighboring Stalingrád. Transportation was by buses, private cars still being a luxury in the Soviet Union.

Stalingrád—now renamed Volgográd—is located on the western bank of the Volga River, a short distance below the dam. It was completely destroyed during its epic defense in World War II. At first those of the inhabitants who had survived and returned were allowed to put up themselves any kind of sheds, utilizing the available debris, and the authorities helped them to do so. But these were being gradually replaced in accordance with a new master plan, which however incorporated as shrines a few of the ruined skeletons of buildings where the Soviet garrison made a "last ditch" stand right on the bank of the Volga River. A number of impressive monuments were going up.

The city architect, a man in his early forties, explained to us the reconstruction plan on a huge model in his offices and then drove with us through the town on our way southwards to the locks at the Volga end of the completed Volga-Don Canal.

The rebuilt greater Stalingrád was to cover a continuous strip of some 50 miles length along the banks of the Volga River. It would be only from 2 to 5 miles wide. In spite of the provision of rapid transit facilities, because of its great length it was to consist of several self-contained centers, located at the sites of previously existing suburbs.

I was sitting next to the city architect on the trip which we made in a special bus and asked him whether Sarépta was going to be the site of one of these self-contained centers. "Sarépta?" he said, "but that is quite a small place, how come you have heard of it?" I told him I had been with the White armies when they held it in December, 1918 (pp. 234–236). He changed the conversation, but some time later pointed with a smile through the window, saying, "There is the railway station of *your* Sarépta!" I admitted that the area had been quite built up since I saw it forty years earlier.

We visited the museum of the defense of Tsarítzyn and Stalingrád—the first name being that of the city during the Civil War of 1917–1920. It contained many interesting items, such as the sword of honor presented to Stalingrád by King George VI of England. As we came in, the young local Soviet engineer who was accompanying us spoke in a low voice to the woman guide who met us and who was to show us around. She gave me a look, which, it seemed to me, displayed a greater degree of curiosity than could have been produced by the mere information that I was going to translate.

She seemed ill-at-ease during the first part of the tour and spoke haltingly, as if she were modifying her usual narrative and was improvising a new one. She became much more fluent when we came to the World War II part. It may have been my imagination, but it looked as if she had been asked not to say anything that might hurt my feelings, since I had been before Tsarítzyn on the White side during the Civil War. This was only one of several incidents which indicated considerate thoughtfulness on the part of our Soviet hosts which I appreciated greatly.

## 4. *New Construction*

On our return trip from the Volga-Don Canal to Stalingrád we stopped at the construction site for a double-walled cofferdam within which a landing pier for a new oil refinery was to be built. The steel sheet piles of the cofferdam were being driven by a vibratory method (Fig. 50) which had been developed in the Soviet Union. Under certain soil conditions this new procedure had considerable advantages over the conventional steam hammers, and we were all very interested in it. We had already been shown two construction sites at Leningrad where vibratory driving was being used —one with considerable success. Trouble developed at the other site, where soil conditions were not suitable for this type of method, but I liked the willingness of our hosts to show us all the aspects of their new procedure—not only the pros but the cons as well.

We saw quite a lot of new housing and other reinforced-concrete construction going up everywhere we went. Prefabrication was used much more extensively than in the United States. One reason is the colder climate and the resulting shorter construction season in the Soviet Union. It is therefore advantageous there to produce the year round standardized reinforced-concrete units at special factory type prefabrication plants, store them and then rapidly assemble them on the site during the short climatically favorable season.

Figure 51 shows a reinforced-concrete girder for a highway grade separation bridge as it was being hoisted into place. It is composed of several factory-made standard prefabricated units which were delivered to the site and then assembled there by post-stressing.

Almost all of the very large amount of new housing construction in Moscow and in other cities is being carried out by similar procedures which greatly accelerate things. Figs. 52 and 53 illustrate this.

In general, economy appears to be the main consideration in all new planning. This is natural in a country which has suffered such terrible devastation from foreign invasions and civil strife over the past half-century. Quality often suffers as a result. Also, in the search for new solutions, as in all experimentation, mistakes are inevitably made, until the "bugs" are ironed out of the new procedures. Some of these have received undue attention in the Western and in the Russian *émigré* press and have sometimes been used for erroneous assertions that they proved the incompetence of Soviet engineers in other than the atomic energy and the rocket fields. In my opinion, they were only evidence of "growing pains" of the rapidly expanding Soviet construction industry. For example, the fact that a few buildings in Moscow had to be provided with cantilevered wire-netting to protect passers-by from falling tiles was frequently mentioned in a derogatory way. As I understand it, what actually happened is this:

Because of a shortage of skilled plasterers in the country in numbers needed for the rapid reconstruction of war-damaged buildings simultaneously with the expansion of new construction, an attempt was made to use factory-made tiles on the façades of some new buildings and, at the same time, to extend construction into months of low sub-zero temperatures. The special heating of materials and other procedures employed however did not work out as well as it was hoped and the occasionally falling tiles are a remnant of that stage of development. The now widely used prefabrication of entire wall and floor panels in special factory-type plants is the present answer to that problem.

Doubtless further "bugs" will be found here and there, as in all new procedures, but my overall impression of civil engineering planning and work in the Soviet Union was one of original creative thinking and of courage in experimenting with new and as yet untried procedures in a continued search for economic and rational solutions.

### 5. *Moscow University*

An example of such experimentation is the architecture of a number of "high houses"—thirty stories and more—which were built during the last years of Stalin's era. The new Moscow State University buildings (Fig. 55) are representative of their style, which has been often jeered at in this country as a copy of the "Woolworth gingerbread" type of architecture. I have never read a mention of the original objective of their construction, which was explained to me as follows by a Moscow architect.

In the old days, Moscow had its own typical silhouette seen from afar. The Kremlin towers (Fig. 54) provided its distinctive feature then, but were gradually blocked out of view as seven- and eight-story buildings went up in their vicinity.

An attempt was made after World War II to restore a semblance of the city's ancient skyline by constructing several thirty-story high buildings along the periphery of one of the outer ring boulevards well outside the Kremlin which is at the heart of the city. Six or seven of them were put up, spaced widely apart. I must say that these high houses do provide a distinctive silhouette to present-day Moscow's skyline and I believe that American city planners will appreciate the point.

A comparison of the photos on Figs. 54 and 55 shows that the resemblance between silhouettes of the ancient Kremlin towers and of the new ones on the outer ring is striking, although the close-up appearance of the latter would probably have gained if some of their fancy outer decorations had been omitted.

The new Moscow State University buildings are not among the high houses on the outer ring boulevard, but dominate the overall scene, since they have been erected on a ridge at the edge of the city overlooking all of Moscow. (It is here that Napoleon waited in vain for its keys in 1812.) The University has no Engineering Department since, just as in old Russia, all engineering training is done by specialized Institutes of the Technological or the Polytechnic types. But it did have a good Department of Geology with a section on Soil Mechanics which served as host to our first seminar.

Over two hundred and fifty persons attended it, many of them having come from other cities and even from other Republics of the Union to meet the Americans—Professor Tsytóvich had sent an invitation to the seminar to all members of the National Association of Soil Mechanics and Foundation Engineering of the U.S.S.R. of which he was chairman—it is a section of the International Society of the same name.

The introduction of the American delegation was done in the same way as we had handled the matter earlier (p. 322)—first the Soviet scientist who presided introduced our chairman, who then presented to the audience, one by one, the members of his delegation. The Soviet speakers referred to each other as "comrades," but to us as "colleagues"—we referred to everyone as "colleagues." A Soviet engineer remarked to me later: "It is a good word, 'colleague'—a neutral one."

It was the first time that I appeared before a Soviet audience and I was deeply moved by the reception it gave me. Of course, most of them were specialists in my field and knew me from my published work; many may have heard that I had a hand in welcoming their delegation to the United States—nevertheless it was most gratifying to me that, as my colleagues on the delegation told me later, I got more volume and length of applause than they did. It was with a lump in my throat that I stood before the smiling friendly faces in the big lecture hall and, later on, presented to them my paper in my native language.

There was much to remind me during my trip of old Russian ways and it seemed to me that the tradition of inner integrity among the intellectuals was basically alive. A visible symbol of this continuity is the emblem which all university graduates are entitled to wear (Fig. 56). Just as in the old days, it consists of a white-enameled rhombus with a gold crest on a blue enamel background within it—only now the crest of the Soviet Union has replaced the Imperial Eagle.

## 6. *Revisiting Old Haunts*

Of all the cities we visited, Leningrád was the one I knew best and, at almost every step, a flood of recollections swept through my mind. The center of the city had been restored from the ravages caused by the continuous bombardment during the 900-day siege it heroically withstood in World War II. Special efforts seem to have been made to preserve the center of Imperial St. Petersburg just as it was in the old days. For instance, the square in front of St. Isaacs Cathedral (Fig. 57) looked quite unchanged to me, although the Cathedral inside—so I was told (we did not go in)—had been converted into an antireligious museum.

The statue of Nicholas I on a rearing horse * was still there, although he had been one of the most reactionary and least popular Tsars—the famous unsuccessful uprising of the "Decembrist" liberal officer group attempted in 1825 to prevent his ascending the throne. The "Astoria" hotel where we stayed, (on the right of the photo), did not seem changed in its outer appearance since January, 1917, when I had dinner there as a young officer. The only new element in the picture was the bus before the hotel which shuttled foreign

---

* The statue has artistic merits and is of some engineering interest since it has only what is technically known as a "two-point support" with considerable bending stresses being thereby created in the two rear legs of the horse. It was protected by sandbags during the siege.

tourists from Helsinki in Finland through the Soviet Union, to Warsaw in Poland, and back.

The beautiful and architecturally well-balanced waterfront of the wide Nevá River also was practically unchanged. The spire of the Peter and Paul fortress had been newly covered with fresh gold leaf and gleamed in the sunlight (Fig. 43). So did the spire of the Admiralty and the domes of other churches. The Central Asian style dome of the Moslem mosque—seen with its minaret in the distance of the righthand part of Fig. 43—was covered, as it was originally, with glazed tiles of a light bluish-green color. I was told that it was still "active"—that is, open for Moslem religious services. I did not embarrass our guides by asking whether they knew who gave the money for its construction—it was Nicholas II (see p. 297).

Such changes as had been made in the central part of the city seemed to be in the direction of restoring the older features of the area, which was treated as a gigantic outdoor architectural museum. Thus, I remember the Winter Palace (Fig. 4) as of a brownish-red color. Now it was painted light olive, with white trim at the windows, as it was supposed to have been just after it was built in the reign of Catherine II. In my opinion, its present appearance is a considerable improvement over what it was half a century ago.

There was however a large amount of new modern construction on the periphery of the city, mainly of new apartment houses for the erection of which prefabricated units were used extensively, although of a somewhat different type than those used in Moscow.

Soil conditions in Leningrád are quite difficult because of peat and soft clay deposits near the surface. So all construction there had to cope with special foundation problems. The Leningrád subway, for instance, was not built from the surface within sheeted and braced trenches, as was predominantly done in New York. Cylindrical shafts had to be sunk first through the upper soft layers into an underlying thick layer of very compact clay of great geological age; from these shafts the subway tubes were then advanced laterally by tunneling.

During the 900-day siege of World War II the city was under constant aerial and artillery bombardment which, together with the falling splinters of antiaircraft defense fire, seriously damaged practically every roof in the town. Since many roofs had to be replaced entirely, it was attempted in many cases to combine this operation with the addition of one or two stories to increase the much needed living space. My Leningrad soil engineering colleagues were kept very busy determining whether the existing foundations could take the added load. In many cases this proved feasible and was actually done—compare the old and the new photos, Figs. 58 and 59, of the building where I began my engineering studies (pp. 198, 199).

I did not enter the building because I took the photograph, Fig. 59, on my way to Pávlovsk. It was early Sunday morning and this is also the reason why so few people are seen out on the street. From conversations with former graduates of this Institute of Engineers of Ways of Communication I learned that my old School had been split into its component parts and expanded. The Railroad Transport Engineers kept the original building, while the Highway and Water Transport Engineers moved out into other structures provided for their new and separate Institutes. The latter group claimed that they were the oldest one and therefore should have been given the honor of occupying the original building, since canal and harbor construction constituted the major part of the Institute's activities when it was founded in 1809–1810, whereas railroads had not even been in existence then.

But the three groups were still linked by the strong *esprit de corps* characteristic of our old school and they all joined in celebrating the 150th anniversary of its founding in December, 1959. So many alumni both of the old Institute and of its younger heirs came to the ceremonies from all over the Soviet Union, that the festivities had to be held in one of the largest theaters of Leningrad.

Our New York alumni group, which included all former students of the Institute whether they had graduated or not, also met that December for an annual dinner, as they had done for years.* I gave them a talk about my trip—Professor Stephen Timoshénko of Stanford, our most venerated living alumnus, had done so the year before about his own visit (Ref. 60). When they heard from me that our 150th anniversary was being celebrated in Leningrád almost at the exact time we were meeting in 1959, there was considerable surprise

---

* I was the "youngest" member, having been of the last (1918) *priyóm*, that is, admission, which was held according to the old procedures and standards. At the first dinner I attended, some thirty men were present. Every year there were fewer, and the list of those of us who had died became longer. Last year there were only about fifteen men present and of these not more than two or three, fortunately including myself, were permitted by their doctors to toss down more than one glass of vodka.

that this was done at all. One point puzzled some of the older men who remembered the centenary celebrations which were held in 1910. Why was the 150th anniversary celebrated a year before 1960?

It turned out that it was the actual opening of the Institute in 1810, the centenary of which had been celebrated before the Revolution, whereas the Soviet authorities must have taken the 1809 date of the order by Tsar Alexander I to form the Institute as the date of its founding. Be that as it may, I was happy to find this spirit of continuity over there, so that I no longer had the weird feeling, as I did at our New York meetings, of probably becoming the "last of the Mohicans" among its living former students. I sent a personal note of anniversary congratulations and got a courteous "thank you" reply from the Director of Railway Transport Engineers at Leningrad.

Although I had wanted to hire a taxi at my own expense for my trip to Pávlovsk, the Leningrad Branch of the Academy of Construction and Architecture, U.S.S.R., provided me with one of their cars for that purpose. As a special touch of attention, the young chauffeur selected to drive that car had been born in Pávlovsk himself. One of my Soviet colleagues, whom I had met before and whom I liked very much, went along with us.

We passed on the way the Púlkovo Heights which had remained in Soviet hands as a protruding salient of their defense lines during the entire siege of Leningrád. The Nazi Army had been unable to take these heights, any more than we had been able to do so in October, 1917. But their intensive bombardment had completely razed the old park which surrounded the famous observatory there.

A short distance further on, I vainly tried to locate the embankment in the shelter of which General Krassnóv had begun dictating to me the order for the retreat of his troops (p. 118). It may have been that of the special railroad branch which led to the Imperial residence palace at Tsárskoye Seló and which appeared to have been leveled since then, but I did not explain to my Soviet companions why I asked them to slow down and even to stop a couple of times.

Both Púshkino * (the old Tsárskoye Seló) and Pávlovsk had been fought over and for many months were in the zone of artillery fire. The entire area was therefore almost unrecognizable for me. Practically all the wooden houses had burned down, stands of fine old

---

* Thus called because the famous Russian poet, Púshkin, had studied at the Imperial Lyceum there before it was moved to St. Petersburg.

pines in the parks had been cut to build entrenchments or were razed by continuous pounding of artillery shells. New growth was sprouting where I remembered fields; new roads with new cottages along them had been built. Only here and there remained old stone houses which I recognized. Some of them had been restored, for instance that of my old secondary school (Fig. 60).

As we drove back from Pávlovsk to Púshkino, I asked to stop at a corner which I thought must be that of Zakharzhévskaya Street where we had lived when the town was still called Tsárskoye Seló. Now the street too had some other name and the corner looked quite different—there were new three-story buildings where I remembered a small fire house with a high wooden tower (*kalanchá*) for fire look-outs. But opposite them I recognized the ruins of a corner wall as having been part of the stone palace of Prince Yussúpov (one of Raspútin's murderers).

My companion stopped two old women as they were walking past us and asked them how long they had lived in the town—since the 1920s they said, but could not remember the old name of that street. Did they remember a fire look-out tower anywhere nearby? "Oh yes!" they replied and pointed to the exact spot where I had said it once stood.

This and a number of other similar incidents appeared to firmly establish my authenticity. When on the next day we were about to visit the Hermitage Museum in Leningrad, a young woman came up to me and said that, in view of my interest in Pávlovsk, she had been asked to take the place of one of the two women art historians who had previously accompanied us on similar non-technical visits. She and her husband were both architects, who were conducting the restoration of the war-damaged Grand Ducal Palace and other old landmarks at Pávlovsk. She stayed with us all day, accompanied us to an ice show in the evening, and we had conversations about Pávlovsk which I think were of considerable interest for both of us. On the previous day I had seen that the outside of the Palace had been already fully restored (Fig. 61) and that the park was being well taken care of too (Fig. 62). But the interior restoration had not yet been fully completed and she and her husband still lived at Tiárlevo, a little place between Púshkino and Pávlovsk which had not changed its name and which I remembered well. A delegation colleague of mine and I drove her after the ice show in a taxi to the suburban station which looked just as it did when as a boy I commuted to school in St. Petersburg from Tsárskoye Seló. Again—and this happened more often in and around Leningrád than elsewhere on this trip—I felt a lump in my throat and my eyes dimmed as scenes from the past repeatedly arose in my memory.

Incidentally, as we entered the Winter Palace that day, we first came to the collection of priceless Rembrandts among which I could not help noticing the famous "Return of the Prodigal Son." But none of our escorts seemed to pay any attention to it.

There was however one incident during my visit to Pávlovsk, the subsequent developments of which had me worried for a while—the only time this happened during my entire visit to the U.S.S.R.

I had been told by my parents that I was born in a little cottage there which adjoined the riding school (*Manézh*), a stone structure. I remembered the latter well, having been taught there as a boy to ride, and I had no trouble locating it now since it was not far from the remnants of an ancient fort which were still standing (Fig. 63). But only the outer walls of the riding school remained now, its windows bricked up, its roof gone. As in the old days it formed part of the outer periphery of a military reservation. Facing it, I could see to the left of it the bombed and burned-out skeleton of what had been the garrison church where I had been baptized and frequently attended services as a boy. To the right, where had stood the cottage in which I was born, was only an empty space, but new stone barracks could be seen in the background.

I wanted to photograph this empty spot, with just the corner of the ruined riding school for back-drop, but my companion intervened—there was an all-Union law which strictly forbade photographing any parts of military installations or units whatsoever. A short distance away I had seen a house on the inner side of which a line of soldiers were waiting. They entered it one by one and then came out into the street and walked away. It looked like a guard house where they were receiving their passes for town leave. I thought there must be an officer on duty there and wanted to go in and ask his permission to take this one particular photograph in the presence of one of their officers, if he so wished. My companion flatly refused to let me do this, but, rather reluctantly agreed to go in and ask permission himself.

He emerged looking rather glum and said that the officer on duty had telephoned his superiors and the answer was: "A law is a law and they had no power to change it." * Thus the spot where I was born proved to be the only one on my entire trip where I was not permitted to take photographs on the ground—all pictures on or from airplanes are generally forbidden. But I took some Russian earth with me from that spot to join to the earth I keep from my father's grave (p. 269).

When we got back to our Astoria Hotel in Leningrad that Sunday evening, our delegation chairman asked me to collect our passports from the Intourist branch office in the lobby where they were kept in a safe—we were scheduled to get back late Monday night when the office would already be closed and were to leave for Stalingrád early Tuesday morning before it opened again. The girl in charge of the passports had already gone home, but another employee went to the safe where they were kept, opened it and rummaged through it. She came back with only six of our seven passports—the one missing was mine. I refused to take any, unless all were returned together, just as they had been handed in.

At dinner I told this to our chairman, who approved my action, but it seemed to alarm at least one of my delegation colleagues who wanted to have his passport back the very next morning, irrespective of what happened to mine.

This was the only night on the trip when I did not sleep well. It seemed just possible that some over-zealous military police or counter-intelligence officer, on learning of my request to photograph the edge of their reservation in Pávlovsk, might have decided to try and advance his career by starting a row over it.

On the next morning I mentioned the incident to the senior of our hosts present in what I thought was a casual manner. He pooh-poohed it. But then I saw him speak to one of the Soviet engineers who were serving as our hosts and the latter stayed behind at the hotel instead of accompanying us on a visit to some harbor construction work.

From there we were scheduled to go directly to the House of Scientists for luncheon, but the professor I had spoken to that morning suggested that we stop first at the Astoria Hotel to pick up the Soviet engineer who had stayed behind. We found him waiting for us in front of the hotel with all our seven passports in his hand. "I saw you were worried," said the professor, as he handed me mine,

* Foreign tourists frequently do not realize this and then get into trouble by photographing some building which happens to have military offices inside.

"so I asked him to look into this. It was just the silly girl last night who missed finding it in the safe!" Maybe so, but this episode and other impressions I got on the trip strongly suggest a much more independent attitude on the part of Soviet scientists and engineers than they are credited with in the West.

But, let us return to our Sunday excursion. After visiting Pávlovsk, we rejoined our delegation at Púshkino and continued with them by car to Petrodvorétz—the old Peterhof. The palace there had frequently served as a summer residence for the Imperial family and was known as the Russian Versailles because of its beautiful park and fountains. The palace itself was smaller than its French prototype, but the view from it, in my opinion, is more beautiful and more impressive since the cascade of fountains before it has the waters of the wide Finnish Gulf for backdrop.

Our guide there was a Leningrád architect who had been a captain in a combat unit of the Soviet Army assigned to defend Petrodvorétz during the Nazi invasion and to save as much of its treasures as possible. He told me a great deal that was interesting about the fighting and the siege of Leningrád. The Soviet troops retreated without fighting from Petrodvorétz so as not to have it damaged and, later, when the German blockade collapsed, did not make a frontal attack on it, but made a landing on the coast of the Finnish Gulf in the enemy's rear. But this did not save the palace. The Nazis had mined the tunnel conduits which supplied water for the fountains and, before retreating, blew up the central portion of the palace, gutting the rest by fire (Fig. 66). The enormous work of restoration done since then can be seen by comparing the photograph of Fig. 66 to the same view, but from further away, as I saw it fifteen years later in 1959 (Fig. 67). A significant detail is that during the reconstruction the Imperial Eagles on the towers were replaced just as they appeared originally—that is with crowns over their heads (Fig. 65). After the February 1917 Revolution and the abdication of Tsar Nicholas II, most of the old eagles were left in their places, but the crowns over them were knocked off (see Fig. 64).

Now, monarchism had ceased to exist as a realistic political issue. On the other hand, the racial policies of the Nazi invaders, their arrogant hostility towards native Slavic cultures and populations, their wanton destruction of Russian shrines and monuments in an attempt to eradicate everything that would contradict their absurd theories of Germanic racial superiority—all this has produced within the Soviet Union a great revival of national consciousness and a genuine interest and pride in Russia's past. The outer signs of this, such as the official recognition of past Russian heroes, for instance of the Generals Souvórov, Koutoúzov and others, in my opinion are very far from being just a temporary wartime concession of the Soviet rulers, as many of my fellow Russian *émigrés* still seem to believe. The revival of national pride and feeling appeared as something very real to me and as coming from the "grass roots." I could sense it in the attitudes of crowds visiting museums, in the way a former Soviet officer would point to the battle-won ribbons on his chest and especially to one which had exactly the same orange and black striped ribbon as did the old St. George Cross,* but was that of the equivalent Soviet combat decoration of *Sláva* (Glory), and by a multitude of other impressions.

I had a strange feeling when we were dining at a well-known Moscow restaurant and I could not help thinking of the days not so long ago, or so it seemed to me, when infuriated mobs tore epaulettes off the shoulders of Imperial Army officers and were singing:

> "Yésh ananásy, riábchiki zhúi,
> Dyén tvóy prikhódit poslédnyi,
> bourzhoúi!"

> (Eat pineapple, chew *riábchiks,*
> Your last day is coming, bourgeois!)

And here I was, eating the same delicacy, the *riábchiks* (p. 26), among the descendants and the successors of the same revolutionaries, many of whom in the big restaurant hall were in uniform with epaulettes on their shoulders which looked just like those of officers of the old days. But most of the faces were different, especially among those of the older people—their features were roughly hewn, indicating their closeness in time to the hardships of tilling the earth in the villages they came from. Sometimes, side by side, would be their offspring with features resembling those of their parents, but already softened by city life.

I was deeply touched by what one of our Leningrad hosts—a much younger man than I—said to me at the airport when we were about

* The only Imperial decoration which had been recognized and which could be worn in the Soviet Union by its citizens, since it was awarded only for valor on battlefields of foreign war.

to board a plane and leave: "Grigóriy Porphyrievich, we are not entirely devoid of an understanding of psychology and we realize what you must have felt revisiting the place of your birth (*rodnýie myestá*). I will not permit myself to express sympathy (*sochoúvstvye*), because in sympathy there is an element of condescension. May I just shake your hand to say good-by." We solemnly shook hands.

### 7. *Impressions of Kíev and the Ukraine*

I found a great many changes in Kíev, as compared to 1917–1918, when I had known it (pp. 79, 137, 206). The appearance of its main street, the Kreschátik, had changed beyond recognition. It had been completely destroyed during World War II—first by delayed action mines which the retreating Soviet troops left in its buildings and which blew up many of the German Army offices when they established themselves in them. The remaining buildings were burned down by the Nazis when they, in turn, retreated two years later. The destruction was so complete that the street was widened from its original 170 feet to 235 feet when it was rebuilt (Fig. 68).

One ancient cathedral in another part of the town was destroyed beyond repair, but fortunately the St. Sophia Cathedral with its priceless Eastern Orthodox eleventh-century mosaics (Fig. 70) remained intact and is now a carefully preserved museum.

It was at Kíev that Russia formally embraced Christianity almost a thousand years ago. Photo Fig. 71, shows a statue of Prince Vladímir,—a saint of the Russian Orthodox Church. It was erected about a hundred years ago on the steep bank of the Dniépr River at Kíev, overlooking the spot where the mass christening of its inhabitants took place in the year 988. The statue is still there.

Kíev is known as "the mother of Russian cities." Those who want to "liberate" the Ukraine from Russia thus want to separate Russia from its cradle.

The term "Ukraine" did not exist when Kíev was founded. A daughter of the Grand Duke Yaroslav who built the St. Sophia Cathedral in 1030 married the French King Henri I and was the mother of King Philippe I. She is known in French history as *"Anne de Russie, reine de France."*

Yaroslávʼs grandson, Vladímir Monomákh, married Gyda, the daughter of the last Saxon King of England, after she fled to Scandinavia following her fatherʼs defeat in 1066 at the Battle of Hastings (Ref. 72, page 336). The great antiquity of the mosaic shown by Fig. 70 can be visualized if one stops to consider that refugees from the Norman conquest of England had worshipped under that dome.

Kíevan Russia flourished until the middle of the thirteenth century when it was laid waste by the Tartar invasion from Asia. With the decline of Tartar power in the fifteenth and the sixteenth centuries, the Ukraine came for a while under Polish and Roman Catholic domination.

The photo on Fig. 72 shows another old monument in present-day Kíev to an important figure in the chapter of Ukrainian history which followed the period of Polish domination—Bogdán Khmelnítzky, who was a Hétman of the "Zaporózhtzy," the Ukrainian Cossacks. In 1648 he led a violent and bloody revolution of the Eastern Orthodox Ukrainian peasants against Polish rule, which succeeded in driving the Poles out of the Eastern Ukraine. Khmelnítzky and his followers then petitioned to be reunited with Russia.

This was agreed to by the Tsar in 1654 (Fig. 73), only after two years of delay and hesitation among his advisors in Moscow, since acceptance of the Ukrainian petition meant war with Poland (Ref. 72, page 128). Over the following years Russian became the literary language of the Ukraine.

The main change in the forty-one years since I had last seen Kíev, however, was in the signs of "Ukrainization" which were in evidence everywhere. Even under the Hétman Skoropádsky the Russian language was predominant (p. 206). Now all the names of the streets were given only in the Ukrainian language; the majority of the newspapers were printed in Ukrainian; primary, secondary and part of the higher education were in the Ukrainian language. The local radio and television were also in Ukrainian.* All this had not just been permitted but had been encouraged by the Soviets although Ukrainian is very similar to Russian (see Fig. 73) and Ukrainians have no difficulty in understanding and in speaking Russian.

These facts are virtually unknown to the United States public,

* I understand that a similar situation exists in the other member Republics of the Soviet Union (Map G, 354).

since the propaganda of émigré separatists about "genocide" of the Ukrainian population has been widely accepted in this country. I will therefore make some relevant comments about the photograph which I took of the monument in Kíev to the Ukrainian poet Tarás Shevchénko which is shown on Fig. 69.

The United States Congress has recently passed a bill, which was sponsored by misguided supporters of émigré separatists, authorizing the erection of a monument to Tarás Shevchénko in Washington. This is about to be actually done near the Capitol. The purpose appears to be to make Americans think that Shevchénko symbolizes the "colonial oppression" of Ukrainians by "Russians."

The Congressmen who voted in favor of this measure were of course unaware of the fact that there are numerous statues to Tarás Shevchénko all over the Soviet Ukraine—the one shown on Fig. 69 is not the largest of them. I have seen photographs of a very big monument to him at Khárkov and of another overlooking a steep bluff of the Dniépr River near the place where he was buried. In addition, he is honored as a popular hero by the Soviets in the Ukraine in many other ways: for instance in Kíev I found that his name was officially given to one of the main boulevards of the city, to its oldest university and to the main state theater; also a special museum commemorates him there (see p. 359).

The promoters of Ukrainian separatism in the United States are largely of Galician origin, the Galicians being a small minority among all Ukrainians in their homeland,—see Map F, p. 353 and p. 39. However, it so happens that they form about 90% of all Ukrainians in this country, which explains their disproportionate influence here.

During my visit to Kíev several incidents took place which I found personally interesting. Thus at a reception dinner given for our United States delegation by the President of the Ukrainian Academy of Construction and Architecture, I was seated next to some high official who came from the Donétz coal mining basin. If I remember correctly, he was the Deputy Minister for Construction of the Ukrainian S.S.R. During a lull in the conversation he asked me whether I had any previous ties to the Ukraine. I mentioned my past visits to Kíev, the fact that my maternal grandmother came from Chougoúyev, where I had spent a summer (p. 10) and that my paternal grandmother had owned the well-known Ríkovsky coal mines. Having a member

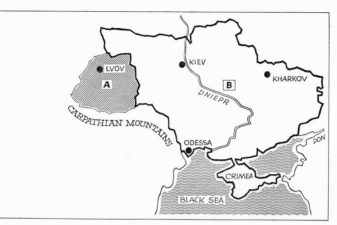

Map F. Area A shown above is the small Austro-Polish part of the Western Ukraine known as Galicia, which for the past 300 years was under Polish or Austro-Hungarian domination. The part B of the map is the Eastern or the Ukraine proper which for 300 years has been united with Russia. (*See p. 39*).

f a family of former Russian industrialists among them produced a momentary chill, but all was immediately friendly smiles again when I added that I had never actually visited the mines since grandmother had disinherited my father (pp. 6, 7, 10).

On another occasion, when we were visiting the ancient Kíevo-Pechérsky Monasteries, some of our younger members noticed an antireligious museum near the entrance to the catacombs which were still under the jurisdiction of the Eastern-Orthodox clergy at that time. My colleagues insisted on being shown what was inside the museum. Our escorts, also young men, went into a huddle and from the way they occasionally glanced in my direction I could see that they were worried that I might be offended if they acceded to the wishes of my colleagues. They then came up to me and asked if I would object to their doing this.

On learning that I would have no objections, they asked whether I would be willing to translate too, since they had no really fluent interpreter with them. They looked somewhat surprised when I answered: "Of course. Why not?" So we went in.

Map G. European borders of the Soviet Union and of its Member Republics after World War II. (*Compare with Map A, p. 44.*)


I expected something much worse than what I actually saw. A
large part of the "Godless Museum" was occupied by pictures con-
trasting the Biblical legend as to how God had created the world
in seven days with what modern science has to say on the matter;
in another section pictures depicted beliefs similar to that of the
Immaculate Conception which had allegedly existed among religions

more ancient than the Christian—for instance in Egypt of the Pharaohs and in Babylon. Some models illustrated the burning at the stake of scientists persecuted for their beliefs during the days of the Holy Inquisition; many pictures presented the clergy in an unfavorable light, for instance a painting of a very young girl being married by a priest to a decrepit but prosperous-looking old man. This Russian painting was a prerevolutionary one and is well-known.

That same afternoon we visited an "active" cathedral; that is, one where Eastern-Orthodox services were still being held. We arrived between services and, as we walked through the church, I dropped behind and left a one hundred rouble note * at the contribution box on the candle-selling desk near the entrance. One of our guides happened to turn around just at that moment and saw me do it.

He said nothing at the time but my actions that day must have appeared contradictory and puzzling to him and to his friends. At any rate, as we were leaving for Leningrád, on the way to the airport the wife of one of our hosts turned to me and said: "Please forgive my feminine curiosity, but we are all *so* interested to know whether you are a believer, or not!?"

I replied that it all depended on what they understood by the word "believer." If they meant by that the belief in God having created the world in seven days—then I was *not* a believer. But I thought that hardly anyone else in the West took this and similar other Biblical legends literally—in this respect their antireligious exhibit was therefore quite out of date. But I liked going to a Russian church occasionally because of its spiritual atmosphere and of the many childhood memories it brought back to me. There were no comments to my reply.

In Kíev, as elsewhere, I was asked by engineers I met questions which, although worded differently, were in effect: "Did I find anything different from what I had expected?" I truthfully replied that I had not thought I would see so many smiling happy-looking young faces on the streets. Then, in turn, I asked whether this was recent. Nobody would actually say that this was the result of developments following the death of Stalin, but the answers amounted to the same thing, such as: "Since things got better after 1953," or "Since Nikíta Sergéyevich † introduced reforms."

* About ten dollars at the rate of exchange then in force.
† Khrushchev.

The farewell at the Kíev airport, as elsewhere, was quite cordial and many of our newly acquired friends came to see us off.

As our home-bound plane taxied away from the airport building at Moscow a large group of scientists and engineers who had been our hosts stood at the gate waving to us until we were out of sight.

I left with the happy feeling that the land of my birth, Russia, was very much alive and was recovering from its terrible ordeals. I use the term "Russia" here in the sense of "Rossíya," meaning the multinational community of its peoples.*

* See p. xxiv.

# Epilogue

My trip to the Soviet Union in September, 1959, coincided with Premier Khrushchev's visit to the United States from which he returned to Moscow a few days before our United States foundation engineering delegation left that city for New York. I therefore had the opportunity to read in the original his impressions of America as printed by *Pravda* and *Izvestia* in the U.S.S.R.

One point intrigued me, namely his impression that, although most Americans wanted peace, some obviously did not since they even intended to "liberate" from the Soviet Union an imaginary country called "Idél-Urál." [1]

To find out more about this, some time after my return to Princeton I looked up the text of the so-called "Captive Nations" U.S. Public Law 86–90 [2] which had been unanimously voted by the United States Congress in July, 1959 (see p. xv). No public debate had preceded its adoption on the recommendation of the Senate's Subcommittee on Internal Security—the Committee on Foreign Relations of the Senate had somehow been by-passed.

The law called upon the President of the United States to proclaim, every year, the third week in July a "Captive Nations Week," officially to manifest to a long list of nations, enumerated by name, the fact that "the people of the United States share with them their aspirations for the recovery of their freedom and independence." The "national independence" of those nations was supposed to have been subjugated by the "imperialistic policies of Communist Russia." However, many of these "nations," such as "Idél-Urál" and "Cossackia," have been integral parts of Russian territories for centuries.

Taken by themselves the annual "Captive Nations Week" observances resulting from Public Law 86–90 may seem fairly innocuous. But, even among anti-Soviet Russian *émigrés* the world over it provoked the greatest indignation and has rightly become known as the "Dismember Russia Week" since the law which created it embodies many features of past plans for dismembering Russia by Kaiser Wilhelm's and Hitler's invading armies in both world wars. Further, coinciding as it did with an intensive rearmament of West Germany, which was encouraged by the United States, the Public Law 86–90

[1] See p. 229 and Ref. 78.
[2] See *Congressional Record,* January 21, 1960, pages 918–920.

increased suspicions within the Soviet Union that America's motive
in all this were far from being purely defensive ones. Therefore
instead of weakening the position of the Communist extremists in th
U.S.S.R., the Public Law 86–90 with its promotion of hatred an
enmity for the Russian people,[2] only strengthened such extremists b
placing them in the enviable position of defenders of national interest
against the threat of renewed foreign aggression. Fears over the
that resurgent German militancy may trigger a new holocaust, in m
opinion, have been strengthened by our P.L. 86–90. Such fears ar
at the root of the recurrent troubles over Berlin and cause Sovie
pressures attempting to neutralize that city.

The military deterrence on which this country has so far concer
trated can be only a temporarily effective step. To make nuclear wa
mutually suicidal is not enough. It is also essential to remove th
causes of justified suspicion which prevent disarmament and, espe
cially, such factors as may cause the opponent to risk anything rathe
than submit to intolerably aggressive designs.

One such factor is our U.S. Public Law 86–90 which should be re
pealed in its present form since it is now directed primarily against th
Russian people and not against the aggressive features of Communisn

As an Appendix to this book I am reproducing on pp. 365, 366
"Statement on U.S. Public Law 86–90" which gives the outstandin
relevant facts and which was signed by sixteen permanent tenure e
emeriti professors of twelve American universities. I am happy t
note that eight of them, that is exactly one-half, are Americans o
non-Russian and non-Slavic origin. Ten are historians, including tw
departmental chairmen. Six others, including myself, had personall
experienced the events of the Russian Revolution and Civil War. I
this connection the name of Professor S. P. Timoshénko—well know
to thousands of young American engineers who have studied h
books—deserves special mention since he was one of the origin
organizers of the Ukrainian Academy of Sciences. He wrote me co
cerning this: "I am of Ukrainian origin, but have never been
samostíynik." [3]

The "Statement" on pp. 365, 366 is reprinted from the *Russic
Review (An American Quarterly devoted to Russia Past and Present*
by permission of its Editor, D. S. Von Mohrenschildt, Professor
Russian Civilization at Dartmouth College. All who have signed th

---

[3] That is a separatist.

"Statement" fully sympathize with the aim of establishing real freedom in the whole world. But one can never achieve this aim by following ways inherited from past oppressors of freedom.

As I became more and more interested in trying to correct the misinformation on which our Public Law 86–90 on the "Captive Nations" is based, and as I studied relevant issues, an amazing picture gradually unfolded itself. Space does not permit me now to go into a detailed analysis of the questionable methods and motives of the sponsors and misled adherents of what the *Washington Post* described in one of its recent editorials [4] as ". . . one of the most artful and arrogant lobbies ever operated by a minority group. . . ." The *Post's* evaluation was concerned with one of the more obvious but comparatively minor manifestations of this lobby's sinister influence.[5] An entire new book would be required to do justice to the much needed task of exposing the enormous harm that the "lobbies" of these pressure groups and their ramifications have done to the moral prestige and interests of this country, and to describe the disunity which they have created among anti-Communists in America and elsewhere by trying to promote "Hate Russia" feelings along with anti-Communism. I hope to write such a book eventually.

In the present book I have given a picture of Russian life as I knew it before and during my native country's time of trials. Some aspects of this picture may serve to emphasize facets of this life which are essential to an understanding of the present but concerning which there is very little knowledge in this country.

The following relevant points emerge from my documented narrative.

In spite of all its faults, old Imperial Russia was far from being the corrupt and backward country [6] with no spirit of individual initiative and enterprise [7] which it is often pictured to have been.

Repeatedly and self-sacrificially Imperial Russia successfully came to the rescue of its Western Allies at decisive moments of World War when they were in really serious trouble.[8] Until the March 1917

---

[4] *Washington Post,* November 12, 1963. See also issues of October 18, 25, November 1, 29, and December 6, 1963.

[5] See p. 352 concerning the Shevchénko monuments in the Soviet Ukraine and the efforts of Ukrainian separatists in this country to get one erected in Washington.

[6] See pp. 22, 164, 168, 198, 199, 245–247; also Refs. 20 and 58.

[7] See background of my own family on pp. 5–7; also Ref. 2.

[8] See pp. 42–46, 50–52.

Revolution the Imperial Russian Army, in spite of its terrible human losses during the preceding two and one-half years of the war, continued to pin down on its front more Austro-German troops than did the combined Anglo-French armies on their front.[9]

These terrible losses were largely the result of an insufficiently developed heavy industry.[10] They and the Tsar's weakness were mainly responsible for the Revolution. Memories of these losses obsessed the next generation and affected its actions. This is why the Bolshevik leaders concentrated on the forced industrialization of the country—at any price—so as to make it independent of foreign armament supplies as rapidly as possible.

Only after the March 1917 Revolution did the Russian Army disintegrate under the unreasonably liberal regime of Kerensky which permitted voting and elections of officers in a war-weary army while it was still engaged in a mortal struggle against a foreign enemy.[11] Memories of this period and of its weakness and aberrations are to a great extent responsible for the absence among many Russians of the unlimited enthusiasm of most Americans for the ballot box.

The Western Allies made a grave mistake in selfishly trying to force their dangerously wounded Eastern Ally to stay in the war— this made a victory of Bolshevism in Russia inevitable.[12] Later on, shortsightedly selfish Western actions during the Civil War managed to alienate even members of the Russian anti-Soviet White armies,[13] a fact well known to the Bolshevik leadership which was reinforced thereby in its distrust of Western capitalism.

Separatist movements of national minorities in Russia prospered only so long as they could be promoted and supported by Austro-German armed forces of occupation in the Ukraine. I give in my present book relevant data concerning the Ukraine [14] and the mythical "Idél-Urál" [15] as well as "Cossackia," [16] which never came into being in spite of persistent Austro-German efforts in that direction.

The United States Congress was misled to believe that the Russian

[9] See pp. 51, 52.
[10] See pp. 48, 49.
[11] See pp. 85–89, 102, 103.
[12] See pp. 107, 108.
[13] See pp. 232–234, 270–272, 279.
[14] See pp. 39, 49, 140, 200, 205–208, 224, 229, 256, 292–293, 350–353. Also Refs. 8, 64a, 64b, 64c.
[15] See p. 229.
[16] See pp. 3, 4, 12, 144–146, 211, 212, 216, 219–223, 225, 266, 270, 298–308, 365. Also Refs. 65e, 65f, 66 and 67.

national minority *émigrés* in this country and their descendants were representative of the attitudes of their minority groups who stayed behind in the Soviet Union. Such beliefs represent a grave miscalculation. Most of these *émigrés* had been tainted by cooperation with past German invaders.

Russian history [17] shows that foreign invaders frequently found some support among individual local malcontents, but that the mass of the population, including the national minorities, invariably rallied around the central government. This happened again and again [18]— for instance in 1709 when the Ukrainian Hétman Mazépa joined the invading Charles XII of Sweden but was not supported by his Ukrainians, the vast majority of whom remained loyal to the Tsar Peter the Great. A similar process was repeated in both world wars.

There is no reason to believe that this will change in the future. The great eastern European land mass which stretches from the Baltic and the Carpathians in the west to the Urals and beyond them in the east and from the Arctic Ocean in the north to the Black and the Caspian Seas in the south is one vast natural economic and defensive entity.[19] Its breakup would spell new hardships and disasters to its component parts, something that most people over there understand very well—especially now when even Western Europe, with many natural barriers between its countries, is attempting to integrate into one entity to remain defensively and economically viable.

One can only wish Western Europe good luck in this endeavor and hope that eventually the East Germans will be able to rejoin their Western countrymen in peace. But our own United States Congress has set almost unsurmountable obstacles to this since no Soviet government can be reasonably expected to give up its present strategic advantages in an armed Central Europe and permit German reunification under Western leadership so long as a copy of past German plans for the dismemberment of Russia remains a law of the land in the United States and dwells in the minds of many misinformed Americans. Nor are most Poles, Czechs and Yugoslavs in their homelands—

[17] See two books, both called *History of Russia*—Ref. 72 by George Vernádsky, and Ref. 53 by Nicholas Riazanóvsky.

[18] In 1607–1612, 1709, 1812, 1917–1920 and 1941–1944.

[19] One of the best analyses of this that I know of has been given by Prof. N. Ouliánov in a speech in New York during a large meeting which commemorated the 1100th anniversary of the founding of the Russian State (see Ref. 47).

who too have suffered so much from past German invasions—likely
to be drawn to us by the present Congressional policies.

During my 1959 visit to the Soviet Union, I met, even in Moscow
itself, members of national minority groups in many high administrative and technical positions. This is only a continuation of past
Russian attitudes.[20] The present educational, cultural and industrial
developments in minority regions of the Soviet Union [21] compare
favorably with those in any other state with a multilingual population. Political freedoms such as are symbolized by the ballot boxes
of the West are lacking but equally so for the Russians as for the
minorities.

As time goes by and the stultifying effects of past foreign invasions
fade away, the need for subordinating individual rights to the objective of national survival through enforced unity will decrease, but
only to the extent that threats from abroad become less menacing.
There are many signs that such an inner relaxation is already taking
place within the Soviet Union. (See also Ref. 30a.) No one can however foretell the exact shape of future developments over there, for
"only Russia can teach us about herself," [22] but I am confident of a
great future for the country within a world at peace if mutual "co-
annihilation" with America can be avoided.

However, one thing is certain—continuation in the West of a "Hate
and Dismember Russia" propaganda can only slow down changes
towards more liberal policies within the U.S.S.R. Our "Merchants of
Hate" [23] should be deprived of the support which they have so far
enjoyed, but which they do not deserve.

As I am writing these closing lines less than a week has gone by
since the dastardly murder of President John F. Kennedy. It is therefore too early to say whether the revulsion against all forms of hate
and violence which has swept the country in the wake of this terrible
tragedy is going to last. But hope is in order. May this movement
towards sanity continue and extend to the field of international relations as well.

[20] See pp. 34, 35, 295–297, 324, 342.
[21] See p. 351.
[22] See pp. 295.
[23] See Ref. 65b.

# APPENDIX

# A Statement on
# U.S. Public Law 86–90

Reprinted from THE RUSSIAN REVIEW,
(An American Quarterly devoted to Russia
Past and Present)

Vol. 20, No. 1, January, 1961
235 Baker Library, Hanover, N.H.

This Statement is prompted by the deep concern of the undersigned about some recent developments in the approach of the United States Congress towards future American-Russian relations, as expressed by the so-called "Captive Nations" Public Law 86–90 of July 17, 1959 and by Congressional speeches on related matters.

The Public Law 86–90 calls in effect for the complete dismemberment of Russian territories according to an overall geographical pattern which closely resembles the one advanced in the past by Pan-German and Nazi invaders of Russia and of the Soviet Union for the aggressive purpose of their political subjugation and economic control.

The language of P.L. 86–90 is in direct contradiction to that of the relevant Presidential Proclamation which does not enumerate the "Captive Nations" and refers to "Soviet" instead of "Russian" Communism. According to State Department letters of May 6, 1960: ". . . the language of the Presidential Proclamation represents official United States Government policy which has been described as one of 'non-predetermination' in the absence of some means whereby the views of the subject people themselves may be verified." We welcome this attitude and hope that the U.S. Congress will adopt it too.

P.L. 86–90 is largely based on historical misinformation supplied to the U.S. Congress. Thus P.L. 86–90 commits the United States to help some mythical "nations" such as "Cossackia" and "Idel-Ural" in the "recovery of their freedom and independence."

Further, P.L. 86–90 speaks of "Russian communism" and of the "imperialistic policies of Communist Russia," thereby by implication equating the terms "Russian," "imperialistic," and "Communist." This intention has been spelled out in print by Congressional Consultants in the preparation of P.L. 86–90. For example, it is stated in the Congressional Record for January 21, 1960, p. 919, that the resolution which became P.L. 86–90 clearly identifies the Russian people as the "enemy" of this country. This allegation is completely false.

The 1917–20 Revolution and most of the Civil War in Russia was not fought between the Great Russians and the Minorities as such. The division ran primarily along economic and social lines. Numerous representatives of minorities took part at all levels on the Red side in the struggle. Many others did the same in the ranks of the Russian anti-Communist movements.

Neither do the present realities of the relations between the Great-Russians and the minorities within the Soviet Union conform to the distorted picture given by the separatist propaganda.

The need is clearly indicated for an official review by the U.S. Congress of the erroneous premises of P.L. 86–90 and for its repeal.

Arthur E. Adams, Prof. of History, Michigan State University.

Oswald P. Backus, III, Prof. of History, University of Kansas.

Robert P. Browder, Chairman and Prof. of History, Univ. of Colorado.

Robert F. Byrnes, Chairman and Prof. of History, Indiana University.

Harold H. Fisher, Prof. Emer. of History, Stanford Univ.; Visiting Prof. of Political Science, Univ. of California, Berkeley.

Andrew Lossky, Assoc. Prof. of History, Univ. of Calif., Los Angeles.

Fred Warner Neal, Prof. of International Relations and Government, Graduate School, Claremont, California.

Nikolai P. Poltoratzky, Assoc. Prof. of Russian, Michigan State Univ.

Nicholas V. Riasanovsky, Assoc. Prof. of History, University of California, Berkeley.

Gleb Struve, Prof. of Slavic Languages and Literatures, University of California, Berkeley.

Edward C. Thaden, Assoc. Prof. of History, Penn. State Univ.

N. S. Timasheff, Prof. Emer. of Sociology, Fordham University.

S. P. Timoshenko, Prof. Emer. of Mech. Engineering, Stanford Univ.

D. W. Treadgold, Prof. of Russian History, University of Washington.

Gregory P. Tschebotarioff, Prof. of Civil Engineering, Princeton Univ.

Serge A. Zenkovsky, Assoc. Prof. of Slavic and East European Studies, University of Colorado.

November 17, 1960.

NOTE: Communications concerning the above Statement, should be addressed to: Prof. G. Tschebotarioff, Engineering Building, Princeton, New Jersey.

# List of References

1. Aten, Marion, and Arthur Orrmont. *Last Train Over Rostóv Bridge,* Julian Messner, Inc., New York, 1961, 340 pp.
2. Bill, Valentine T. *The Forgotten Class,* Praeger, New York, 1959.
3. Browder, Robert Paul, and Alexander F. Kerensky. *The Russian Provisional Government,* Volume III, Stanford University Press, 1961, 1,875 pp.
4. Chebotarióv, P. G. *Krátky Ócherk Istórii 6-oy Leib Gvárdii Donskóy Yegó Velíchestva Bataréi (Brief Sketch of the History of the 6th Leib-Guard Don His Majesty's Battery),* St. Petersburg, Golike & Vilborg, 1905, 191 pp.
5. Chebotarióv, P. "Geróyam Léipziga" ("To the Heroes of Leipzig"), *Rússky Invalíd,* No. 213, 1913, St. Petersburg.
6. Chebotarióva, Valentína Ivánovna. "Handwritten Journal": (a) Vol. I, 152 pp., July 14, 1915 to April 14, 1917; (b) Vol. II, 92 pp., April 15, 1917, to January 5, 1918.
7. Chevigny, Hector. *Lord of Alaska—Baránov and the Russian Adventure,* Viking Press, New York, 1942, 320 pp.
8. Díky, Andrew I. *Undistorted History of the Ukraine-Russia* (in Russian). Vol. I (through the 18th century); Vol. II (19th and 20th centuries). Bookstore of the *Nóvoye Rússkoye Slóvo,* New York, 1961.
9. Deníkin, A. I. *Ócherki Roússkoy Smoúty (Sketches of the Russian Strife),* Vol. IV—The Armed Forces of the South of Russia (in Russian), Berlin, 1925, 245 pp.
10. Detaille, Edouard. *Les Grandes Manoeuvres de l'Armée Russe,* Paris, Boussod, Valadon & C-ie, 1886.
11. Don Historical Commission. *Donskáya Lyétopis* (Don Annals) (in Russian), 3 Volumes, Belgrade, 1923.
12. Durant, Will. *The Story of Philosophy,* New York, Simon & Schuster, 1953, 412 pp.
13. Fineberg, J. English translation from the 1942 Russian edition, *The History of the Civil War in the USSR,* Vol. II (Oct.–Nov. 1917), London, Lawrence & Wishart, Ltd., 1947.
14. Footman, David. *Civil War in Russia,* Faber and Faber, London, 1961, 328 pp.
15. Forman, Sidney. "Lessons in Leadership. Alexander V. Suvórov," *The Military Engineer,* July–August 1958, Washington, D.C., p. 287.
16. *Free Word,* Carpatho-Russian Monthly, 4th year of publication, P.O. Box 992, Newark 1, N.J.
17. Ganussóvsky, B. "Cossacks and Cossackians" (in Russian), New York, *Nóvoye Rússkoye Slóvo,* March 8, 1960.

368

18. Golovíne, N. N. *From the History of the Campaign of 1914 on the Russian Front—Plan of the War* (in Russian), publication of the Main Administration of the Alliance of Russian Military Invalids Abroad, Paris, 1936, 279 pp.

19. Górky, Maxim. *My University Days,* New York, Boni and Liveright, 1923, 327 pp.

20. Goulévitch, de Arsene. *Czarism and Revolution,* translated from the French by Couriss, N. I. Omni Publications, Hawthorne, California, 1962.

21. Greene, F. V. *The Campaign in Bulgaria, 1877–78,* London, Hugh Rees Ltd., 1903, 261 pp. (Abridged from 1879 book by same author.)

22. ———. *Army Life in Russia,* Charles Scribner's Sons, 1880, 326 pp.

23. Ignátiev, A. A. *Piatdesyát Lyét v Stroyú (Fifty Years in the Ranks)* (in Russian), Moscow, 1950, Volume 2, 446 pp.

24. *l'Illustration,* "Le Colonel Artamónov," January 13, 1900, Paris, p. 32.

25. ———, "La Crise de l'Armée Russe," Supplement to the September 8, 1917 number, distributed with the December 22, 1917 issue, Paris.

26. ———, "Chevaliers Mendiants–Un Regiment de Cosaques a Paris," April 7, 1928, Paris, pp. 332–333.

27. Joffre, Field Marshal of the French Army. *The Personal Memoirs of Joffre,* English translation by Colonel T. Bentley Mott, 2 volumes, New York, Harper & Brothers, 1932.

28. Kennan, George. *Siberia and the Exile System,* 2 volumes, New York, The Century Co., 1891.

29. Kennan, George Frost. *Russia Leaves the War,* Princeton University Press, 1956, 544 pp.

30. ———. *Decision to Intervene,* Princeton University Press, 1958, 513 pp.

30a. ———. *On Dealing with the Communist World,* Harper & Row, 1964, 57 pp.

31. Knox, Sir Alfred, Major General. *With the Russian Army 1914–17,* 2 volumes, London, Hutchinson & Co., 1921.

32. *Koubansky Kalendar* (in Russian) published by The Kuban Chancellery, Belgrade, 1931.

33. Krassnóv, N. N., Jr. *The Hidden Russia; My Ten Years as Slave Laborer,* translation from the Russian with foreword by Brig. Gen. Frank L. Howley, Henry Holt & Co., New York, 1960, 341 pp.

34. Krassnóv, P. N. "Na Vnútrennem Frónte" ("On the Inner Front"), *Arkhív Rússkoy Revolútzii,* 2nd ed., Vol. I, pp. 97–190, Berlin, 1922.

35. ———. "Vsevelíkoye Vóysko Donskóye" ("The Grand Army of the Don"), *Arkhív Rússkoy Revolútzii,* Vol. V, pp. 190–321, Berlin, 1922 (in Russian).

36. Loúkomski, Georges. *Charles Cameron,* London. Nicholson & Watson —The Commodore Press, 1943.

37. Ludendorff, Erich von. *Ludendorff's Own Story*, 2 volumes (in English), New York, Harper & Brothers, 1919.

38. McCormick, Robert R. *With the Russian Army*, New York, Macmillan, 1915.

39. Mélnikov, N. M. *Yermák Timoféevich* (in Russian), Published by "Rodímy Kráy," Asnières (Seine), France, 1963, 146 pp.

40. Museum of the Leib-Guard Cossack Regiment of H.M. The Emperor of Russia. "Leib-Kazakí—Stihí i Pésni" ("Leib-Cossacks—Poems and Songs") (in Russian), Paris, 1936, 64 pp.

41. Naoúmenko, V. *Velíkoye Predátelstvo (The Great Betrayal)* (in Russian), All-Slavic Publishing House, New York, 1962, 288 pp.

42. The *Nation* Magazine. editorial: "Wanted: an Atlas." April 23, 1960, New York.

43. The *Nation* Magazine. editorial: "Mark on Your Calendar." June 23, 1962, New York.

44. *Nóvoye Vrémya,* Russian language daily, published in St. Petersburg, microfilms available in New York Public Library:
    (a) No. 13295, 17(30) March 1913, p. 4;
    (b) No. 13296, 18(31) March 1913, p. 2;
    (c) No. 13306, 28 March (10 Apr.) 1913, pp. 4–5;
    (d) No. 13307, 29 March (11 Apr.) 1913, p. 4;
    (e) No. 13333, 26 April (9 May) 1913, p. 3;
    (f) No. 13629, 20 February (5 Mar.) 1914, p. 4;
    (g) No. 13630, 21 February (6 Mar.) 1914, p. 3;
    (h) No. 13632, 23 February (8 Mar.) 1914, p. 4;
    (i) No. 13646, 9(22) March 1914, p. 4;
    (j) 13680, 14(27) April 1914, p. 3.

45. *Oktiábr'skoye Vooruzhénnoye Vosstánie v Petrográde (October Armed Uprising at Petrográd)*, Documents and Materials. Published by Academy of Sciences, USSR, Moscow, 1957.

46. Ópritz, I. N. *The Leib-Gvárdii Cossack H.M. Regiment in the days of the Revolution and of the Civil War, 1917–20* (in Russian), V. Siánsky, publisher, Paris, 1939, 363 pp.

47. Ouliánov, N. *Istoríchesky Ópyt Rossíyi (The Historical Experience of Russia)*, Bookstore of *Nóvoye Rússkoye Slóvo,* New York, 1962, 32 pp.

48. Oushakóv, D. I., Prof. (editor). *Tolkóvyi Slovár Rússkago Yazyká (Comprehensive Dictionary of the Russian Language)*, OGIZ, Moscow, 1935, Vol. I.

49. Parry, Albert. "John B. Túrchin: Russian General in the American Civil War," *The Russian Review* (An American Quarterly devoted to Russia Past and Present), Vol. 1, No. 2, April 1942, The Baker Library, Hanover, N.H.

50. Polyakóv, I. A. *The Don Cossacks in their Struggle against the Bol-*

*sheviks* (in Russian), Munich, 1962, 388 pp. (Written at Zagreb, Yugoslavia, in 1925.)

51. ———. "The President of the 'Cossack Supreme Representation,'" *Rossíya*, New York Russian-language daily, 4 Sept. 1958.

52. Reed, John. *Ten Days that Shook the World*, New York, Boni and Liveright, 1919.

53. Riazanóvsky, Nicholas V. *A History of Russia*, Oxford University Press, 1963, 711 pp.

54. Sentinelle, La, *"Tschassowói"* (in Russian), No. 446(7), July 1963, Ixelles 4, Bruxelles.

55. ———, *"Tschassowói"* (in Russian), No. 447(8), August–September 1963, Ixelles, Bruxelles.

56. Shólokhov, Mikhaíl. *And Quiet Flows the Don*, translated from the Russian, Putnam & Co., Ltd., London, 1934, 755 pp.

57. *Soil and Foundation Engineering in the U.S.S.R.*, Highway Research Board Special Report No. 60, National Academy of Sciences, Washington, D.C., 1960, 188 pp.

58. Tarsaídze, Alexandre. *Czars and Presidents—The Story of a Forgotten Friendship*, McDowell-Obolensky, New York, 1958, 383 pp.

59. Timasheff, N. S. *Nóvoye Rússkoye Slóvo* (in Russian) letter, July 7, 1963.

60. Timoshénko. *Engineering Education in Russia*, McGraw-Hill Book Co., 1959, 47 pp.

61. Tkatschéw, Borís. "There Never was a Cossackia," *Nóvoye Rússkoye Slóvo*, New York, May 15, 1960.

62. *The Truth*, Weekly Publication of the Russian Brotherhood Organization of the USA, 61st year, 1732 Brandywine St., Philadelphia 30, Pa.

Other Carpatho-Russian periodicals:

62. (a) *Karpátskaya Rus*, Lemko Press, 556 Yonkers Avenue, Yonkers, New York.
    (b) *Svit*, weekly published at 84 East Market Street, Wilkes-Barre, Pennsylvania.
    (c) *Viéstnik*, monthly published at McKee's Rock, Pa. Editor: V. Rev. Andrew Slepecky, 106 North Morris Str., St. Clair, Pennsylvania.

63. Tschebotarióff, Gregory P. "Perpetuating Nazi Myths" (letter), *The New York Times*, Jan. 25, 1960.

64. ———. "Public Law 86–90" (letter), *The New York Times Magazine*, Sept. 11, 1960.

65. ———. A series of articles in the New York Russian-language daily *Nóvoye Rússkoye Slóvo:*
    (a) "The Captive Nations of Lev Dobriansky," June 8, 1960;

(b) "Concerning the Merchants of Hate," June 17, 1960;

(c) "Who is the Misinformer?" Exchange of letters with Timothy Herasymóvich, June 26, 1960;

(d) "A Call for the Repeal of Public Law 86–90," February 5, 1961;

(e) "Cossackia and Lev Dobriansky," November 30, 1963.

(f) "Cossackian 'Rumour Factories,'" May 5, 1964.

(*Note:* English translations of the above articles can be obtained from the author.)

66. ———. (and fifteen other permanent tenure and emeriti professors of twelve American universities). "A Statement on U.S. Public Law 86–90," *The Russian Review* (an American Quarterly devoted to Russia Past and Present), Vol. 20, No. 1, January 1961, 235 Baker Library, Hanover, N.H.

67. ———. "The Cossacks and the Revolution of 1917," *The Russian Review* (an American Quarterly devoted to Russia Past and Present), Vol. 20, No. 3, July 1961, pp. 206–216, 235 Baker Library, Hanover, N.H.

68. ———. "The Captive Nations," an illustrated Address to the Present Day Club of Princeton, New Jersey, on February 21, 1962, 52 pp.

69. ———. Comments on Book by Joseph Mackiewicz. *Rússkaya Mysl* ("La Pensée Russe") (in Russian), Paris, August 10, 1963, No. 2032.

70. Túrchin, John B. *Chickamauga*, Chicago, Fergus Printing Co., 1888, 295 pp. (From Series: "Noted Battles for the Union during the Civil War in the United States of America.")

71. Vernádsky, George. *Kievan Russia*, Yale University Press, 1948.

72. ———. *A History of Russia*, Yale University Press (4th revised edition, 1959, now available paperbound), 512 pp.

73. Víroubova, Anna. *Memories of the Russian Court*, New York, The Macmillan Co., 1923.

74. *Vólne Kozáctvo*, Prague, No. 96, January 10, 1932.

75. Weinbaum, Mark E. *I Odín v Póle Vóin* (A single Man in the Field can be a Warrior) in Russian, *Nóvoye Rússkoye Slóvo*, March 28, 1962.

76. Wolkónsky, Alexandre, Prince. *The Ukraine Question—The Historic Truth versus the Separatist Propaganda,* English translation under the direction of William Gibson, Ditta E. Armani, Rome, 1920, 236 pp.

77. Wrangel, P. *The Memoirs of General Wrangel* (in English), translated by Sophie Goulston. Duffield & Company, 1930, 356 pp. Printed in London.

78. Zenkóvsky, Serge. *Pan-Turkism and Islam in Russia*, Harvard University Press, 1960, 347 pp. Chapter XI: "Idél-Urál Dreams."

# Name Index

Abrámov, Fyódor Fyódorovich (Russian General, a Cossack), 239, 247–248, 252–253

Adams, Arthur E. (American Professor), 366

Afanássiev (Russian lieutenant-colonel, a Cossack), 252, 261

Akagi, Toshinobu (Japanese engineer), Fig. 41

Alékhin (chess champion), 69

Alexander (King of Yugoslavia), 283

Alexander I (Tsar of Russia), 17–18, 25, 198

Alexander II (Tsar of Russia), 32, 36, 296

Alexander III (Tsar of Russia), 32, 223, 296

Alexándra Fyódorovna (last Empress of Russia), 52–59, 61–62, 77–78, 190–193, 195–197, 217; Figs. 16, 28

Alexéi Nikoláyevich (Heir to the throne and only son of Tsar Nicholas II), 54, 193

Alexéiev (Russian General), 62, 146, 218

Alsop, T. (author's friend), 320–321

Alsop (columnists), 321

Álya (author's sister), see also Bill, Valentine T., xxiii, 52, 195, 259–261, 278–279, 290

Anastasíya Nikoláyevna (Grand Duchess, 4th daughter of Tsar Nicholas II), 53, 198

Andreau (Russian officer), 33

Andreoletti (Russian engineering student), 32

Andréy Vladímirovich (Grand Duke of Russia), 75–77, 185

Anne de Russie (Queen of France), 350

Angas, W. Mack (Vice Admiral, CEC, USN, ret.), 322

Artamónov (Russian Colonel, a Cossack), 15–16, 36

Aten, Marion, 259, 267, 368

Avédikoff (Russian Sergeant, a Cossack), 14; Fig. 7

Axten, J. (Secretary to Mr. J. P. Morgan), 287

Azhógin (Russian Captain, a Cossack), 122

Azzola (Austro-Hungarian officer), 291

Backus, Oswald P., III (American Professor), 366

Baklánov (Russian General, a Cossack), 36

Bákmanson (Russian painter), 14, 214

Barkán, D. D. (Soviet Engineer), 326

Beggs, George E. (Princeton Professor), 290

Beloússov (Bolshevik administrator), 309

Benkendorff (Russian Imperial Court official), 194

Beseler, von (German General), 49

Bethmann-Hollweg (German Chancellor), 40

Bézruk, V. M. (Soviet Professor), 323; Fig. 40

Bill, Alfred Hoyt (author's father-in-law), xxv

Bill, Edward C. (author's brother-in-law), 290–291, 304

Bill, Florence Dorothy (see Tschebotarioff, Mrs. Gregory P.)

Bill, Valentine T. (author's sister), see also Alya, 290–291, 304, 368

Bismarck (German Chancellor), 40

Bogáyevsky, Afrikan Petrovich (Russian General, a Cossack and Don Atamán), 221, 237, 253, 268, 299

Bronk, D. W. (American scientist), 326

Broussílov (Russian General), 50–52, 62, 70, 84, 144, 257

Browder, Robert P. (American Professor), 366, 368

Brussílov (see Broussílov)

Budiónny (Red cavalry leader), 263, 266–267

Burggraf, Fred (American engineer), 316–318

Buturlín (author's classmate), 67
Byrnes, Robert F. (American Professor), 366

Cameron (18th-century Scottish architect), 19
Catherine II (Empress of Russia), 31–33, 342
Cazalet (British Army Captain), 234–237
Chaperon de la Raye (Russian officer), 33
Charles XII (King of Sweden), 17, 35, 361
Chatelain (Russian officer), 33
Chebotarióv, Iván Grigórievich (author's uncle), xxiii, 60
Chebotarióv, Grigóriy Porphýrievich (see Tschebotarióff, Gregory P.)
Chebotarióv, Grigóriy Yákovlevich (author's grandfather), 5–6, 198, 212
Chebotarióv, Porphýry Grigórievich (author's father), xvii, xxiii, 3, 7, 10–15, 18, 27, 30, 35–36, 38, 41, 46–49, 54, 59, 69, 70, 76, 200, 207, 213, 259, 261–263, 269, 368; Figs. 1, 14, 33
Chebotarióv, Yákov (author's great-grandfather), 4–5
Chebotarióva, Valentína Ivánovna (author's mother), xxiii, 19–20, 27, 49–50, 52–62, 69–70, 77, 107, 111–113, 116, 120, 136–137, 185, 187–188, 190–195, 213, 244–245, 368; Figs. 2, 15, 16
Cheriachoúkin, Alexándr V. (Russian General, a Cossack), 8, 200, 206, 267–268, 275–278, 280–284
Chernetzóv (Russian Captain, a Cossack), 146–149, 155, 157–162, 171
Chevigny, Hector, 368
Churchill, Winston, xvi
Clapier de Colongue (wife of author's maternal uncle), 33
Congreve, Sir Walter Norris (British General), 276–277, 280
Coúriss, Elizavéta Nikoláyevna (mother of Nika Couriss), 191, 201
Coúriss, Níka (see Coúriss, Nikolái Ivánovich)
Coúriss, Nikolái Ivánovich (author's boyhood friend), 21, 34, 279, 369

Cragg, Roland H. (Anglican clergyman), 280–281, 286
Creighton (Russian Army Colonel), 34

Danílova, Lyólia (author's cousin), 258–261, 264, 269
Deníkin, Antón (Russian General), 35, 146, 218, 221, 225–226, 228, 230, 237, 245, 256, 258, 270, 368
Deníssov (Russian officer, a Cossack, Commander of Don Army), 220, 226–228, 237
Detaille, Edouard (French painter), 18, 368; Fig. 12
Díky, Andrew I., 368
Dimítry Pávlovich (Grand Duke of Russia), 61, 76
Dodds, Harold W. (Princeton President), 290
Doubéntzov (Russian Captain, a Cossack), 155
Doubiágskaya, Olga Sergéyevna (author's maternal grandmother), 8–9, 120, 190; Fig. 3
Doubiágsky, Iván Stepánovich (author's maternal grandfather), xxiii, 8; Fig. 3
Doubiagsky, Nikolai Ivanovich (author's maternal uncle), xxiii, 33, 136
Dragomírov (Russian General), 226–229
Drozdóvsky (Russian Colonel), 211, 265
Durant, Will, 368
Dybénko (Bolshevik leader), 121–123, 127

Ebersole, A. A. (YMCA Secretary), 284–285
Ehrenberg, J. (German engineer), 298
Eichelmann (Ukrainian émigré professor), 301
Erdély, Ásya (harpist), 9, 34
Erlich (French Army Lieutenant), 231–235

Farafónov (Russian Colonel, a Cossack), 241
Ferdinand (King of Bulgaria), 11
Fineberg, J., 368

Fisher, Harold H. (American Professor), 366
Fouquet (French Army Captain), 231, 233
Folimónov, Iván (Russian Captain, a Cossack), 77, 97, 165, 184
Folimónov, Nikolái (Russian Captain, a Cossack), 97; Figs. 22, 23
Footman, David, 368
Forman, Sidney, 368
Franz Ferdinand (Archduke of Austria), 41
Fry (English tutor), 21–22

Ganussóvsky, B., 368
Gedróitz, Princess, Véra Ignátievna (surgeon), 53, 55, 57, 62–63, 192; Fig. 16
Gedróitz, Prince (author's classmate), 34
George VI (King of England), 337
Geringer (Lady-in-Waiting), 194
Goheen, Robert F. (Princeton President), 320
Golovíne, N. N. (Russian General and historian), 41, 369
Goltgauer (Russian Colonel), 25, 67
Gólubov (Russian Colonel, a Cossack), 160, 171, 173–174
Górky, Maxim (writer), 96, 369
Goulévitch, de Arsène, 369
Greene, Arthur M. (Princeton Dean), 290
Greene, F. V. (U.S. Military Attache to St. Petersburg, 1876), xxv, 13, 369
Gyda (daughter of Harold, last Saxon King of England and wife of Vladímir Monomákh), 350–351

Hadland, Edith (English governess), 21
Hahn (court photographer), 23
Hammerstaedt, Friedrich, Figs. 38–39
Hanna, William Selim (Egyptian engineer), 289
Heering, Dimítry Edouárdovich (author's boyhood friend), 21, 34
Heering, Edouárd Edouárdovich (Russian General), 19, 33
Heering, Mítya (see Heering, Dimítry Edouárdovich)

Hindenburg, von (German Field Marshal), 45
Hitler, Adolf, xiv–xv, xviii, 300–301, 303, 306; Figs. 38–39
Hughes (industrial pioneer in Donetz basin), 6

Ignátiev, Count (Russian Colonel, later Soviet General), 258, 369

Járov (Cossack émigré choir leader), 252
Jilínsky (Russian General), 43
Joffre (Field Marshal of France), xviii, 42–43, 45, 50, 369

Kaledín, A. M. (Russian General, a Cossack and Don Ataman), 139, 143–144, 146–151, 154, 166
Karachán, Piótr Petróvich (Russian General, a Tartar), 34, 138
Kárpov (author's classmate), 67
Kennan, George, ix, 29–30, 369
Kennan, George F., ix–xii, xxvi, 29, 108, 369
Kennedy, John F., 362
Kerensky, Alexander F., 85–87, 100, 107–110, 121–125, 128–129, 131–133, 137–138, 144, 165, 175, 191, 194, 219, 360; Fig. 21
Keyes, Terence H. (British officer), 226–227, 230, 233, 269
Kharlámov, V. (President of Don Kroug), 145
Khitrovó, Margaríta (sister of mercy), 192, 196
Khmelnítzky, Bogdán (17th-century Ukrainian Hétman), 351; Fig. 72
Khopiórsky (Russian Lieutenant, a Cossack), 97, 147, 149, 152–156, 159–160
Khreschatítsky (Russian General, a Cossack), 120
Khrushchév, Nikita S., 7, 331, 355, 357
King & Gavaris (New York consulting engineers), 290
Knírsha (Russian Lieutenant), 124–125, 128–129
Knípper, Lev (composer), 23–24, 312
Knox, Sir Alfred (British General), 50–52, 113, 369

Kochenhausen, von (German Major), 221

Koegler, F. (German Professor), 289, 297–298

Kolchák (Russian Admiral), 175, 229–231, 245, 256

Konkóv, Iván Grigórievich (Russian Captain, a Cossack), 97, 161–163, 168–169, 171, 174, 177; Figs. 22–23

Konstantín Konstantínovich (Grand Duke of Russia), 19

Kornílov, L. (Russian General, a Siberian Cossack), 107–108, 123, 146–147, 167, 170, 218–219

Korolkóv (Cossack émigré painter), 307

Korovichénko (Russian Lieutenant Colonel, Kerensky's appointee), 191

Kossel, Max (German engineer), 309

Kossel, Paul (German engineer), 288, 308–310

Kóssov (Russian Captain, a Cossack), 91, 97–99; Figs. 22–23

Koulgávov (Russian Captain, a Cossack), 123–124, 128, 215

Koutoúzov (Russian Field Marshal), 349

Kouznetsóv (Russian Corporal, a Cossack), 96–97, 153, 181–182

Kozlóvsky, Prince (Russian officer), 279

Krassnóv, Nikolái Ivánovich (grandfather of General Piótr Krassnóv), 231

Krassnóv, N. N. (nephew of General Piótr Krassnóv), 307–308, 369

Krassnóv, Peter (see Krassnóv, Piótr N.)

Krassnóv, Piótr N. (Russian General and Atamán of Grand Army of the Don), xvii, 107, 109–138, 141, 195, 200–201, 212–217, 219–222, 225–227, 229–234, 237–238, 244, 269, 271, 299, 301–308, 312, 344, 369; Figs. 24, 26, 29

Krassnóv, Zinóvy (Russian Lieutenant, a Cossack), 97, 141–143, 161, 164–165, 171, 174, 177–178; Figs. 22-23

Krassnóva, Lýdia Fyódorovna (wife of General Piótr Krassnóv), 107, 111–113, 120, 131, 133–134, 136–137, 195, 214, 302, 304–305, 307

Krýmov (Russian General), 108–109

Krýnine, D. P. (American Professor), 313

Kutáysov, Count (Russian Colonel), 76–77

Lacy (U.S. Ambassador), 316, 320

Lagouténko, V. P. (Soviet Architect), Fig. 52

Lavergne, G. (French Artillery Captain), 38

Lenin, Vladímir I., 86–87, 123, 132, 188, 314

Lévkin, M. M. (Soviet engineer), 325; Fig. 41

Litvínov, I. M. (Soviet engineer), 321, 323–324; Fig. 40

Loewenhaupt (Swedish General), 32

Loewenhaupt (Russian engineering student), 32

Lóssky, Andrew (American Professor), 366

Loúkomski, Georges, 369

Ludendorff, Erich von (German General), xviii, 43–48, 370

Lunachársky (Bolshevik Commissar), 132

McCormick, Robert (American Army Colonel), 34–35, 79–82, 370

Makhnó (Ukrainian anarchist), 224, 256

Makínsky, Prince, 34

Mámontov (Russian General, a Cossack), 251–252, 266

Mannerheim, Baron (Russian General, a Finnish Swede), 34

Marchand (French Commandant), 15

Marie Antoinette (last Queen of France), 55, 77

Maríya Fyódorovna (Dowager Empress, widow of Tsar Alexander III of Russia), 32, 57

Maríya Nikoláyevna (Grand Duchess, 3rd daughter of Tsar Nicholas II), 53, 191, 197

Maríya Pávlovna (Grand Duchess of Russia), 113

Márkov (Russian Colonel, a Cossack), 133–135

Máydell, Baron (Russian officer, Inspector of Artillery, Don Army), 253–254, 258, 264–268, 270

Mays (English tutor), 22–23

Mazépa (Ukrainian rebel Hétman), 17, 35, 209, 361

Medem, Sophie, Baroness von (godmother of author's sister), 197, 284–285, 305

Mélnikov, N. M. (Don Cossack émigré writer), 370

Menelik (Negus of Abyssinia), 15–16

Mewes, M. G. H. (British correspondent), 87

Mikhaíl Alexándrovich (Grand Duke of Russia, Inspector of Artillery, end of 19th century), 13

Mikhaíl Alexándrovich (Grand Duke of Russia, brother of Tsar Nicholas II), 101, 133

Mikhaíl Fyódorovich (First Tsar of Románov dynasty), 17, 332

Mikháilov (Soviet Professor), 309–310

Mitskévich (Bolshevik Commissar, a Lithuanian), 126–128

Mitskévich (Russian General, a Pole), 25–26

Mohrenschild, von, Dimítry (American Professor), 359

Morgan, J. P. (financier), 286–287

Mouravióv (Russian gendarme colonel), 121, 126–129, 138, 175

Mouravióv, B. (Soviet architect), 348; Fig. 65

Mrozóvsky (Russian General), 61

Nakhichevánsky, Khan (Russian General, a Tartar), 34

Naouménko, V. (Kuban Cossack officer), 41

Napoleon I (Emperor of France), 17–18, 340

Neal, Fred Warner (American Professor), 366

Nazárov (Russian General, a Cossack and Don Atamán), 166–167, 170

Nefiódov (Russian Captain, a Cossack), 252

Neviadómsky, Pável Richárdovich (Russian Colonel, a Pole), 34, 282

Nicholas I (Tsar of Russia), 32, 296, 341

Nicholas II (last Tsar of Russia), 9, 12, 32, 77, 84–85, 192–193, 197, 217, 296–297, 342, 348; Fig. 5

Nikolái Nikoláyevich (Grand Duke of Russia), 43, 77, 303–304

Nikoláyev (Ukrainian officer), 206

Nikólin (Russian gendarme captain), 29–30

Nollet (French Army Colonel), 38

Novogrebélsky (Russian Captain, a Pole), 37, 188–189

Oldenbúrgsky (Russian Prince), 25, 64–68

Ólga Nikoláyevna (Grand Duchess, 1st daughter of Tsar Nicholas II), 53, 56–61, 78, 191; Figs. 16–18, 20

Ópritz, Ilyá (Russian General, a Cossack), 240, 370; Figs. 10–11

Ótzoup (photographer), 23

Ouliánov, N. (historian), 361, 370

Oupórnikov, Anatóly (Russian Colonel, a Cossack), 81–82

Oupórnikov, Borís Nikoláyevich (Russian Captain, a Cossack), 97; Figs. 22–23

Oupórnikov, Nikolái Nikoláyevich (Russian Colonel, a Cossack), 73, 82, 90, 94–95, 97, 159, 166, 169, 177–178, 180–181, 215, 239; Figs. 22–23

Oushákov, D. I. (Soviet Professor), 370

Pannwitz, von, Hellmuth (Nazi General), 300, 307

Parry, Albert, 370

Paul I (Tsar of Russia), 20, 27, 32

Peck, Ralph (American Professor), Fig. 41

Peter the Great (Tsar of Russia), 17, 33, 144, 209, 332, 361

Peter III (Tsar of Russia), 32

Petliúra (Ukrainian separatist leader), 224

Podtiólkov (Russian Sub-lieutenant, a Cossack), 82–83, 99, 149–151, 153–154, 160, 180–181, 185, 209–211

Pólshin, D. I. (Soviet Professor), Fig. 46

Poltorátzky, Nikolái P. (American Professor), 366

Polyakóv, Iván A. (Russian officer, a Cossack, Chief of Staff of Don Army), 211, 237, 370

Ponomarióv (Russian artilleryman, a Cossack), 150–151, 180

Poole, F. C. (British General), 225–233

Popóv (Russian Lieutenant Colonel, a Cossack), 120, 126–131

Popóv, B. P. (Soviet Professor), 317

Pótulov (Russian Major), 29–30

Pougachévsky (Bolshevik leader), 172–177, 182

Pourishkévich (right-wing member of the Douma), 61

Poutiátin, Prince (author's classmate), 23

Prentis, E. A. (American engineer), 313

Prokófiev (composer), 9

Ramacharaka (Hindu Yoga), 97, 153, 182

Ramsey (Russian Baroness), 33

Raspútin, Grigóriy Efímovich (sinister adventurer), 54–55, 58, 61–62, 70, 76, 192, 194, 345

Reed, John (American Communist), 110, 117, 131–132, 371

Rehbinder, Count (Russian Colonel), 75–76, 113, 118, 185

Rennenkampf (Russian General), 43

Riazanóvsky, Nicholas (American Professor), 361, 366, 371

Ríkovsky, Fyódor (author's cousin), 312

Ríkovsky, Praskóvia Petróvna (author's aunt), 312

Ríkovsky, Piótr (Russian Cossack General), 6

Ríkovskaya, Praskóvia Ivánovna (author's paternal grandmother), 6–7, 10, 76, 213, 352

Robeson, Paul (American singer), 334

Rosenberg (Hitler's aide), 24

Roshál (Bolshevik leader), 129–130

Roumiántsev (Russian 18th-century Field Marshal), 31

Samokísh (Russian battle-painter), 214

Samsónov (Russian General), 43

Sanders, Liman von (German General), 39

Schedróff (Russian Corporal, a Cossack), 15; Fig. 8

Schlieffen, Count von (German General), 42, 45

Scott, Georges (French battle-painter), 299

Semilyétov (Russian Colonel, a Cossack), 167

Sergéy Mikháilovich (Grand Duke of Russia), 11

Shevchénko, Tarás (Ukrainian poet), 351–352, 359; Fig. 69

Shokóly (Russian Army Captain), 34, 72–73, 159

Shólokhov (Soviet writer), 160, 210–211, 371

Sidórin (Russian officer, a Cossack, Commander of Don Army), 253, 268

Sikórsky, Ígor (airplane designer), 22

Simmons, Arthur A. (American Congregational Minister and YMCA Secretary), 281–285; Fig. 37

Skoropádsky, Pável (Russian General, German puppet Hétman of the Ukraine), 200–201, 209, 212, 224

Slaschióv (Russian General), 271

Solomón (author's classmate), 23, 159, 287

Sómova, Mrs. (Secretary to Whittemore's Committee), 286

Souvórov, Alexander V. (Russian 18th-century Field Marshal), 31, 349

Souvórov (Russian Colonel, a Cossack), 147, 149–153, 160

Spaláykovich (Serbian diplomat), 38

Spencer, White & Prentis (New York engineers), 290, 312–313

Spinoza (philosopher), xiii, 68

Spiridónov (Russian Sub-lieutenant, a Cossack, later a Captain), 82, 209–211, 254

Stalin, Joseph V., xiv–xv, 6, 314, 332, 355

Stanton (British Major), 266

Strúve, Gleb (American Professor), 366

Tarássov-Rodiónov (Russian Lieutenant), 125, 129–130

Tarsaídze, Alexandre, 371
Tatiána Nikoláyevna (Grand Duchess, 2nd daughter of Tsar Nicholas II), 53, 56, 58–63, 77–78, 191, 193–197, 217; Figs. 16–18, 27
Taylor, Harold (American educator), 319
Ter-Stepanián, G. I. (Soviet engineer and geologist), 335
Terzaghi, Karl (engineer), 289
Thaden, Edward C. (American Professor), 366
Tikhomírov, sisters (daughters by first marriage of author's maternal grandmother, Doubiágsky), 9, 201
Timásheff, N. S. (American Professor), 367, 371
Timoshénko, Stephen (American Professor), 328, 343, 358, 367, 371
Tito, J., 300
Tkatschéw, Borís Ivánovich (Russian officer and Kubán Cossack Atamán), 223, 270, 371
Todt (German engineer), 297
Tokár, R. A. (Soviet engineer), 323, 326; Fig. 40
Toundoútov, Prince (Russian Colonel, a Kalmuck), 35
Treadgold, D. W. (American Professor), 367
Trotzky, Lev (Bolshevik leader), 121, 123, 127–129, 138
Tschebotarióff, Gregory P., Mrs. (author's wife), v, xix, xxv, 290, 305; Fig. b' (p. 187)
Tschebotarióff, Gregory P. (author), xx–xxi, xxiii, 60, 90, 129, 138, 172, 267–268, 293, 313, 331, 333, 350, 367, 371–372; Fig. b (p. 187); Figs. 15, 19, 23, 26, 30, 34–37, 41, 64
Tsytóvich, N. A. (Soviet Professor), 316–318, 322–323, 326, 328–329, 332, 340; Figs. 40, 44
Turchanínoff, Iván Vassílievich (see Turchin, Basil)
Turchin, Basil ("Lincoln's Cossack General"), 13, 370, 372

Vélho, Baron, Vladímir Ivánovich (Russian General), 33
Vernádsky, George (American Professor), xxv, 361, 372

Vikéntiev (author's classmate), 23
Vilchkóvskaya, Varvára Afanásievna (wife of Colonel Vilchkóvsky), 54, 57, 192; Fig. 16
Vilchkóvsky (Russian Colonel), 54
Víroubova, Ánna Alexándrovna (Lady-in-Waiting), 53, 55–56, 61, 372; Fig. 16
Vladímir (Prince and Saint of the Russian Orthodox church), 350; Fig. 71
Vladímir Alexándrovich (Grand Duke of Russia), 328
Vladímir Monomákh (Grand Duke of Kíev), 350
Vladýkin (author's artillery school classmate), 74
Voldemar (teacher of Latin), 64–66
Voldemaras (premier of Lithuania; see Voldemar)
Vysheslávtzev (Russian artillery captain), 74

Weinbaum, Mark E. (editor), xxv, 372
Weygand (Marshal of France), 271
White, Lazarus (American engineer), 289–290
Whittemore, Thomas (American archaeologist and Director, Committee for Education of Russian Youth), 286–288, 293–295
Wilhelm II (German Kaiser), xv, xviii, 35, 49, 220, 357
Wolkónsky, Alexandre, Prince (Roman Catholic Convert), 372
Wrangel, P., Baron (Russian General), 136, 237, 256, 270–271, 279, 299, 372
Wrangell (see Wrangel, P.)

Yaroslávi (Grand Duke of Kíev), 350
Yudénich (Russian General), 256
Yussúpov, Prince (one of Raspútin's murderers), 61, 345

Zenkóvsky, Serge A. (American Professor), 367, 372
Zveguíntzev (Russian Colonel), 227–228
Zveguíntzev, Sásha (author's boyhood friend), 228

(*There are 32 pages of photographs in this book, Figures 1 through 73.*)

# Subject Index

Abyssinia, Russian expedition to in 1898, 15–16

America (*see* United States)

American, help to Russian Refugees, 281–288, 293–294
mistakes of officials in cultural exchanges with USSR, 317–323, 332–334
volunteer from Texas in South Russia, 259, 267
Y.M.C.A., 281–285; Fig. 37

Austria-Hungary, aims in the Balkans of, 38
explosive bullets, manufacture and use by in World War I, 187
military defeats of by Russia in 1914 and 1916, 46–47, 50–52
promotion of Ukrainian separatism by (*see* Russia, foreign plans for dismemberment of)
subjugation of Slavic nations in, 39
support by its prisoner detachments of Bolshevik Red Army, 163

Baptist proselytizing activities, 282–283

Bolsheviks, causes for success of, 236–238
seizure of power by in October 1917, 108–109

Britain (*see* England)

Bulgaria, German influences in, 11
ties to Imperial Russia, xxi, 13–14, 37–38, 296

Byzantium, spiritual cradle of Eastern Orthodoxy in Russia, xxi, 293

"Captive Nations Law" (U.S. Public Law 86–90), mythical nations included in (*see* "Cossackia" and "Idél-Urál")
passage of, xv, 357, 365–366
suspicions aroused by, 357–358

Carpatho-Russians, 39–40, 47, 371

Catholic Church (*see* Roman Catholic Church)

"Cossackia," objectives of creation of term, 145, 270, 300–301
support of by Nazi Germany, 298, 301, 357
by Ukrainian separatist émigrés, 301, 352–353, 358–359
by U.S. Congress, xi–xii, xv, 298, 301, 357–358, 365–366
(*see also* Russia, plans for dismemberment of)

"Cossackians," records which contradict present claims of, 110, 216–217, 223, 301–308

Cossacks, attitudes towards non-Cossacks, 36, 145–146, 215, 222, 253–254
dress of, 12, 300; Figs. 1, 7–8, 10, 33, 38, 39
in emigration, 299–305
in World War II, 300–301, 304, 306–308
origins of, 3–4
privileged position of in Russian Empire, 4
"self-determination" of in 1917, 98–100, 144
stabilizing influence of during first 1917 revolution, 98, 100, 109–110, 145
(*see also* Don, Kubán, Térek Cossacks)

Don Cadet Corps, 7, 213, 259, 261–264, 267–268, 275–284; Fig. 33

Don Cossacks, anti-Red uprising, spring of 1918, 208–212, 215
defection to the Reds early in 1918, 149–162, 166, 171–172
Deníkin's Volunteer Army, relations with in 1918, 218–222, 225–230, 237–238
subordination to in 1919, 237–238
recriminations with after 1919–1920 defeat. 266–267, 270

Don Cossacks, German occupiers of the Ukraine in 1918, cooperation with, 200, 206–207, 214
Imperial Guard Units, Leib Guard Cossack Regiment, 17–18, 239–242, 299; Figs. 10–12
Atamánsky regiment, 15–16, 213, 239, 260–261
Guard Cossack battery, 8–9, 12–18, 73–77, 79–84, 89–99, 102–103, 139–143, 149–154, 160, 180–182, 185–186, 299; Figs. 1, 4–9, 22–23
Imperial Russian Army, service in, 4
Kerensky's Provisional Government, support of in 1917, 100, 144–145
(see also Cossacks)

Egypt, author's life at Ismailia, 275–283
service with Austrian Building Company in, 288
service with Government of, xiii, 288–289, 295
England, church of and Russia, 281
evacuates some of White Russian refugees, 269, 275–276
occupies Batoúm and Bakú oil wells, 233, 271, 279
sends missions, volunteers and supplies to White Armies, 225–236, 245–247
English agents encourage abortive anti-Red uprising at Yaroslávl, 189
attitudes towards non-White races, 295
help Russian refugees in Egypt, 276–278
teachers in Russia, 20–22
Esthonia, 32

Foundation Engineering (see Soil Mechanics)
France, acknowledges Russia's decisive role in World War I, 42–47
temporary help of to General Wrangel, 270–271
French, nationals in pre-revolutionary Russia, 20–21, 33, 37–38
officers and troops in South Russia, 1918–1920, 229, 231–234

French, officials of Suez Canal help Russian refugees, 276–279, 283
policies during Russian Civil War, 189, 225, 232, 270–272
relations with their World War I British allies, 231, 278–279

Galicia, province of Austria-Hungary, 39, 46, 48, 352–353, Maps A, B and F
Germans, in pre-Soviet Russia, 21–24, 32–33, 35, 253–254
pressure the Don Cossacks to proclaim "independence" in 1918, 221
friendly to Russian émigrés after World War I, 291–292
Germany, anti-Slavonic attitudes of, xviii, 40
author's studies and work in, 284–289, 291–293
"Drang nach Osten," of, 38–39, 44
plans of for Russia's dismemberment before and during World War I, 39–41, 49, 88, 200–209, 223–224, 365
revival of after World War I, 292–293, 360, 365
plans of to transform Russia into its economic colony, 40–41
Polish lands, pre-World War I colonization of, 40, 44, 292
starts World War I at peak of its military preparedness, 41
strategic error of at start of World War I, 45
Great Russian (see Russian language, Great Russian)
Greece, past ties to Imperial Russia, 11, 13, 231, 296
"Greens," the, origin of term and activities of, 250–251

"Hazing" in Russian schools, 25–28, 66–68

"Idél-Urál," mythical nation of, xv, 229, 357, 365–366
(see also Russia, plans for dismemberment of)
l'Illustration, Paris illustrated French language weekly, 15–16, 87–88

Jews, in Germany, during 1920's, 293
    in Russia (*see* Russian Jews)

"Klúkva," explanation of term, 16
Kouschóvka, meeting at, 225–229
Kubán Cossacks, 12, 218, 223, 254,
    256, 270, 299–300; Figs. 38–39

Latvia, 32
Leipzig, battle of in 1813, 17–18

Marne, battle of, 42–46
Mazurian Lakes, battle of (*see* Tan-
    nenberg)
Miháilovsky Artillery School, the, 7–8,
    69–74

Nagáika, Cossack riding whip, 28
Novogeórgievsk, siege of, 48–49, 54
*Nóvoye Rússkoye Slóvo*, New York
    Russian language émigré news-
    paper, xxv

Peremýshl, siege of, 47; Fig. 13
Poland, past wars with Russia, 5, 17
    1920 war against the Soviets, 270–
        271
Polish officers in Russian Army, 34, 36,
    83–84, 188–189, 282
"Pravovédeniye," Imperial Russian
    School for Jurisprudence (Law
    School), 24–26, 52, 64–69
Princeton University, xiii, 71, 290, 320–
    323
Provisional Government (*see* Russia,
    Provisional Government of)
Púlkovo, first field battle of Russian
    Civil War, 113–120

Roman Catholic Church, crusades of
    against the Eastern Orthodox,
    xviii, 17, 283
    need for reconciliation of with East-
        ern Orthodox, xviii, 362
    support given by to Ukrainian sepa-
        ratism, 39
Románov dynasty, origin of, 17
    foreign blood in, 32
    members of (*see* Alexánder I, II, III,
        Mikhaíl Fyódorovich, Nicholas I,
        II, Paul, Peter, Tsars of Russia;

Románov dynasty, members of, Alexéi,
    Andréi, Dimítry, Konstantín,
    Mikhaíl, Nikolái, Sergéy, Vladí-
    mir, Grand Dukes; Anastasíya,
    Maríya, Olga, Tatiána, Grand
    Duchesses)
Rossíya, term applied to Russian State,
    xx, xxiv, 219, 356
*Rossíya*, New York Russian language
    émigré newspaper, 88
Russia, abolition of state vodka mo-
        nopoly in 1914, 143
    America, future relations with, xx,
        362
        past friendly relations with, xiv,
            xxv
    American present hostility towards,
        sources of, ix–xi, xiv, xvi, 357–
            359
    decisive help of to Western Allies in
        World War I, 42–47, 50–52
    engineering education in, before and
        during Revolution, 5, 198–199,
            285
        after the Revolution (*see* Soviet
            engineering education)
    foreign invasions of in the past, 17,
        361
    foreign languages in, teaching of, 20–
        22
    foreign plans for dismemberment of,
        before and during World War I,
            39–41, 49, 88, 200–209, 223–224
        during and after World War II,
            xv–xvi, 292–293, 357, 360, 365–
                366
        (*see also* "Captive Nations" U.S.
            Public Law 86–90)
    frustrates in 1914 German plan for
        winning World War I, 42–46
    liberation by of Balkan Christians
        in 19th century (*see* Russo-
            Turkish wars)
    Moslems in, 34, 101–102, 297
    multinational origin of its upper
        strata, xxiv, 32–35
    Provisional Government of, defers
        to Petrograd Soviet "Order No.
            1," 85–88
    causes of its failure, 107–109
    Románov dynasty of (*see* Románov
        dynasty)

Russian, aims differ from Communist ones, xv, xvii, xxv, 18, 365–366
alphabet, xxi, 309
(*see also* Russian language, transliteration of)
Army, education for, 7, 19, 30, 69–74
in World War I, before March 1917 Revolution, 42–52
after March 1917 Revolution, 85–88; Fig. 21
field guns of, 71, 168, 246–247
shortage of ammunition in 1915, 47–48
"bánya" (steam bath), 179–180
calendar (pre-revolutionary or "old style"), 3
Constituent Assembly (All-Russian), 145, 189
customs, xxiii–xxiv, 27–32
Jews, before and during 1917 Revolution, 23, 100, 217
after 1917 Revolution, xxv
(*see also* Soviet Jews)
language, Byélorussian, xxi
Great Russian, xiv, xxi, 3, 8
transliteration of into the Latin alphabet, xxi–xxiii
Ukrainian, xxi, 8–9
(*see also* Ukrainian language)
monarchists after Revolution, xx, 137, 188, 193, 207, 217–219, 225, 348
non-white races, attitudes towards, 34–35
peasants, good nature of, 183–184, 187–188
intelligence of, 96, 255
White Armies (*see* White Armies of Russia)
Russo-Japanese War of 1905, 16–17, 22–23, 53
Russo-Turkish Wars, xxv, 8, 12–14, 31, 296

St. George, Imperial Russian order of, 5, 14, 114, 202, 349; Figs. 7, 29
Sarépta, village near Stalingrad, 235, 337
Serbia (*see* Yugoslavia)
Soil Mechanics, author's work in, xviii, 289–290, 318
definition of term, 289

Soil Mechanics, example of intuitive use during Russian Civil War, 255
International Conferences on, 297–298, 314–315
U.S.-U.S.S.R. exchange delegations in, xvi, 316–356
Soviet Union, civil engineers in, 309–315, 324; Figs. 40–42, 44–47, 52, 56, 65
courtesies shown to author in, 326–327, 331–332, 337–338, 340–341, 348–350
education of minorities in their own language, 351
engineering education in, 328–330, 343–344
Jews in the professions of, 324
reconstruction after World War II, 336–340, 342–343, 350
renewed pride in Russia's past, 333–334, 348–349
soil engineering exchange delegation from U.S., reception of, 326–338

Tannenberg, battles at, 42–47
Terek Cossacks, 12, 299–300

Ukraine, history of, outline, 350–353
failure of to support invading Charles XII of Sweden in 1709, 17, 361
Germans in occupation of in 1918 promote puppet "independent" governments, 88, 200–209, 223–224, 360, 365
Soviet rule in, 351
Ukrainian Bolsheviks, 140–141, 208–209, 223–224, 350–356
language, xxi, 3, 39, 351; Fig. 73
(*see also* Russian language)
poet Shevchénko, 351–352; Fig. 69
separatists from Galicia, promotion of by Austro-Germans, 39–40
by U.S. Congress, xv, 352
Uniates, 39
United States, Public Law 86–90 (*see* "Captive Nations")
Russia, distorted image of at present, ix–xi, xiv, xvi, 359–362
friendly relations with in the past, xiv

Versailles, Treaty of, 293
Volunteer Army (see White Armies of
    Russia)


White Armies of Russia, Kolchák's Si-
    berian Army, 126, 245, 256
  North-Western Army under Yudé-
    nich, 256
  Volunteer Army, Beginning of under
    Alexéyev and Kornílov, 146
  Crimean epilogue of under Wran-
    gel in 1920, 136, 270–272
  defeat of by Reds in fall of 1919,
    256–257, 266–267, 269–270

White Armies of Russia, Volunteer
    Army, "Icy March" of, 218
  successes of in first half of 191
    under Deníkin, 245, 247, 251
    253, 255–256

Yálta, U.S.-U.S.S.R. agreement at, xi
Yaroslávl, anti-Red uprising at, 188
    189
Y.M.C.A. (see American Y.M.C.A.)
Yugoslavia, past ties of to Imperial
    Russia, xxi, 11, 13, 37–39
  post-revolutionary asylum in for
    Russian émigrés, 283–284, 298
  (see also Alexander, King of)

## DATE DUE

| | | | |
|---|---|---|---|
| 1 √ 19 | | | |
| JAN 4 1973 | | | |
| APR 2 7 1976 | | | |
| | | | |
| | | | |
| | | | |
| | | | |
| | | | |
| | | | |
| | | | |
| | | | |
| | | | |
| | | | |
| | | | |
| | | | |
| | | | |
| | | | |